FRANK LLOYD WRI

MASTERWORKS FROM THE
FRANK LLOYD WRIGHT ARCHIVES

GHT DRAWINGS

BY BRUCE BROOKS PFEIFFER

ABRADALE PRESS/HARRY N. ABRAMS, INC., PUBLISHERS, IN ASSOCIATION WITH
THE FRANK LLOYD WRIGHT FOUNDATION AND THE PHOENIX ART MUSEUM

TO EDGAR KAUFMANN, JR., LONGTIME FRIEND AND COLLEAGUE

Project Director: Margaret L. Kaplan
Editor: Charles Miers
Designer: Bob McKee

Library of Congress Cataloging-in-Publication Data
Pfeiffer, Bruce Brooks.
Frank Lloyd Wright drawings : masterworks from the Frank Lloyd
Wright archives / by Bruce Brooks Pfeiffer.
p.   cm.
"In association with the Frank Lloyd Wright Foundation and the
Phoenix Art Museum."
Includes index.
ISBN 0–8109–8143–2
1. Wright, Frank Lloyd, 1867–1959—Archives.   2. Architectural
drawing—United States—Catalogs.   I. Wright, Frank Lloyd,
1867–1959.   II. Title.
NA2707.W74A4   1996
720'.22'22—dc20   96–3898

CONTENTS

ACKNOWLEDGMENTS
JAMES BALLINGER AND BRUCE BROOKS PFEIFFER
303

PREFACE

FOR AN ARCHITECT THE ACT OF DRAWING is essentially a means to an end: the putting down on paper of ideas in the imagination with the goal of building a building. In this respect, an architect's drawing is not unlike a composer's notes on staff paper. Both the architect and the composer are faced with identical situations: to make the graphic representation of creation so precise, so clear and readable, that others may interpret, understand, and bring the work to life. The contractor and his workmen must be able to build the building as envisioned by the architect; the conductor and his musicians must be able to produce the sound and nuance as it was originally written by the composer. But the drawing of an architect, like the score of a composer, is—in itself—of relatively less importance than the end result. It is the building that becomes the final embodiment of the idea; the drawing represents the first tangible evidence.

Frank Lloyd Wright lucidly recorded his ideas on paper; thereafter, they were translated into three dimensions. By this process he produced a new architecture for the twentieth century. He preferred to call this new architecture "organic architecture." Throughout his lifetime he continually defined and explained this term, but perhaps never so succinctly as when he said, "Any building that is organic, anywhere in time, will be appropriate to time, appropriate to place, and appropriate to man."

Added to the tangible results of his genius—seen in the great many buildings that he built, as well as in the drawings for unbuilt buildings that may yet be built—is a special benefit, a special bonus as it were, that we are privileged to savor and enjoy. He was a master draftsman and a sensitive artist as well as a towering innovator in the world of architecture.

This special gift was noticed by another great architect and draftsman, Louis H. Sullivan. In the spring of 1887 Wright came to the office of Adler and Sullivan in Chicago to apply for a job. Sullivan asked the young man to go home, prepare some drawings, and bring them back in a few days. When Sullivan subsequently saw the draftsmanship of Wright, he did not know who this twenty-year-old lad from Wisconsin was, but he did perceive that he had a great talent for drawing, a talent that Sullivan desperately needed as work proceeded on the large Chicago Auditorium commission. (One of the drawings Wright made to show Sullivan is in this collection; page 124).

When the president of Florida Southern College, Dr. Ludd Spivey, came to Frank Lloyd Wright in 1938 and asked the architect to design a new college campus for him, Spivey told Wright that he was seeking him as much for his philosophy as for his architecture. Wright replied that the two were inseparable. It is the same with his drawings—they are inherently woven into his work and underlying philosophy; we cannot see one without being aware of the other. Nevertheless, this volume, published in conjunction with an exhibition of drawings at the Phoenix Art Museum, is aimed primarily at the drawings themselves, with some explanation of the works and projects they represent. It was decided, as we began the selection of drawings for the exhibition and this book, to divide the work into various categories. Nine categories were finally determined, including a separate category in which one building alone, the Imperial Hotel, could be studied from many different aspects.

Within each division the work is presented chronologically, except in the case of the Imperial Hotel, where all the drawings shown were done within a span of time concurrent with the architect's presence in Japan, on and off from 1916 to 1922. One other exception to the chronological format is Part Seven, a section that deals with several types of projects—a sort of miscellaneous potpourri. Here chronology has been thrown to the wind and works are grouped by type, regardless of time. Drawings for a bridge of 1915 stand next to those for one of 1949; an automobile design of 1920 next to one of 1958.

THE FRANK LLOYD WRIGHT ARCHIVES

The drawings illustrated in this volume represent but a minuscule fraction of the drawings in the Frank Lloyd Wright Archives. The archives, stored at Taliesin West in Scottsdale, Arizona, were actually begun when Frank Lloyd Wright opened his architectural practice in Chicago in 1893. In 1932 Wright and his wife founded the Taliesin Fellowship, a school for architecture and the allied arts based on apprenticeship training. Eight years later he established the Frank Lloyd Wright Foundation. Out of the holdings of his early practice and of the foundation's have grown the Frank Lloyd Wright Archives.

The quotations of Frank Lloyd Wright used in this volume are taken for the most part from transcripts of his talks and conversations with the apprentices in the Taliesin Fellowship. These transcripts cover a ten-year period from 1949 to 1959. Other quotations are taken from both his published and unpublished writings. It should be noted that sections from Wright's autobiography vary in different editions (1932, 1933, 1938, and 1943, as well as three copies of the book in the archives that he heavily annotated).

Frank Lloyd Wright saved more than his drawings, which he closely and carefully guarded throughout his life. He also collected and preserved his correspondence, manuscripts, photographs, books, periodicals—anything pertaining to his work as well as to his family and ancestors. Another major portion of the archives is his art collection of Asian and European objects, including prominent examples of Japanese prints and screens and Chinese ceramics and sculpture.

Wright's sense of his place in history is revealed too by his diligent saving of various items from his childhood—parts of the Kindergarten Gifts (patterns designed by Friedrich Froebel) given to him by his mother in 1876 and the English cathedral woodcuts that she carefully cut out and hung on the wall of his room just before he was born in 1867. His love of beautiful objects is evident throughout the collections, even extending to his personal library: rare editions of William Blake, a set of four volumes of *A Monograph of Trogons* by John Gould, Curtis's *Botanical Magazine,* and a first edition of Samuel Butler's *Hudibras.* There is also a series of folio volumes entitled "Dessins des Maîtres," in which all of the plates are exquisite lithographs of paintings and drawings by artists from Rembrandt to Watteau. After a trip to Russia in 1937, Wright brought back color lithographs of Russian fairy tales and lithographic scenes of the palaces and monuments of Saint Petersburg. His was a most catholic taste, and the full scope of it, as seen in his collections, further interprets his remark, "I can well do without the necessities of life as long as God gives me the luxuries."

On his eightieth birthday, during a breakfast party held for him in the large studio at Taliesin, in Spring Green, Wisconsin, he reminisced about the drawings and the projects that had their birth in that space—from Midway Gardens and the Imperial Hotel to Fallingwater, the Johnson buildings, and the Guggenheim Museum. He pointed to the doorway connecting the house to the studio, where twice—first in 1914 and then again in 1925—a devastating fire had totally destroyed his living quarters. Each time the fire had been stopped before reaching the studio. "It was as if God questioned my character," he told us, "but not my work."

These were not the words of a vain man, nor of an arrogant man. Wright once made the "quip" that he preferred honest arrogance to insincere humility. He later regretted the remark; it was thrown back in his face over and over again throughout his lifetime. But his statement about the fires and Taliesin and the preservation of his work merely points out his conviction about his mission as an architect, his belief in his work, his dedication to the goal of bringing an element of beauty in touch with human life whenever and wherever he could.

Over twenty-one thousand original drawings reside in the archives at Taliesin West. That so many drawings exist—and most of them in fine condition—seems a miracle indeed, considering the two fires at Taliesin and considering over the years Wright moved his office from Chicago to Oak Park, from Oak Park back to Chicago, and then to Taliesin in Wisconsin. He moved later to Los Angeles, to Tokyo, and then back again to Los Angeles. For the last twenty-one years of his life he had also changed his place of work twice annually—spending summers in Taliesin in Wisconsin and winters in Taliesin West in Arizona.

At times it appeared that Wright was somewhat casual about his drawings—exhibiting them generously and publishing them often. They were never kept under lock and key but rather in cabinets near to the drafting room where he worked. The longer he lived, the more he returned to his earlier drawings to make notes and comments on them, to annotate them, sometimes working on the architectural lines themselves as well as adding written texts. A drawing from the nineteenth century will have, for example, a note written in 1930, and then another written in 1950, and so forth. His drawings were always available to those around him, his draftsmen, and, later, his apprentices. But he knew their worth, and he knew their value to posterity. He intended Taliesin West to be the repository of his life work and said so in a recorded talk to the Taliesin Fellowship in 1951:

Whatever disposition is made of my drawings, I intended them to be kept at Taliesin [West]. That is going to be the Taliesin of the future—the repository of all those drawings and of that work. You may wonder why we are spending all this time and effort in expanding and making Taliesin more or less permanent. It is because it is going to be the only repository of this work in which you have become interested and to which you have contributed. If anyone wishes to learn about it or see it firsthand, authentically, this is where they are going to go to see it.

ABOUT THE DRAWINGS

Frank Lloyd Wright's drawings fall into five distinct categories: conceptual sketches, preliminary studies, presentation drawings, development drawings, and working drawings. In this volume, working drawings are not shown except in the section on the Imperial Hotel.

CONCEPTUAL SKETCHES

Conceptual sketches, as the designation implies, are those drawings done entirely by Wright; they represent the first record of the project on paper, his ideas as drawn entirely by his hand. Several of these are reproduced in this volume. They are less easy to read and understand than the final presentation renderings made for the clients, but the poetry and beauty of them cast a special spell. And as his output increased, as he gained more and more experience not only in drawing but recording the ideas, these conceptual sketches became simpler and were imbued with a clarity that is startling. They likewise become easier to study because of that clarity. In his later years Wright came to regard these as his most valuable drawings and frequently sketched in a red square, his personal logo, and signed the drawing with his typical "FLLW" and the date. Even the sketchiest and most cursory of these conceptual drawings has a discipline set within it, a well-ordered sense of conveying the essential message: the idea of the building. He told us that his friend and early associate Cecil Corwin would sit at the drafting board making sketch upon sketch until the paper was covered with a morass of smudges, all in an attempt to provoke the idea. That was not the way Wright worked.

To his apprentices, on September 12, 1953, he explained:

You all want to design things. You want to learn how to design things. Well, you don't learn how to design things by sitting at a drafting board with a pencil in your hand, and with T-square and triangle. That's what this talk this morning chiefly means, and that's why I'm giving it to you. I never sit down to a drawing board—and this has been a lifelong practice of mine—until I have the whole thing in my mind. I may alter it substantially, I may throw it away, I may find I'm up a blind alley; but unless I have the idea of the thing pretty well in shape, you won't see me at a drawing board with it. But all the time I have it it's germinating, between three o'clock and four o'clock in the morning—somehow nature has provided me with an hour or more of what might be called insight. . . . So this design matter is not something to do with a drawing board. It is something that you do as you work, as you play. You may get it in the middle of the tennis court and drop your racket and run off and put it down. That is the kind of thing that it is. It is fleeting, it is evanescent. It's up here where you have to be quick and take it.

PRELIMINARY STUDIES

In the preliminary studies for a project, the work of the draftsmen and, later, of the apprentices is combined with Wright's own sketches. But sometimes the studies are all his. In the case of Unity Temple (page 88), he wrote that he had made over thirty-five studies before he settled on the scheme as we see the building today. He did not keep those studies, and he later told us that he regretted destroying them. It certainly is a great loss for us today, but in 1906 Wright was less conscious of building up an archive than building buildings.

PRESENTATION DRAWINGS

The presentation drawings, which constitute the greatest number of works in this volume, are those drawings made to show clients. Customarily, they include a building's plan (or plans if a second story was intended) and perspective. These are highly collaborative drawings, because once the idea was down on paper, via the conceptual sketch, and then developed to his satisfaction, via the preliminary studies, Wright instructed his draftsmen as to the kind of view he wanted, from what angle, and requested whatever other drawings he felt necessary to explain the scheme to his clients—further elevations or sections. But we see his hand in these drawings, for after the mechanical perspective had been laid out and developed he would come in and render the drawing, adding color, shading, foliage, people, birds, flowers—whatever he felt would give it life and vitality.

Beginning with his work for Louis Sullivan, Wright had this gift to come upon another draftsman's drawing and work it over, breathe life into it, make it sing. In the Adler and Sullivan office he recollected how Paul Mueller, contractor for the firm, would bring a drawing to his table and say, "Here, Wright, can't you do something with this? Nift it up a little." "And I'd nift it," he told us.

The presentation drawings are obviously the most interesting to the widest range of people because they are intended to be easily read. They are also intended to promote the idea of the project. In reality they form a sort of sales document so the client can get a glimpse of the charm of the building even if he is not too adept in reading plans.

In the early years of Wright's work, the perspectives were mostly done in ink, watercolor, and watercolor wash. He had a well-trained drafting force at his Oak Park studio, including Marion Mahony, Walter Burley Griffin,

Louis Rasmussen, Birch Burdette Long, and Taylor Woolley. Others were skilled in the production of working drawings and details for interior design, windows, furniture. Hugh Garden, Allen Weary, and Charles Morgan were professional delineators outside the studio whom Wright used for certain renderings. Taylor Woolley and Wright's son Lloyd accompanied Wright to Florence to prepare the drawings for a monograph of his work published by Ernst Wasmuth in Berlin in 1910. (This monograph, the first of Wright's work, contains one hundred plates of his drawings and is titled *Ausgeführte Bauten und Entwürfe* ["Executed Buildings and Projects"]. Its appearance in Europe in 1910, along with a companion volume of photographs the next year, had a profound influence on European architects and architectural students, especially in Holland and Germany.) Lloyd was an especially gifted and talented draftsman. The drawings he prepared for his father are among the finest in the collection; his own work is equally beautiful.

Wright closed and disbanded his Oak Park studio in 1909, spent 1910 in Europe, then reopened his office in downtown Chicago in 1911, and eventually settled at Taliesin in 1911. From 1915 to 1922, he traveled back and forth from Tokyo to Los Angeles. Again he built up a support staff of draftsmen, many of them Japanese, German, Austrian, or Czech, including architects Werner Moser, R. M. Schindler, Richard Neutra, and Kameki and Nobu Tsuchiura. By 1924, after returning from Tokyo, there were few commissions coming into his office, and he let most of his staff go. But the San Marcos commissions for Alexander Chandler, starting in 1928 and going forward with the design of the great resort hotel San Marcos-in-the-Desert (page 184), necessitated another surge of drafting. This time Wright brought in Heinrich Klumb, Donald Walker, Vladimir Karfik, George Kastner, Frank Sullivan, and, later, George Cronin. Lloyd also joined his father to help with the Chandler drawings, and Paul Mueller, Adler and Sullivan's contractor (who also built the Imperial Hotel), supplemented the team. But the stock-market collapse at the end of 1929 brought an abrupt halt to the hotel scheme, and many of the studio force were let go.

It is a pity that there is no exact record of which draftsman did which drawing throughout these early and middle years of Wright's career. Sometimes Wright himself, going over the drawings many years later, would write in the name of the draftsman who made or worked on a particular drawing. Many of the drawings that were specially prepared for a European exhibition of Wright's drawings in 1931 were done by Klumb and Okami, another studio draftsman. (This was an exhibition of drawings, photographs, and models that Wright first organized in 1930 and that was shown in several cities across the United States. In 1931 it traveled to Holland, Belgium, and Germany, winning awards and honors for Wright and further enforcing the strong impression his work had made twenty years before in the Berlin publications and five years before in the Dutch publication *Wendingen*, devoted to Wright's major works and edited by H. Th. Wijdveld.) In 1951 Wright again reviewed his work for a far larger exhibition, including drawings, murals, models, and photographs, that toured Europe under the title *Sixty Years of Living Architecture*.

With the founding of the Taliesin Fellowship in 1932, however, the record becomes clearer. At least many of the original apprentices from the early thirties are still living and have responded to our call for information about which drawings they worked on. But the finest draftsman of them all is undoubtedly John Howe, who came to Taliesin in 1932 and remained until after the architect's death in 1959. Nearly every apprentice who came to Taliesin and underwent training in the studio took on some work, to a greater or lesser degree, in this preparation of the preliminary drawings. Certain Fellowship members, along with John Howe, figured most prominently in this work: John deKoven Hill, Curtis Besinger, Peter Berndtson, Charles Gordon Lee, Allen Lape Davison, Stephen Oyakawa, Ling Po, Alvin Louis Wiehle, John Rattenbury, David Wheatley. By no means a complete list, it nonetheless points out those who contributed the most.

If Wright's work was to be successful, his clients had to be able to "read" the idea clearly and succinctly from the drawings shown to them. It was, therefore, in the general interest of getting the work built that Wright took great pains to train his draftsmen in the earlier years of his practice, and then his apprentices, during the last twenty-seven years of his life.

DEVELOPMENT DRAWINGS

That category of drawings called, arbitrarily, "development" drawings is mainly the work of draftsmen problem solving: working out details, plans, sections, and elevations pertaining to how a building was to be put together prior to the final stage, the working drawings, from which the building was actually built.

But on many such development drawings Wright then went to work to explain, by means of his own additional sketching, how a problem was to be solved. It was his life-long custom when he was still in doubt about a detail to put in the margin of the drawing a large encircled question mark and to connect it with a line to the actual detail on the drawing.

Perhaps the greatest value of his drawings lies in the fact that Wright loved to draw. He spoke of the seductive feeling of facing a sheet of clear, white paper stretched out on the drafting board before him while he held a handful of colored pencils. He was a swift draftsman—once the idea was clear in his mind, it came quickly onto paper. He maneuvered his T-square and triangle with a beautiful dexterity; it was a joy to watch him draw, to watch the lines appear so effortlessly—and sometimes not without humor. In 1958 he was preparing a series of interior views of the Guggenheim Museum, in construction at the time, in order to show the museum's director and board of trustees how paintings and drawings could be best exhibited. One perspective shows a group of people looking at a large Kandinskyesque painting, except for a small girl who has turned away from the painting and is looking down the open well of the museum into the building below, obviously more intrigued with the view than with Kandinsky. Wright came in to sign the drawing, picked up his pencil, and without even bothering to sit down, sketched a little yo-yo in the out-stretched hand over the parapet edge held by the little girl. He turned to those of us in the studio, and with that wonderful twinkle in his eyes, said, "Boys, in all this endeavor we must never lose sight of a sense of humor."

The more each drawing bears his own hand upon it the more that drawing exudes his love for making a design, for the actual act of drawing itself. Many drawings here are highly collaborative, others the work entirely of his draftsmen. But the light of his genius permeates all of them, and in the final analysis the work is irrevocably his.

—Bruce Brooks Pfeiffer

ABOUT THE WORK

When a drawing or design for a building was made but not executed or constructed, the word project *follows in parentheses the title throughout the headings in this volume. All other illustrations included in this book are designs for structures that were built, even if the buildings were subsequently demolished (such as the Larkin Building and the Imperial Hotel). Dates assigned correspond to the conception of the work, when it was first put down on paper. The Guggenheim Museum, for example, was a design idea conceived in 1943. It underwent many revisions until construction began in 1956. But the salient fact remains that the concept of the work dates to 1943 in the oeuvre of Wright.*

PART ONE

RESIDENTIAL DESIGNS

THE FIRM OF ADLER AND SULLIVAN did not, as a rule, accept commissions for residential work. They designed and built auditoriums, opera houses, commercial buildings, and office buildings. Occasionally one of their clients would ask for a house design, and in those rare instances where they accepted the commission, the work was invariably turned over to Wright. He was, by 1890, "Chief of Design," the senior draftsman, with several draftsmen working under him. Along with residential commissions for the clients of Adler and Sullivan, Wright also designed Sullivan's own summer home in Mississippi and a town house for Sullivan's brother in Chicago. However, when Wright took on private clients, doing the work at home in the evening in the little studio on the second floor of his Oak Park home, Sullivan considered it "moonlighting." A heated argument along with accusations arose, and Wright quit the firm. More than twenty years passed before there was a reconciliation.

In 1893, right after leaving Adler and Sullivan, Wright set up his own architectural practice in Chicago's Schiller Building, although Oak Park, a nearby suburb, remained his place of residence. His first client was William H. Winslow of River Forest, Illinois. The famed Winslow House of 1893—still standing and in remarkable condition—was a new statement in American domestic architecture that paved the way for the houses Wright was creating in rapid succession. Although its plan was quite conventional, the Winslow House presented a totally new elevation. An important statement came to the fore in the treatment of materials for this house. The golden roman brick, white cast stone, and dark brown terra-cotta frieze of the upper story are left in their natural condition without application of paint or covering. Each material's characteristic texture and color are respected. Instinctively, from the very beginning of his work, Wright had a sensitive and sympathetic attitude toward the nature of whatever material he employed, at a time in architecture when natural materials were painted, veneered, and disrespected in every possible way.

As his residential work progressed from 1893 to 1900 (a span of just seven years), Wright forged into totally uncharted waters, responding to the problems of building a home on the Midwest prairie, in a democratic society, in the twentieth century. To him this context precluded the use of the "architectural styles" that abounded at that time, and he developed plans with more open, flowing interior spaces than had been seen before; they became known, in fact, as the "open plan." His use of extended horizontal lines inspired the term "streamlined" to describe his work. On the basically flat, if not monotonous, prairie he saw that those extended horizontal lines were more harmonious. As he opened the spaces within the home, doing away with needless partitions and doorways, he also opened the interior to the exterior by using screens of glass—either French doors giving onto extended terraces or running bands of windows on the second-floor level, set well back under broad projecting roofs. The roof lines themselves he brought down to a gradual, graceful slope; the fireplace and chimney masses he broadened so that one generous mass would carry the

flues for several fireplaces and the heater. He abolished the basement, considering it to be an unpleasant hole in the damp ground, and the attic, which he saw as a difficult space adding height to a building totally unbecoming to the prairie. The result: long, low buildings tied to the ground that brought the inhabitants within into a relationship with the natural world without.

It was not a style Wright was after, but rather solutions for better residential design. As the terrain has been subsequently developed and landscaped, those early houses are now set within a dense suburban environment. But at the turn of the century, when they were built, they stood quite isolated in a sparsely landscaped plain.

In developing this new type of house design many factors were at work at the same time: respect for the site and for the natural characteristics of materials and the aim of making the plan more flexible, with fewer partitions, fewer doors, more open space within, more generous use of glass windows and glass doors. In addition, all his woodwork details employed straight lines, cutting the wood clean and even, conserving the lumber as much as possible. Explaining this principle to his apprentices, in later years, he said:

> Now you have here the whole psyche of modern architecture, of the negation, that is. There was a denial of the hand-carved, decorated torture that used to get into woodwork in that day. That was the negation. . . . everything was straight line, everything was done with a T-square and triangle. There isn't a pattern on those early houses in the windows, there isn't a chair, there isn't anything in the house that wasn't done with a T-square and triangle. I doubt if there is a free-hand mark in the whole collection. That was what I felt to be the best interpretation of the machine as a tool—to find work that it could do well, and I found it.

By 1911, Wright had built ninety-six houses in and around the suburbs of Chicago and designed some seventy more. (In other words approximately every six weeks for eighteen years a new set of working drawings was produced by Wright and his draftsmen in the Oak Park studio.) By far the majority of these houses were for flat suburban lots (although the Hardy House in Racine was on a steep precipice overlooking Lake Michigan). In 1911 with the Sherman Booth House, Wright had another dramatic site to design a house for, a wooded ravine, and in the same year, he built his own home, Taliesin, whose structure closely followed the brow of a hill in southwestern Wisconsin. The plans of both the Booth House and Taliesin were fluid, far less formal than the designs for the Willits and Ullman houses. Rooms open directly onto flagstone or concrete terraces flush with the ground level rather than onto raised terraces such as at the Robie and Coonley houses. The reason for raising the floor in those prairie-site houses was to get as much overlook across the prairie as possible. Taliesin, on the other hand, is perched above the trees on a hillside, overlooking water gardens below, pastures, meadowlands, and the Wisconsin River beyond. As more and more interesting sites were made available by new clients around the nation, Wright's designs responded to the specific conditions wherever possible.

At the close of an extended period of work on the Imperial Hotel in Japan, from 1916 to 1922, Wright moved to Southern California. The four concrete block houses (pages 30–31) in Los Angeles, all built in the mid-1920s, were a revelation in the treatment of this generally despised material, the concrete block. Wright bestowed a poetry and beauty in his handling of the blocks that has never been rivaled. The new location, new conditions, and new climate produced an entirely new architectural grammar. Wright left California and returned to the Midwest after 1924. He had little residential work until he was called to Arizona in 1928–1929 by Alexander Chandler to design a resort hotel and detached residences. The work for Chandler was interrupted by the stock-market collapse in the fall of 1929; the architect returned with his family to Wisconsin with only a small portion of the commission due him and faced a period of six years in which little work came his way. There was a home for his cousin Richard Lloyd Jones in Tulsa, Oklahoma—a block house of a different scheme and application than the California ones—and a home in Minneapolis for Malcolm Willey, dean at the University of Minnesota. In the completed Willey home and an earlier project designed for it lie the embryo for the Usonian houses that followed.

Fallingwater, the Johnson Wax Administration Building, and the Johnson home "Wingspread" were commissions that came to Wright at a time when he had little work, and the abundantly creative way in which the architect responded shows the amount of creative energy that was obviously stored up within him waiting to pour out. While designing these major commissions Wright pioneered an entirely different phase of residential design: the modest, moderate-cost home for the average American family, which he called the "Usonian" house, borrowing Samuel Butler's term for the United States of America.

Moderate-cost housing was a lifelong concern of Wright's. The largest percentage of Wright clients during the Oak Park years, from 1893 to 1911, were upper–middle-class businessmen, and the homes he designed for them were generally large and generous, both in size and detail. There were exceptions, of course, but Wright was clearly not the architect for the average working man. At the same time, he strongly believed that the average American was entitled to a home that could also be a work of art. He once qualified that belief, saying, "I believe a house is more a home by being a work of Art."

He knew that if the maxim was to apply to the lower-income home, it would require either prefabrication or a systems-built method of construction. It meant, he explained, that the home would have to go to the factory, rather than skilled labor coming onto the building site. From 1915 to 1917 he designed a series of prefabricated gouses called the American Ready-Cut System. The key to the system was that each piece of lumber was precut in the factory, then brought to the site, assembled, and plastered. Nine hundred and sixty-six drawings, from sketches to hundreds of working drawings, were produced at Taliesin to put the system to work. There was a great variety of designs and sizes, but all derived from the same units. Several of these houses were built in Milwaukee and other places in the Midwest. They were not exactly prefabricated as such, but they were an innovative thrust in that direction. His block houses for California hinted once again at a systems-built method of construction.

In 1937 Wright tried once again in California to develop a prefabricated home by means of sheet metal. He called the scheme the "All Steel Houses," and proposed building one hundred houses on a hillside location in Los Angeles. Each house had a unique design, but the system of construction and all the detailing were standardized, thereby reducing the unit cost. This proposal, too, was abandoned and remained only in project form.

In 1936 Wright began to develop another type of house construction. He proposed the design for a client in South Dakota, Robert Lusk, but it was so revolutionary that the banks and lending institutions made it impossible for the clients to get a building loan, much less a building permit. The next year, however, the system was developed for the Herbert Jacobs House in Madison, Wisconsin. A concrete floor is set over heating coils in a bed of gravel directly on the ground; brick wall masses carry most of the supports for the flat roof; the other walls are made of wood and plywood, laminated with insulating building paper between and held together by screws. The wall outside is also the wall inside, and no finish work is required once the wall is screwed together and mounted. The roof framing is made up of laminated 2×4's in three offsets, producing a 2×12 roof without using expensive 2×12 lumber. French doors reach from floor to ceiling. Heating, kitchen, and bath facilities are grouped together in one central location, with a small basement below for the heater. "A modest house," Wright wrote, "this Usonian house, a dwelling place that has no feeling at all for the 'grand' except as the house extends itself in the flat parallel to the ground."

Scores of homes utilizing this basic system were built across the nation from Massachusetts to California, each one its own individual design, depending upon site, client, requirements, and budget. Contractors at first were loath to get caught up in a "new" idea, and so Wright sent his apprentices to the various clients to hire subcontractors and supervise construction. The system was simplified so that even the furniture could be built according to the architect's design by the carpenters on site, rather than going to expensive cabinetmakers.

Wright often told his apprentices that he seemed to be destined to be a "residence architect." Houses certainly comprised the vast majority of his architectural commissions.

In his later life he sometimes maintained that he would not take on any more commissions for less than a million dollars; but an anxious young couple would approach him with the conviction that they would have nothing but a home designed by Frank Lloyd Wright, even if it put them into debt for the rest of their lives. He could not muster the heart to refuse them. He continued, right up to the time of his death, to design homes for moderate-income families, one of his last designs being a simple prefabricated house that would fulfill this quest of being more a home "by being a work of Art."

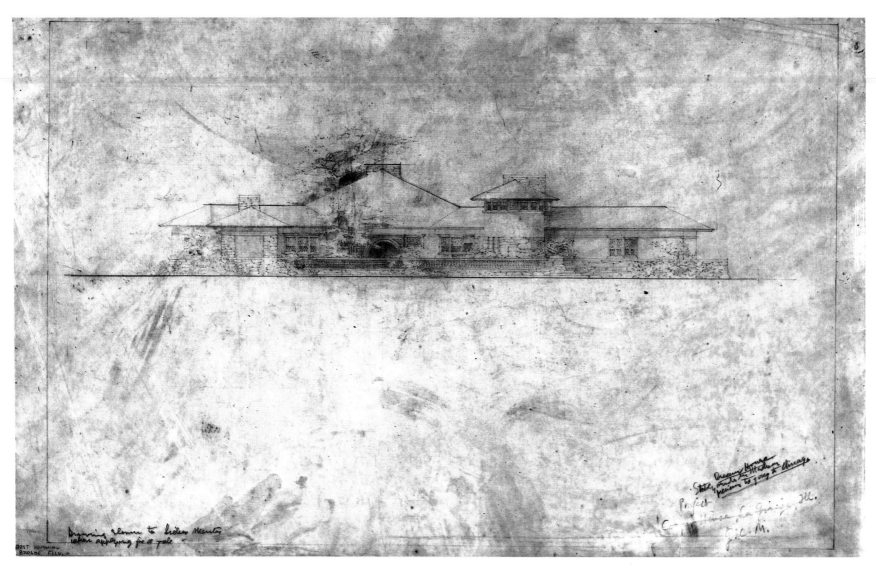

"DRAWING SHOWN TO LIEBER-MEISTER" *(PROJECT). 1887. ELEVATION. PENCIL ON TRACING PAPER, 26 × 15". FLLW FDN# 8701.001*

IT WAS THIS elevation drawing that convinced Louis Sullivan to hire the twenty-year-old Wright as a draftsman in 1887. On the lower left corner Wright has documented the work, "Drawing shown to Lieber-Meister when applying for a job." This note was put on the drawing sometime in the mid-1940s; ten years later, Wright noted on the sheet, "Dream house—study made in Madison previous to going to Chicago," referring to a study plan from which this elevation was then prepared. Both the plan and elevation were adapted in 1890 for a house for Henry Cooper, a client in La Grange, Illinois (page 13).

There is a careful balance between the rendering of the foliage and of the building itself in this drawing, and it portrays, even at this early point in Wright's career, that special balance between the two that he would always honor. It is a delicate drawing that obviously appealed to Sullivan, a master draftsman himself.

(opposite top)

BASED ON A SKETCH plan made by Wright in Madison, this more formally developed plan corresponds closely to the specifications of the previous elevation. Again the architect made notes on the drawing much later in his life: "Made while at U. W. before going to Chicago—1885." Eighteen eighty-five was actually the date when he started to study under A. D. Conover at the University of Wisconsin. It was the following year that he was admitted as a "special student" at the university.

However, the character and rendering of this plan would better suggest a date of 1890, when Wright was already working for Louis Sullivan and had gained much more drafting experience.

(opposite)

WILLIAM WINSLOW was Wright's first client when he opened his own architectural practice in Chicago in the spring of 1893. The elegance and proportion of the house bespeaks a mastery of the art of architecture from the very beginning of Wright's career. Certain Sullivanesque traits are still with him, however, as seen in the terra-cotta frieze that ran around the exterior of the entire second story. But the low, broad, projecting roof and the honest use of materials become, in this residence, a clear forecast of work to follow.

This particular drawing was prepared in Florence in 1910 for use in the German publisher Ernst Wasmuth's folio of Wright's drawings, *Ausgeführte Bauten und Entwürfe von Frank Lloyd Wright.* Along with the perspective, it gives a hint of the ground plan and some of the cast-stone details at the entrance to the house.

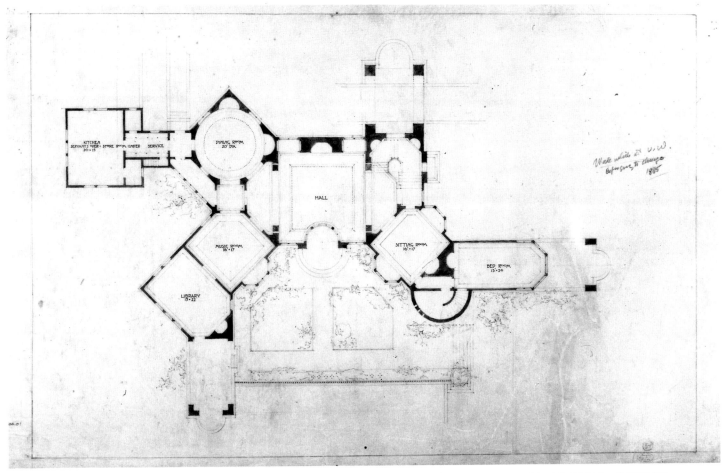

HENRY N. COOPER HOUSE (PROJECT), LA GRANGE, ILLINOIS. 1890. PLAN. INK ON TRACING PAPER, 26 × 16". FLLW FDN# 9004.001

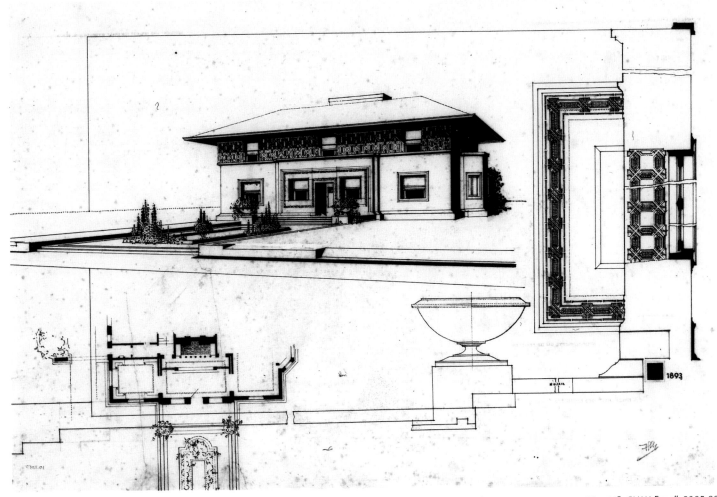

WILLIAM H. WINSLOW HOUSE, RIVER FOREST, ILLINOIS. 1893. PERSPECTIVE, PLAN, AND DETAILS. INK ON TRACING PAPER, 23 × 16". FLLW FDN# 9305.001

A . K . M c A f e e H o u s e *(project), Kenilworth, Illinois. 1894. Perspective. Watercolor and watercolor wash on art paper, 29 × 10". FLLW Fdn# 9407.001*

THIS WATERCOLOR RENDERING of the A. K. McAfee House gives further evidence of the new direction in residential design that Wright was taking. The connection between building and ground is emphasized by the concrete stylobate and extended terrace walls. There is an obvious lack of foundation planting — the traditional habit of planting shrubs and bushes along the front façade of a house. Window openings are grouped together in bands, in place of individual holes cut into the walls; the actual windows themselves are open-swinging rather than double-hung. The chimney masses are broad and generous. The "prairie house," as this architecture would soon be called, was being born.

H . J . U L L M A N H O U S E *(project)*, O A K P A R K , I L L I N O I S . *1904. P E R S P E C T I V E .*
P E N C I L O N T R A C I N G P A P E R , 19 × 11". F L L W F D N # 0411.002

THIS DELIGHTFUL PERSPECTIVE of the Ullman House, another prairie house for Oak Park, can almost be described as a miniature. The drawing measures a diminutive nineteen inches by eleven inches, but from paper edge to paper edge the sheet is filled with the image of the house, the surrounding trees along the rear of the property, and the sidewalk in the foreground. Provision seems to have been made for a title block at the bottom edge of the drawing, but this was never achieved. Despite the small size of the drawing, the plans and elevations reveal a house of almost eight thousand square feet. The living room reaches up two stories, the dining room (on the left of the house) is grand and spacious. Both living and dining rooms have windows on three sides, and on the third level are bedrooms opening onto balconies on both sides of the building.

This particular drawing is not often published to represent the Ullman House, but it is selected here because it shows the vitality of Wright's hand at work on the perspective. Some of his editing of the ground line seems to have been done much later than 1904; he frequently took out drawings made many years earlier and went to work on them. The greatest amount of annotation occurred at the times when he was selecting drawings for an exhibition: first in 1930, again in 1940, and lastly in 1950. Part of this drawing was damaged, at the right edge, and a paper fill was inserted many years ago. The handwritten caption, "Ullman house project," is not by Wright but by Henry Russell Hitchcock, done when he was reviewing Wright's drawings for the 1940 show of his work at New York's Museum of Modern Art.

THE CURTIS PUBLISHING Company of Philadelphia, publishers of *Ladies' Home Journal,* commissioned Wright to design a house as part of a series it sponsored of "Modest Suburban Houses Which Can Be Built at Moderate Cost." The elevation is a typical conceptual sketch done by the architect. Much later it was labeled, "Original of the Ladies' Home Journal House. FLLW."

On the perspective Wright has twice indicated "FLLW del." to put on record that the entire drawing was done by him. As with the elevation made for Louis Sullivan in 1887 (page 12), the delicate balance between building and landscape is carefully preserved. The sketch elevation, as well, is entirely by the hand of Wright. But the elevation represents a conceptual drawing, with its inevitable foliage and plants drawn in at the same time as the lines of the building. It shows, even at this early date, Wright's concern for landscaping and natural planting as an inherent part of architecture.

When the house was published in the February 1901 issue of *Ladies' Home Journal,* Wright provided the text material, a portion of which expressed his feelings about the prairie town and this dwelling: "The exterior recognizes the influence of the prairie, is firmly and broadly associated with the site, and makes a feature of its quiet level. The low terraces and broad eaves are designed to accentuate that quiet level and complete the harmonious relationship."

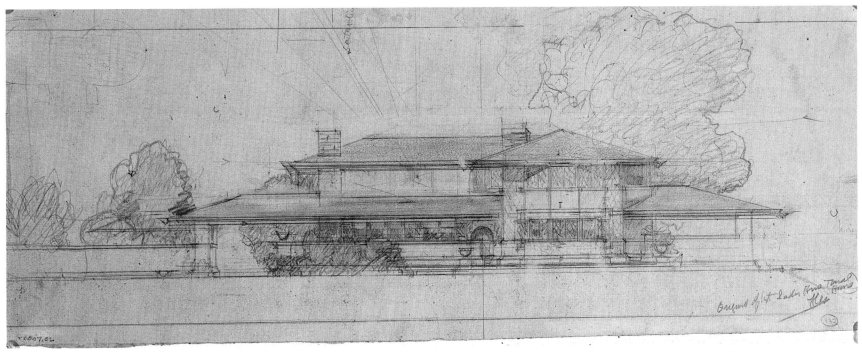

"A Home in a Prairie Town" for *Ladies' Home Journal* (project). 1900. Elevation. Pencil and color pencil on art paper, 20 × 18". FLLW Fdn# 0007.002

"A Home in a Prairie Town" for *Ladies' Home Journal* (project). 1900. Perspective. Watercolor and watercolor wash on art paper, 25 × 15". FLLW Fdn# 0007.001

IF THERE WAS EVER a drawing by Wright that emphasized his love for and the lessons he learned from the Japanese print, it is this tall, vertical rendering of the Thomas Hardy House. Placed on the sheet of paper at the extreme top edge, the building itself, drawn free-hand in ink lines, is by no means lost, despite its vertical setting on a bluff at the lake's edge. On the contrary, the drama of the intended voids in the drawing intensifies the drama of the architecture.

This was one of Wright's first commissions for a dwelling situated on a site that was not a typical suburban lot. His response to the challenge is evident in the rendering.

THOMAS P. HARDY HOUSE, *RACINE, WISCONSIN.*
1905. PERSPECTIVE. WATERCOLOR AND WATERCOLOR WASH
ON ART PAPER, 6 × 19". FLLW FDN# 0506.003

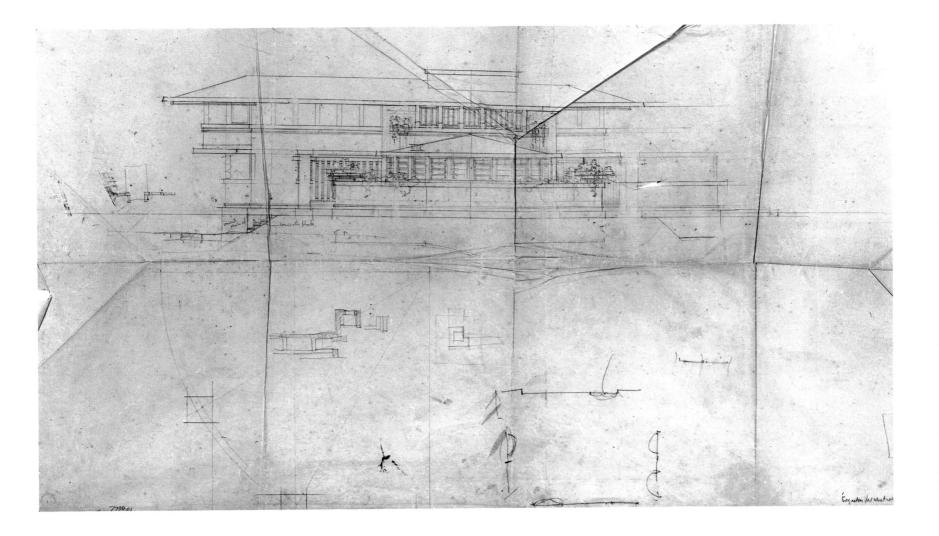

THE MILLARD HOUSE was built in a heavily wooded section of Highland Park, Illinois. This early sketch for the house is shown here in place of a more famous perspective so as to give an example of how Wright "thought" on paper while creating a new design. After Wright made such a drawing, the work was turned over to a competent draftsman. Seventeen years after this house was built, in 1923, the client's wife, Alice Millard, built another Frank Lloyd Wright house, the well-known "La Miniatura" in Pasadena, Wright's first concrete textile-block house.

GEORGE MADISON MILLARD HOUSE,
HIGHLAND PARK, ILLINOIS. 1906. ELEVATION.
PENCIL ON TRACING PAPER, 35 × 19".
FLLW FDN# 0606.017

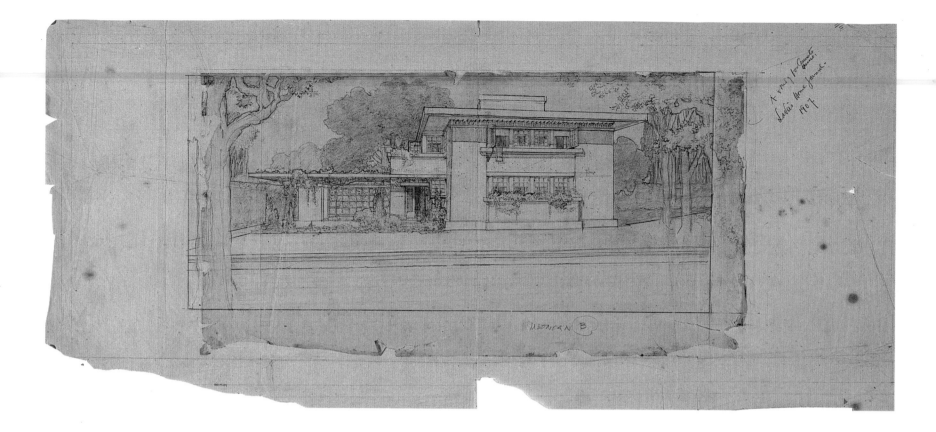

ONE AFTERNOON in the mid-1950s Wright said to his apprentices: "Bring out the *Ladies' Home Journal* Fireproof House. It was a good plan then, and now, fifty years later, it is still a perfectly good plan. We are going to modify it for the Erdman pre-fab second scheme." At the same time he put on the drawing the label "Usonian B," to designate the plan's new assignment.

In the 1906–1907 version the house was to be built of poured concrete—walls, floor slabs, and roof slabs—thereby making it fireproof. The original commission was given to Wright by the Curtis Publishing Company. His solution to the problem of creating a fireproof structure was to use poured concrete, so successfully implemented in the construction of Unity Temple (page 88). In the April 1907 issue of *Ladies' Home Journal,* Wright described not only the house but the construction details as well. A cost estimate is also included, pricing the house—for the Chicago area—at five thousand dollars. There is another rendering for the same project, done by Marion Mahony in brown ink, with her monogram tucked into the foliage at the front right. Her style of rendering is always recognizable in the meticulous treatment of the foliage; so meticulous, in fact, that it almost becomes the predominant element in the drawing.

In this drawing, Wright moved the house to the right of the sheet of paper and redrew a strong marginal line to blot out some of the tree foliage on that side. Obviously, he felt it produced a better rhythm in the overall drawing, and it is interesting to see how, on a drawing that was no more than a preliminary sketch, he has taken pains to "correct" the image so as to satisfy himself.

FIREPROOF HOUSE FOR *LADIES' HOME JOURNAL* (PROJECT). 1906. PERSPECTIVE. PENCIL ON TRACING PAPER, 33 × 15".
FLLW FDN# 0614.004

WRIGHT'S EARLY DRAWINGS abound with these thumbnail sketches, wherein the architect made a small study simply to clarify the work for himself. Sometimes they appear on the general elevation or section on which he was at work; more rarely, they are on small separate sheets as seen here.

The Tomek House, built in Riverside, Illinois, not far from the Avery Coonley House, was one of Wright's most successful prairie houses. The sketch perspective is taken from an oblique angle at the short end of the house and does not reveal the long, extended structure that the building actually is. Like the Coonley House, the main living-room–dining-room area is on the second level, the bedrooms above. Ground level is reserved for storage, heating, and laundry. The general plan of this house served as a prototype for the Robie House, designed two years later.

F. F. TOMEK HOUSE, *RIVERSIDE, ILLINOIS. 1907.*
CONCEPTUAL PERSPECTIVE. PENCIL ON TRACING PAPER, 11 × 10".
FLLW FDN# 0711.035

WILLIAM NORMAN GUTHRIE HOUSE (PROJECT), SEWANEE, TENNESSEE. 1908. PERSPECTIVE. PENCIL AND COLOR PENCIL ON TRACING PAPER, 26 × 13". FLLW FDN# 0813.001

A PROJECT FOR Wright's friend William Norman Guthrie, this house for a site in Tennessee was not built. Guthrie seemed to be a man of dreams unrealized, at least as far as his architectural projects were concerned (page 92).

The house, dated 1908–1909, was eventually built, however, for Frank J. Baker in Wilmette, Illinois, much as it is seen here. The perspective is in brown ink on fine tracing paper. The paper has somewhat yellowed with age, producing a soft overall tone in harmony with the lines of the drawing. Red pencil lightly designates the tile roof, and in later years Wright went over the foliage and tree trunks in graphite pencil to give them more punctuation. The placement of the house on the sheet of paper, close to the top, as well as of the title block on the lower left, almost as a part of the foreground foliage, demonstrates Wright's unique way of drawing perspectives. The tall trees disappear beyond the upper edge of the paper and truly give the impression of a building set by itself in a quiet, southern forest.

THIS DRAWING is a superb example of draftsmanship on the part of an Oak Park studio assistant. It was executed in freehand with black ink, using a quill pen. Only a few touches of color have been included: some light red to designate the tile roofs; vertical blue lines for the sky; blue for the water coming down the small ravine over and around which the house was to be built.

The commission for Sherman Booth, a lawyer and friend to Wright, gave the architect a rare chance to design a home for a particularly unusual site. Entrance to the dwelling is via a bridge that spans the ravine. The tall structure in the center is a large, two-story living room, with bedrooms extending out to the right and dining, kitchen and servants' quarters over the entrance at the other corner of the living room. A guest wing can barely be seen running behind the dining/kitchen wing. The way in which the tree foliage vanishes into the almost nonexistent border of the drawing demonstrates a freer, more relaxed approach to the perspective as a whole.

SHERMAN BOOTH HOUSE *(PROJECT), GLENCOE, ILLINOIS. 1911. PERSPECTIVE. SEPIA INK ON ART PAPER, 38×36". FLLW FDN# 1118.004*

MRS. THOMAS GALE HOUSE, OAK PARK, ILLINOIS.
1909. PERSPECTIVE. WATERCOLOR ON ART PAPER, 17 × 13".
FLLW FDN# 0905.001

WRIGHT HAS DATED this perspective "1904" and signed it "FLLW." The attribution is actually about five years before the correct date of the project, and the style of his handwriting on this drawing corresponds more to a date in the 1920s than in the early part of the century. He referred to this drawing, when showing it to his apprentices in 1951, as the "progenitor of Fallingwater" (not comparing the sites, of course, but rather the cantilevered roofs and balconies that are so prominent a feature of Fallingwater, built thirty years earlier; page 41). The drawing is a curious sort of collage: the skyline over the house and the tree trunks in the rear are drawn on a separate sheet of heavy beige paper set behind the rendering of the house itself and the foreground planting. On the reverse side of the background sheet is the inked title, "Pattern study for wall decoration on the Booth house Frank Lloyd Wright Architect April 1911."

We must deduce that the drawing was made sometime after 1911, probably for an exhibition, and not made to show to Mrs. Gale, whose house was already built by this time (page 24).

OVER AND OVER, Wright spoke of and wrote about his admiration for the Japanese print: "It was the great gospel of simplification . . . the elimination of all that was insignificant." We see him trying to achieve these goals in his work in general, and we see this taking place in the manner in which he made his perspectives, or directed their making. In this view of the Francis W. Little House, for example, the foreground is left practically empty while the tree line above and behind the house is so delicately rendered as to become hardly more than an indication of the trees. The house itself is outlined in brown ink, the wall masses, which were actually brick, are left plain. Some shadow lines and shading in the greenery has been added in graphite pencil, and color is used only in small touches: blue for Lake Minnetonka in the distance and some red and blue

for the hollyhock blossoms that rise as an unexpected surprise in the otherwise void foreground.

The client, Francis Little, had a previous house built by Wright in Peoria, Illinois, at the turn of the century. Over the ensuing years he became a strong supporter and patron of Wright's, providing him with the funds for his trip to Germany and Italy in 1910–1911. A most conservative businessman, Little sternly criticized his architect's personal life, but at the same time he always stood by him and was ready to help whenever he could.

Originally intended as a summer home on the shores of Lake Minnetonka, this house eventually became the Littles' permanent residence. The house was demolished in the 1960s; its living room is now installed in New York's Metropolitan Museum of Art and its library in the Allentown Museum in Pennsylvania.

"NORTHOME," F. W. LITTLE HOUSE, *WAYZATA, MINNESOTA. 1912. PERSPECTIVE. PENCIL AND COLOR PENCIL ON TRACING PAPER, 37 × 17". FLLW FDN# 1304.003*

TALIESIN, FIRST BUILT in 1911, was originally intended to be a home for Wright's mother, Anna Lloyd Wright. But on the architect's return from Europe with his companion Mrs. Cheney, his mother encouraged him to take the house, then in construction, for himself. At that point the drawings, which read originally "Cottage for Anna Lloyd Wright," were retitled "Taliesin, Country Home for Frank Lloyd Wright."

In 1914 the house, seen on the far right of this view, was demolished by a fire set by an arsonist who also took the lives of seven people. Wright returned from Chicago to find a charred ruin smoldering on the hill brow and Mrs. Cheney, her two children, an apprentice, two workmen, and the gardener's son lying dead in the courtyard. It was a tragic blow from which few men could have recuperated, but Wright had a strongly resilient nature, though the tragedy cut deeply into him, as he wrote in his autobiography. A commission that arrived at the same time from Japan to build a new structure for the Imperial Hotel in Tokyo (pages 270–280) rescued him from his grief and gave him the needed change of scene and work. His design for the rebuilding of Taliesin—Taliesin II—not only replaced the living quarters that had been consumed in the fire, but also expanded the existing studio, farm buildings, and workshops.

This rendering of the building shows the studio in the center, living quarters for draftsmen and workmen on the left, and a new residence wing, Wright's private living quarters, on the right. Although only his quarters had been destroyed, he intended, as this drawing shows, to amplify and extend the studio and adjacent areas.

Across the top of the sheet, almost imperceptible to the eye, is the title "TALIESIN COUNTRY HOME OF FRANK LLOYD WRIGHT ARCHITECT," and farther down the sheet on the far left is another, much clearer title block reading, "Preliminary Study of TALIESIN Spring Green, Wisconsin."

The drawing is rendered in black ink on gray tracing linen, with the leaves of the trees and some of the foliage in gray watercolor. All the lines are drawn freehand; the stone walls and flower gardens are especially typical of Wright's own drawing technique.

But Taliesin II was destined once again to be struck a blow by the hand of fate: in 1925 a raging summer storm sent a bolt of lightning into the living quarters, igniting some electrical and telephone wires and destroying the living quarters. But this time, as there was no loss of life, the rebuilding by Wright was less painful; Taliesin III still stands today.

F. C. BOGK HOUSE, WISCONSIN,
1916. ELEVATION. PENCIL ON TRACING PAPER, 25 × 16".
FLLW FDN# 1602.011

F. C. BOGK HOUSE, MILWAUKEE, WISCONSIN.
1916. PERSPECTIVE. PENCIL ON TRACING PAPER, 19 × 25".
FLLW FDN# 1602.010

TWO DISTINCTLY DIFFERENT elevations, based on the same plan, were proposed by Wright for this town house, which he designed in 1916. On the first drawing he later wrote, "Study City Dwelling for Bogk—Milwaukee 1912"; on the second, more conventional one, he noted, "Study for City House Bogk—Milwaukee—FLLW."

The site was a very constricted city lot, with no particular view or prospect. But the elevation is treated, in both cases, with an intricate articulation of windows, brickwork, and concrete lintels. Especially in the second scheme, the one chosen and eventually built, the architect went to great lengths to delineate the sculptural quality of the street façade. Certainly 1912 is not the accurate date; rather the commission came in 1916,

when he was working on the Imperial Hotel. Certain elements about the elevation can be closely related to the elevations he was concurrently designing for the hotel in Tokyo.

Wright often played havoc with the assignment of dates on his own work, as these drawings attest. But sometimes he was precisely accurate, as in the case of the Imperial Hotel. Scholars have consistently placed its date as 1915, but Wright consistently placed it at 1913. A recently discovered letter from the client Hayashi proves that by August 1913 Wright was sure of the commission and had determined that the structure should be of concrete and masonry to guarantee it was fireproof.

"*FIRST STUDY* for Barnsdall Dwelling Hollywood 1913 FLLW" has been penciled in at the very top edge of this rendering. It is one of the few Wright drawings in which the lines of the building, in this case the extended terraces and terrace walls, are cut off by the paper's edge. The image, in other words, occupies the entire sheet. It is a delicately drawn aerial view, mostly in a soft graphite pencil, with no color except for the pale green in the trees and bushes. The house was intended to be a poured-concrete structure, like Unity Temple (page 88), but was changed to wood frame and cement plaster for the most part. Ornamental hollyhock sculptures (Barnsdall's favorite flower) do not appear in this rendering, but they were constructed for the house in poured concrete.

This work demonstrates Wright's reaction to another climate and region: Southern California. The house is built on the top of a hill, basking in the hot California sunshine. Window openings onto the hill are recessed and relatively few in number, while the openings into the patio court, in the center of the house, are full-length French doors leading to grass lawns, pools, and fountains.

The house was designed and constructed between 1919 and 1922, while the architect was traveling back and forth to Tokyo; the client herself was constantly traveling, too. Under these circumstances it is a miracle the house was built at all, albeit the finished product was not altogether according to Wright's wishes.

But despite the difficulties and setbacks, it stands today as a great statement of a type of architecture he felt belonged more to the region than do the imitations of Spanish missions that prevail in Southern California.

"HOLLYHOCK HOUSE," ALINE BARNSDALL HOUSE, *LOS ANGELES, CALIFORNIA. 1917. AERIAL PERSPECTIVE. PENCIL AND COLOR PENCIL ON TRACING PAPER, 19 × 18". FLLW FDN# 1705.002*

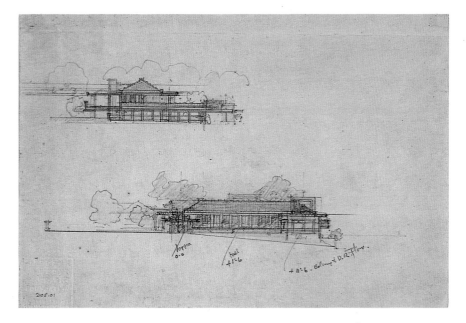

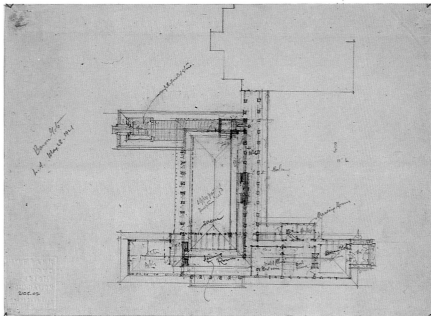

NOT MUCH IS KNOWN about this commission—in Wright's hand the main floor plan has been titled "Baron Goto L.A. May 28, 1921," referring to the client and the date that the sketches were made in Los Angeles. Other drawings in the Frank Lloyd Wright Archives are labeled "Prime Minister's House" and appear to be developed from these three sketches. That Baron Goto and the "Prime Minister" are one and the same person is only speculation.

These three drawings are included here for the pleasure of seeing how Wright drew—the precision with which he made the small plans, with dimensions given for each room, and the delightful elevations. Each sheet measures eleven by seven and a half inches. The project is obviously for a very large house; the sketches are hardly more than "miniatures."

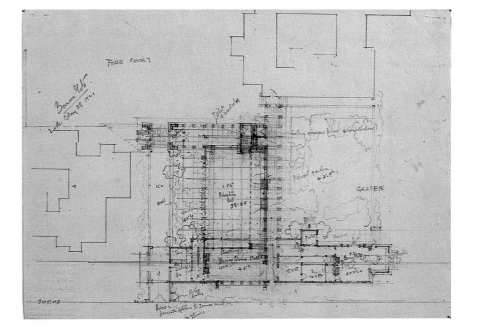

ACROSS THE TOP of one of the preliminary plans for this block house, Wright has penciled in the title, "Study for Block House—Textile Block Construction Los Angeles 1920–1921." This description was the architect's way of explaining the method of reinforcing the structure's concrete blocks with thin rods of steel that run horizontally and vertically inside the hollow grooves of the blocks: a type of weaving is what he sought, with concrete blocks and steel reinforcing each other. Although he classified this particular design as just one of his block houses, such as the Millard, Free-

man, Storer, and Ennis houses, it utilizes a great deal of poured concrete as well. The plan is rather formal, and the perspective certainly suggests monumental formality. There are three levels to the house: the ground floor contains living and dining areas and a kitchen; the second level provides two bedrooms and a study, all three rooms having access to the roof terrace; and a third level, a sort of belvedere, also provides access to roof terraces on either side of the house. Many of Wright's California houses, starting with the Barnsdall House, make use of roof terraces—as is appropriate for

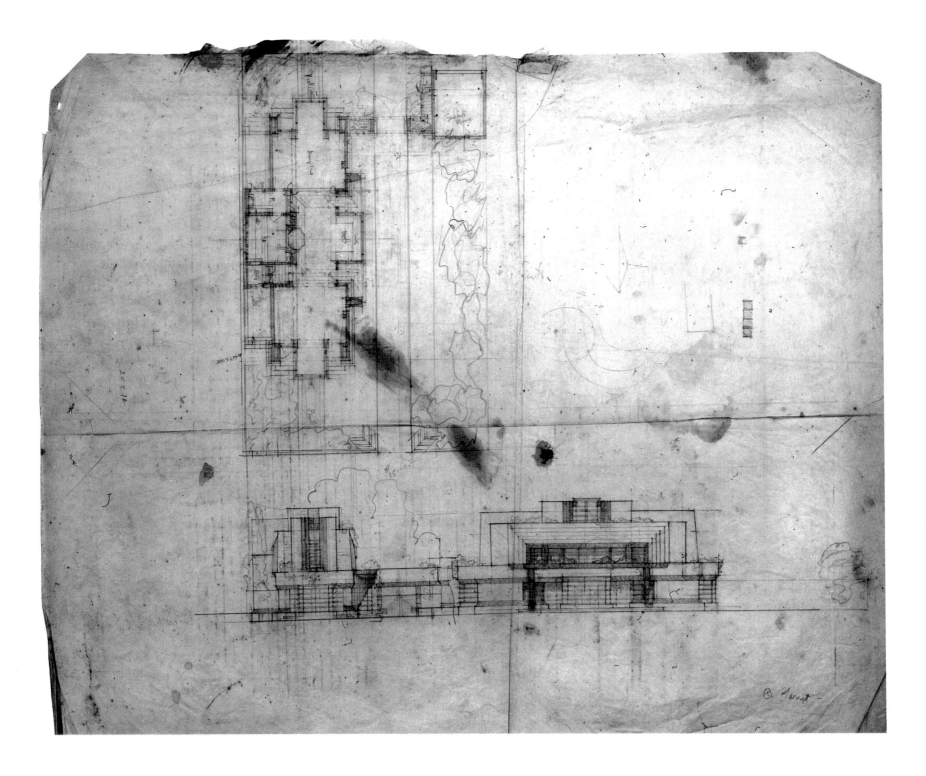

a climate that is gentle and conducive to outdoor living most of the year. The decorative elements in the concrete were achieved, as in Unity Temple (page 88), by pouring concrete into a mold in which steel or wooden blocks pattern the form. In 1901 Wright wrote and delivered a famous paper entitled "The Art and Craft of the Machine." Patterning, as shown here and in the other block houses for California done at this time, is a clear example of what he meant when he maintained in the paper that the machine must be "a tool in the hands of the artist."

The 1921 date seems questionable because of the detail of mitered glass, or glass that covers a corner without a wooden sash. Wright's first use of this detail, as constructed, appeared in the Freeman House of 1924. The same detailing of sash and glass in long horizontal bands is seen here.

STUDY FOR BLOCK HOUSE (PROJECT), LOS ANGELES, CALIFORNIA. 1921. PLAN. PENCIL ON TRACING PAPER, 33 × 29". FLLW FDN# 2103.002

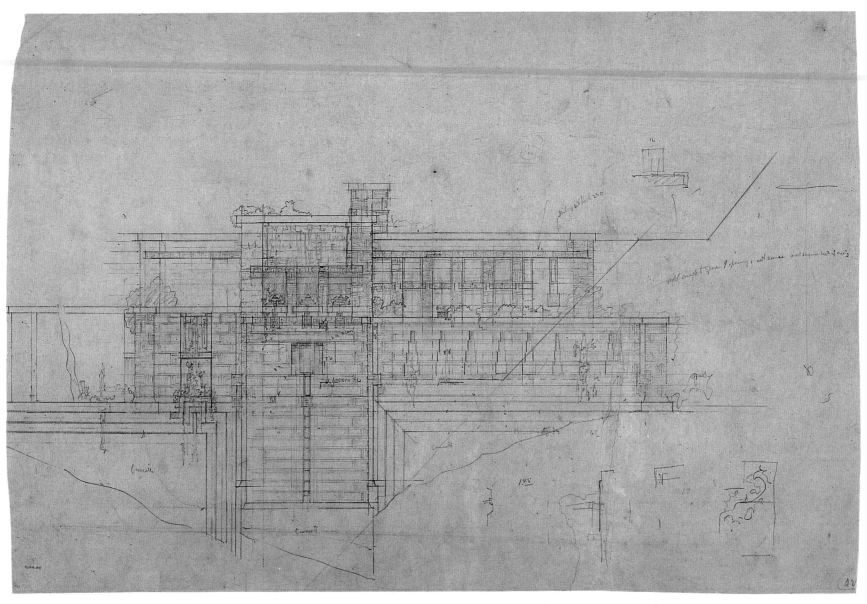

DOHENY RANCH RESORT *(PROJECT)*, LOS ANGELES, CALIFORNIA. 1923. ELEVATION. PENCIL ON TRACING PAPER, 30 × 18". FLLW FDN# 2104.002

THE DOHENY RANCH development gave Wright the opportunity to show how a landscape and an environment could be preserved and respected by architecture. The drawing represents a group of houses in the Hollywood hills. The bridges and roadways were designed by the architect as well.

On this perspective Wright has written, "Doheny Ranch Project—Hollywood Hills Development—Block houses—Roadway built with houses as architecture—Contours of hills undisturbed." On another drawing in the series he has written, "The whole becomes a terraced garden suitable to the region." In 1931, before the European exhibition of his work, where this particular drawing was shown, he wrote the additional caption, "An attempt to preserve the native beauty of the Hollywood hills by preserving all natural contours and growth—embroidering the hills with architecture, the road itself becoming architecture as a part of the houses themselves."

Except where the roadways cross over bridges, themselves beautiful architectural features, they run behind the houses and let the buildings grace the landscape. The perspective gives a tantalizing glimpse at what could have been, had the client had the vision to build it—in contradistinction to the bulldozing and gutting of the hills that has since occurred.

The detail front elevation of one of the houses shows the grammar of the architecture throughout the entire scheme: poured-concrete and patterned-concrete block, similar to the four concrete block houses of his design built at the same time.

(OVERLEAF: DOHENY RANCH RESORT. *PERSPECTIVE; DETAIL)*

DOHENY RANCH RESORT *(PROJECT), LOS ANGELES, CALIFORNIA. 1923. PERSPECTIVE. PENCIL AND COLOR PENCIL ON TRACING PAPER, 30 × 13". FLLW FDN# 2104.005*

CHARLES E. ENNIS HOUSE, LOS ANGELES, CALIFORNIA. 1923. ELEVATION. PENCIL ON TRACING PAPER, 40×22". FLLW FDN# 2401.001

CHARLES E. ENNIS HOUSE, LOS ANGELES, CALIFORNIA. 1923. PERSPECTIVE. PENCIL AND COLOR PENCIL ON TRACING PAPER, 40×20". FLLW FDN# 2401.003

THE ENNIS HOUSE is one of four famous concrete block houses Wright built in Los Angeles upon his return to California from Japan. The first block house was for a former client from Highland Park, Alice Millard (Mrs. George Madison Millard; page 19); following on the heels of that commission came the houses for Storer and Freeman and then Ennis.

The Ennis House is by far the largest of the four; it is a two-bedroom house with a living room, dining room, and guest room. The rest of the opus is taken up by terraces and retaining walls and steps and stairs leading to various levels. The house itself is practically one great retaining wall set into the steep hillside. By 1954 Wright regarded the Ennis House somewhat adversely, and he confessed, "I built the Storer House up on the hill, it's a little palace, it looked like a little Venetian palazzo. Then I built the Freeman House, then there was finally the Ennis House, which was way out of concrete-block size. I think that was carrying it too far—that's what you do, you know, after you get going, and get going so far that you get out of bounds. And I think the Ennis House was out of bounds for a concrete-block house."

Nevertheless, for sheer beauty in an architectural conceptual elevation, the Ennis drawing is one of his most powerful examples. And the perspective, rising over an isometric partial plan at the bottom of the sheet of paper, is also a drawing of exceptional quality. There is no framing, no border lines, no title block on the rendering. The draftsmanship, as well as the artistry, is impressive: each block is minutely detailed, each element of the house graphically explicit.

Wright's touches can be detected in the shading, the foliage, and the manner in which he outlined the building. A simple title has been added by the architect at a later date in his own handwriting: "Perspective drawing of Ennis House Hollywood Los Angeles." The 1920–1921 date is not accurate; the working drawings are dated January 1924, which would logically place the conceptual and preliminary drawings sometime in 1923.

"A STUDY FOR A HOUSE on a steep bank—overlooking a great plain—hot winds" is the 1931 caption for this work. The drawing is precisely rendered in clean, black ink lines on white tracing paper, showing a view of the house above a plan at the edge of the sheet. The formal composition of the drawing is broken by tall trees on one side and an architectural feature on the other.

MRS. SAMUEL GLADNEY HOUSE (PROJECT),
FORT WORTH, TEXAS. 1924. PERSPECTIVE AND PLAN.
INK ON ART PAPER, 35 × 26". FLLW FDN# 2502.003

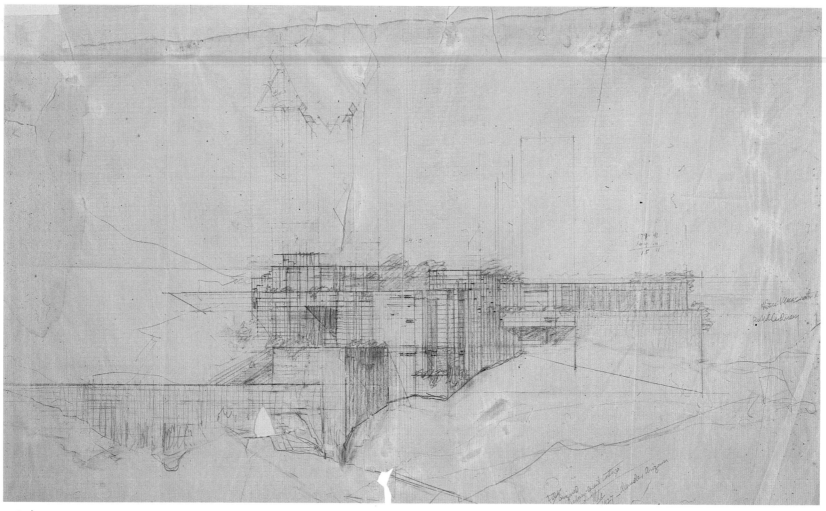

RALPH AND WELLINGTON CUDNEY HOUSE *(PROJECT)*, CHANDLER, ARIZONA. 1928. CONCEPTUAL ELEVATION. PENCIL ON TRACING PAPER, 31 × 19". FLLW FDN# 2706.001

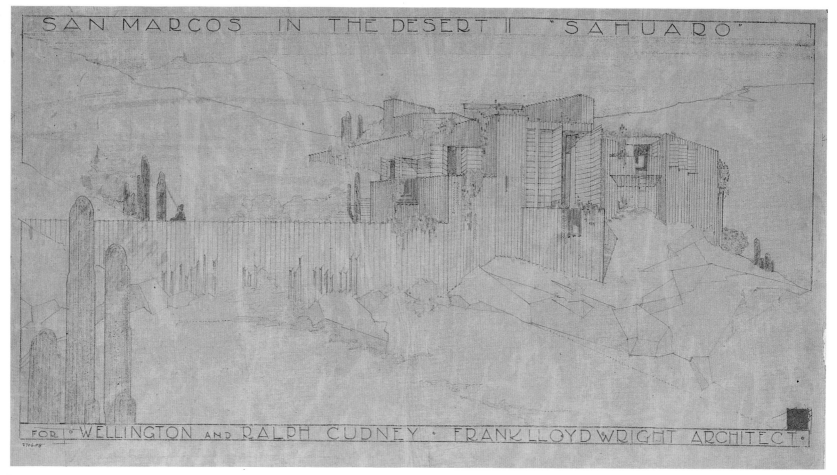

RALPH AND WELLINGTON CUDNEY HOUSE *(PROJECT)*, CHANDLER, ARIZONA. 1928. PERSPECTIVE. PENCIL AND COLOR PENCIL ON TRACING PAPER, 22 × 19". FLLW FDN# 2706.008

PERSPECTIVE VIEW

SAN MARCOS IN THE DESERT. MOUNTAIN COTTAGE FOR MRS. OWEN D. YOUNG — FRANK LLOYD WRIGHT. ARCHITECT

FOR A RESORT called San Marcos-in-the-Desert Wright designed two separate cottages, one at each end of the hotel's great terrace. The Cudney brothers, for whom this project, named "Saguaro," was designed, were New York financiers who were also partly financing the construction of the main hotel. The saguaro is a typical cactus of the Sonoran desert—the type of desert that stretches from the state of Sonora in Mexico up into Arizona and New Mexico. Three tall stalks of the cactus, which ordinarily are taller than people, appear in the perspective drawing to illustrate the natural form that provided the inspiration for the house itself.

The conceptual elevation, in graphite pencil on tracing paper, is complex and intricate, as is the "cottage" itself.

HERE WRIGHT has taken the concrete-block form and turned it at an angle of 45 degrees in a rich application of geometry that naturally blends the house into the environment. The rocks and cactus seem to have found a sympathetic companion in this structure. As we study Wright's designs for the Arizona desert, we can be frankly alarmed at the type of housing and construction in general that instead grew up in the Phoenix region: uncomfortable and unbecoming imitations of colonial, Spanish, ranch-modern, and other "styles" that do not take into consideration the climate or the landscape.

OWEN D. YOUNG HOUSE *(PROJECT)*, *CHANDLER, ARIZONA. 1928. PERSPECTIVE. PENCIL AND COLOR PENCIL ON TRACING PAPER, 32 × 24".* *FLLW FDN# 2707.002*

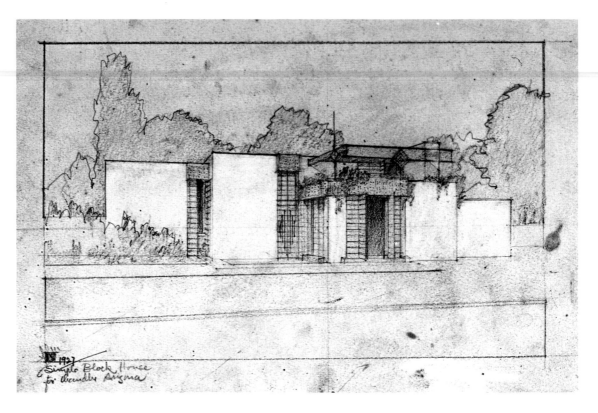

CITY BLOCK HOUSE *(PROJECT)*, CHANDLER, ARIZONA. 1928. PERSPECTIVE. PENCIL AND COLOR PENCIL ON ART PAPER, 14 × 12". FLLW FDN# 2708.001

"A SIMPLE BLOCK house for Chandler, Arizona," written at the bottom of this perspective, denotes exactly what the architect had in mind for this project. By "block house" he did not mean the concrete textile-block construction used for the California houses a few years earlier; rather he meant a typical small dwelling on a city block. In this case, the house was intended for the town of Chandler, Arizona, and intended to be part of a subdivision of several similar houses. The materials are wood frame and cement stucco, the form is obviously quite simple: square rooms with narrow openings for tall glass windows. For the particularities of the climate, the window area is kept to a minimum, while the upper level opens onto a large roof deck with a canvas awning. The living room faces the front of the lot, with a dining room, kitchen, and breakfast nook behind. The ground level provides for a guest room and a studio-bedroom as well. The master bedroom on the upper level measures a generous twenty feet by thirty-five feet.

Wright was to make several modifications of this plan during the next five years, providing more bedroom space, a garage with maid's room, and an enclosed garden yard. But the general configuration of plan and elevation would remain as it is seen here.

RICHARD LLOYD JONES, as the name implies, was a relative of Frank Lloyd Wright's—his cousin—and the son of Jenkin Lloyd Jones, the Chicago Unitarian preacher. The Welsh strain in Wright's ancestral line was a strong one: all of the Lloyd Joneses were colorful, powerful, temperamental, and often very difficult individuals. They came from a pioneering background, and each and every one of them carried that banner through life. Cousin Dick, as Richard Lloyd Jones was called, was no different. He left his native Illinois-Wisconsin background and came to Tulsa to run a newspaper. At a time—1929—when the rest of the nation was suffering from the stock-market crash and the Depression, Jones was successful in his publishing venture and was determined to build a suitable home for himself and his family.

The house is very large, to say the least, and built on a grand scale. It is a one-of-a-kind work, with no predecessor or follower in Wright's oeuvre. In the 1931 catalog for the showing of his work in Belgium, Holland, and Germany, Wright described this work: "The dwelling house without walls. The palisades with steel sash and glass between substituted. The interior space robed with textiles and light modified by movable screens—both features of the architecture."

The term "palisades" refers to the alternating vertical members of concrete block and glass. At the terminals of the wings, glass enclosures extend out and up as conservatories for indoor plants and trees. One such enclosure is seen on the perspective where the line of the house reaches out toward the sidewalk.

RICHARD LLOYD JONES HOUSE, TULSA, OKLAHOMA. 1929. PERSPECTIVE. PENCIL AND COLOR PENCIL ON TRACING PAPER, 25 × 10". FLLW FDN# 2902.004

EVERYONE AT TALIESIN was excited about the prospect of the commission from Edgar Kaufmann to design his home in western Pennsylvania. His son, Edgar, Jr., had been an apprentice in the Taliesin Fellowship and had encouraged his father first to help finance the making and exhibiting of the Broadacre City model and then to build this weekend house near a series of water cascades in Mill Run. Wright had visited the site, a deep shady glen in a forest. A rushing stream, Bear Run, flowed through the site and was bordered by rhododendron bushes. The architect had walked over the property while Edgar and his wife, Liliane, explained how they entertained their guests there: sunbathing on the large flat ledges of stone, sliding down the rocks into the falls, letting the cascades of water pour over them.

When he was back at Taliesin, Wright wrote to Kaufmann that "the visit to the waterfall in the woods stays with me and a domicile has taken vague shape in my mind to the music of the stream." But the design remained in his mind for quite some time: there was not a line on a piece of paper. His apprentices were getting anxious over the situation: here was the first major commission he had received in many years. A long drought between commissions had occurred after the stock-market collapse in 1929 and the termination of the San Marcos projects for Alexander Chandler (page 189). There had only been the one large house for his cousin Richard Lloyd Jones and a smaller house in Minneapolis for Malcolm Willey in 1932. By 1934 Wright had turned his full attention to the design and model of Broadacre City, a study in decentralization. But these were projects only, nothing concrete to go into construction.

When Wright one day received a phone call from Edgar Kaufmann asking about the sketches for his house, the architect jauntily invited his client to come to Taliesin, where he would show him something. The anxiety of the apprentices who heard this exchange, namely Edgar Tafel and Robert Mosher (who would both figure prominently in the construction and supervision of the Kaufmann house), turned to troubled concern. There was not a line on paper, and Wright was inviting the client to see the work! But what the apprentices failed to realize at that time (they would learn to understand it better as they worked at Taliesin) was that the design was indeed there, in Wright's imagination, fully complete and ready to pour out on paper. And pour it did. He sat down and produced in the span of a few hours the design for Fallingwater. By the time that Kaufmann arrived, basic plans for the three levels were sketched and the elevation prepared, showing the relationship of the house to the rock ledges, the surrounding trees, and the cascading water. Kaufmann was at first astonished that his architect had placed the house over the waterfall, not up the slope looking at it. "Not to look at your waterfall, but to live with it," was Wright's reply.

In subsequent weeks more drawings were made and taken to Pittsburgh. Although the design flowed rapidly from Wright's imagination onto paper, there was a great deal of modification required to make that vision a reality.

This perspective shows the house in relation to the cascades. It portrays a view that, in reality, is not possible to see without going farther down the falls and climbing up into a tree to get to a higher elevation. The real essence of Fallingwater is that almost mystical blend of man and nature that Wright achieved in this building. It is difficult to qualify his work, or classify it. He himself rarely did so, but he once confessed that Fallingwater "is a great blessing—one of the great blessings to be experienced here on earth."

(OVERLEAF: FALLINGWATER. PERSPECTIVE; DETAIL)

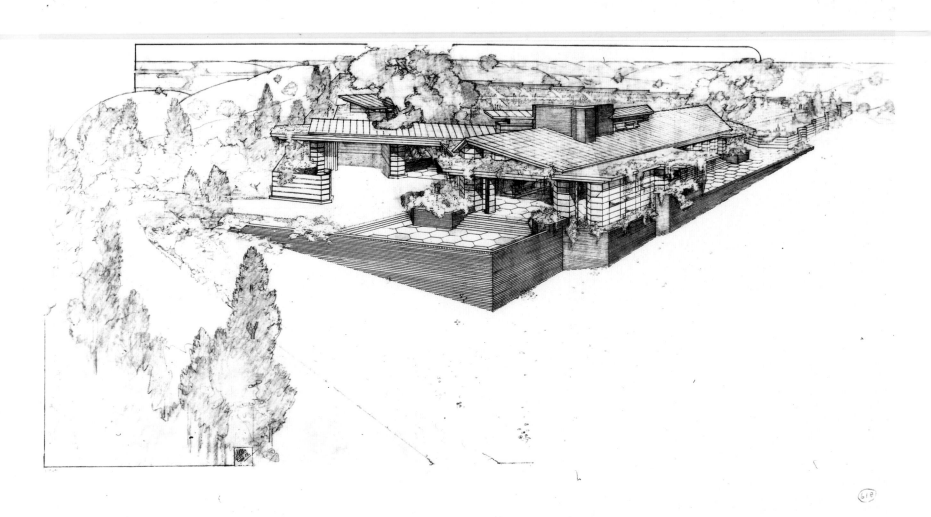

PAUL AND JEAN HANNA HOUSE, *STANFORD, CALIFORNIA. 1936. AERIAL PERSPECTIVE. PENCIL ON PAPER, 36×22" FLLW FDN# 3701.001*

DEVELOPING ANOTHER innovation in plan type, Wright employed the hexagonal unit as the basis for this residential design. He gave this home for Paul and Jean Hanna the name "Honeycomb House." Built of brick, copper, and glass, the house takes advantage of the California clime. Sections of glass doors in the living room and playroom fold away to the sides, opening the rooms fully to the outdoor terraces. The aerial view shows this effect on the living-room side. Every detail, every feature, every bit of furniture had to be specially designed to conform to the hexagonal nature of the plan. From this prototype plan Wright went on to design dozens of other homes based on the same unit system, or variations of it.

In this ink and graphite pencil drawing, there is a delicate shading in the pencil areas that brings out subtle tones of gray, which lie quietly in repose across the paper — a consort to the black ink lines of the house itself.

THE JOHNSON WAX Company Building was in construction in 1937 (page 248). It was a complicated building due to Wright's many innovations in construction technique and use of materials. At the same time, Fallingwater was also in construction, some seven hundred miles to the east near Pittsburgh. The large and expansive house for Herbert Johnson himself (page 46) was also on the boards concurrent with the two works cited above. In the midst of these major commissions, Wright suddenly revolutionized the moderate-cost home-building industry with this design for a house for a journalist and his family in Madison, Wisconsin.

Every aspect of the Jacobs House pioneered a new path in small-home construction, especially the floor-heated concrete slab and the wooden sandwich walls (composed of a plywood core with building paper on either side and boards and battens then fastened down with brass screws on both sides). The wall construction was conceived as something that could easily be done in a factory or on the building site, with the completed walls then raised on site. All the various details of this method of building that Wright called the "Usonian house" were explained in his book *The Natural House*, published in 1954. The Jacobs House was the prototype for many dozens that followed across the nation, from New England and the South to California.

The drawing illustrated here is actually two separate perspectives joined together: the upper one shows the house as seen from the garden side of the property, the lower one as seen from the street side. Both drawings are monochromatic, rendered in sepia rose pencil with only a few touches in graphite pencil. The way in which each of the drawings is "framed" by skyline and foliage creates a charming effect that is intensified by the two views being placed together as one.

HERBERT JACOBS HOUSE, *MADISON, WISCONSIN. 1937. PERSPECTIVES. PENCIL AND COLOR PENCIL ON TRACING PAPER, 33 × 22". FLLW FDN# 3702.002*

HOUSE FOR HERBERT JACOBS
MADISON, WISCONSIN
$5,500.

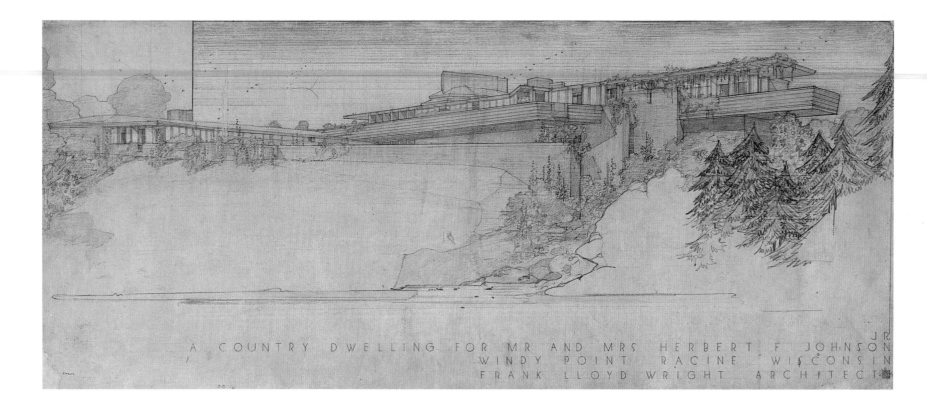

A COUNTRY DWELLING FOR MR AND MRS HERBERT F JOHNSON JR
WINDY POINT RACINE WISCONSIN
FRANK LLOYD WRIGHT ARCHITECT

IN THE WINTER of 1934–1935, Wright and his apprentices migrated from cold, sub-zero Wisconsin to Chandler, Arizona, where they worked—mostly out of doors, bathed by the warm desert sunshine—on the preparation of the Broadacre City models. Their experience in the desert convinced the architect that he would make a winter camp in Arizona. But it was not until 1937–1938 that he found the site for Taliesin West, as this new camp was to be called, and began construction.

The building that he and his apprentices built, literally with their own hands, is a complex one: it was added to, changed, revised, rearranged, expanded, and modified each winter, when Wright returned to the desert, for a period of twenty-two years. But the basic idea of the structure remained constant: over a massive base of desert masonry walls, a superstructure of red- wood and canvas provided soft, translucent light for the rooms below. This startling combination of two such distinctly opposite materials—stone walls and stretched white canvas—produced a totally new effect in architecture, at once massive and protective, rugged like the mountain ranges, and ephemeral, delicate, almost transitory.

"TALIESIN WEST," FRANK LLOYD WRIGHT RESIDENCE AND STUDIO, *SCOTTSDALE, ARIZONA. 1937. AERIAL PERSPECTIVE. PENCIL AND COLOR PENCIL ON TRACING PAPER, 104 × 23". FLLW FDN# 3803.003*

FROM A CENTRAL, three-story living room—a tall tepeelike form—four wings extend in each direction: one for the master bedroom, seen to the right on this perspective, one for the children, one for guests, and the last for the kitchen and servants' areas. Given this plan, Wright named the opus "Wingspread" and likened it to an earlier work of his, the Avery Coonley House in Riverside, Illinois, because of what he called the "zoned plan." The Coonley House was not so precise in its divisions of zones, nor as large. And the Coonley House, although placed on a generous suburban site, was still a home in a suburban environment. Here, at Wingspread, the prairie surrounds the house. In the center of the tall living room a great brick mass acts as a dividing feature to segregate the room's various functions: entrance hall, living space, dining space, and mezzanine library. Each of these spaces has its own fireplace opening onto it from the central mass. The roof is pierced with small, square skylights, while tall French doors on each of the four sides of the great hall give onto gardens, terraces, and a swimming pool.

''WINGSPREAD,'' H. F. JOHNSON HOUSE, WIND POINT, WISCONSIN. 1937. PERSPECTIVE. PENCIL AND COLOR PENCIL ON TRACING PAPER, 40 × 17". FLLW FDN# 3703.002

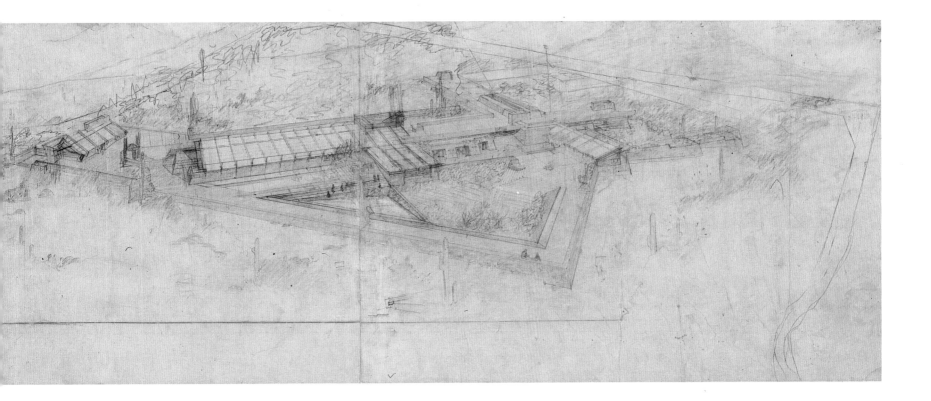

JUST AS THE Pauson drawing (page 54) reflects the delicate mystery of the desert in Arizona, the Pew drawing reflects the lush green landscape of southern Wisconsin. The main feature of the site is Lake Mendota, seen from the balconies of the house and through the branches of the trees. As with many such renderings laid out and started by the members of the Taliesin Fellowship, Wright has added his own touches, evident in the water and foliage, the shading of the embankment, and the outlining of the tree trunks. Wesley Peters, Wright's son-in-law and an engineer, acted as contractor for this moderately priced home for a university professor and his family. The house was in construction at about the same time as Fallingwater (page 41), and many of the site conditions are somewhat similar: a shady glen, steep slope, and the presence of water. Fallingwater, of course, was placed in a much deeper glen, on a far vaster tract of land, and was more luxurious in every way. But when Peters remarked to Wright, "We should call the Pew house the 'poor man's Fallingwater,'" the architect corrected him, saying, "No, Wes. We shall call Fallingwater the 'rich man's Pew house.'".

JOHN C. PEW HOUSE, SHOREWOOD HILLS, WISCONSIN. 1938. PERSPECTIVE. PENCIL AND COLOR PENCIL ON TRACING PAPER, 36 × 22". FLLW FDN# 4012.002

THE YEARS FROM 1934 to 1939 are studded with many new and innovative types of designs by Wright for works ranging from office buildings to private dwellings. It was in the development of the residence plan, chiefly, that Wright explored new directions in the general configuration of rooms and spaces. The Jacobs House saw the "L"-shaped plan, almost never used before, take best advantage of a city lot by its placement at the corner of the property, thus freeing up the rest of the land and allowing all of the rooms of the house to open onto gardens and lawn. The Hanna House ventured into the first use of the hexagon as a unit. The Jester House, for the first time in Wright's work, employs the circle as the basic design unit. By spacing the circular modules on a square grid, mostly apart from each other, the architect was able to avoid the tight constriction of the interstices that would have resulted if the circles all touched. Dining and work areas and a small bedroom were also designed to avoid constriction. The lounge, or living room, is the largest of the circles. The central patio, roofed over but open on the sides, is the focal point for the circular spaces. All doors leading into the patio are full-length French doors, protected by the patio roof from sun or rain. The windows that face out form a narrow band at eye level, creating a continuous "scroll" out of the surrounding landscape.

During a period of eighteen years, Frank Lloyd Wright tried to build variations of this house for ten different clients. It seems that the circular plan frightened them away, and when they complained about the circle, he would say, "But man's pattern of mobility is certainly circular; only the military walks 'square.'" Nevertheless, regardless of size or location, the design went unbuilt until an adaptation of this house was constructed at Taliesin West in 1971.

RALPH JESTER HOUSE, PALOS VERDES, CALIFORNIA. 1938. PERSPECTIVE AND PLAN. PENCIL AND COLOR PENCIL ON TRACING PAPER, 35 × 33". FLLW FDN# 3807.003

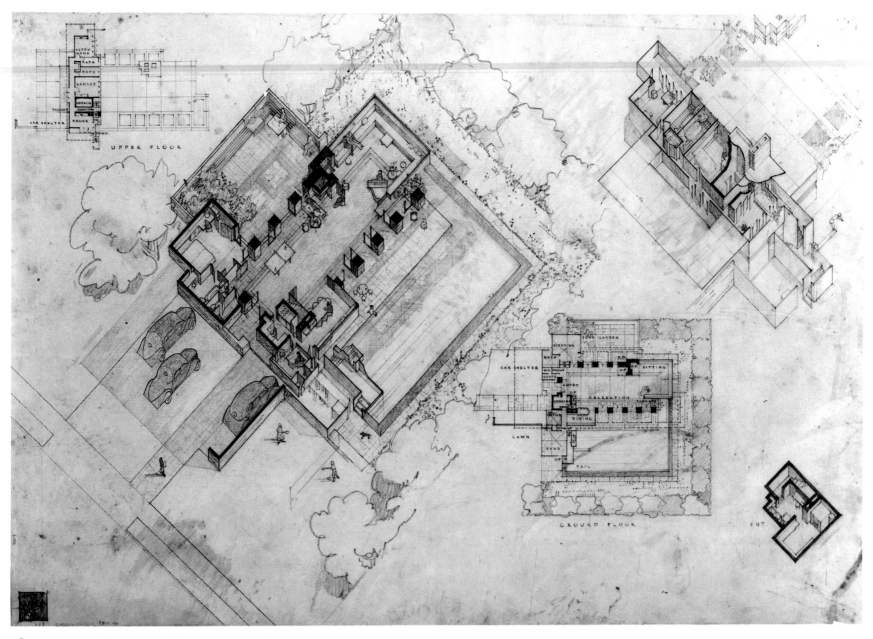

IN 1938 LIFE *MAGAZINE* and the *Architectural Forum,* both owned by Time-Life, Inc., sponsored a series of house projects at various prices showing potential clients traditional designs by contemporary architects as well as designs by modern architects. Frank Lloyd Wright was one of the architects chosen to design a nontraditional house in the 5,000-dollar bracket.

The plan of Wright's submission is actually the same, in general concept, as his design of the Jester House (page 49), but here the units are square and rectangular rather than circular. The open patio of the prototype house is enclosed (the client was in Minneapolis where such open living would be unfeasible). The master bedroom is on the ground level, but an upper level provides three additional bedrooms for the children.

The drawing is one of the best in Wright's Usonian house series, done all in rose and sepia colored pencils, with the blossoms of the hollyhocks touched up in brown ink. Off to the left, tucked among the foliage, can be seen—for an interesting contrast—the typical American dwelling of the time.

Below the perspective Wright has written, "For a Usonian family in these United States - The Blackbourns - Minneapolis - Minnesota." Close to his signature square with the date, "Aug 15/38," he added, "To Howard M—from FLLW." The drawing was dedicated to Howard Myers, editor of *Architectural Forum* and a friend of Frank Lloyd Wright's. It was through Myers's dedicated persistence that the two *Forum* issues of January 1938 and January 1948 were given over entirely to Wright's work.

The clients preferred the Wright design for their house to the alternate one—a Colonial design. But the lack of bank financing forced them to accept the more traditional scheme. They were warned, as were many of the clients for these early Usonian homes, that the walls would not support the roof, that floor heating was impractical, that the combination of living-dining room was undesirable, that the kitchen—as a workspace adjacent to the main living area—was also undesirable, and in general the design would have no resale value.

50

BLACKBOURN HOUSE FOR *LIFE* MAGAZINE (PROJECT), MINNEAPOLIS, MINNESOTA. 1938. PERSPECTIVE. COLOR PENCIL ON TRACING PAPER, 36×24". FLLW FDN# 3806.001

BLACKBOURN HOUSE FOR *LIFE* MAGAZINE (PROJECT), MINNEAPOLIS, MINNESOTA. 1938. INTERIOR PERSPECTIVE. SEPIA INK ON TRACING PAPER, 32×23". FLLW FDN# 3806.007

(OVERLEAF: BLACKBOURN HOUSE. PLAN; DETAIL)

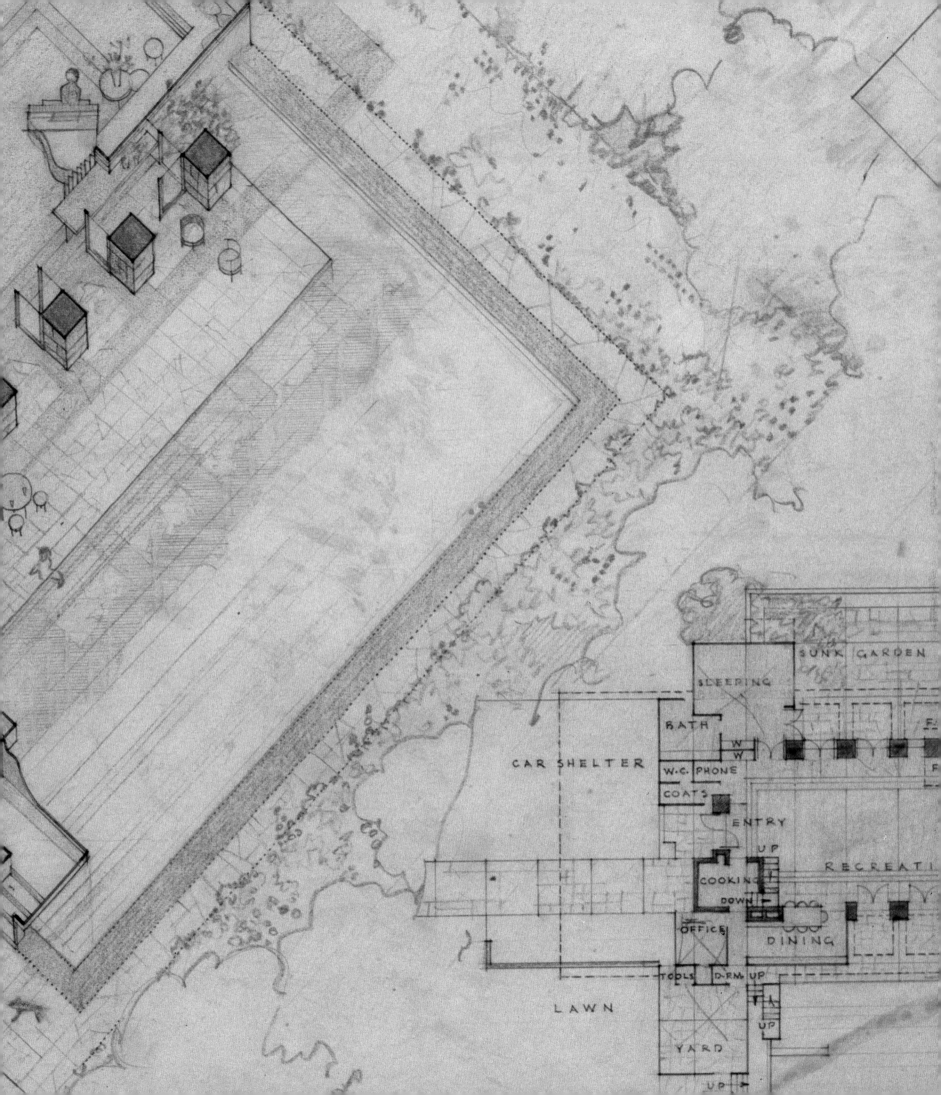

SUNK GARDEN

SLEEPING

BATH

CAR SHELTER

W.C. PHONE

COATS

ENTRY

UP

COOKING

DOWN

RECREATI

OFFICE

DINING

TOOLS   D.RM UP

LAWN

UP

YARD

UP

ONE OF THE UNDERLYING principles of all of
Frank Lloyd Wright's work was the relationship of building to site; this interaction became something at which
he was a great master. In his earlier homes this was not
the challenge that he was later afforded because most of
them were built in suburban Chicago and Oak Park on
typical city lots.

When he had a fine site, especially when he had a
difficult site, his reaction to it produced an equally
special design. This relationship of the dwelling to its
environs is nowhere better expressed, on paper at least,
than in this rendering for the Rose Pauson House. Desert and building, rocks and wall, even the mists and
mountains, are wedded together in a rendering of exquisite poetry and poignancy. The coloring and shading
shows his sense of the Sonoran desert—vast, silent,
mysterious, and, indeed, delicate: for once the desert
terrain is interrupted or disturbed, it never regains its
equilibrium, never grows back as it was before. This
sense of a timeless but fragile quiet is reflected in the
perspective drawing.

On the lower left Wright has written, "A desert house
just completed for the Pauson Sisters Phoenix Arizona.
Cost - $7500.00 complete."

ROSE PAUSON HOUSE, PHOENIX, ARIZONA
(DEMOLISHED). 1939. PERSPECTIVE. PENCIL AND COLOR
PENCIL ON TRACING PAPER, 29×15". FLLW FDN# 4011.002

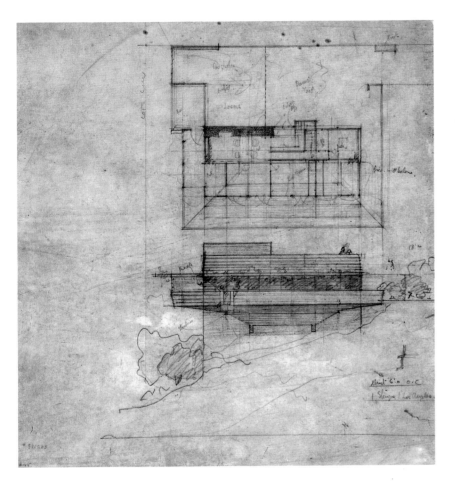

THE ARCHITECT'S conceptual plan for this house is simple: a rectangular form containing a living-dining room by the fireplace mass at the left, two bedrooms, and a kitchen and bathroom on the right—the entire house placed on a brick pedestal with a terraced balcony for living room and bedrooms riding out over the treetops. The site was steep, and the building is brought to the back of the property line, where there is a car shelter and paved court, leaving the rest of the site undisturbed. The scale figure standing on the terrace by the parapet reveals that the house is a relatively small one, compact in plan, but taking great advantage of the cantilever principle.

GEORGE STURGES HOUSE, BRENTWOOD HEIGHTS, CALIFORNIA. 1939. CONCEPTUAL PLAN AND ELEVATION. PENCIL ON TRACING PAPER, 14 × 15". FLLW FDN# 3905.003

GEORGE STURGES HOUSE, BRENTWOOD HEIGHTS, CALIFORNIA. 1939. PERSPECTIVE. PENCIL AND COLOR PENCIL ON TRACING PAPER, 37 × 22". FLLW FDN# 3905.002

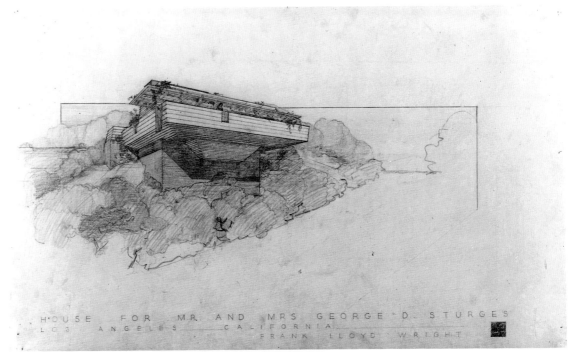

HOUSE FOR MR. AND MRS. GEORGE D. STURGES
LOS ANGELES CALIFORNIA
FRANK LLOYD WRIGHT

HOUSE FOR MR. AND MRS. E. A. SMITH . . PIEDMONT PINES
FRANK LLOYD WRIGHT ARCHITECT

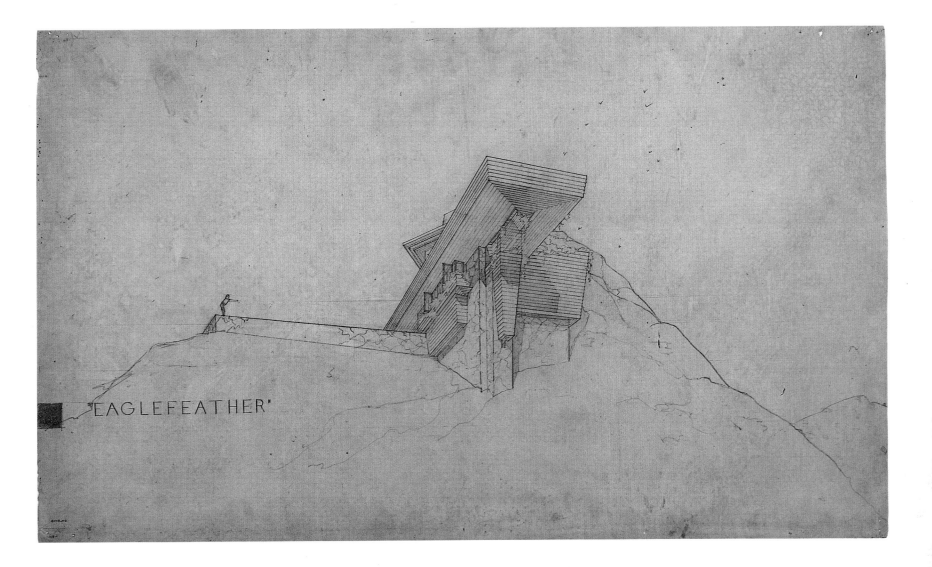

"EAGLEFEATHER"

IN 1921–1922 Wright designed a group of vacation cabins for Lake Tahoe, California (page 181). The site was a steeply sloped pine forest bordering a lake, and the designs for the cottages placed in the forest were inspired by the surrounding fir trees. The project was never realized, but sixteen years later he designed a home for E. A. Smith in Piedmont Pines, California, in a similar situation.

The base of the house is built of stone masonry set into a wooden form. Concrete was poured in and around the stones, and the form was then removed when the mix hardened. Above this substantial fortress of heavy masonry, the house itself rises as a pure abstraction made from pine wood—the natural material of the surrounding site. Like the Tahoe project, the house was never realized.

E. A. SMITH HOUSE (PROJECT), PIEDMONT PINES, CALIFORNIA. 1939. PERSPECTIVE. PENCIL AND COLOR PENCIL ON TRACING PAPER, 22 × 23". FLLW FDN# 3811.001

ARCH OBOLER was a radio and film writer-producer, specializing in horror films and radio programs such as "Lights Out" and "Suspense." Wright named the house he designed for him on a mountaintop in Malibu, California, "Eaglefeather." The head-on view selected for this collection since it is the view most rarely seen, highlights the extended parapet that soars out from the hillside to look over the mountains, meadows, and the sea beyond. The building is in three levels, the living room becoming, as would be expected, a cinema when desired. Bedrooms and the study—called in this case "Sanctum"—are on the lower levels, and a swimming pool, surrounded and supported by stone masonry walls, extends to the left of the house. A poised figure, ready to take a dive into the pool, completes the rendering.

"EAGLEFEATHER," ARCH OBOLER HOUSE (PROJECT), MALIBU, CALIFORNIA. 1940. PERSPECTIVE. PENCIL AND COLOR PENCIL ON TRACING PAPER, 37 × 22". FLLW FDN# 4018.002

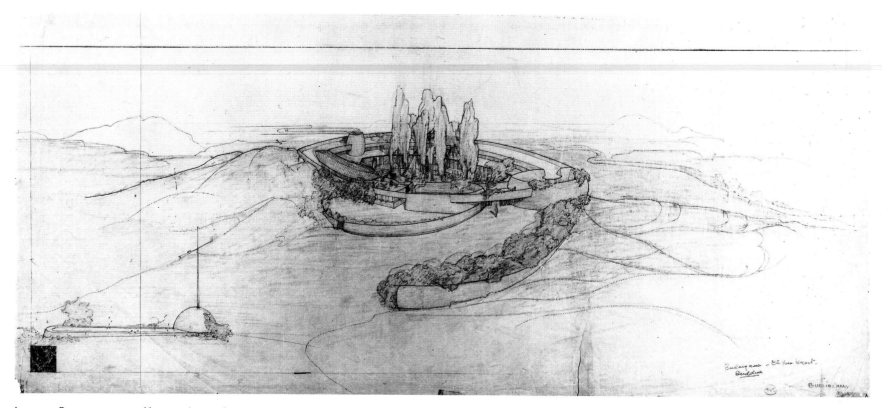

"BURLINGHAM—EL PASO DESERT—SAND-DUNE," Wright wrote on this perspective. If ever there was a dwelling that reflected the nature of its site, it is this house, which seems to be but another one of the desert's sand dunes. The architecture is so appropriate to the landscape that one would be hard put to imagine any other design for the same location.

On another drawing Wright made the notation, "House for a sea of swirling sands," thereby explaining the nature of the plan: curvilinear, closed to the outside for the most part, opening onto a patio-oasis within.

The material was to be adobe, typical of the region, prompting Wright to refer to this opus as the "Pottery House."

THE BLACK INK plan and section for these homesteads are typical of the genre of drawings that Wright had his apprentices prepare for "publication": in other words, an explicitly simple type of drawing that is easily readable. The project was for a group of houses in the Detroit area that were to be constructed of rammed earth with banks of grasses and moss bermed against the walls for insulation. Construction was begun on a prototype, but the war intervened, building materials were unavailable, and the project was abandoned.

The rendering demonstrates the simple nature of the entire design, and coloring on the berm indicates the effect of planting it with a variety of ground covers, making it a carpetlike feature nestling up to the building.

Unlike most renderings, this is done mainly in brown ink with color pencils instead of graphite pencil with ink employed only for touches.

COOPERATIVE HOMESTEADS HOUSING *(PROJECT)*,

DETROIT, MICHIGAN. 1942. PLAN. INK ON TRACING PAPER,

35×18. FLLW FDN# 4201.026

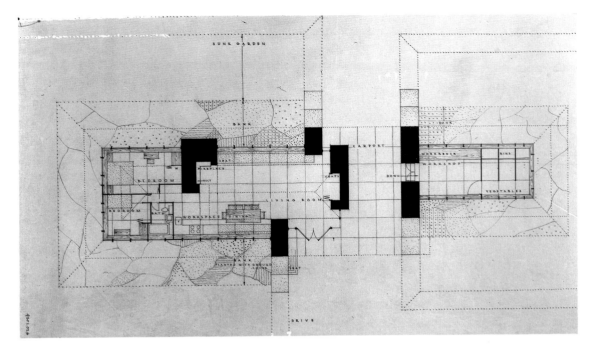

COOPERATIVE HOMESTEADS HOUSING *(PROJECT)*,

DETROIT, MICHIGAN. 1942. PERSPECTIVE.

INK AND COLOR PENCIL ON TRACING PAPER,

34×20. FLLW FDN# 4201.009

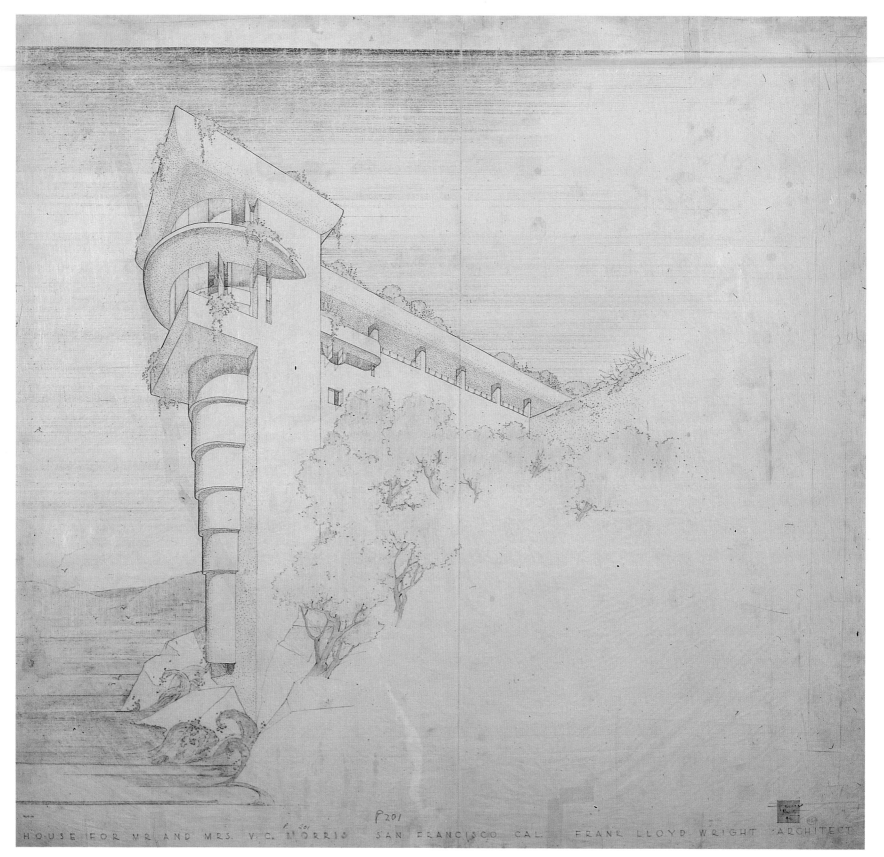

HOUSE FOR MR AND MRS. V.C. MORRIS   SAN FRANCISCO CAL.   FRANK LLOYD WRIGHT ARCHITECT

''SEACLIFF,'' V. C. MORRIS HOUSE (PROJECT), SAN FRANCISCO, CALIFORNIA. 1945. PERSPECTIVE. PENCIL AND COLOR PENCIL ON TRACING PAPER, 42 × 40". FLLW FDN# 4303.004

FRANK LLOYD WRIGHT
DWELLING FOR MR AND MR WILLIAM R SLATER
WARWICK · RHODE ISLAND

WILLIAM SLATER HOUSE *(PROJECT)*, WARWICK, RHODE ISLAND. 1946. PERSPECTIVE. PENCIL AND COLOR PENCIL ON TRACING PAPER, 34×22". FLLW FDN# 4504.002

(opposite)

LONG, HORIZONTAL, ground-hugging lines form the grammar we most associate with the work of Frank Lloyd Wright—at least in his residential architecture. Here, however, for a house on the cliff near Golden Gate Bridge, San Francisco, he stacked the living arrangements in a vertical succession that becomes one with the cliff site itself. The top level is a circular space for living and dining; French doors open onto a terrace overlooking the sea. The parapet is made of metal bars, so that the view from inside will not be impeded. The level below the roof contains the master and mistress bedrooms, with study and storage vault for works of art. The small study doubles as a guest room. The third level down in the circular shaft provides two more guest rooms with the sea view, while servants' rooms are placed in the part of the building that reaches back to engage the cliff.

The reinforced concrete roof edges above the living room turn up to hold soil for a roof garden that stretches all the way back to the entrance drive and garage. "A house to the ocean, a garden to the neighbors," as Wright described it.

While working drawings were being prepared, the Morrises commissioned Wright to design a shop for them on Maiden Lane in San Francisco. They went ahead and built the shop, but even after two revisions of plans for the house, it was never built. At one point Wright referred to this condition as "the little steamboat that blew its whistles, then had to return to shore for more firewood." The Morrises never had the means to continue the house project, but they remained steadfast friends of the architect's. Wright encouraged many of his later clients to go to the Morris Shop on Maiden Lane for furnishings for their houses, particularly crystal, glass, silver, and tableware.

(above)

THE DESIGN for this New England home is a development of a house plan Wright tried twice before. The first time, for northern Wisconsin, Wright named the project "Below Zero." The second time it was proposed again for Wisconsin, near Racine. Both earlier schemes were considerably smaller than this, occupying the main section seen here on the right, with living room and two bedrooms. The Slater version extends a longer bedroom wing to the left.

The roof line rises high on one side and sweeps down almost to the ground on the other, expressing the sense of shelter required in colder climes. Glass French doors are kept to a minimum, included only under the protective roof over the living room. The tree growing through the roof is a typical solution used frequently by Wright to save an existing tree without having to alter the chosen location of the building.

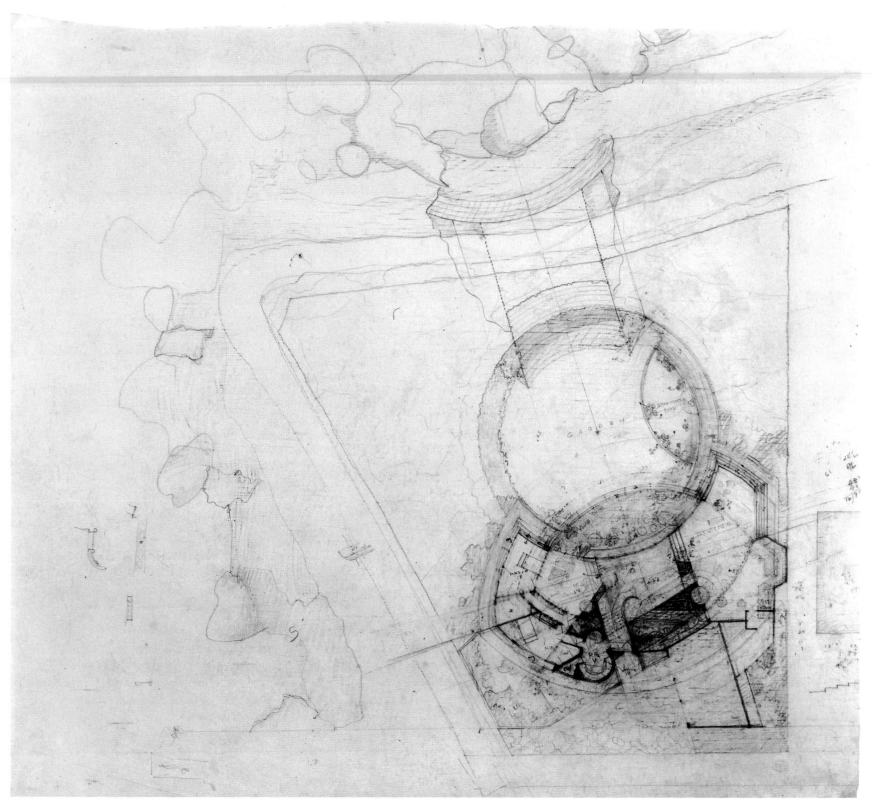

"THE WAVE," STUART HALDORN HOUSE *(PROJECT)*, CARMEL, CALIFORNIA. 1945. PLAN. PENCIL AND COLOR PENCIL ON TRACING PAPER, 36×32". FLLW FDN# 4502.004

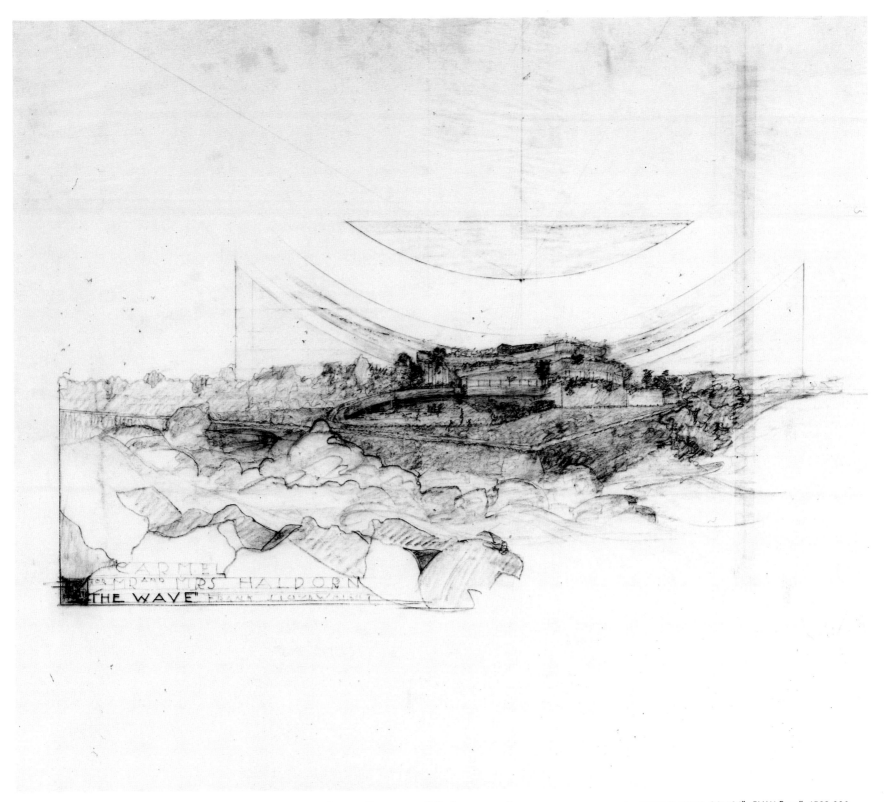

THE PLAN FOR the Haldorn House solved two vexatious problems in a most ingenious way: one, the lot is relatively small, although it faces the expanse of the ocean; two, a public road passes right along the front edge, next to the sea. By pulling the plan all the way back to the property line on two sides, as the sketch reveals, the house makes the most of the space between it and the boulders at the edge of the sea. The house is terraced, stepping up in elevation, from entrance court to tall living room at the front; a sunken garden is scooped out under a bridge to give access to the waterfront.

"The Wave," Wright explained, "is a suggestion to the Haldorns for an appropriate, luxurious, steel-and-masonry shelter on a completely exposed ocean front where heavy surf breaks high over great rocks piled on the shore. The steel fenestration opening only beneath on account of wind, the sunken garden (excavated earth transferred to the top of the house for insulation) and the terrace for recreation are its main features."

Wright's sketch view (this was not the final perspective made for the clients) is indeed a most unusual one, with his treatment of the rocks, the waves, and the swirling sky clouds above almost as turbulent as the sea below.

HOUSE FOR MR AND
FRANK LLOYD WRIGHT

"THE SOLAR HEMICYCLE" was Frank Lloyd Wright's name for the style of design wherein the walls of a house are curved against the northern exposure, opening the rooms to the southern. Just as Herbert Jacobs had been the "first" to build the Usonian house in 1937, he was the first, in 1944, to build a solar hemicycle plan. The curve on the north is piled with a berm up to the second-story windows as protection and insulation against the cold in winter as well as the heat in summer. The tall, two-story glass windows on the southern side are shielded by a generous projecting flat roof acting like a sun hat in summer to shield the glass but tilting back in winter, as the earth's axis tilts, to allow the warming rays into the interior. The mezzanine, or second floor, that contains the bedrooms is hung from the roof rafters by steel rods, thus doing away with walls for support from below that would encumber the free flow of space on the ground floor.

The Jacobs House was a prototype as well as a moderately low-cost building, much of the labor being done by the clients themselves. The Marting House, on the other hand, is more "polished" in all its details.

E. L. MARTING HOUSE (PROJECT), NORTHAMPTON, OHIO. 1947. PERSPECTIVE. PENCIL AND COLOR PENCIL ON TRACING PAPER, 43 × 22". FLLW FDN# 4713.001

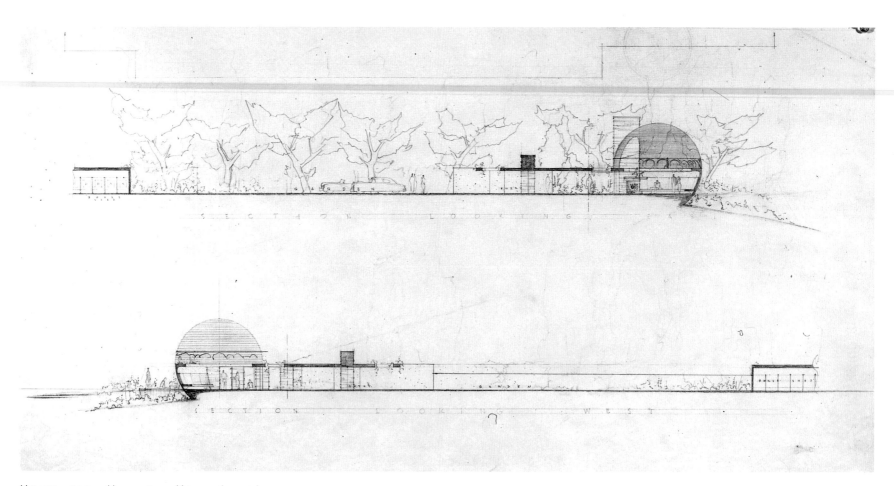

Huntington Hartford House (PROJECT),

Hollywood, California. 1947. Section.

Pencil on tracing paper, 37 × 25".

FLLW Fdn# 4724.005

THE PLAN FOR the Hartford House conforms closely to that of the Ralph Jester scheme, except that the open patio in the earlier project is here glazed in, with glass doors between the stone piers. The building is really more a clubhouse than a dwelling, with provision for entertaining, dining, and swimming. The rooms that ordinarily would form the bedroom wing are used here for showers and changing. The pool itself is set into the hillside, held up by a great concrete retaining wall. The living room, as the sections show, is lit by a dome of glass tubes.

HUNTINGTON HARTFORD HOUSE (PROJECT), HOLLYWOOD, CALIFORNIA. 1947. PERSPECTIVE. PENCIL ON TRACING PAPER, 37 × 22".
FLLW FDN# 4724.006

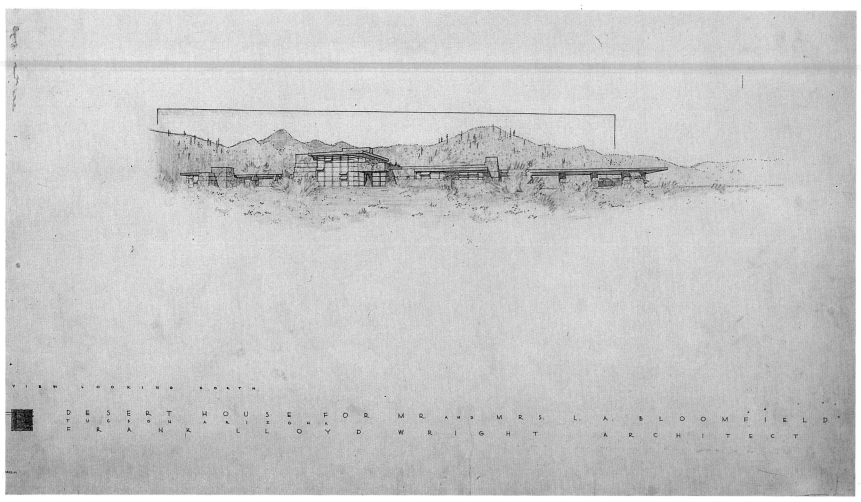

LOUIS BLOOMFIELD HOUSE *(PROJECT), TUCSON, ARIZONA. 1949. PERSPECTIVE. PENCIL AND COLOR PENCIL ON TRACING PAPER, 36 × 22". FLLW FDN# 4902.001*

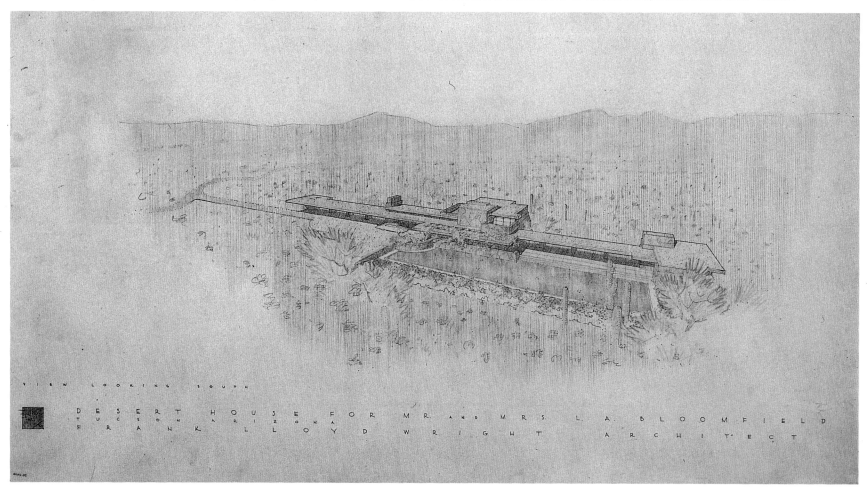

LOUIS BLOOMFIELD HOUSE *(PROJECT), TUCSON, ARIZONA. 1949. AERIAL PERSPECTIVE. PENCIL AND COLOR PENCIL ON TRACING PAPER, 36 × 22". FLLW FDN# 4902.002*

ALMA GOETSCH AND KATHERINE WINCKLER HOUSE (PROJECT), OKEMOS, MICHIGAN. 1949.

PERSPECTIVE. PENCIL AND COLOR PENCIL ON TRACING PAPER, 35 × 26". FLLW FDN# 5006.013

(opposite)

IT WAS RARE for Frank Lloyd Wright to make two renderings for a house of moderate dimensions, but the aerial view and the ground view, combined, clearly reveal the character of this design for desert living outside Tucson. The view from below places the house in context with the arid landscape and the distant mountain ranges. From the aerial view we get a glimpse, on the other side, of the small oasis, walled in next to the main portion of the house. Tucson receives all its water from underground wells. Water, therefore, is a rare commodity for this desert city, and the lush planting that other desert cities, such as Phoenix, can afford due to canals bringing water from the mountains is not available. The aerial view shows a small water course, running the periphery of the enclosed garden to supply water to a narrow band of flowers and shrubs. All the rest of the landscaping around the house is desert planting in character, for the most part leaving the native flora on the site untouched. A two-story living room is in the center of the scheme, with a dining room, a kitchen, and a small mezzanine serving as a study. To one side stretches the bedroom wing, terminating with the carport, while on the other side a covered pergola connects the main residence to a shop and guest cottage.

The materials, as shown in these drawings, were to be chiefly stone and concrete, laid up in the manner of Taliesin West (page 47). Two sets of working drawings were prepared, one for a building of stone, the other of adobe, but the scheme was never built.

(above)

IN 1939 ALMA GOETSCH and Katherine Winckler, two school teachers in Okemos, Michigan, built a Usonian house designed by Wright as part of a community of homes for eight teachers. The execution of the other six dwellings was curtailed because the banks considered the design unacceptable as a plan type and claimed that no house by Frank Lloyd Wright would have any resale value. Misses Goetsch and Winckler went ahead, however, and built their small home.

Ten years later they came back to their architect and wanted a larger design, with more living space and studios. Shown here is the design Wright made for them, conceived at first in red brick. In the working drawings the material was changed to standard concrete block. This was a common occurrence when bids for a masonry material came in too high, and Wright willingly went ahead and specified an alternative.

The drawing makes a lovely circumstance of the lake in front of the house, which extends, by means of two simple blue lines, through the architect's red square logo and out beyond the frame.

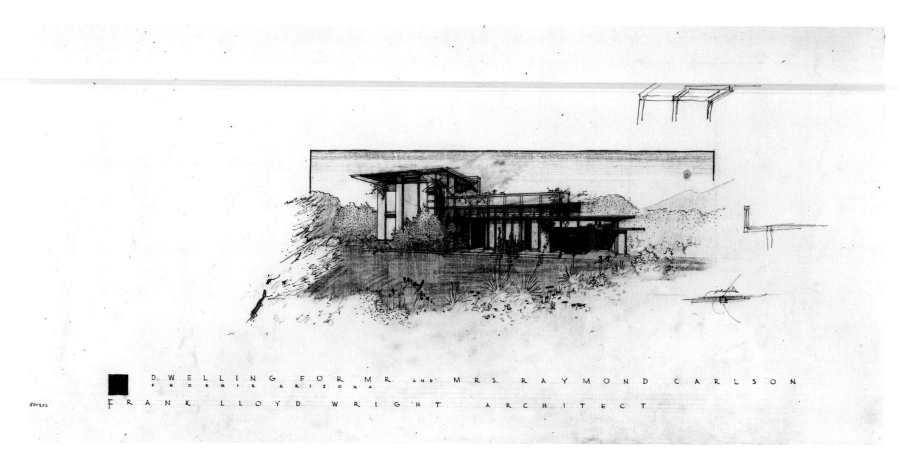

RAYMOND CARLSON HOUSE, *PHOENIX, ARIZONA. 1950. PERSPECTIVE. PENCIL AND COLOR PENCIL ON TRACING PAPER, 36×32". FLLW FDN# 5004.003*

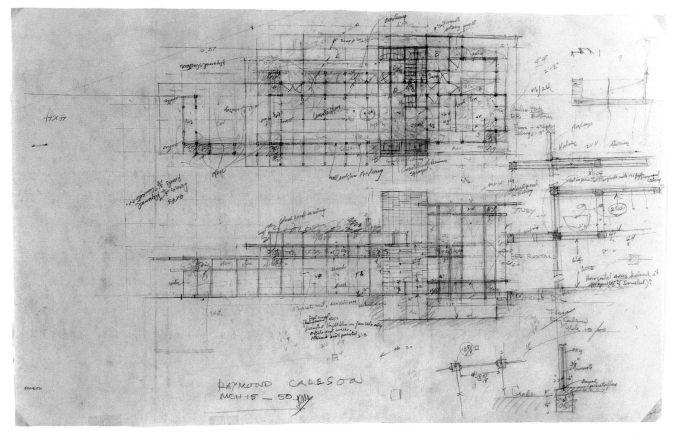

RAYMOND CARLSON HOUSE, *PHOENIX, ARIZONA. 1950. CONCEPTUAL PLAN AND ELEVATION. PENCIL ON TRACING PAPER, 28 × 18". FLLW FDN# 5004.002*

ORDINARILY WRIGHT would never have accepted a commission to design a home in a crowded tract development, but this was all the property that the Carlsons could afford. Raymond Carlson was editor of *Arizona Highways* magazine and had been a long-time personal friend of the Wrights'. Many times he published the architect's Arizona buildings in his magazine, beginning with a now-rare issue of May 1940 that first presented Taliesin West, nearing completion, to the public. For that issue Wright wrote an important article entitled "To Arizona," counseling against overdeveloping the desert around Phoenix.

For the Carlsons, Wright undertook to design a small, innovative little home that would suit them and their budget and still be a work of art. The house is on three levels, a split-level down into the ground for dining and kitchen, a level flush with the ground for the living room, a half level up (above the kitchen-dining area) for two small bedrooms, and a study—roof terrace on the top. The construction method was something that had never been done before: 4 × 4-inch posts of redwood (a very inexpensive wood at that time) support gray Masonite panels. The redwood is lacquered a bright turquoise blue so as to protect it from drying out and splintering in the desert sun. The house is surrounded by a hedge of oleanders, a tall, thick tropical bush with fragrant white and rose flowers in season. The dining-kitchen level has windows that look out, at eye level from a seated position, into surrounding flower beds. The study and roof deck give a view over neighboring houses, as on a ship's bridge. The house is small, compact, and charming in every way, creating its own little world in what otherwise is a typical tract lot.

On the architect's conceptual plan and elevation he has covered the sheet with notes, diagrams, structural designs, and construction details that make this one of the most extensive and complete drawings in the collection, from the point of view of the amount of information recorded on it. He first signed the sheet on the lower right "FLLW / Ray Carlson Mch 10/50." But then after doing more work on the drawing, he retitled it below "Raymond Carlson Mch 15 - 50 FLLW."

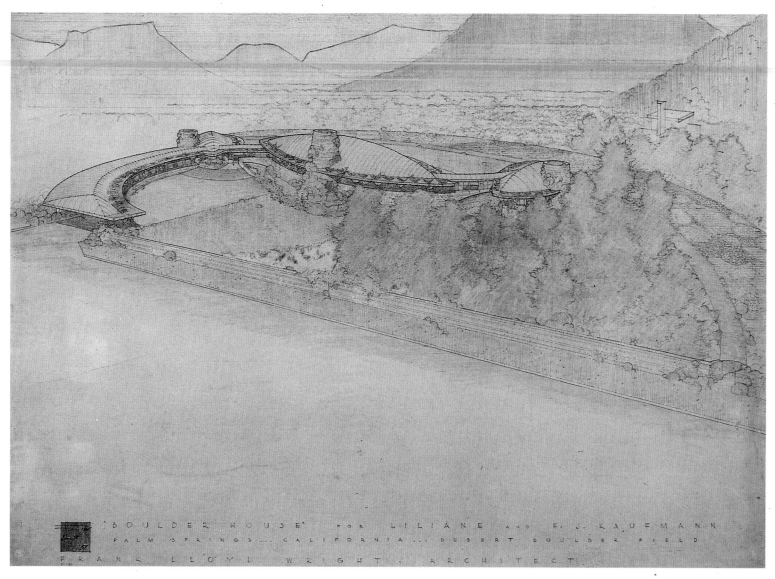

"Boulder House," Edgar J. Kaufmann House (project), Palm Springs, California. 1951.
Perspective. Pencil and color pencil on tracing paper, 35 × 26". FLLW Fdn# 5111.001

WRIGHT EXHIBITED no favoritism with his clients. The fact that he could spend such time and effort working to develop a moderately priced house—indeed a new house-construction system altogether—for a newspaper journalist and his family while he was at work on other, far larger commissions bears out this claim. But by the time he was designing this house for the Kaufmann family, a strong personal relationship had developed between him and the Kaufmanns and their son Edgar, Jr.

The Kaufmanns had taken to wintering in California's sunny, warm Palm Springs and had built a home there, but the house did not fulfill their needs; in fact they found it to be quite unlivable. Too many exposed and unprotected glass surfaces brought the sun into the rooms when shade and cool were more desirable. The family was also going through a time of some personal difficulties, and Wright hoped that by creating a lovely residence for them in their winter habitat he could offer some help and comfort to them the way he had with their home in the western Pennsylvania woods.

"Boulder House" was his personal prescription for them, a circular opus set into a desert landscape strewn with native rocks. Loath to look back upon his work and compare any one house with any other, he did, however, when referring to this work, tell the Kaufmanns that "this was one of my best."

The drama of the entire project, both as a work of architecture and as a building suited to its terrain, is captured in Wright's conceptual elevation. The two perspectives are exciting drawings, some of the best-made drawings by his apprentices, and filled with his own touches throughout. However, it is the concept elevation that stirs the most excitement with a freshness and vitality that a finished presentation drawing can rarely capture.

The main living area is the central section, with master bedroom and study; a bridge connects the guest wing on one side; on the other side is the dining room, connecting to kitchen and service facilities. Mrs. Kaufmann put in a special request for a pool in which she did not have to swim laps back and forth, "with no place to go," as she said. Wright's solution was to make the pool a moat going around the periphery of the main section of the house with bridges crossing over it. This way she could leave her Indian bath, next to her dressing room, via a "water gate," come out into the open-air pool, and swim around the house.

(OPPOSITE TOP)

"Boulder House," Edgar J. Kaufmann House (project), Palm Springs, California. 1951. Conceptual elevation. Pencil and color pencil on tracing paper, 36 × 17". FLLW Fdn# 5111.003

(OPPOSITE BOTTOM)

"Boulder House," Edgar J. Kaufmann House (project), Palm Springs, California. 1951. Perspective. Pencil and color pencil on tracing paper, 35 × 26". FLLW Fdn# 5111.002

BOULDER HOUSE FOR LILIANE AND E. J. KAUFMANN
PALM SPRINGS CALIFORNIA DESERT BOULDER

FRANK LLOYD WRIGHT ARCHITECT

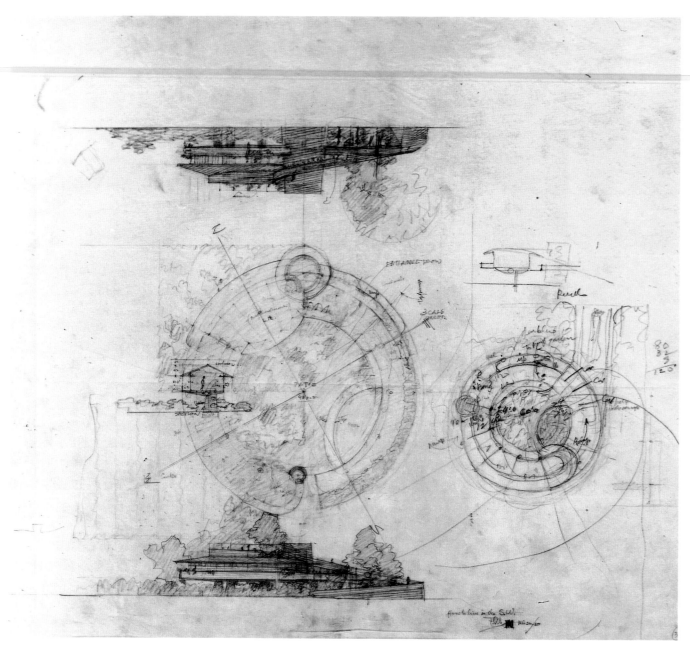

''HOW TO LIVE in the Southwest'' is the name Wright gave to his proposal for a home for his son David Wright, who was living in Phoenix. The property was a large flat tract of land surrounded by citrus trees with the sculptural Camelback Mountain in the distance. From ground level the view of the mountains was obstructed by the orchards in the area, and Wright felt that the first prerequisite for a house in that location was to get it up off the ground and onto a level from which the mountains could be seen. Also, elevating the house above the hot desert floor appealed to him, and so he set the building on spacious concrete piers, creating a shade garden through which breezes could circulate

and help cool the house above. A ramp accessed the upper, dwelling level, part of the wide ramp planted in flower gardens.

The conceptual drawing in red pencil is a romantic sheet containing his first sketch for the building in free hand. Working from this sketch, and using his compass and triangle, he further developed the idea into plan, sections, and elevations. These he then rendered with colored pencils. The section is carefully dimensioned, even at this early stage. He signed the concept, "How to live in the S.W. FLLW Mch 30/50".

The two perspectives easily explain the raised nature of the house: one taken from the south, drawn in sepia ink and with delicate graphite pencil touches, shows the approaching ramp with its garden; the other, a development drawing made entirely in pencil, gives a glimpse from inside of a small plunge pool, the house's supporting concrete piers, and the shade gardens beneath the dwelling.

(OVERLEAF: ''HOW TO LIVE IN THE
SOUTHWEST.'' PLAN; DETAIL)

VIEW FROM SOUTH
HOW TO LIVE IN THE SOUTHWEST
FRANK LLOYD WRIGHT ARCHITECT

"HOW TO LIVE IN THE SOUTHWEST," DAVID WRIGHT HOUSE,
PHOENIX, ARIZONA. 1950. PERSPECTIVE. PENCIL ON TRACING PAPER, 36 × 23". FLLW FDN# 5030.003

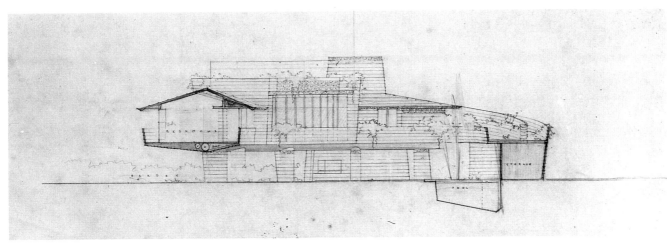

"HOW TO LIVE IN THE SOUTHWEST," DAVID WRIGHT HOUSE,
PHOENIX, ARIZONA. 1950. ELEVATION. PENCIL AND SEPIA INK ON TRACING PAPER, 36 × 18". FLLW FDN# 5011.002

"HOW TO LIVE IN THE SOUTHWEST," DAVID WRIGHT HOUSE,
PHOENIX, ARIZONA. 1950. PERSPECTIVE. PENCIL ON TRACING PAPER, 36 × 14". FLLW FDN# 5030.005

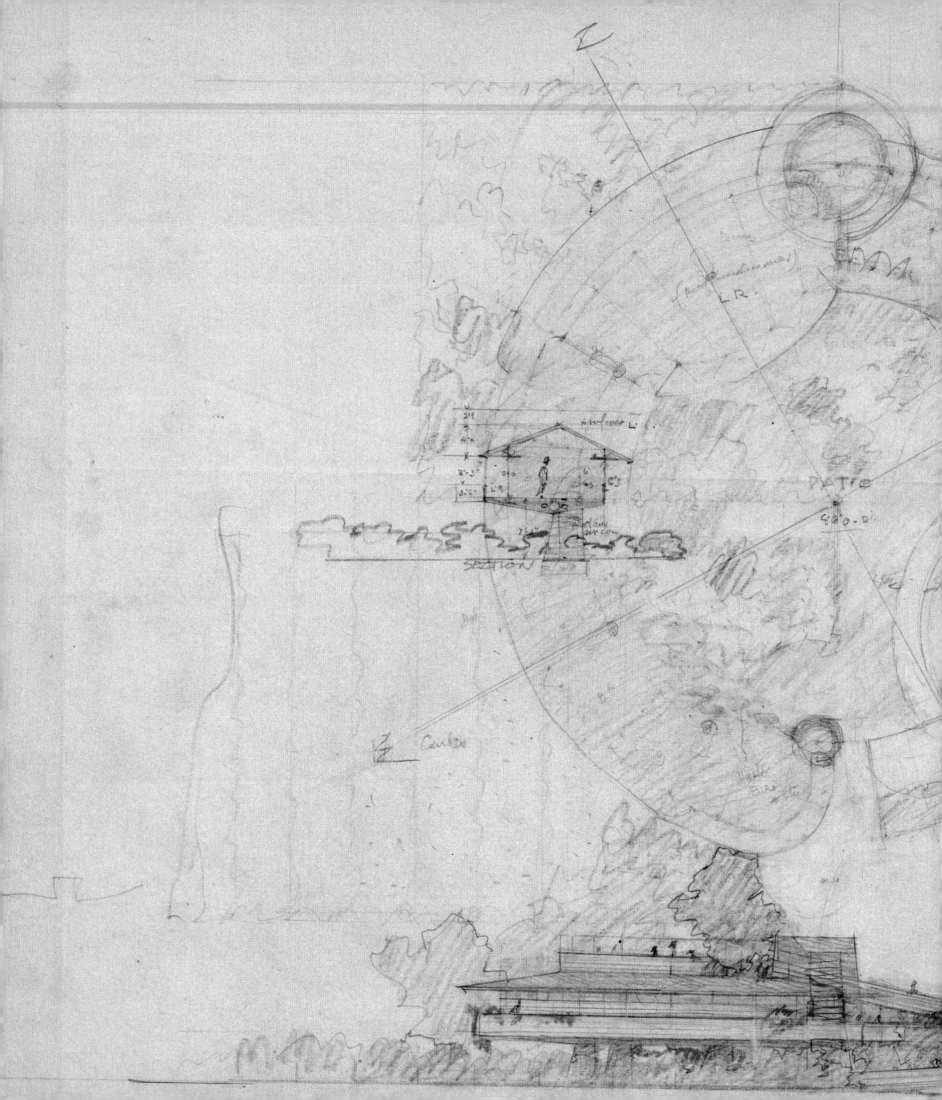

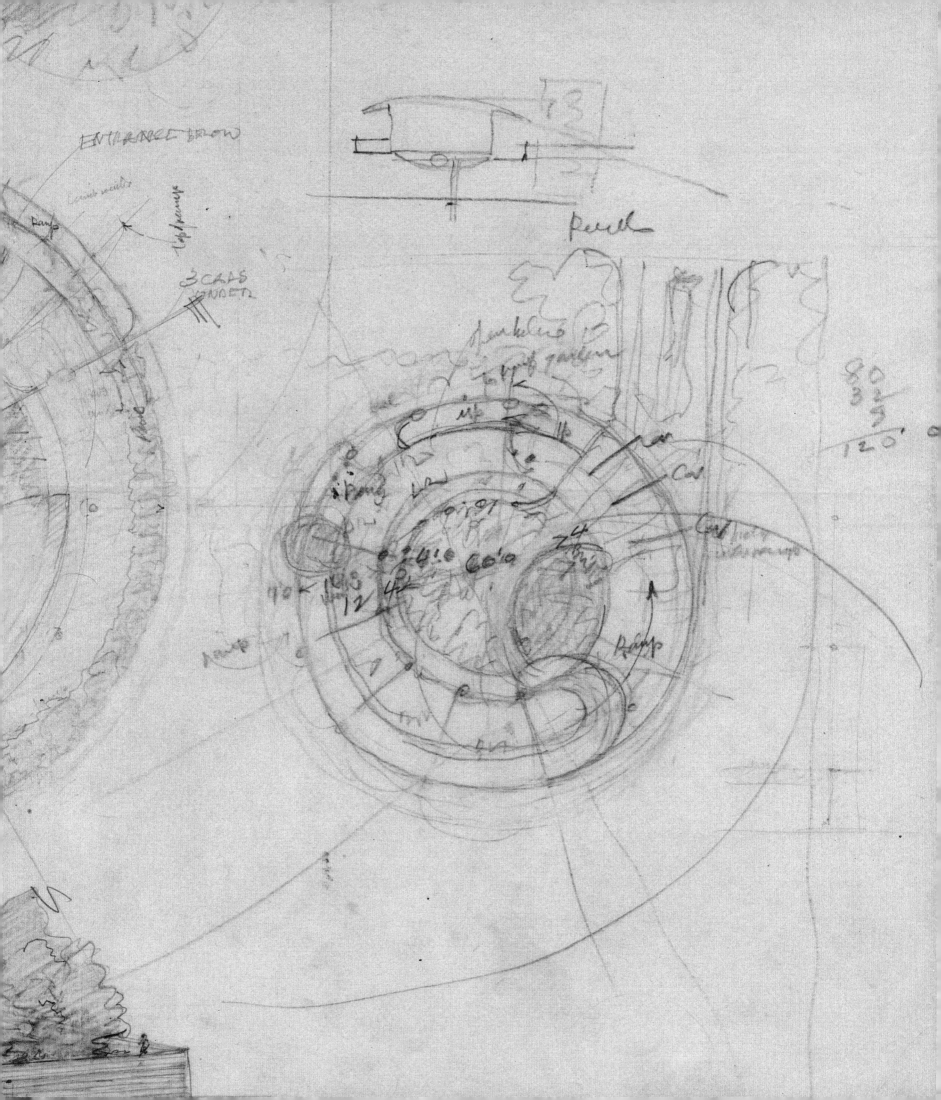

VIEW FROM NORTHEAST
POINT VIEW RESIDENCES
FOR THE EDGAR J. KAUFMANN CHARITABLE TRUST
FRANK LLOYD WRIGHT ARCHITECT

POINT VIEW RESIDENCES was intended as an apartment tower for retired families. It was to be built on a river bank overlooking Pittsburgh. The client was the Edgar J. Kaufmann Charitable Trust, a foundation set up by Kaufmann and his son Edgar, Jr. The idea for the project stemmed from an apartment Wright designed for Elizabeth Noble in Los Angeles in 1929. The Noble apartments were never built, but here Wright expanded and elaborated on the scheme. The plan is symmetrical with an even number of apartments on either side of the building, but the division is such that the apartments are on alternating levels. This would automatically provide for more privacy. If the floor slabs connected through, the steel and concrete would carry sound and noise as well, but with this solution each apartment's floor slab ends at the central dividing wall.

Some apartments are on one level, others are duplexes; the plan for each floor varies. Parking garages and storage facilities are located in the concrete pedestal at the base of the tower. Exterior balcony edges are of poured concrete, the white surface exposed and left natural, with stamped copper plates. The drawing is carefully made, executed with the fine workmanship that Wright had developed in apprentices such as John Howe. But the quickly drawn lines, by Wright, accentuating the cliff drop and going right down and through the title block, show the mastery with which he could add touches that make a fine rendering into an exciting drawing.

POINT VIEW RESIDENCES *(PROJECT), PITTSBURGH, PENNSYLVANIA. 1952. PERSPECTIVE. PENCIL AND COLOR PENCIL ON TRACING PAPER, 31 × 37". FLLW FDN# 5222.001*

VIEW IN GARDEN COURT

SEASHORE DWELLING FOR MR. MAX HOFFMAN
NORTH MANURSING ISLAND, RYE, NEW YORK
FRANK LLOYD WRIGHT ARCHITECT

THE PERSPECTIVE of the first scheme for the Max Hoffman House here shows only the living room, with a great copper-roofed high-pitched ceiling, and the circular pool swinging out over Long Island Sound. Hoffman owned the Jaguar concession for the United States, and later the Mercedes one. He was a short, lithe, energetic Viennese with grand schemes and great business prowess. Wright was designing a Jaguar showroom for him on New York's Fifth Avenue when Hoffman asked for a house to be built on Manursing Island in Rye, New York. When these designs were ready to be sent to Hoffman in New York, Wright showed them, as was his practice, to his wife, Olgivanna. She said: "Frank, I think that you have designed too grand a house for Max Hoffman; he is a small man and seems, despite his business skill, to be somewhat shy. His real love is cars, especially the

fast, speedy Porsche. It is my feeling that he will find this proposal too large for him." Wright, however, felt confident that Max Hoffman would respond favorably to the plans. Hoffman did not: "But it is too big for me. I could never live in a house that large." And so Wright went to work again. It was to take three tries before Hoffman was pleased.

Meticulous in his knowledge of fast racing cars and meticulous in business, Hoffman turned out to be meticulous as a client as well. No detail escaped him, he wanted everything to be absolutely perfect, and his letters to the architect are filled with distrust of anyone connected with his house, from contractor to workmen. The house he finally got was beautifully put together in every detail, although it was not the elegant "baronial" scheme shown here.

MAX HOFFMAN HOUSE *(PROJECT), RYE, NEW YORK. 1954. PERSPECTIVE. PENCIL AND COLOR PENCIL ON TRACING PAPER, 50 × 36". FLLW FDN# 5504.006*

IN ANOTHER ATTEMPT to try to get his friends and clients Lilian and Vere Morris situated in a house on their cliffside property, the architect proposed this revised plan. The new scheme placed the house further down the cliff, on a more sloped site, whereas the first scheme was at the very edge of a high promontory. The disposition of rooms here is more horizontal, whereas in the first building it was primarily vertical. The larger circle contains the living room, with windows and doors opening all around onto a circular balcony towards the sea and a grassy slope and garden behind. Another, small circle is for the workspace (kitchen) and dining, and on the opposite side of the living room is a wing for the bedrooms. The tall slender mass of concrete that rises out of the house and extends up to the road above is labeled, with Wright's connecting line and writing, "Elevator." The other writing on the lower part of the view has been partially erased, and the meaning of what he wrote is therefore not clear. It obviously refers to the reinforced concrete masses and retaining walls, and the last part reads, "Imagine a quake might be fine in the circumstances. Affection, FLLW."

On one of the other sketch sections the diagram shows the central support for the house is basically a dendriform, or mushroom-shaped, column, like those for the Johnson Wax Administration Building (page 248). The shaft of the column penetrates into the ground and the house is balanced on it, like a tray held overhead on the hand of a waiter. This is basically the same construction principle that saved the Imperial Hotel in the Kanto quake of 1923. Wright saw it equally applicable to this earthquake-prone area.

The drawing is thoroughly edited by Wright, as can be seen in the foliage along the cliffside, the details of the house itself, and especially the play of waves and rocks and sea birds at the base of the cliff.

"SEACLIFF," V. C. MORRIS HOUSE (PROJECT), SAN FRANCISCO, CALIFORNIA. 1955. PERSPECTIVE. PENCIL AND COLOR PENCIL ON TRACING PAPER, 35 × 22". FLLW FDN# 5412.001

VIEW FROM NORTH:
"GRANDMA HOUSE" FOR THE H. C. PRICE FAMILY
PARADISE VALLEY, ARIZONA.
FRANK LLOYD WRIGHT ARCHITECT

THE "GRANDMA HOUSE" was Wright's answer to a request by Harold Price's wife for a winter home near Phoenix where she could entertain and play with her beloved grandchildren. The house was under construction at the same time that Wright was building an office tower for her husband in Bartlesville, Oklahoma. By using standard concrete block, but in this novel fashion of having the courses of block protrude one above the other, a quiet elegance and modern way of living was achieved. Instead of having the block piers rise up to the ceiling, thin steel pipe columns, with decorative cubes of metal welded on, support the roof in a delicate fashion that makes the whole covering seem to float over the substantial block walls and piers. Lights, set into the column at the point where the steel post emerges, shine up against the ceiling, further accentuating this sense of a floating ceiling. The central portion of the plan is an open atrium, with a fountain in the center, living and dining rooms to the right, and bedrooms for the Prices and their visiting grandchildren to the left. At the far left end an enclosed play yard was built so that the small children would be safe from the desert and secure from wandering. When the children grew up, Wright then converted this space into a larger, more elegant master bedroom suite.

H. C. PRICE HOUSE, PHOENIX, ARIZONA. 1954.
PERSPECTIVE. PENCIL AND COLOR PENCIL ON TRACING
PAPER, 51 × 20". FLLW FDN# 5419.001

ALLADIN
FOR MR. JOHN GILLIN
HOLLYWOOD, CALIFORNIA
FRANK LLOYD WRIGHT ARCHITECT

''ALLADIN,'' JOHN GILLIN HOUSE (PROJECT), HOLLYWOOD, CALIFORNIA. 1956. PERSPECTIVE. PENCIL AND COLOR PENCIL ON TRACING PAPER, 44×30". FLLW FDN# 5528.004

JOHN GILLIN, a geologist from Texas, had built a Frank Lloyd Wright house in Dallas in 1951. Basically a two-bedroom dwelling, it was extremely large and rambling because of Gillin's life-style: he loved to entertain and throw large parties.

When Gillin contemplated having a residence in Hollywood in addition to his Texas one, Wright produced this design for him and called it "Alladin." It is another one of those homes placed on the brow of a hill, stretching in one level from the pool terrace and living room at the left to the covered pergola and barbeque pavilion far right. Behind the covered pergola is a garden court, grassy lawn, and flower beds. The entrance is on the other side of the living room, not visible in this perspective, but it provides carport, service area, and rooms for servants and the caretaker. The roof of the living room rises above the line of the other roofs; the room is spacious and airy within, with a spectacular view of Los Angeles. The two bedrooms next to the living room have the same eastern exposure to the sprawling city below. Working drawings were completed for the scheme, but there were some problems in acquiring the property, and Gillin chose not to go ahead with the house.

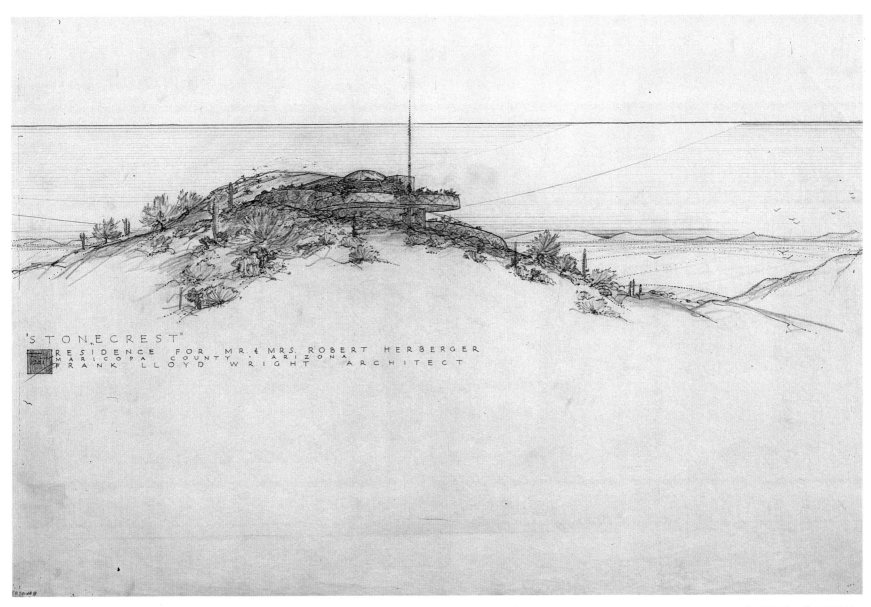

"STONECREST"
RESIDENCE FOR MR. & MRS. ROBERT HERBERGER
MARICOPA COUNTY · ARIZONA
FRANK LLOYD WRIGHT · ARCHITECT

"STONECREST," G. R. HERBERGER HOUSE *(PROJECT), SCOTTSDALE, ARIZONA. 1955. PERSPECTIVE. PENCIL AND COLOR PENCIL ON TRACING PAPER, 34 × 30". FLLW FDN# 5830.008*

"*STONECREST,*" a home for Robert Herberger not far from Wright's Taliesin West, epitomizes the architect's consideration of placing a house in relation to its hill site. He warned, "Once you put the house on the top of the hill, by so doing you destroy the hill!" Here the house projects out from the brow like another one of nature's stone outcroppings. To further blend the home to the site, the building materials are desert stone set into wooden forms with concrete poured in to secure them. The forms were then removed to reveal a "desert masonry rubble stone wall," as Wright once described it.

The scale of Wright's work is always a surprise when one encounters it. Where his buildings may appear monumental in photographs, we are constantly startled to discover the sense of humanizing scale present in all he did.

The perspective of this house achieves what no photograph could: it portrays a rather large three-level house as a modest companion to its desert environs.

A PREVIOUS OWNER of this site had leveled off the uppermost hilltop to form a flat plane upon which to eventually build a home. In the process, the hilltop itself had been destroyed; two other adjacent, lower hills were also part of the same property. The new client, Helen Donahoe, wanted a residence that would also provide two guest houses for her sons and their families when they came to visit her. Wright rode over the site, not far from his own home at Taliesin West, and saw the leveled hill. Ordinarily he admonished any architect against building on the very top of a hill and "negating the very reason for placing a building that should be a part of the landscape." But by building on the brow of the hill, the way he did with Taliesin (Wisconsin), the hill crown remains as an integrated feature of the dwelling. With the Donahoe House, he set out to make a

design that would literally replace the hill in stone and concrete.

The main house, in the center of the complex, was the focus of the three buildings—called the Donahoe Triptych—with ample living and dining space, master bedroom, and further guest rooms on the same level as a swimming pool. Entrance, library, office and dining room are at ground level; the bedroom level is above this one, and a top level contains the living room. A wide outside ramp extends from the ground level car court to the living room three floors above.

Terraces set on bridges that span over the drive at one side and a craggy, rock-filled ravine on the other connect the main house to the two guest houses. The character of the rock and concrete masonry, similar to that of Taliesin West and the Rose Pauson House—both

Arizona buildings—helps to place the three houses in the natural context with the region.

The architect's first sketch plan, made on a land parcel map, barely shows the outline of the three dwellings. But right below this hint of a plan he has made a thumbnail perspective, again in a very sketchy manner, but clearly indicative of the idea he had in mind.

The finished rendering shown here is one that has never been published before. It is more "in the rough" than the usually published one, and obviously much more in his own hand. The drawing was signed late in March 1959, only a few days before Wright's death. It constitutes, therefore, one of—if not the last—renderings to be worked upon and signed.

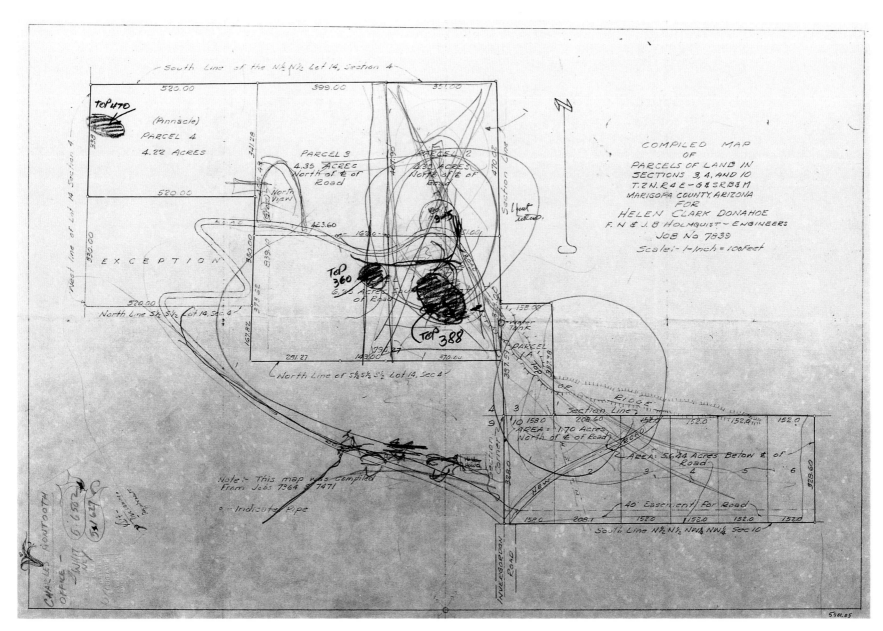

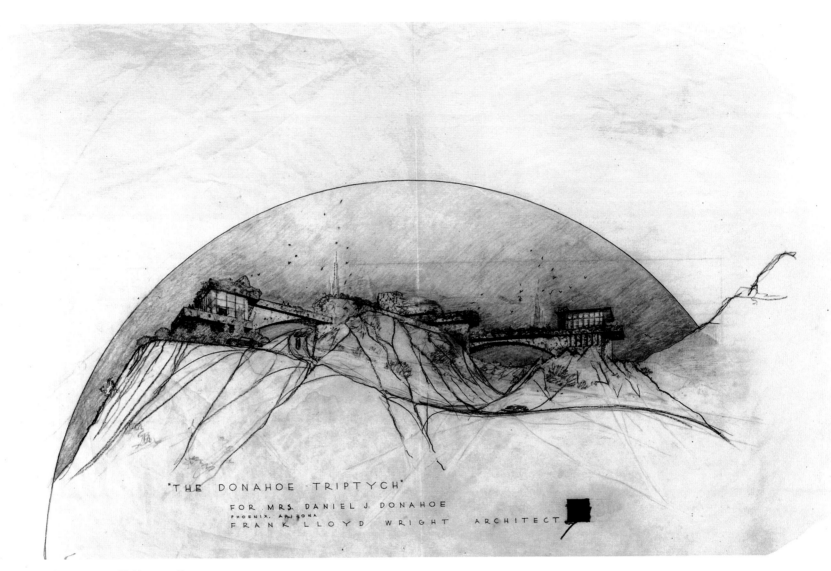

"THE DONAHOE TRIPTYCH"
FOR MRS. DANIEL J. DONAHOE
PHOENIX, ARIZONA
FRANK LLOYD WRIGHT ARCHITECT

"DONAHOE TRIPTYCH," HELEN DONAHOE
HOUSE (PROJECT), PARADISE VALLEY, ARIZONA. 1959.
PERSPECTIVE. PENCIL AND COLOR PENCIL ON TRACING PAPER,
58 × 36". FLLW FDN# 5901.020

(OPPOSITE)

"DONAHOE TRIPTYCH," HELEN DONAHOE
HOUSE (PROJECT), PARADISE VALLEY, ARIZONA. 1959.
PLAN. PENCIL AND COLOR PENCIL ON SEPIA PRINT,
27 × 18". FLLW FDN# 5901.005

PART TWO:

RELIGIOUS STRUCTURES

"*I ATTEND THE GREATEST* of all churches. And I put a capital N on Nature and call it my church," Frank Lloyd Wright said in a television interview with Mike Wallace in 1957. "If I belonged to any one church, they couldn't ask me to build a church for them. But because my church is elemental, fundamental, I can build for anybody a church."

Wright's own religious background was Unitarian, and he was steeped since childhood in the American transcendental tradition. His faith developed quite naturally into the fundamental, elemental approach to religion that he spoke of in 1957, at the age of ninety. In the Wallace interviews (there were two of them), he also remarked: "I'm building a synagogue in Philadelphia, a Unitarian church in Madison, a Greek Orthodox church in Milwaukee, and a Christian Science church in California." The next year, 1958, he would design a mortuary chapel for himself, his immediate family, and members of the Taliesin Fellowship, as well as a chapel for the University of Oklahoma. The year he died, 1959, he received a commission for another Greek Orthodox church, this time in San Francisco. His death came before he was able to put his sketches down on paper clearly, but he spoke several times of the design he had in mind.

In 1886, when Wright was still living in Madison and attending the University of Wisconsin, his family built a chapel, called Unity Chapel, in their ancestral graveyard near Spring Green, Wisconsin. The architect was Joseph Lyman Silsbee, but the young Wright made the design for the interior ceiling. Seventy years later he would point to that ceiling and say, "Here was my first work, in straight-line square patterns, done with Silsbee for my uncle Jenkin Lloyd Jones." In 1887, when he had already left home and gone to work for the architectural firm of Adler and Sullivan in Chicago, Wright designed a Unitarian chapel in Sioux City, Iowa. The young Wright was still under the influence of Silsbee and the shingle style—the predominantly rustic combination of shingle walls and roofing invariably resting on a rustic fieldstone foundation, which typified American vernacular architecture at the turn of the century. His chapel as published in *Inland Architect* in June 1887 shows a plan not dissimilar to the family's chapel in Wisconsin.

In 1897 his uncle Jenkin Lloyd Jones again commissioned a church building, this time for All Souls' Church in Chicago. The new structure, Abraham Lincoln Center, was to be a social as well as religious center for the local Unitarian community. Wright went into partnership with another architect, Dwight Perkins, for the job, but the completed building, started in 1903, bore little resemblance to his original plans.

Thus, the famous and greatly influential Unity Temple (page 88) can be said to be Wright's first religious structure, designed solely by him and built as he would have it. A monolith of poured concrete, in 1906 it was a revolution unto itself and to the world of modern architecture. It made use of poured concrete not just as construction material but as an aesthetic statement. The use of poured concrete was beginning in architecture at this time, but the forms it took usually were adapted to the traditional styles and modes common to the building vocabulary of turn-of-the-century America. In contrast to this imposing modern monolith of concrete, the building he designed, also of 1906, as a memorial chapel for the Pettit family in the Belvedere Cemetery, Belvedere, Illinois, speaks an entirely quieter, more humble language (page 89).

Over the next fifty-three years Wright's designs for religious structures expanded and changed: sometimes they are complex, such as the vast Steel Cathedral for William Norman Guthrie (page 92); others are extremely simple, such as the Greek Orthodox church in Milwaukee (page 100). There were instances when an idea was put on paper and developed but not realized, yet it served as the seed for another project. The Steel Cathedral of 1926, for example, flowered into the Beth Sholom Synagogue in 1954, constructed in Elkins Park, near Philadelphia (page 99).

When he referred to his church as "Nature," always qualifying it "with a capital N," he did not mean his joy from the association with nature—the trees and flowers, the fields and lakes, the cliffs and outcroppings of rock. Although those elements were very dear to him and figured strongly in his work, what he really was referring to was the profound study of underlying principles. He studied the principles at work in nature, such as the taproot of the pine tree and its cantilevered branches or the tall stalk of the saguaro with its hollow interior surrounded by a rim of slender ribs (like reinforcing rods in a concrete or concrete-block structure), and translated those principles into modern building techniques that in no way imitated nature but were inspired by it. The taproot foundation and cantilevered floor slabs became, for him, among the consistent principles upon which he designed all his tall buildings.

He saw, foremost in nature, a constant adherence to principle, sometimes subtle, sometimes powerful, sometimes cruel, but always consistent. He spoke often about looking "into the nature of whatever is" to find its meaning. This was by no means limited to his religious structures; it permeated each and every aspect of his work. But he was a deeply religious man, and in designing edifices for the religions of others he strove to find those symbols, which he incorporated into the very fabric of the buildings, that would be an inspiration to the congregation and would express something of the philosophy underlying each sect. He saw a unity in various religious philosophies rather than a complexity; he saw a certain oneness that sprung, again, out of principle rather than out of individual application. His way of explaining these ideas was often in terms of the simple flowers of the field, where he pointed out that one principle was at work in all of them but in an infinite variety of visual forms, styles, and shapes. This again was that Nature, with a capital "N," that forever intrigued him and led him to say, "All the more because I study Nature do I revere God, because Nature is all the body of God we will ever know."

UNITY TEMPLE WAS a distinctive break with traditional ecclesiastical architecture. It adhered to no particular "style," as was commonly cherished by churches of all denominations in the United States at the turn of the century. It has no steeple, no high, steeply pitched Gothic Revival roof, no classical portico in the Greco-Roman tradition. The general form of the church takes its "grammar," as Wright termed it, from its construction technique: wooden forms into which concrete was poured. Once the concrete was set, the forms were removed to reveal the building as we see it today. No further surfacing or coating was required. The freshly exposed concrete was washed down to reveal the rough-textured aggregate that gives the exterior surface its character. Interior surfaces were then plastered. For ornamental details in keeping with the poured concrete, wooden blocks were inserted inside the forms to produce geometric patterns on the piers and capitals. The character of the ornament itself was derived from these blocks of wood. Everything was thus integrated and related: form, structure, ornament. Wright went beyond the dictum of his master Louis Sullivan, who said, "Form follows function," and developed the approach that "form and function are one."

Auguste Perret was pioneering an architecture of poured concrete at about the same time, in France, and was the first in Europe to use the material in a way appropriate to its nature, without covering it with a veneer of brick, stone, or plaster. But Perret still adhered, in the early stages of his career, to more conventional, if not classical, design standards. Unity Temple, on the other hand, is a totally new statement in the use of material and design.

The square—the dominant module in this church—reflected, to Wright's way of thinking, the Unitarian faith: unity through simplicity, through solidarity. The larger square structure houses the temple, the smaller one the secular rooms of the church. Access to both sections, contrary to all previous tradition, is via a quiet, low entrance set between the two cubes. As the site is on a busy city street, the windows are placed high above a screening wall of poured concrete to afford privacy and quiet within. To provide further lighting, both sections of the building have skylights, but the glass is patterned in warm, sunny tones of amber and gold. Even on a cloudy day the interior seems to be bathed in sunlight.

On the side of the interior perspective Wright wrote, in 1950, the following notation: "The unlimited overhead. Interior space enclosed by screen-features only. Idea later used in Johnson Bldg, Racine Wis." The architect was pointing out the "destruction of the box," as he called it in later years. This aim of his to take architecture away from the old language of boxy rooms cut with holes for light and air was fully achieved in Unity Temple after earlier experiments at the Hillside Home School in 1902 and the Larkin Building in 1904 (page 237). Wright admitted that both of those earlier buildings were headed in this direction more by feeling and instinct than by definite intention.

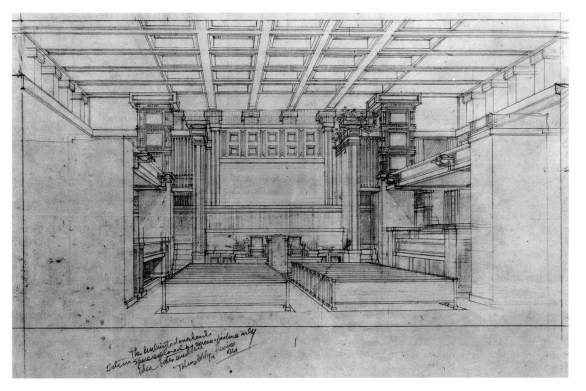

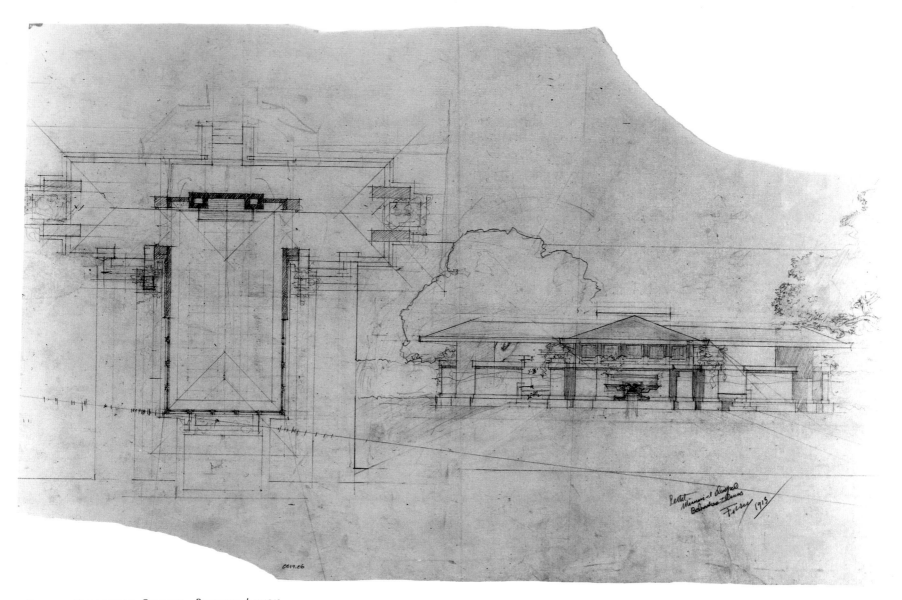

PETTIT MEMORIAL CHAPEL, BELVEDERE, ILLINOIS.
1906. PLAN AND ELEVATION. PENCIL ON TRACING PAPER,
29 × 18". FLLW FDN# 0619.006

THE EXTERIOR RENDERING for Unity Temple is typical of the type of presentation drawings made by Wright and his studio before 1920. It is a drawing made to show a client what a building would look like or to show the general public at an exhibition or in a publication. The plan and elevation of this small memorial chapel, on the other hand, was made for the architect himself and for his draftsmen. In this context, it is a conceptual drawing: the plan and its accompanying elevation represent Wright's first record of the work, made on the same sheet. It is also a drawing made for "office work" only; the diagonal line running along the paper just outside the plan was most likely put there by one of the draftsmen making the mechanical perspective. The small vertical marks along the line represent

the various vertical elements in the plan as they are plotted into perspective.

The chapel was designed for the Pettit family's plot in the Belvedere Cemetery. As a memorial chapel it is not a grand monumental expression but rather a simple, almost residential, type of building for family gatherings to reflect and meditate in a quiet environment. A fireplace, heart and hearth of the home to Wright's way of thinking, is central to the project and further emphasizes the human, rather than monumental, quality of the chapel. An important feature to notice is the careful attention Wright has given to the trees and foliage around and behind the chapel. On all his drawings, even in the very earliest stages of the work, he made the building and its natural surroundings come together to

form a relationship that he considered essential: nature's beneficent presence in the lives of people.

On the drawing Wright has written, "Pettit Memorial Chapel Belvedere, Illinois, FLLW 1913." The number 159 was circled in red, indicating that this drawing, along with nearly 750 others, was selected by Wright for inclusion in the exhibition "Sixty Years of Living Architecture," which premiered in Philadelphia in 1951. The show, the largest architectural exhibition ever assembled, traveled on a four-year tour to Italy, Switzerland, Germany, Holland, and France, then to New York, Mexico, and Los Angeles. It was during the summer and fall of 1950 that the architect, in making his selection, annotated many of his drawings.

(OVERLEAF: UNITY TEMPLE. *PERSPECTIVE; DETAIL)*

FROM THE SIMPLE, almost homelike, memorial chapel of 1906 (page 89) to the soaring Steel Cathedral for a million people of 1926, Wright made an extraordinary leap in design concept and technology. In between, in 1915, he had designed a Catholic church for Zion, Illinois, based mostly on the idea of Unity Temple but much larger and more conservative. The church was never built, and it was ten years before another ecclesiastical commission—the Steel Cathedral—came his way. The project arose out of Wright's association with his friend William Norman Guthrie, for whom he had designed a home in Sewanee, Tennessee, in 1908 (page 22). The house was not built, and Guthrie subsequently moved to New York to be the pastor of a small Episcopal church, Saint Mark's in the Bouwerie. Guthrie was a dynamic person and also a dreamer. He proposed that Wright build a vast cathedral that would house many churches of different denominations under one roof. This elevation is the result of that dream. (There are only three drawings extant from the commission, a plan and two elevations. The elevations differ but show two solutions based on the same plan.)

A massive, airy structure of steel and glass rises above a group of poured-concrete cathedrals, chapels, and temples. The small dots along the lower lines represent people, giving a sense of the overall scale of the intended edifice. Notes and calculations abound across the elevation. On one side Wright has even calculated the division of his fee payments. Based on a total building cost of $300,000 (this was in 1925–1926; it would, naturally, figure in the millions by today's costs), he made his proposal as follows: "7500 payable when sketches are complete. 12500 when plans are ready to build. 5000 when work is practically complete."

The building was to be constructed as a gigantic steel tripod, designated on the drawing as "rigid vertical—suspended" and "rigid lateral—suspended"; in other words, it was to be a structure not unlike a suspension bridge. The central mass rising over a basic hexagonal plan was to be a tall, vast space—called "The Hall of the Elements"—with light pouring into the individual chapels and with a great court in the center of the structure.

In 1931 the drawings were exhibited in Belgium, Holland, and Germany. The caption the architect wrote for that exhibition was simply, "Steel Cathedral embracing minor cathedrals, New York City, 1925. A study of the devotional church of churches." In 1932 Wright assigned the building on the other elevation to be a "Commercial Arts Festival" and relabeled all the details in keeping with this concept. But in 1934, he again labeled the drawing "Broadacres Cathedral" in conjunction with his design of the Broadacre City model.

The building was a visionary concept, as were many of his works of this period, both in design and engineering. In the late 1920s there were few architectural commissions coming to Wright, due in some respects to his turbulent and controversial personal life-style. But when a commission did arrive, he poured a great amount of creative energy into it. Taken as a group, these unbuilt projects of the late 1920s comprise a record of new concepts in building that have still to be realized. But they are not dreams: they were designed, as was all of his work, with the fullest intention of being built according to the methods and technologies of the twentieth century. The concern with the fee was typical of Wright's practical nature: in order to work, he had to live, support his family, and pay his studio staff. At this time in his life he was also rebuilding his home, Taliesin, after a fire in the summer of 1925 had totally destroyed his living quarters.

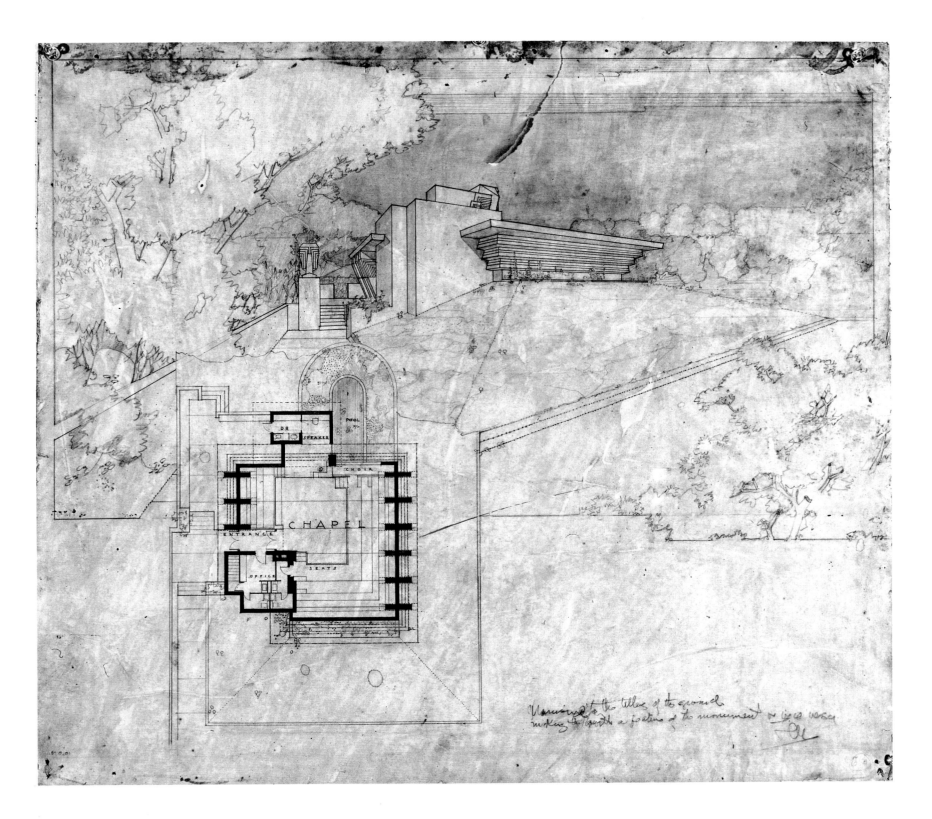

"MEMORIAL TO THE SOIL" (PROJECT), WISCONSIN.
1936. PERSPECTIVE AND PLAN. PENCIL ON TRACING PAPER,
25 × 22". FLLW FDN# 3710.001

ALTHOUGH THIS PROJECT goes by the title "Memorial to the Soil," on the drawing Wright has written "Memorial to the Tillers of the Ground. Making the earth a feature of the monument, or vice versa." This crisply rendered view, in graphite pencil, demonstrates Wright's predilection for strong geometric precision in organizing masses of concrete and architectural details. Although the drawing was executed by an apprentice at Taliesin, Wright softened the surrounding landscape with his usual touches, especially the berm that is built up to the front of the structure. Varying mosses and grasses have been depicted, albeit with no color, yet with a deftness in graphite pencil that shows the architect's skill in the art of drawings as well as design.

There is little on record about the history of this commission; only a suggestion from a local Wisconsin group who asked for a small chapel design for their pastoral property. Even before the drawings were completed, however, the commission was dropped. But Wright was determined to see the idea fixed on paper and developed at least into a clear record of his thoughts. He obviously liked the project enough to include it in the January 1938 issue of *Architectural Forum* devoted solely to his work.

BEGINNING IN 1938 Frank Lloyd Wright designed an entire campus at the request of Dr. Ludd Spivey, president of Florida Southern College. The architect described the opus as "Floridian" in character. The first structure to be built was the Anne Pfeiffer Chapel. As the other buildings (some of which did get built, some left only as projects) bear a relatively low profile in the flat citrus-orchard landscape facing a lake, the tower of the chapel is the one strongly vertical element dominating the site. The tower is actually a "lantern": between two masses of poured concrete daylight filters into the sanctuary below through vines and plants that grow in suspended concrete planting boxes on each side of the tower.

Specially cast concrete blocks form the lower walls of the chapel. In the perforations of the blocks are set small squares of stained glass. As in Unity Temple, built over thirty years earlier, the interior space is accentuated by the presence of light drifting down to the room. In Unity Temple, daylight comes from the obvious skylight above; here it comes from a variety of overhead sources. Just where supports for the lantern tower itself might be expected, there are further skylights. This is the miracle of reinforced concrete and steel put to work to create a magical effect of light and openness.

The choir is placed on the second level, above the lectern and pastor's platform and behind a lattice screen wall, again made from specially cast concrete blocks. Despite the use of concrete and concrete block, which are usually regarded as machine-made industrial products, the building has a quiet and poetic harmony, creating its own contemplative atmosphere.

SHORTLY AFTER WRIGHT'S death in 1959 his widow, Olgivanna Lloyd Wright, was once asked how she would define, or explain, his genius. "Genius, you must understand, is really undefinable," she replied. "By its very nature it eludes categorizing. Where it comes from is also elusive. With my husband there were many elements that contributed to it, however, including his upbringing, the powerful influence of his mother, aunts and uncles, the music of his father, his life on the farm as a young boy, his close association with Louis Sullivan and Dankmar Adler, these all contributed to it. But the actual source will ever remain a mystery, as it does with all great geniuses throughout time. But if I were to describe one powerful element of his genius, I would have to say that it was his enormous power of absorption."

In talking to his apprentices at Taliesin, Wright continually advised them to "go through life with an open hand, rather than a shut fist, and ideas will come to you when you least expect them." He derived ideas from myriad sources, and once an idea got hold of him, he took it and worked it out in whatever he was creating. He was not possessive of ideas; he was not concerned with their source but rather with how they could apply or be applied. The astounding variety of forms in his architecture is proof of his ability to tap a great source of inspiration in what he called "the realm of ideas."

The idea for the plan and elevation of this Unitarian church for Madison, Wisconsin, came as the result of a conversation Wright had with Olgivanna. "I have a new commission," he told her, "to design a small church for the Unitarian congregation in Madison. But I haven't an idea in my head." She replied: "You have designed churches on the form of a square and on the form of a rectangle and hexagon. Why not a triangle? The triangle is really a symbol of aspiration. And couldn't you make the roofline like the hands held together in the attitude of prayer?"

From this simple query, the idea was born, and he soon made the first sketch. Throughout their life together there were many instances when Olgivanna sparked an idea and Wright took hold of it. She later observed: "I could never design a building such as the Unitarian church, but I know from the experience of living with him that he responds to ideas with unbelievable speed. That is the genius in him, that he can grasp, from a small suggestion, the vision of a great concept."

The chief configuration of the plan is a combination of two triangles, a larger one and a smaller one, placed together on their flat sides. The church sanctuary is located in the larger triangle, open to and connected with the smaller triangle, behind which space is provided for social functions. From the low ceiling over this secular space the roof projects up to the prow of the sanctuary and terminates over a prow of glass windows behind the pulpit. During services the pastor stands in front of this prow and the choir is on a balcony above him. On one side of these two triangular spaces a Sunday school wing extends; on the other are the church's entrance, foyer, toilets, and kitchen. The unusual angle of the perspective was deliberately used so that the drawing could go on the cover of the Unitarian magazine Christian Register. The format of the journal was vertical, but the drawing was originally horizontal. Wright chose to "compromise" between the two and let the image run diagonally across the cover.

As with all small churches, the budget was very limited. The contractor, Marshall Erdman, went into considerable personal debt to try to get the building finished, and Wright, in the summer of 1952, brought in the Taliesin Fellowship to help with interior detailing. His apprentices worked from early morning until late in the evening; Wright himself was on the site a great deal of the time despite his other work in the drafting room back at Taliesin, some thirty-six miles away. The dining room and theater at Hillside had burned that spring, and Wright was planning new construction, adding one more burden to the work placed on him. But he did not want to see this church building fail, so he was willing to contribute his time and labor, and those of the Fellowship's as well, to see it through to the end.

Recently discovered among Wright's papers is a brief "caption" he wrote for this drawing: "Aspiration—the Unitarian Meeting House. Unity—the ideal of Unitarianism appears in Madison as a structure preaching what the congregation professes to believe. In concrete form—the Unitarian Ideal."

Unity Temple achieved the same interpretation of the Unitarian faith forty years earlier by means of a harmony built out of squares (page 88). But Unity Temple was set in an urban environment. With the church in Madison, Wright encouraged the congregation to go out into the country. The great windows at the prow overlooked trees and meadows and Lake Mendota in the distance. In time, the city eventually grew out and around the building, but enough land was secured to keep a barrier of greenery despite the proximity of new buildings.

PFEIFFER CHAPEL, *FLORIDA SOUTHERN COLLEGE,*
LAKELAND, FLORIDA. 1938. PERSPECTIVE. COLOR PENCIL
AND PENCIL ON TRACING PAPER,
36 × 21". FLLW FDN# 3816.003

UNITARIAN CHURCH, *SHOREWOOD HILLS, WISCONSIN.*
1947. CONCEPTUAL SKETCH. PENCIL ON TRACING PAPER,
33 × 43". FLLW FDN# 5031.002

UNITARIAN CHURCH, *SHOREWOOD HILLS, WISCONSIN.*
1947. PERSPECTIVE. INK ON TRACING PAPER,
21 × 18". FLLW FDN# 5031.016

HARRY JOHN DORMITORY *(PROJECT)*,
OCONOMOWOC, WISCONSIN. 1949. PERSPECTIVE. COLOR
PENCIL ON TRACING PAPER, 33×20". FLLW FDN# 4909.007

FATHER JOHN, a Catholic priest in Oconomowoc, Wisconsin, commissioned Wright to design a "dwelling" for him that would also accommodate a group of orphans to whom he gave shelter. The main floor is a two-story space, seen through the tall open windows at the front of the perspective. On the balcony, which runs the full length of the building's interior and extends out of doors, the dormitory facilities are located (with the father's private quarters at the far end). On the right of the drawing, a berm can be seen. This mound of earth was to slope up to the building on the north side to provide insulation against the cold in winter.

The spire rises above a small chapel. It denotes the ecclesiastical nature of the project and gives a certain striking drama to what in reality is a rather simple, residential building.

DR. PEYTON CANARY, the president of the Southwest Christian Seminary, a small college near Phoenix, contacted Frank Lloyd Wright early in 1950 to discuss the design for a new campus. Canary's office was about twenty miles from Taliesin West, so he received an invitation to come for an interview. Canary explained that he wanted a new architectural program, including a chapel, auditorium, administration offices, seminar rooms, and more—an entire agricultural layout with homes, farms, and gardens. He also explained, at the very beginning of his request, that although the seminary had a beautiful tract of land, some seventy-three acres surrounded by mountains in the desert beyond Phoenix, they had no money: "It may be foolish and presumptuous of me even to think of trying to secure your services as an architect. But I know I am no fool for wanting that service. I came to challenge you to lay out the grounds and design the buildings of the Southwest Christian Seminary on a lovely bit of land we own. All this must be economical, substantial, and definitely beautiful. The beauty which we build must sing with

the joy of its own loveliness." Wright responded characteristically: "I hardly see how I can find the time and energy to help you, but somehow I will do it. Go back and tell your friends and colleagues I am proud to be the architect of your seminary, and will help you in every way I can."

Clearly Wright was intrigued by the challenge to design not only a group of buildings but to lay out the entire campus, including the farms. He created a triangular grid pattern for the whole property and placed the main structure diagonally across from the main access road.

The long elevation shown here places the chapel at the far left, connected to the administration building, lookout tower, auditorium, classrooms, seminar rooms, and library. Next to the main chapel is a freestanding bell tower. The aerial perspective shows the entire development, including this structure and the surrounding farms and citrus groves. The length and scope of the central building, described above, was such that Wright preferred to show the work by means of the long eleva-

tion. It is the only presentation drawing of its kind in the entire collection. "Architecture here combines Tillage and Building," Wright wrote. "A building scheme wherein each contributes to the other. The patterns of tillage become the patterns of building and the patterns of building become the patterns of tillage."

The seminary was able to pay an initial but relatively small fee for the presentation drawings. They hoped to use the drawings to help raise funds for the buildings. This was a practice that Wright fervently avoided throughout his career, and the exception he made in this instance only further proves his keen interest in the project. But as the sponsors were unable to get funding or financing, the plans were finally abandoned. In 1971, however, the Reverend William Boice of the First Christian Church remembered the project (he had been associated with Dr. Canary), contacted the architect's widow, and secured the permission of the Frank Lloyd Wright Foundation to build the church in Phoenix.

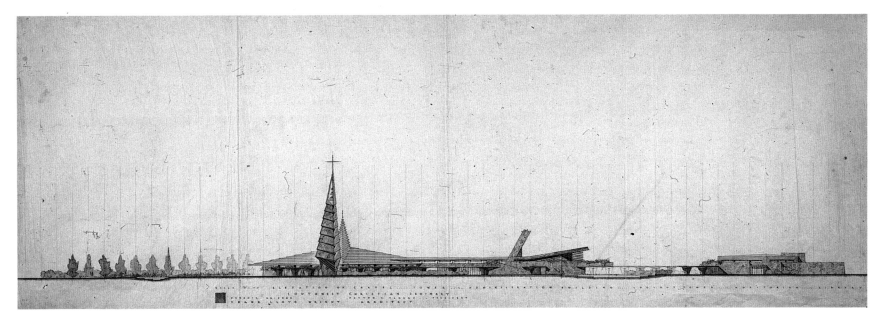

SOUTHWEST CHRISTIAN SEMINARY (PROJECT),
PHOENIX, ARIZONA. 1950. ELEVATION. COLOR PENCIL
ON TRACING PAPER, 96 × 39". FLLW FDN# 5033.005

SOUTHWEST CHRISTIAN SEMINARY (PROJECT),
PHOENIX, ARIZONA. 1950. PLAN. INK ON TRACING PAPER,
89 × 46". FLLW FDN# 5033.002

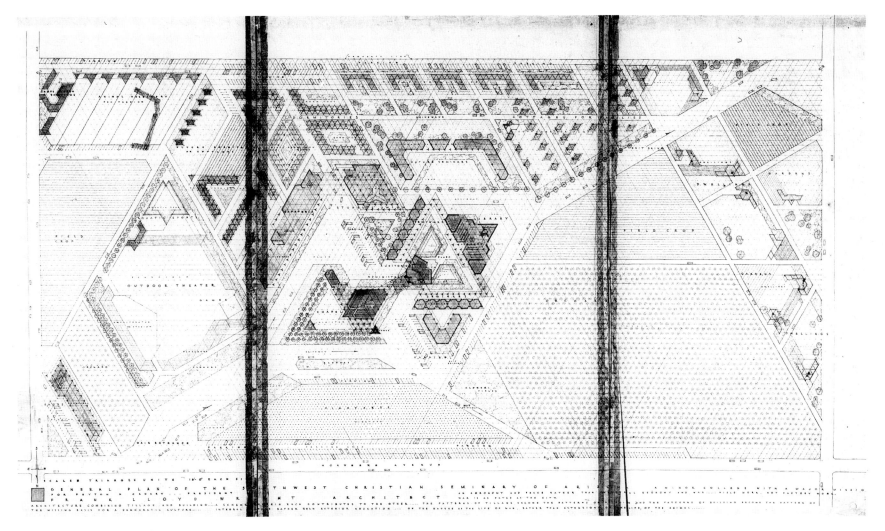

THE PROPERTY SURROUNDING Edgar Kaufmann's house Fallingwater (page 41) is famous for its rhododendrons. In this design for a small family chapel to be built upstream from the main house on a flat piece of land, Wright selected that shrub for the title of the work. The stonework of the chapel was to have the same grammar as that of the house downstream, but the roof was to be composed of crystalline panels of glass and copper. Diamond-shaped windows pierce the stone wall under a protective overhang.

Other than the method of constructing the stone walls, the overall design is quite different in all aspects from that of Fallingwater. The house, built for daily living and entertaining above the water cascades, makes use of several reinforced-concrete cantilevered terraces and balconies in and among the trees and foliage. The site is apparently dramatic and the house well matched to it. The chapel was to be built on a quieter location and was to serve, naturally, quite another function.

The perspective, drawn by an apprentice at Taliesin, has the architect's usual added flourishes in the treatment of the trees and shrubbery. The chapel was to be a memorial to Edgar Kaufmann's wife, Liliane, who had recently died, but the family had a simpler monument in mind, and the project was dropped.

RHODODENDRON CHAPEL (PROJECT), MILL RUN, PENNSYLVANIA. 1953. PERSPECTIVE. PENCIL ON TRACING PAPER, 34 × 19". FLLW FDN# 5308.001

WRIGHT'S PLAN FOR a great pyramidlike structure composed of glass and steel rising out of a concrete mass was finally realized in this synagogue for the Beth Sholom congregation in Elkins Park, Pennsylvania. The prototype for the building is obviously the Steel Cathedral of 1925–1926 (page 92), but the scale of the prototype is here greatly reduced, although the synagogue is still an imposing structure. The original presentation drawings were never returned to the architect's office; apart from the great amount of working drawings required to get the building constructed, only Wright's conceptual sketches and this small view record his early work on the commission.

The architectural lines on this perspective have been extensively modified and edited by Wright, including the color designation of stained-glass windows in certain tall elements of the translucent roof. On the lower right of the perspective the architect has written, "Scheme 1. American Synagogue for Beth Sholom—Rabbi Cohen. May be increased up to 10,000 seats or diminished to 500—Various forms by modification of planes—infinite. FLLW."

Wright described the building as a "luminous Mount Sinai." Inside, the light coming from overhead is silver in the morning, golden in the afternoon. At night the light within the temple radiates, as the sketch lines on the perspective indicate. Wright saw the structure into construction, but the temple was consecrated in September 1959, five months after his death.

BETH SHOLOM SYNAGOGUE, ELKINS PARK, PENNSYLVANIA. 1954. CONCEPTUAL SKETCH. COLOR PENCIL AND PENCIL ON TRACING PAPER, 29 × 18". FLLW FDN# 5313.001

CHURCH FOR THE
MILWAUKEE · WISCONSIN
FRANK LLOYD ·WR

ANNUNCIATION GREEK ORTHODOX CHURCH,

WAUWAUTOSA, WISCONSIN. 1956. CONCEPTUAL SKETCH.

COLOR PENCIL AND PENCIL ON TRACING PAPER, 36 × 30".

FLLW FDN# 5611.001

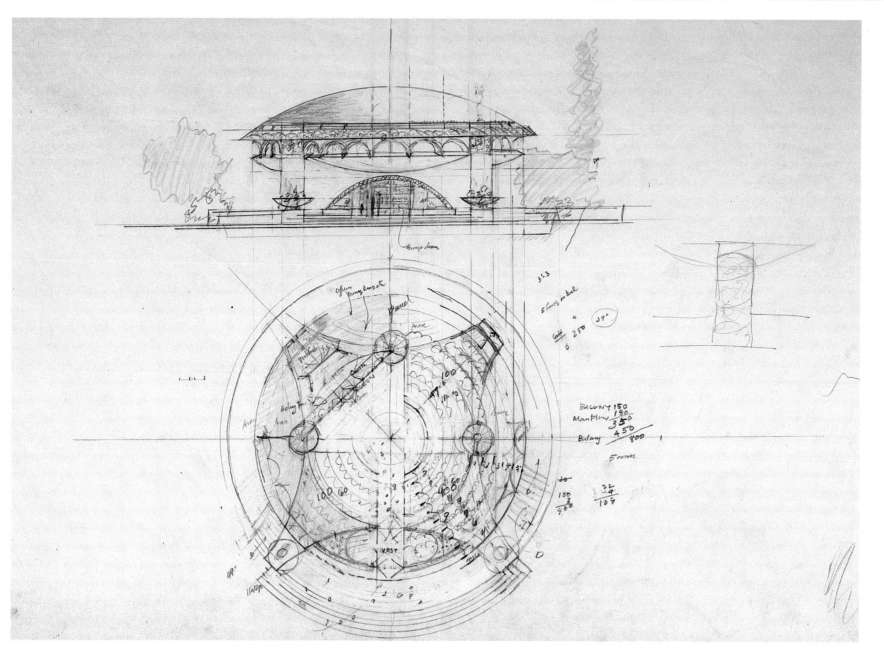

WHEN HE RECEIVED a commission for a church for the Milwaukee Hellenic Community, Wright consulted his wife, who was brought up in the Greek Orthodox faith, about the predominant symbols of the church. "The cross and the dome" was her reply. The heritage of the Greek Orthodox church greatly interested him because of his own admiration for Byzantine architecture. He often referred to the remarkable domes of the early Byzantine churches, Hagia Sophia in particular. "The arch was Byzantine," he wrote, "and is a sophisticated building act resulting in more sophisticated forms than the lintel of the Mayan, Egyptian or Greek. Yet it is essentially primitive masonry. Byzantine architecture lived anew by the arch. The arch sprung from the caps of stone posts and found its way into roofing by way of the low, heavy, stone dome. Its haunches were well down within heavy walls. It was a flat crown showing above the stone masses punctured below by arches. The Byzantine sense of form seems neither East nor West but belongs to both."

Wright's architectural interpretation of these two forms, or symbols—the dome and the cross—shows his acute sense of abstracting the essence of an idea for the Milwaukee church and then translating it into terms and methods relative to modern times and technology. The plan is a Greek cross, and the building rises on arches that support the upper level, or balcony. The roof dome rises above an inverted dome, or bowl, that is the balcony. His conceptual sketch demonstrates this very clearly and shows the marvelous relationship between plan and elevation. On the plan below the elevation Wright has drawn both levels: the part enclosed by the cross is on ground level; the encircling lines beyond the cross supports represent the balcony level.

On the conceptual elevation Wright has partially colored in the dome surface with a blue pencil, the only color in the entire drawing, reflecting another aspect of ancient architecture that intrigued him, that of Persia: "The Persian was born, or had become, a true mystic," Wright wrote. "And because he was a mystic, this particularly developed man of the white race naturally loved blue." The impression of the blue domes in Persian architecture, which he saw only in illustrations, was reinforced by yet another precedent: "I remember going to Palermo some years ago to see the mosaics of Monreale. I had just got into the Cathedral square and lifted my eyes to that great work when to the left I saw— or did I see it—for some moments I thought I dreamed— there against the sky—no, not against it, of it, literally of the sky was a great dome of Racca blue."

Among the unpublished manuscripts in the Frank Lloyd Wright Archives is one that contains several short descriptions, in Wright's own hand, of his buildings. For the Greek church he wrote, "Worship à la Byzantium. The domed religion of antiquity at home in modern times—the Romance of its Past distinguished."

And again, in a letter of September 9, 1958—when the project was well into the working drawing stages— Wright explained, "This edifice is in itself a complete work of modern art and science belonging to today but dedicated to ancient tradition—contributing to Tradition instead of living upon it."

The building went into construction the year the architect died. Archbishop Iokavos dedicated the completed edifice in a moving service attended by the architect's widow and apprentices.

IN 1957 THE HOTEL Claremont in Berkeley, California, commissioned Wright to design a chapel for weddings. It was to be located in a garden at the front side but connected to the main building. The elevation shows Wright's first design, a small chapel with a covered passageway to the hotel. The very sketchy plan is somewhat similar, but on a much smaller scale, to the plan for the Greek Orthodox church (page 100). Encircled on the sheet of paper is Wright's working title for the project, "Rococo Wedding Chapel."

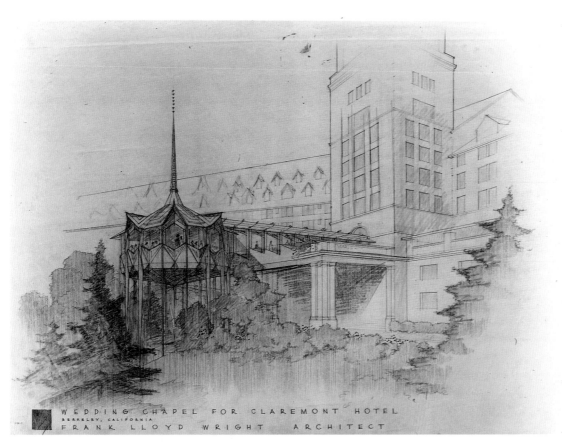

WEDDING CHAPEL FOR CLAREMONT HOTEL
BERKELEY, CALIFORNIA
FRANK LLOYD WRIGHT ARCHITECT

WEDDING CHAPEL FOR HOTEL CLAREMONT
(PROJECT), BERKELEY, CALIFORNIA. 1957. PERSPECTIVE.
COLOR PENCIL ON TRACING PAPER, 35×26".
FLLW FDN# 5731.001

SHORTLY AFTER MAKING his first sketch for the wedding chapel, his so-called rococo design, Wright learned that the extension from the hotel to the chapel would have to be connected to the second floor. This second design resolved that problem, putting the chapel on slender, delicate "legs," like those of a crane or heron, with the connecting passageway coming out from the older building behind. There were times when Wright would break his own "rules" and do so very successfully. He detested the International Style, especially buildings that were glass boxes set on pilotis, or slender poles. He frequently referred to the International Style as "Neither international, nor much style." Such buildings he saw as devoid of a necessary connection to the site and to the ground, as well as devoid of a sense of human scale. Here he used pilotis, but the chapel has a graceful charm in keeping with his own idiom.

TRINITY CHAPEL (*PROJECT*), NORMAN, OKLAHOMA.

1958. CONCEPTUAL SKETCH. COLOR PENCIL ON PAPER,

10 × 8". FLLW FDN# 5810.002

IN 1958 WRIGHT received a commission to design a chapel for the campus of the University of Oklahoma in Norman, Oklahoma. The work came by way of the Joneses—a local Tulsa family.

One morning while Wright was reading his mail, his wife asked him about the new job for the chapel in Oklahoma. This small thumbnail sketch, made with a blue pencil that he had in his pocket and sketched on an advertisement for Praeger Art Books, was his reply. The final perspective is nothing more than a clearer rendition of the small first sketch. The chapel is raised off the ground to provide covered parking underneath; access is via six ramps, two coming off each corner of the triangular-shaped chapel. The chapel itself is flèche, tower, and church all within one form. The concrete walls rise to support a copper roof, and diamond-shaped stained-glass windows are set into each side of the building. The stone lions, shown at the terminal of each ramp as it reaches ground level, are an interesting touch, in some ways quite unrelated to the commission as a whole. Wright had recently purchased two ancient Chinese lions and placed them on the low walls that extended out from the Hillside Home School building in Wisconsin. As the lions strongly appealed to him, he added a "touch" of ancient China to this modern chapel.

Above the word "ARCHITECT," Wright has written, "TO NATURE The Sectless Chapel."

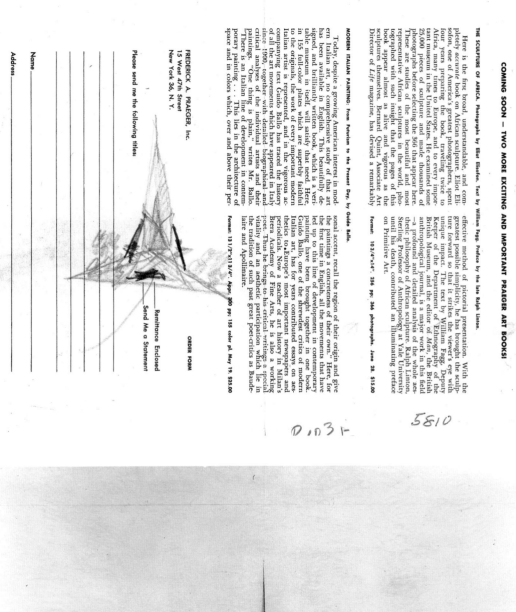

TRINITY CHAPEL (*PROJECT*), NORMAN, OKLAHOMA.

1958. PERSPECTIVE. COLOR PENCIL AND INK ON TRACING PAPER,

49 × 36". FLLW FDN# 5810.001

(*OVERLEAF:* TRINITY CHAPEL. *PERSPECTIVE; DETAIL*)

PART THREE

HIGH-RISE BUILDINGS

WRIGHT'S FIRST EXECUTED DESIGN for a high-rise structure was the windmill tower "Romeo and Juliet," built in 1897 for his two aunts, Nel and Jane Lloyd Jones, at the Hillside Home School. The school, which was the first coeducational home school in the nation, was located near Spring Green, Wisconsin, in the ancestral Lloyd Jones valley (and not far from the Silsbee Unity Chapel). The architect called the windmill tower his first "engineering-architecture"—the structure of the tower and its form were combined into one entity, each directly related to the other. Not truly a high-rise as such, it nevertheless was an early statement about what Wright believed a tall building should be. To emphasize its significance in the overall scope of his work, he continually included it in publications and exhibitions throughout his life.

Wright had had early training and experience in creating tall buildings first as a draftsman and later as chief of design for the firm of Adler and Sullivan. Chicago witnessed a rapid growth of skyscrapers following the fire of 1871, which had leveled the city and made possible a new beginning in architecture and engineering. (The invention of the elevator, "The up-ended street," as Wright called Otis's innovation, was perhaps the chief development in enabling architects to construct tall buildings.) Firms such as Burnham and Root and Holabird and Roche, along with Adler and Sullivan, competed with each other for high-rise commissions.

With twentieth-century technology applied both to materials and building methods, the tall building was possible. But the early structures were tall only by consequence, not by aesthetic determination. They consisted of heavy, boxy masses of concrete and masonry stories piled one upon the other until a certain height was achieved. It took the genius of Louis Sullivan to find an aesthetically appropriate expression for the tall building. In his autobiography Wright recollected the moment: "When he brought the drawing board with the motive for the Wainwright Building outlined in profile and in scheme upon it and threw it down on my table, I was perfectly aware of what had happened. This was Louis Sullivan's great moment, his greatest effort. The skyscraper as a new thing beneath the sun, an entity imperfect, but with virtue, individuality, beauty all its own—was born."

In the typical Adler and Sullivan high-rise, all vertical design elements were accentuated, brought forward from the general surface of the building, and the horizontal elements—window sills, floor-level separations—were set back. The effect was immediately of predominant verticality. The vertical motifs were usually left unadorned—simple, sleek masonry masses—while the set-back elements were richly ornamented. Sometimes the combination was reversed: the tall masses richly decorated, the recessed horizontal fixtures left clean.

The Press Building, a project for San Francisco in 1912, was Wright's way of expressing the tall building. It was to be built in reinforced concrete, a monomaterial structure quite unlike the conglomerate of materials Adler and Sullivan used for the structure, ornamentation, and interior decoration of their high-rises. Twelve years later, Wright's National Life Insurance Building, another unbuilt project for Chicago, was even taller and had cantilevered floors carrying walls of copper and glass. The old post-and-beam form of construction was abolished. Indeed lessons Wright had learned from the construction of the Imperial Hotel in Tokyo (1915–1922) were applied here for the first time in a high-rise design: the plan called for a system of central core supports carrying concrete slabs; each floor balanced like a tray on a waiter's hand. The flexibility of this scheme, the balanced cantilever, had saved the Imperial Hotel from destruction during the great Kanto quake of 1923. If the exterior walls had been the supporting members of the building, the movement of the trembler would have collapsed the building like a house of cards. The principle of cantilever and reinforced-concrete floor slabs had amply proved itself; it became the basic principle of every high-rise building Wright designed.

In 1929, for the Saint Mark's Tower in New York—one of Wright's innovative projects for his friend and client William Norman Guthrie (Steel Cathedral, 1926, and a house in Tennessee, 1909)—he devised a "tap-root" foundation system to supplement the central support and cantilevered-floor construction. The tap-root, as he called it, was a deep extension into the earth of a building's main concrete and steel core. Although the Saint Mark's Tower was not built, variations on its structural system were designed by Wright during the next twenty-five years; the original design, in a somewhat modified and refined form, eventually was built in Bartlesville, Oklahoma, for the H.C. Price Company, (page 120).

In 1932 Wright wrote *The Disappearing City*, his first book on decentralization. During the late 1920s he became aware of the dangers of overcrowded cities, and his book was one of the first to expound on moving the city out into the landscape, not as a suburban sprawl but as a beautifully organized design solution. One of the illustrations in the book is a photograph of the New York City skyline showing smoke belching up from a network of skyscrapers. The conditions look mild compared to those of today, but the effect is still ominous and threatening. Beneath the photograph Wright has placed the caption, "Find the citizen." Two years later he designed and built a model of just such an organized community, which he called "Broadacre City." Features of the landscape are wedded to the requirements of modern living in a spacious environment never before envisioned by architects or planners.

The major cities, such as New York, had grouped their skyscrapers into massive clusters reaching into the sky, cutting out light and air and creating dark, noisy canyons on the streets below. Wright's solution was to site tall buildings in such a way that they would be free and clear of each other. Beginning with Saint Mark's and continuing through the Grouped Towers (1930), the Crystal Heights (1939), the Rogers Lacy Hotel (1946), the Price Tower (1952), the Golden Beacon (1956), and the Mile High (1956), he developed the concept of the tall building standing in its own park, isolated from other tall buildings. As his career progressed, as he saw the International-Style skyscrapers built across the nation and around the world, Wright conceded that high-rises were a necessary evil, but in his own work he reiterated that they should never confine or dehumanize life.

THIS COMMISSION for a skyscraper office building came to Wright in 1911, when his office was in transition. He had returned from a year's sojourn in Europe, had closed his Oak Park studio, had moved his practice first to the Fine Arts Building in Chicago and then to Orchestra Hall, and was building a new home and studio for himself at Taliesin, in southwest Wisconsin. Perhaps the office moves account for the fact that no record of this job or the client is to be found among Wright's papers. One drawing carries the notation, "For the Spreckles estate," but there is no formal title block on the drawing sheet. The Spreckles family of San Diego controlled much of the city, including the utility and ground-transportation companies, as well as the shipping and sugar industries in Hawaii. After John D. Spreckles acquired a newspaper in San Francisco, *The Call Bulletin,* the design for a skyscraper was requested. The final plans for the structure show neither the name of the client nor the building itself; they are simply titled, "Design for Reinforced Concrete Skyscraper— Slab Construction."

On one of his notes about the building, Wright explained that it would be built using a slip-form, just as tall concrete grain elevators in the Midwest and West were built. This type of construction did away with expensive and cumbersome scaffolding and forming; once the floor and walls for each story were poured, the formwork was moved up to the next level. The building therefore was to be a concrete structure, reinforced by steel. A reinforced-concrete cantilever is used in this building only for the projecting roof at the top. Two years later, in the Imperial Hotel in Tokyo, Wright expanded this cantilever principle to all the floors and roofs. Here, the stability and strength necessary to withstand California's earthquakes were achieved by the steel reinforcements in the slab construction.

The sketch elevations, one of the front of the proposed skyscraper and the other of its profile, actually show two structures, one about half the height of the other, but both employing the same design. A small thumbnail sketch view reveals the two new buildings attached to an existing edifice. The projecting roof at the top was intended to carry spotlights that would illuminate the entire façade and the entryway on the street below. The overall articulation of vertical elements, with the window lines set well back, reveals the influence of Louis Sullivan, but the simplicity of form and clean lines are strictly Wright's own touch.

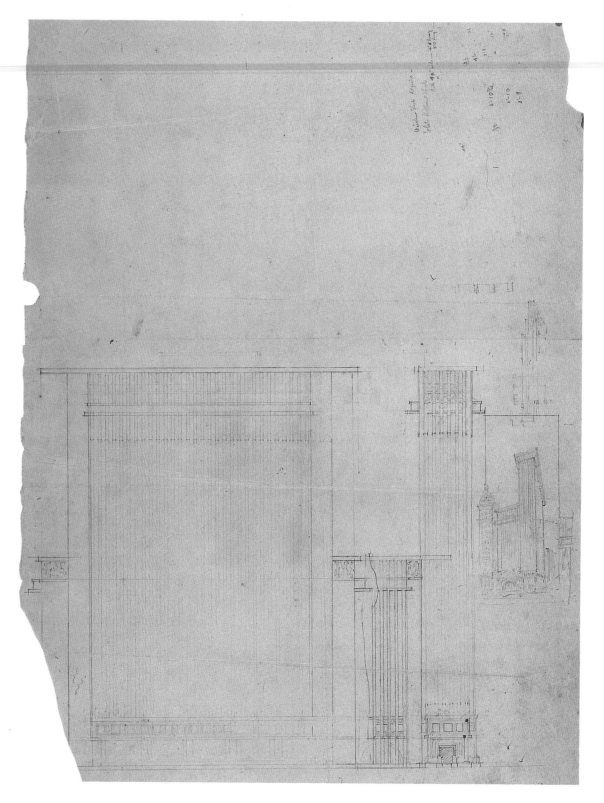

Press Building for *The San Francisco Call* (project), San Francisco, California. 1912. Perspective. Ink and pencil on linen, 19 × 39". FLLW Fdn# 1207.001

NATIONAL LIFE INSURANCE BUILDING (PROJECT), CHICAGO, ILLINOIS. 1924.

PERSPECTIVE. INK ON ART PAPER, 36 × 46". FLLW FDN# 2404.001

NATIONAL LIFE INSURANCE BUILDING (PROJECT), CHICAGO, ILLINOIS. 1924.

PERSPECTIVE. PENCIL ON TRACING PAPER, 18 × 24". FLLW FDN# 2404.005

IN THIS 1924 BUILDING, the skyscraper is born again. A totally new system of construction was introduced, with cantilevers at work throughout the entire structure. All of the building's supports are centrally located, the concrete masses revealed as they rise out of the top of the building. The floors are cantilevered, reinforced-concrete slabs, the window walls are screens only, composed of glass and copper and hung from the slab edges. Compared with other high-rises in the United States at this same time—heavy stone masses decorating a steel post-and-beam frame—the National Life building soars into the sky: a lightweight, pristine structure. The second view, rendered from ground level, emphasizes the contrast between Wright's vision and the buildings on either side of it.

The client, Albert M. Johnson, president of the insurance company, made it explicitly clear to Wright from the beginning of the project that he would "grubstake" him twenty thousand dollars to prepare plans for a new kind of skyscraper using the structural principle that had saved the Imperial Hotel during the disastrous Kanto quake the year before. Although Johnson kept his word and paid for the designs, he lacked the courage to build the building. In writing about the commission and its client, Wright recollected, "Intensely interested in ideas, I believe, though not himself the kind of man inclined to build, he seemed rather the type called conservative who, tempted, will sneak up behind an idea, pinch it in the behind and turn and run. There is this type of man bred by our capitalistic system, not the

captain, nor the broker or the banker but a better sort not quite contented with the commonplace, not quite courageous enough to take risks. I have met many such men." Nonetheless, because of his innovation of the reinforced cantilever, Wright was anxious to set a new direction for the tall building in the United States—to create a skyscraper appropriate to the twentieth century.

Wright's notes in the 1931 exhibition catalog refer to this structure: "Cantilever balanced construction—walls eliminated—glass wall screens pendant in metal setting substituted. A standardization along modern industrial lines to lighten and cheapen and make more humanly effective the 'skyscraper'."

IN 1926 WRIGHT came to grips with the problems of constructing several skyscrapers in a limited urban area. He called the project "Skyscraper Regulation." Two years after the design for the National Life Insurance Company (page 110), his basic structural solution to the high-rises was a continuance of the reinforced-concrete slab construction with a screen wall of glass and stamped metal. Taking four, eight, or more, if desired, conventional city blocks in an equally conventionalized grid plan, he sited the tall buildings in such a way that they would not create dark caverns. Some of the high-rises have north-south axes, others east-west. The rooftops provide planting areas for green gardens and parks, and the medians on the street are also wide enough for planting trees and foliage. The ground level is reserved for vehicles; the second level is a sidewalk that bridges the streets below, keeping pedestrian passages free of automobile traffic. At certain places the sixth-floor level is also a pedestrian walkway spanning blocks with gardens and roof terraces. Thus, the plan humanizes the necessary evil of dense urban architecture, offering a jewellike cluster of geometric shapes interspersed with light, air, and green plantings.

On the plan and its accompanying elevation, Wright has titled the project, "SKYSCRAPER REGULATION Augmenting the Gridiron. Remodelling of the city— beyond these provisions the city should spread out— FLLW Jan 1926." This idea that "the city should spread out" prompted him, six years later, to write *The Disappearing City,* his first detailed thesis about urban planning.

On these drawings he was still seeking a bearable solution for the present-day city. His handwritten notes throughout the plan explain the scheme block by block, indicating height restrictions, setbacks, parking areas, placement of tall towers, and landscaping. Further notes indicate specifications for power lines, utilities, elevator towers, subway entrances, alleyways, and major access routes to the buildings. As with many of his conceptual plans, Wright has indicated several possibilities and conditions all on one sheet, making it difficult to decipher his exact intentions except as they are illustrated.

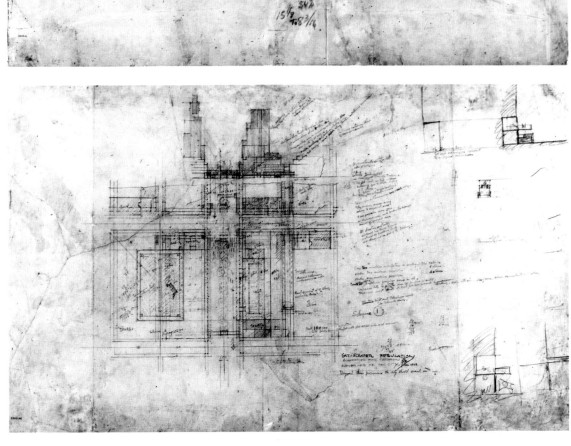

SKYSCRAPER REGULATION *(PROJECT). 1926.*

ELEVATION. PENCIL ON TRACING PAPER, 35 × 20".

FLLW FDN# 2603.001

SKYSCRAPER REGULATION *(PROJECT). 1926.*

PLAN AND SECTION. PENCIL ON TRACING PAPER, 34 × 20".

FLLW FDN# 2603.004

WILLIAM NORMAN GUTHRIE, the colorful and quixotic pastor of Saint Mark's in the Bouwerie, was the client for this apartment tower, which was to stand in the park adjacent to his church. Rent from the apartments was to help support the church. At one point in the project, a complex of three towers was considered. Each apartment is a duplex—a two-story living room with bedrooms on the upper level, and there are four apartments to each floor; the building is nine double-stories tall. Notes for Wright's European exhibition of 1931—a model of Saint Mark's was made for this show—contain Wright's explanation of the design: "The cantilever or principle of balanced construction seen in the skyscraper for the National Life Ins. Co.—adapted to quadruple plan for duplex apartments in New York City. Conservation of space by way of furnishing standardization all combining to bring to the building the scientific attainments of the well-built machine."

The purpose of the axonometric plan was simply to permit the client and his board of trustees to "look" into the plan with a degree of perspective that a flat plan could not reveal. Wright had discovered that few clients could really read plans very accurately. If the project was an especially complicated one, he always insisted on presenting the plans himself, in person. His own explanation would lead the client from room to room and point out the various features of the project. Although the drawing is a plan, the identification of it states, "Interior view of living rooms" and "Interior view of bedrooms." The axonometric makes quite clear the structure of the building as well, denoting the four darkened areas of the supporting core and the light, screenlike nature of the exterior surface.

In this case, the client and his board were far away from the architect's office, and Wright hoped that this planned solution would suffice. But there were still doubts and arguments that went on for some years among members of the board, mostly over their concerns about a nontraditional building. Despite the urging of Guthrie to erect the building, the board prevailed, and the project was abandoned.

SIMPLY TITLED "Grouped Towers," Wright has expanded here the Saint Mark's Tower into a string of five double towers, each twenty-six floors high. As with the earlier project for Dr. Guthrie, the apartments are duplexes, but six are planned for each level rather than four. The towers are connected at their corners so as to provide more light and air than a side connection would allow, and the connections themselves create open terraces on each living-room level. The perspective is rendered from an angle that does not show this connection, but the ground-floor plan, called "pedestal," makes the spacing of the six towers clearly evident. The site for the proposed group was a narrow park on Chicago's Lake Shore Drive at Pearson Street. Wright has carefully preserved the park in his placement of the towers.

The dirigible and motor cars in the drawing are examples of other machine-age elements as they relate to this machine-age high-rise.

SAINT MARK'S TOWER (PROJECT),
NEW YORK CITY. 1929. AXONOMETRIC PLAN.
PENCIL ON TRACING PAPER, 24 × 34".
FLLW FDN# 2905.039

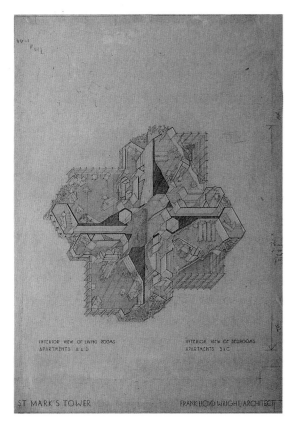

SAINT MARK'S TOWER (PROJECT),
NEW YORK CITY. 1929. PERSPECTIVE.
PENCIL ON TRACING PAPER, 24 × 40".
FLLW FDN# 2905.002

GROUPED TOWERS (PROJECT), CHICAGO, ILLINOIS. 1930. PERSPECTIVE. PENCIL ON TRACING PAPER, 29 × 20". FLLW FDN# 3001.001

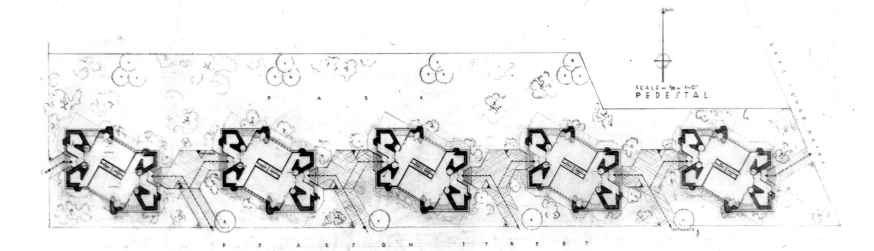

GROUPED TOWERS (PROJECT), CHICAGO, ILLINOIS. 1930. PLAN. PENCIL ON TRACING PAPER, 35 × 12". FLLW FDN# 3001.003

THE GOLDEN BEACON
CHICAGO ILLINOIS
FRANK LLOYD WRIGHT, ARCHITECT

ROGERS LACY HOTEL (PROJECT),
DALLAS, TEXAS. 1946. INTERIOR PERSPECTIVE.
COLOR PENCIL ON TRACING PAPER, 31×22".
FLLW FDN# 4606.010

ALL OF THE PRINCIPLES Wright used in his high-rise buildings—central-core supports, cantilevered floor slabs, nonsupporting screen walls hung from the slabs—are present in the 1946 Rogers Lacy Hotel, but each successive floor of the nine-story main block and of the tower that rises out of it is larger than the one beneath it. A tall, saillike stack at the right of the glass tower contains utilities and provides a further stabilizing element.

The entire surface of the building was to consist of diamond-shaped panes of double-thickness frosted glass with glass wool insulation. This would allow a softly diffused light to permeate the interior. The main block of the hotel houses public rooms, shops, stores, galleries, and some guest rooms. All interior spaces open onto sunlit balconies, and a great atrium court inside rises from a cluster of water gardens. The ground floor was treated as one open space, focusing on the atrium, with screened-off areas for the lobby, reception, bar, café, and dining room. The screening walls were movable to accommodate whatever changes in room function the hotel deemed necessary. The level below was to be the kitchen, with ramps up to the main floor in various locations. The further basements were to provide parking space beneath the hotel. As with the rendering of the National Life building (page 110), the contrast of the light, crystalline building is seen in relation to the conventional buildings on either side. In the tower, duplex suites were planned as well as individual guest rooms. The interior perspective shows a typical living room of one of the duplex suites, with its translucent glass wall. Today, this window wall could be realized by use of plastics. Indeed, Wright remarked toward the end of his life that plastics would become the most appropriate building materials as the world continues to use up or wantonly destroy most of the natural ones.

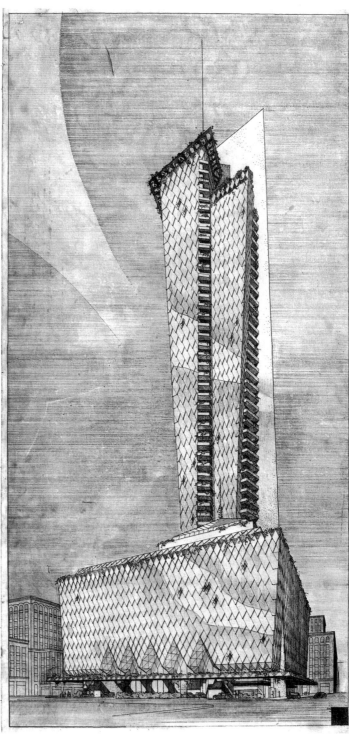

ROGERS LACY HOTEL (PROJECT),
DALLAS, TEXAS. 1946. PERSPECTIVE.
COLOR PENCIL ON TRACING PAPER, 25×54".
FLLW FDN# 4606.001

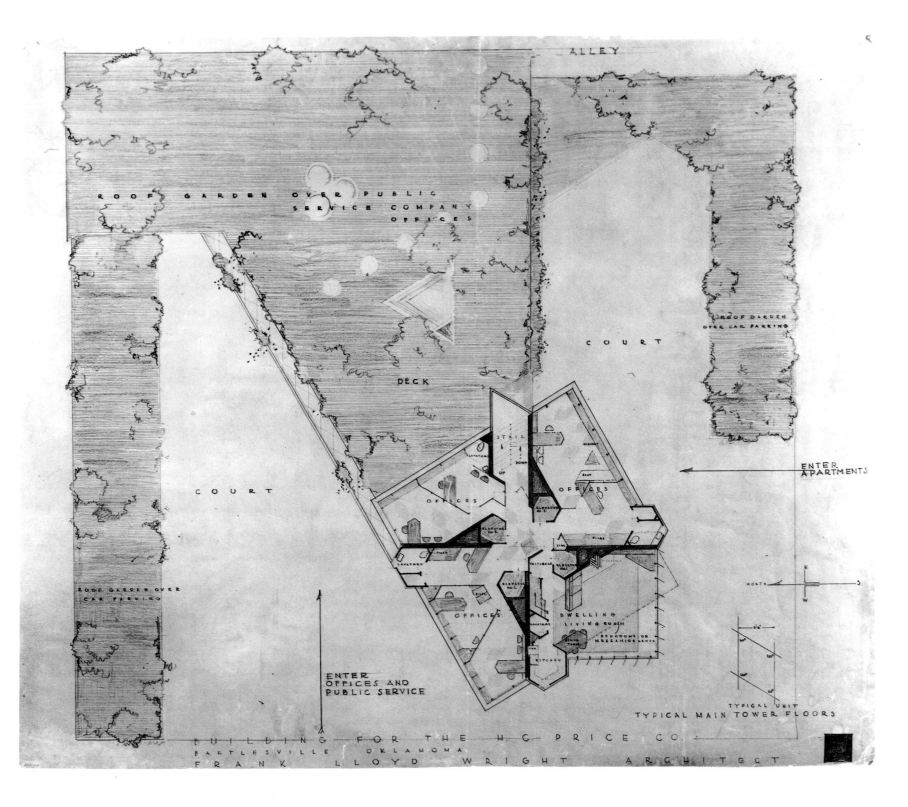

ALLEY

ROOF GARDEN OVER PUBLIC
SERVICE COMPANY
OFFICES

ROOF GARDEN
OVER CAR PARKING

COURT

DECK

ENTER
APARTMENTS

COURT

STAIR

LAVATORY

DOWN

UP

OFFICES

OFFICES

CLOSET

SEAT

ELEVATOR
NO. 4

ELEVATOR
NO. 3

LAVATORY

FILES

FILES

LAV.

VESTIBULE ELEVATOR
NO. 1

ROOF GARDEN OVER
CAR PARKING

ELEVATOR
NO. 2

OFFICES

FILES

LAVATORY

DWELLING
LIVING ROOM

BEDROOM ON
MEZZANINE ABOVE

KITCHEN

E

NORTH

W

ENTER
OFFICES AND
PUBLIC SERVICE

TYPICAL UNIT

TYPICAL MAIN TOWER FLOORS

BUILDING FOR THE H C PRICE CO.
BARTLESVILLE OKLAHOMA
FRANK LLOYD WRIGHT ARCHITECT

THE TOWER FOR THE H. C. Price Company, in Bartlesville, Oklahoma, was considered by the architect to be a "compromise." Hal Price, Sr., had come to Taliesin in the early summer of 1952 to ask Frank Lloyd Wright to design a two-story office structure for his pipeline company, along with parking space for about ten to fifteen vehicles. When he returned at the end of the summer to see his plans, Wright showed him a proposal to build a twenty-two-story version of the Saint Mark's Tower (page 112), with duplex apartments running up one quadrant of the building, rental offices on the other sides, and Price Company offices at the top. Price was startled at this suggestion to venture into real estate, so, in Wright's words, architect and client "compromised and built a nineteen-story tower instead."

H. C. PRICE TOWER, *BARTLESVILLE, OKLAHOMA. 1952.*
PLAN. PENCIL AND COLOR PENCIL ON TRACING PAPER,
45 × 36". FLLW FDN# 5215.006

H. C. PRICE TOWER, *BARTLESVILLE, OKLAHOMA. 1952.*
PERSPECTIVE. PENCIL AND COLOR PENCIL ON TRACING PAPER,
34 × 44". FLLW FDN# 5215.004

THE ILLINOIS

MILE - HIGH CANTILEVER
SKY - CITY TO HONOR
THE STATE OF ILLINOIS
AND CITY OF CHICAGO

528 FLOORS FROM GRADE TO LANDING OF TOP FLOOR ELEVATOR

MEMORIAL TO

LOUIS H SULLIVAN SON OF CHICAGO
FIRST MADE THE TALL BUILDING TALL

ELISHA OTIS
INVENTOR OF THE UPENDED STREET

JOHN ROEBLING
FIRST STEEL IN TENSION ON THE
GRAND SCALE THE BROOKLYN BRIDGE

LIDGERWOOD NAVAL ARCHITECT
FIRST OCEAN LINER KEEL MAKES
IT WHAT IT IS TODAY.

COIGNET & MONIER OF FRANCE
REINFORCED CONCRETE.
THE BODY OF OUR MODERN WORLD

SALUTATIONS

EDUARDO TORROJA SPAIN
ENGINEER

PROFESSORS BEGG F-CROSS
SCIENCE OF CONTINUITY

PROFESSOR PIER LUIGI NERVI
ENGINEER ITALY

DR. J.J. POLIVKA ENGINEER
UNIVERSITY OF CALIFORNIA

MAILLART ENGINEER
SWITZERLAND

FRANK LLOYD WRIGHT SON OF CHICAGO

HONORARY DEGREE OF ENGINEERING
TECHNISCHE HOCHSCHULE OF DARMSTADT, GERMANY

HONORARY DEGREE OF ENGINEERING
TECHNISCHE HOCHSCHULE OF ZURICH, SWITZERLAND

FIRST SUCCESSFUL APPLICATION OF PRINCIPLE OF
CONTINUITY HORIZONTAL DERIVED VERTICAL STEEL
IN TENSION APPLIED TO EARTHQUAKE - PROOF
CONSTRUCTION. THE PRINCIPLE OF THE CANTILEVER
VERTICAL APPLIED TO THE TALL BUILDING.
THE FIRST TAPROOT FOUNDATION

STATISTICS:

GROSS AREA ..... 18,462,000 SQ.FT.
DEDUCT 2,000,000 SQ.FT. FOR
DUCK-SHAFT, STRUCTURAL CANTI-
SOOMF, AUDIENCE HALLS, ETC.

NET RENTABLE AREA .... 13,047,000 SQ.FT.

PROBABLE COST ..... 70% CURRENT/CONVENTIONAL COST
PER SQUARE FOOT

OCCUPANCY ..... 55,000 PERSONS

TOTAL OCCUPANCY
IN AUDIENCE HALLS .. 75,000 PERSONS

GRAND TOTAL ..... 130,000 PERSONS

PARKING ..... 15,000 CARS
100 HELICOPTERS

57 80 FEET

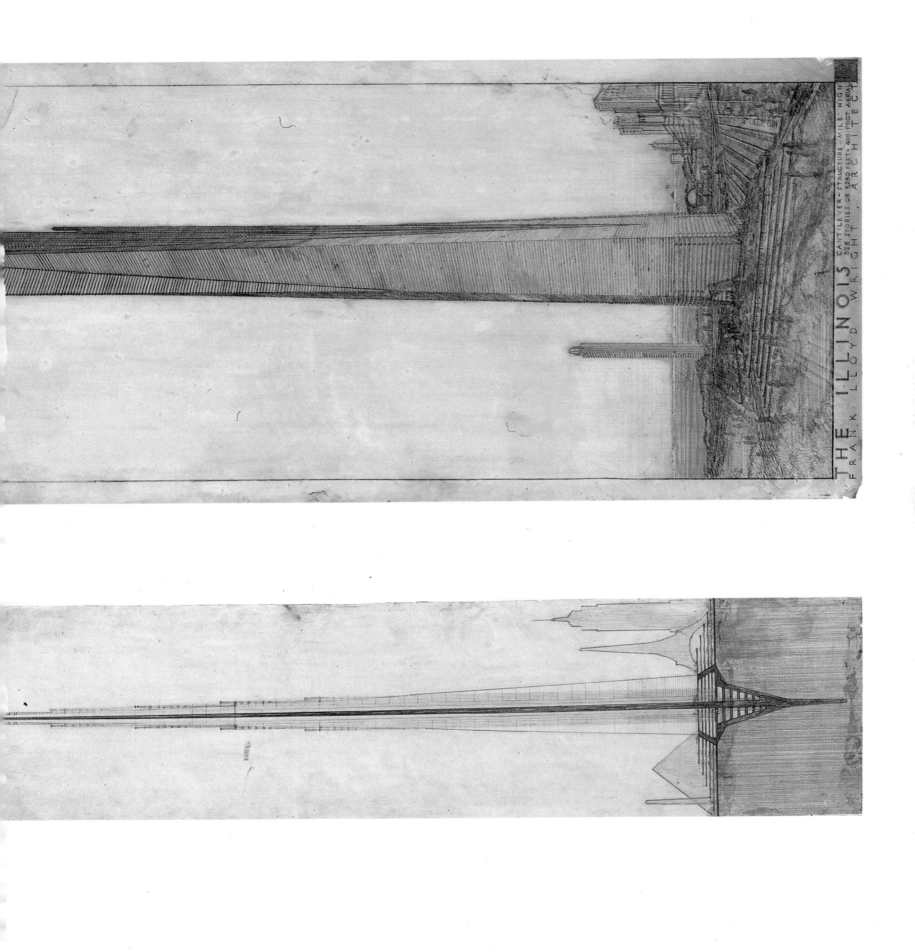

THE ILLINOIS CANTILEVER - STRUCTURE ½ MILE HIGH
528 STORIES OR 5280 FEET · 400 FOOT AERIAL
FRANK LLOYD WRIGHT, ARCHITECT

(Inside left foldout)

CHARLES GLORE, THE CLIENT for whom this tower was designed, commissioned Frank Lloyd Wright to build a house in Lake Forest, Illinois, in 1950. Six years later he asked Wright to design a fifty-story apartment building for Chicago. The first sketches of the project were labeled "Glore Tower," but when the rendering shown here was made, the use of gold-anodized aluminum on the stamped sheet-metal surfaces of the building prompted Wright to call it "The Golden Beacon." Like Saint Mark's (page 112) twenty-five years earlier, it was to be an apartment building but with the addition of a restaurant and club rooms on the top floors. The site was on Lake Shore Drive adjacent to the famous Lake Shore apartment buildings of Mies van der Rohe. (Wright has included Mies's building in the perspective, at the left.) The low three-story structure at the base of the tower is a parking facility; the remainder of the property was to be turned into a green garden park. The project, however, never progressed further than the preliminary drawing stage.

The inclusion of the Mies van der Rohe towers in the corner of the rendering is an interesting footnote. Wright and Mies enjoyed a warm and amiable friendship despite the great differences in their views of architecture. The glass box buildings, as built by Mies and the others following his style, were—to Wright—in every way detestable. They represented, to him, a strong rebuttal against humanity. He described the United Nations Building in New York as "rising like the back of the hand against humanity, a symbol more fascist than democratic." Large exposed glass areas are a constant hazard in tall buildings, and in some cases a deadly threat to the pedestrians on the streets below. They necessitate great expense both for heating and cooling, they expose the occupants to the sun year round and make it mandatory to provide all manner of added interior window covering as protection. In the Golden Beacon, as in Saint Mark's and the Price Tower (page 120), all exterior glass has been carefully shielded by louvers, made either horizontal or vertical—depending on the building's siting in relation to the sun—and as an integral part of the building itself.

THE GOLDEN BEACON (PROJECT),

CHICAGO, ILLINOIS. 1956. PERSPECTIVE.

COLOR PENCIL AND GOLD INK ON TRACING PAPER, 23 × 47".

FLLW FDN# 5615.004

(Inside right foldout)

FOR THIS BUILDING of 528 stories, rising one mile above the ground, stability was naturally the architect's primary concern. The section drawing shows the structure's tap-root foundation, which Wright used to liken to a rapier, or sword, with its handle stuck into the ground. This foundation had already proved successful in constructing tall buildings for the Johnson Wax Company in Racine, Wisconsin, and in the Price Tower in Bartlesville, Oklahoma (pages 248 and 120–121). At ground level a stack of five terraces provides parking space for cars and helicopters. The plan of the tower is a double triangle: "Of all forms of upright structure," Wright pointed out, "the most stable is the tripod: pressures upon any side are immediately resisted by the other two." The outer walls of the tower slope in as it rises, but the elevator shafts rise vertically, emerging out from the tower walls the higher they rise. "Elevator transit is by atomic power; specially designed elevators five units high begin to load where the escalators leave off at the fifth floor," Wright wrote. The terraces below give access to four separate entrances, each with its own freeway and parking facilities; each terrace is landscaped with green gardens and fountains. At the base of the section Wright has indicated the relative heights of other tall structures: the pyramid of Cheops at Giza, the Eiffel Tower in Paris, and the Empire State Building in New York. At the far left is his own Golden Beacon (page 115), visible also on the perspective drawing standing in the distance.

Above the section his legend reads:

THE ILLINOIS Mile-High Cantilever Sky City to honor the State of Illinois and City of Chicago. 528 floors from grade to landing of top floor elevator. Memorial to: Louis H. Sullivan—First made the tall building tall/Elisha Otis—Inventor of the up-ended street/John Roebling—First steel-in-tension on the grand scale:/The Brooklyn Bridge/Lidgerwood, naval architect—First ocean liner keel. Makes it what it is today/Coignet and Monier of France—Reinforced concrete. The body of our modern world./Salutations:/Eduardo Torroja, Engineer, Spain/Professor Beggs-Cross, science of continuity/Professor Pier Luigi Nervi, Engineer, Italy/Dr. J. J. Polivka, Engineer, University of California/Maillart, Engineer, Switzerland.

This "memorial" and "salutations" on Wright's part further illustrate that aspect of his genius that his wife once pointed out: from the ideas of his predecessors and his contemporaries, he was able to distill various achievements and combine them into his work. Shortly after the design was shown and published, Wright remarked to his apprentice Richard Carney while they were driving in his car one day, "Mile high? Why stop there? Why not two miles, or even five miles, if need be?"

THE MILE HIGH ''ILLINOIS'' (PROJECT),

CHICAGO, ILLINOIS. 1956. PERSPECTIVE.

COLOR PENCIL AND GOLD INK ON TRACING PAPER, 24 × 96".

FLLW FDN# 5617.002

THE MILE HIGH ''ILLINOIS'' (PROJECT),

CHICAGO, ILLINOIS. 1956. SECTION.

COLOR PENCIL ON TRACING PAPER, 12 × 96".

FLLW FDN# 5617.001

VIEW FROM THE SOUTH
BUILDING FOR THE H.C. PRICE CO.
BARTLESVILLE, OKLAHOMA
FRANK LLOYD WRIGHT · ARCHITECT

PART FOUR

CIVIC AND CULTURAL BUILDINGS

WRIGHT LOVED THE THEATER. All kinds of dramatic performances thrilled him: the plays of Shakespeare, vaudeville, musicals, modern drama, and cinema, too. Whenever he went to New York City, especially during the last years of his life when he kept an apartment at the Plaza Hotel, he saw as many theatrical performances as he could. In both Taliesins—in Wisconsin and Arizona—theaters designed by Wright existed in the buildings used by the Taliesin Fellowship. These theaters were more like cabarets: dining took place in the same hall as the theatrical or musical event.

During the season in Wisconsin, there was a dinner every Saturday evening, followed by a movie. Griffith, Eisenstein, and René Clair were the great film directors Wright admired: "Griffith gave us the close-up, Eisenstein the montage, and René Clair put the third dimension into cinema," he explained. In 1937, when Wright and his wife were invited to Russia to attend a congress of architects, he met Sergei Eisenstein, who was in the throes of making the film *Ivan the Terrible*. When the Wrights returned to the United States, Eisenstein sent fourteen reels of the uncut film for them to see.

Wright believed that the conventional design of theaters, in which the audience is placed in one area looking at the performers in another, was unpleasant. "I came to the conclusion," he said, "that the proscenium was a thing of the past, and to force the performance through a hole in the wall to the audience in one room, and the performance in another room, was all that was the matter with the drama, with the stage, the theater. If it were brought about that the audience and the performers were sympathetically related to each other, and the stage equipped so the transformations of scenery could be affected in an instant, then the drama would have new life."

From his exposure to theater in Japan, namely Kabuki, Wright learned the benefits of the revolving stage. From his training with Adler and Sullivan—particularly with Dankmar Adler, who was an engineer—he learned about acoustics. "Acoustics is not yet arrived at the point where it is an exact science," Wright said in a lecture in 1958. "You have to have had some experience in building buildings for sound in order to arrive at good results. Adler, who built the Chicago Auditorium, was called a great sound engineer, but he, himself, knew by experience what he knew. He never had to reduce it to a science. . . . Even today [the Chicago Auditorium] is the best room for opera in the world."

In 1915 Wright began his work in theater design for Aline Barnsdall (page 132). She was an oil-business heiress, originally from Pennsylvania, who met the architect first in Chicago, where she took part in setting up an experimental community theater. She later moved to southern California and asked Wright to design a complex that included a theater for large-scale productions, a motion-picture auditorium, residences for directors and actors, and a shopping center, all grouped together on a large property in the center of Los Angeles. In his theater design for her, the first thing Wright accomplished was the removal of the proscenium, incorporating the stage into the same room as the audience. He worked for five years on designs for this theater, but the commission never went beyond the preliminary stages.

In 1931 Wright designed three theater projects for Woodstock, New York (pages 140–141). In the final scheme, which he called, simply, the "New Theatre," he arrived at the flexible solution of a revolving stage, seating the audience around the performers rather than lining up rows of chairs in front of the stage. "A three-quarter view of anything is more interesting than the straight-on view. It gives depth and perspective," he explained. The 1931 project was abandoned but then revised some years later for a theater in Hartford, Connecticut, in 1949. That project, as well, was dropped. It was not until 1955 that he had the chance to see his theater scheme built, as the Dallas Theatre Center in Texas.

When he wrote his book *When Democracy Builds* in 1945, Wright made reference to a rather remarkable vision he had about the future of musical performance and cinema:

Where desired by the homemaker, cinema, like the theater, having the people for producer, would go from director and camera to every home. Entertainment both as sound and as vision would become something freely imagined, well executed, and continuously distributed by subscription like a circulating library. No censorship! . . . Meantime great music would mean something more and more to be distributed to the people, like the cinema. Music would also become a vital cultural affair—the culture of the Usonian family at home. The chamber-music concert would naturally again become a common pastime at home, growing until it again amounted to a culture beyond mere entertainment. It should be no uncommon accomplishment for children to read music readily, play some wind or stringed instrument well. Universal music culture, like the culture of music in the days of the recorder, should come alive again for us. No piano is enough. Knowledge of music and reading it in score should be as universal a practice as reading books, reading the funnies, the reading of plans or reading the stars.

He put his theory into practice at Taliesin. On his return from London in 1939 he brought back a selection of recorders—ranging from soprano to bass—and started a recorder choir. A chorus was already an established tradition. Apprentices rehearsed every morning and performed on Sunday evenings following dinner in Wright's living room. Violins, cellos, flutes, clarinets, and stringed bass were often organized into a chamber ensemble at these concerts, too. When apprentices joined the Fellowship with some skill with an instrument, they were immediately "built-in" to the ensemble. Since the very men and women playing in the ensemble were also helping to construct Taliesin's buildings and working on the farm there, Wright delighted in introducing them to his guests as "our farmer-laborer quartet." Musicians were frequently guests: Paul Robeson, Marcel Grandjany, Artur Rodzinski, and Sergei Koussevitsky spent time at Taliesin. Following a public concert in Madison, Wright once invited performer Sophie Breslau to drive to Taliesin—thirty-six miles away—where she gave a private concert to the Wrights and the Fellowship that very same evening until past one o'clock in the morning.

Wright's appetite for music was insatiable, and he constantly suggested that the mind of the composer was similar to that of the architect—they were of the same species. Beethoven was his great idol: "In Beethoven's music I sense the great mastermind, conscious fully of the qualities of heartful soaring imagination that are godlike in a man. . . . Beethoven's music is in itself the greatest proof of divine harmony alive in the human spirit I know. . . . When I build I often hear this music and, yes, when Beethoven made music I am sure he sometimes saw building, like mine in character?"

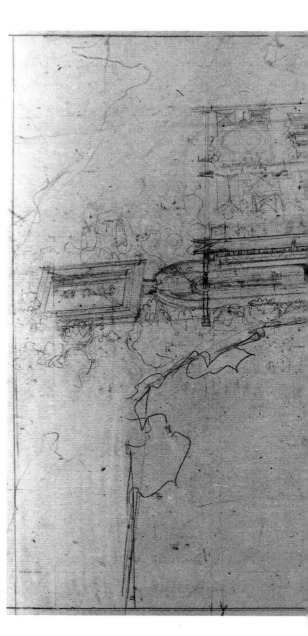

ORNAMENTAL DETAILS FOR THE CHICAGO AUDITORIUM, *CHICAGO, ILLINOIS.*

1888. CONCEPTUAL SKETCH. PENCIL ON TRACING PAPER, 9 × 9". FLLW FDN# 8801.001

THIS IS THE ONLY DRAWING that remains of those Wright made while working for Louis Sullivan on the Chicago Auditorium. The young draftsman quickly caught on to Sullivan's decorative idiom. "Fragment of bronze—newel-post head—Auditorium Chicago," Wright wrote on the small study sometime in the mid-1950s.

Nearly seventy years after this sketch was made, Wright was having lunch with his publisher Ben Raeburn and his client Edgar Kaufmann, Jr., at the Plaza Hotel. They discussed the art of drawing, especially as it related to ornament. Raeburn asked Wright if his use of the T-square and triangle in ornamental details was the result of not having as pronounced a facility for freehand drawing as Sullivan. "Not at all," Wright replied. "I turned to the T-square, compass, and triangle because

of the machine. Lieber-meister [as he called Sullivan] was a great master of freehand drawing, but the machine did not interest him. Nor the materials he used. I believed that the machine was here to stay in the twentieth century, and I should find a way of letting it express beauty." He went on to explain how Sullivan would begin a design. Wright took a large menu in his hand and began to draw on the back of it while he was talking. "Sullivan began with a seed-pod, and let his lines flow out from it," he explained. Raeburn recollected, "[Wright] hardly seemed to be looking at the paper, but kept explaining Sullivan's method of drawing. Suddenly we looked down on the menu and there, before our eyes, was an exquisite, absolutely perfect Louis Sullivan drawing, in glorious freehand."

THESE FEW (of many) sketches for an amusement park on Chicago's South Shore reveal something of Wright's working method. The design underwent several modifications and revisions, beginning with the aerial views, rendered entirely by Wright himself, and concluding with the formalized plot plan, obviously the work of one of Wright's draftsmen. Interestingly, the treatment of the design changes in relation to the site: in the first scheme the park stretched out into the water; it was later confined to a little bay, accommodating the natural protrusions of the land.

The origin of the Wolf Lake commission remains a mystery, at least as far as material in the Frank Lloyd Wright Archives is concerned. Certainly, it was an ambitious work at a very early stage in Wright's career—he had been practicing architecture for only two years. The 1893 Columbia Exposition, in Wright's opinion, was a great tragedy because it heralded Neoclassical forms as the style to imitate. Reflecting on the exposition in later years, he wrote, "I was confirmed in my fears that a native architecture would be set back at least fifty years." The design for Wolf Lake shows a waterfront situation, such as existed at the Columbia Exposition, but Wright has enhanced the shore with an architecture inherently appropriate to the site.

WOLF LAKE AMUSEMENT PARK *(PROJECT),*
NEAR CHICAGO, ILLINOIS. 1895. PERSPECTIVE STUDY.
COLOR PENCIL AND PENCIL ON TRACING PAPER, 26 × 14".
FLLW FDN# 9510.003

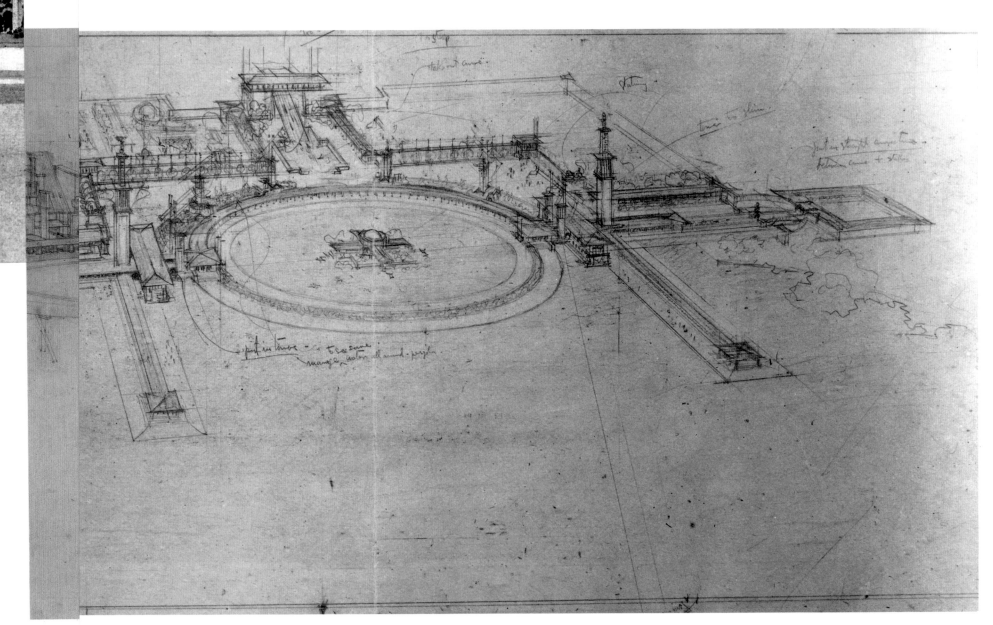

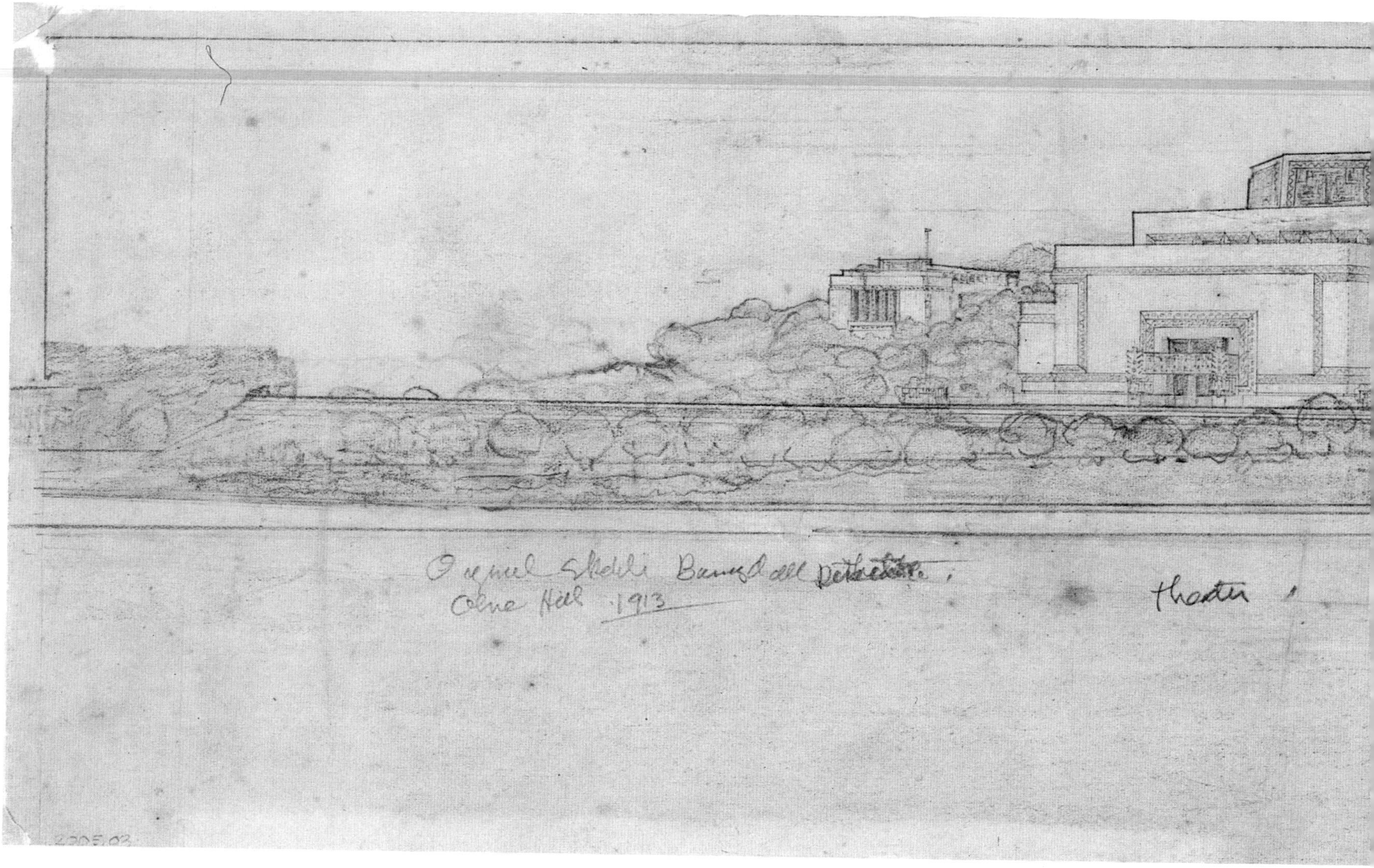

Original Sketch. Barnsdall Detractive.
Olive Hill 1913

theater

Side Elevation. FOR MODEL
BARNSDALL THEATRE Drawing of 1918-1920

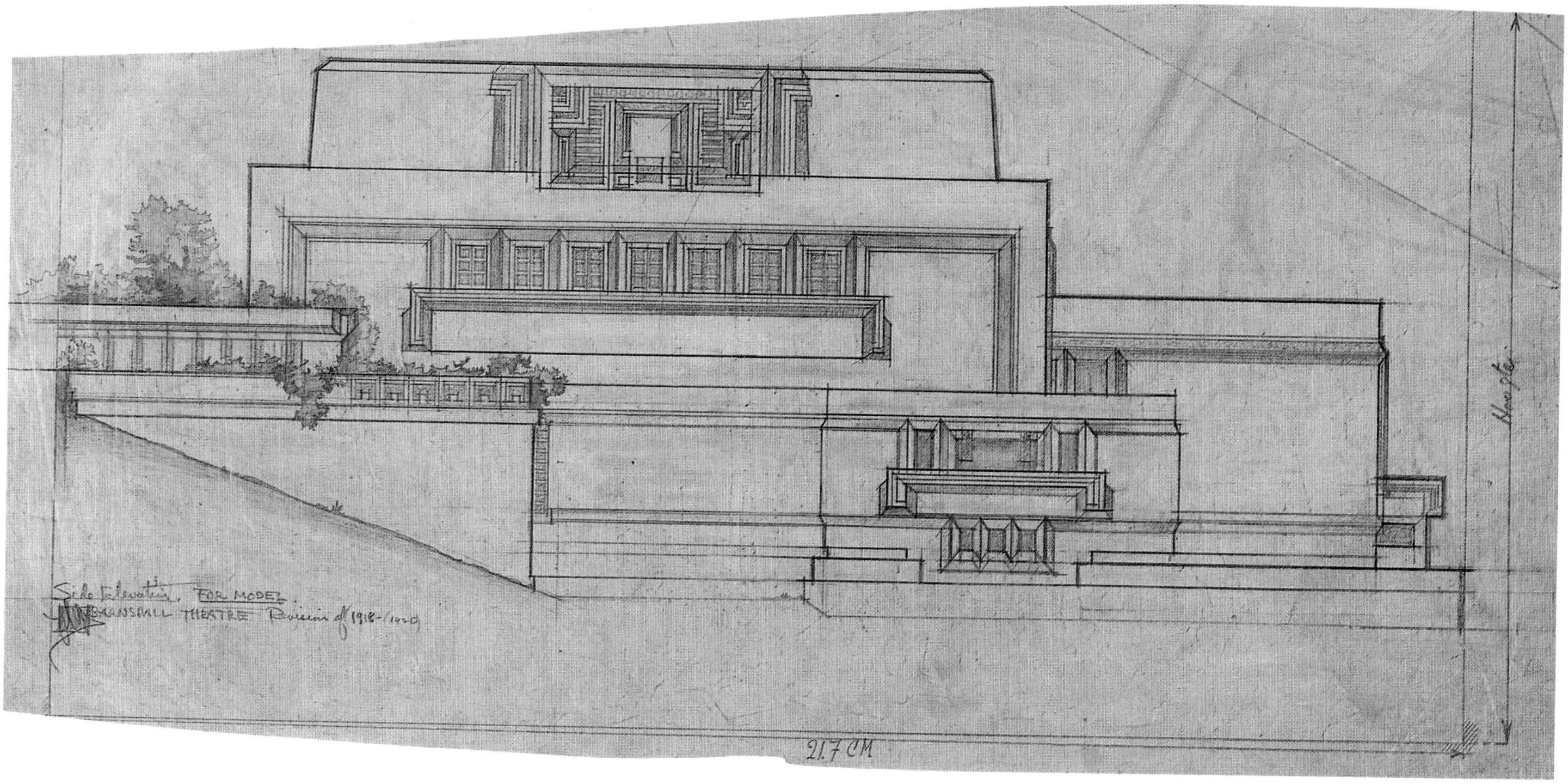

21.7 CM

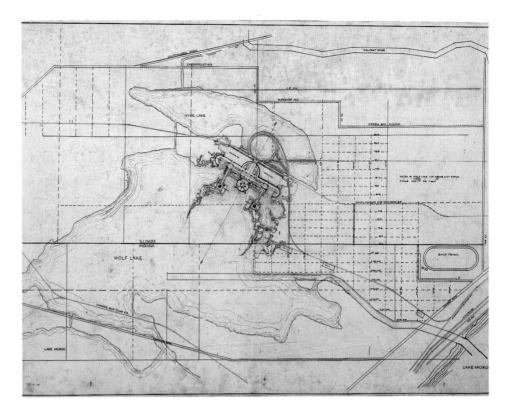

WOLF LAKE AMUSEMENT PARK *(PROJECT)*,
NEAR CHICAGO, ILLINOIS. 1895. PLAN.
INK AND PENCIL ON LINEN, 32 × 24".
FLLW FDN# 9510.017

EXHIBITION BOOTH 1901

0706.01

THIS EXHIBITION PAVILION, which represented the Larkin Company at the tricentennial celebrations of Jamestown, Virginia, was built of wood frame and plaster. When the exposition ended, the building was demolished. The drawing is a softly muted composition of varying tones of gray, executed in watercolor and watercolor wash; some of the outlines for building and foliage are emphasized with graphite pencil.

As with the Wolf Lake commission (page 125), Wright chose to create a building expressive of American culture—in contrast to the European imitations that flooded most fairs and expositions of architecture at the turn of the century. The Larkin Company was a leading mail-order business, as important to the nation in 1907 as the large corporations that were represented thirty-two years later at the New York World's Fair.

LARKIN COMPANY EXPOSITION PAVILION, *JAMESTOWN, VIRGINIA. 1907 (DEMOLISHED). PERSPECTIVE. WATERCOLOR AND WATERCOLOR WASH ON ART PAPER, 24 × 8". FLLW FDN# 0706.001*

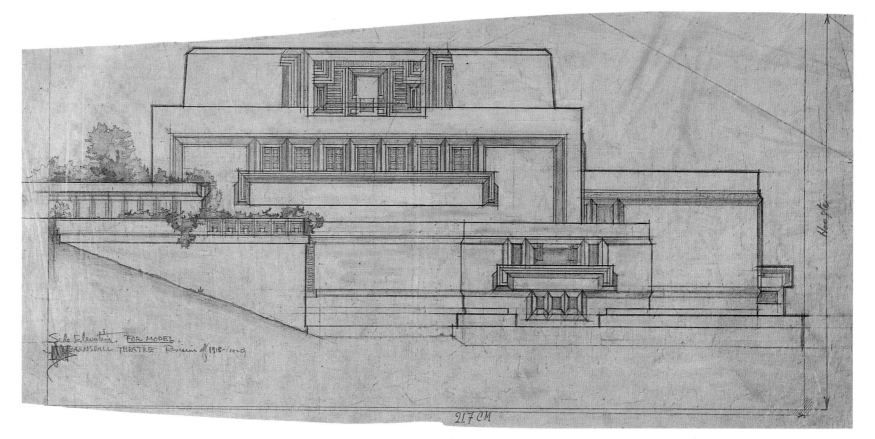

Original Sketch Barnsdall Residence.
Olive Hill 1913

theatr.

Side Elevation. FOR MODEL.
BARNSDALL THEATRE Revision of 1918-1920

21.7 CM

THIS EXHIBITION PAVILION, which represented the Larkin Company at the tricentennial celebrations of Jamestown, Virginia, was built of wood frame and plaster. When the exposition ended, the building was demolished. The drawing is a softly muted composition of varying tones of gray, executed in watercolor and watercolor wash; some of the outlines for building and foliage are emphasized with graphite pencil.

As with the Wolf Lake commission (page 125), Wright chose to create a building expressive of American culture—in contrast to the European imitations that flooded most fairs and expositions of architecture at the turn of the century. The Larkin Company was a leading mail-order business, as important to the nation in 1907 as the large corporations that were represented thirty-two years later at the New York World's Fair.

LARKIN COMPANY EXPOSITION PAVILION, JAMESTOWN, VIRGINIA. 1907 (DEMOLISHED). PERSPECTIVE. WATERCOLOR AND WATERCOLOR WASH ON ART PAPER, 24 × 8". FLLW FDN# 0706.001

CARNEGIE LIBRARY (PROJECT),

PEMBROKE, ONTARIO, CANADA. 1913. PERSPECTIVE.

PENCIL ON TRACING PAPER, 24 × 13". FLLW FDN# 1306.001

LIKE SEVERAL OF WRIGHT'S early bank buildings (and like Unity Temple), this library has massive brick or concrete walls topped with high windows to allow natural light into the rooms. No plan exists for the building, but the objective seems self-evident: heavy masonry walls provide privacy and quiet within for a building set, most probably, in a busy urban or suburban location.

The imposing, fortresslike appearance of the masonry walls is alleviated by the long horizontal window line and projecting roof. The ornament set within the windows also humanizes the building; planting boxes and surrounding foliage relate the structure to the site.

THE DATE OF THIS unbuilt project has been besieged with a plethora of different attributions, most of them assigned by Wright himself. In the general records of his work compiled in preparation for the 1931 European exhibition of his drawings, the view appears on one list as "Motion Picture Theatre—1897" and on another as "Moving Picture Theatre—1900." On yet another list, compiled in 1949, Wright dated the theater as a work of 1908. (It is not listed at all in Henry Russell Hitchcock's oeuvre catalog In the Nature of Materials.)

On the perspective, Wright wrote the date 1897 on the top of the sheet and, later, at the bottom left as well. But the details of the sculpture of the façade, so reminis-

cent of statues at Midway Gardens (page 178), and the style of the automobile and the people's dress would seem to place the rendering around 1915 at the earliest. When he used this drawing as an illustration in his 1957 book A Testament, Wright again recorded its date as 1897. Why he kept insisting on situating the work at the end of the nineteenth century, despite the design evidence, is a mystery that remains unsolved. The plan provided the cinema with a large screen that could be removed, allowing the stage to be used for live productions. In the foyer are two separate areas for shops or stores.

CINEMA SAN DIEGO (PROJECT),

SAN DIEGO, CALIFORNIA. 1915. PERSPECTIVE.

WATERCOLOR AND WATERCOLOR WASH ON ART PAPER,

15 × 19". FLLW FDN# 0517.002

MOVING PICTURE THEATRE
1867 – L.

1917 Perspective by Jou Rasmusen

FRANK LLOYD WRIGHT ARCHITECT 1897

San Diego 190-

THEATRE, OLIVE HILL 2005.01

THEATER FOR ALINE BARNSDALL *(PROJECT)*, LOS ANGELES, CALIFORNIA. 1915–1920. CONCEPTUAL SKETCH. PENCIL ON TRACING PAPER, 7 × 5". FLLW FDN# 2005.001

ALINE BARNSDALL was a difficult client, perhaps one of the most difficult Wright ever encountered. She was rich, restless, and mercurial. When she came across a situation she could not solve, or chose not to face, she booked passage on a steamship and left the country for a while. But through the many years of working for her on theater designs and on her own home, Wright exhibited the patience of Job. For more than five years, beginning in 1915, he worked on this theater project, accommodating her continual changes. At one point it was to be a large theater for an audience

of more than 1,500 people. At another time, the capacity was reduced to 600 people. Throughout all the stages of design, one feature prevailed: there was always a thrust stage and never a proscenium arch.

The section drawing best explains the theater: the stage is one with the seating area. No traditional fly loft is used; instead the scenery is brought up from below on a hydraulic lift. Above the main stage is a rehearsal stage and a library with access to an outdoor terrace. Dressing rooms and scenery storage and work areas are located beneath the theater on two basement levels.

The perspective drawing also shows some of the other buildings Wright planned for Miss Barnsdall's theater complex. He has labeled them "Theatre," "Clubhouse," and "Aline Barnsdall"—referring to the Hollyhock House (hidden behind the cluster of olive and eucalyptus trees), which was actually built. In addition to these buildings, Wright drew plans for a motion-picture theater, terraced housing, residences for directors, and stores flanking the base of the hill for Miss Barnsdall, installed in her house at the top of the hill, to oversee.

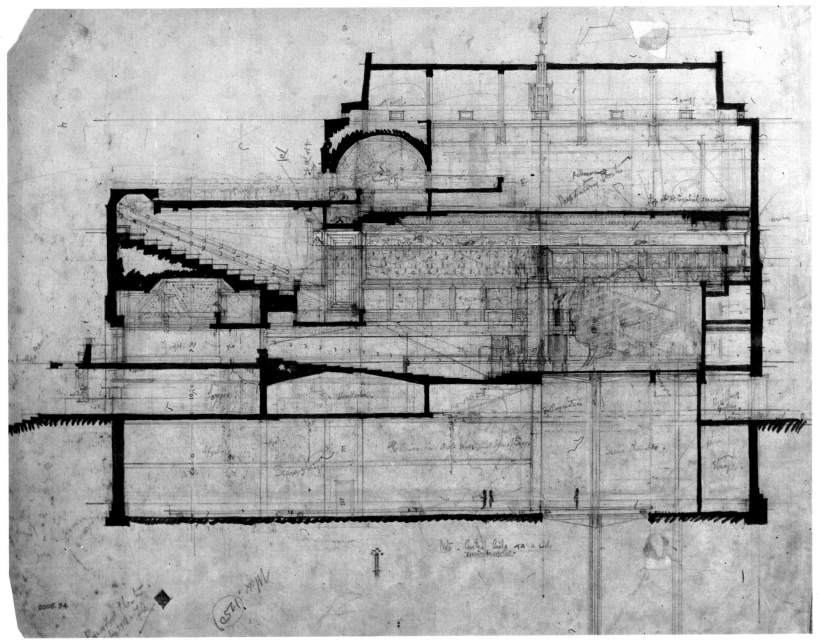

Theater for Aline Barnsdall (*project*), Los Angeles, California. 1915–1920. Section. Pencil and ink on tracing paper, 22 × 17". FLLW Fdn# 2005.034

Original Sketch Barnsdall Residence
Olive Hill 1913

theatre

Side Elevation, FOR MODEL
BARNSDALL THEATRE Revised 1918-1920

21.7 CM

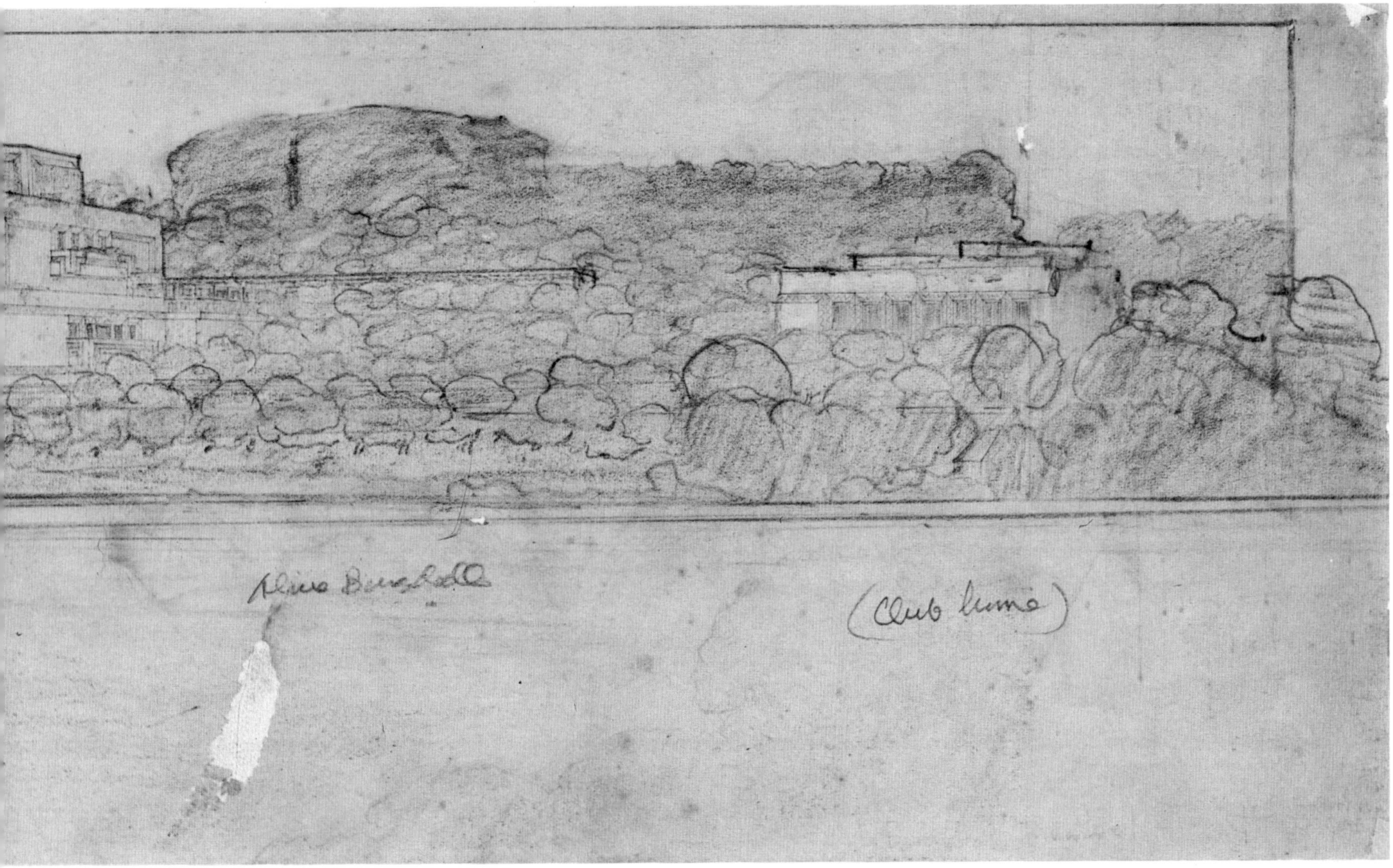

Aline Barnsdall

(Club house)

THEATER FOR ALINE BARNSDALL (PROJECT),
LOS ANGELES, CALIFORNIA. 1915–1920. PERSPECTIVE.
COLOR PENCIL AND PENCIL ON TRACING PAPER, 23 × 7".
FLLW FDN# 2005.003

THEATER FOR ALINE BARNSDALL (PROJECT),
LOS ANGELES, CALIFORNIA. 1915–1920. ELEVATION.
GRAPHITE PENCIL AND INK ON LINEN, 30 × 14".
FLLW FDN# 2005.006

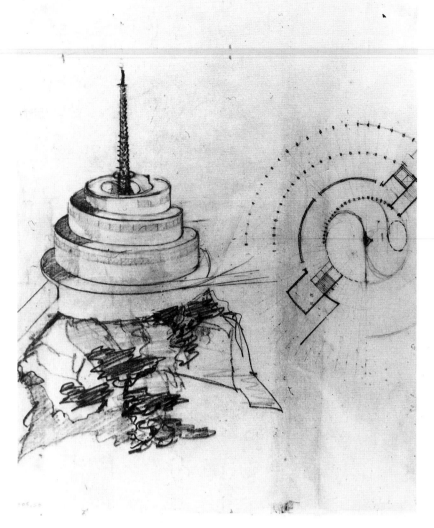

GORDON STRONG PLANETARIUM (PROJECT), SUGAR LOAF MOUNTAIN, MARYLAND.
1924. CONCEPTUAL SKETCH. PENCIL ON TRACING PAPER, 7 × 8". FLLW FDN# 2505.023

GORDON STRONG PLANETARIUM (PROJECT), SUGAR LOAF MOUNTAIN, MARYLAND. 1924.
CONCEPTUAL SKETCH. PENCIL ON TRACING PAPER, 12 × 12". FLLW FDN# 2505.058

IN THE 1931 EUROPEAN EXHIBITION of his drawings, Wright captioned this project, "Automobile Objective for Gordon Strong, Sugar Loaf Mt., MD. 1924. A planetarium with winding ramps going up and coming down over it—so without getting out of the car the scenery might be viewed. Somewhere to go in the car and especially for the car." Wright included parking facilities at the base of the structure for the people who chose to enter the planetarium. Supplementary smaller ramps for pedestrians scale the exterior.

Wright made over sixty-five drawings for this project, most of them versions and revisions of the design concept. On the finished perspective, for example, a tower can faintly be seen behind the clouds. In some sketches, this tower stood beside the main building, but in this final drawing it has been deleted. The first studies, as shown here, reveal a much simpler elevation than was finally developed. But in the completed rendering, the surface of the structure—cast concrete—combines simple, sweeping spiral lines with a delicate integral ornament. As with Unity Temple (page 88), the building took its form from the material out of which it was to be built.

Gordon Strong was a businessman based in Chicago. Strong liked the idea of the project but lacked the courage to build it. There were altercations between architect and client, and the project was soon dropped. In 1929 Wright asked for the return of the sketches, stating that he had in mind "an art gallery to be built in Europe." No documentation exists that can further explain this reference, but as early as 1929 the architect was obviously concerned with spirals in building. In a public building, especially, he saw them as the natural solution for circulating people within a given space.

(OVERLEAF: GORDON STRONG PLANETARIUM.

PERSPECTIVE; DETAIL)

GORDON STRONG PLANETARIUM *(PROJECT)*, SUGAR LOAF MOUNTAIN, MARYLAND. 1924. ELEVATION. PENCIL ON TRACING PAPER, 20 × 14". FLLW FDN# 2505.031

GORDON STRONG PLANETARIUM *(PROJECT)*, SUGAR LOAF MOUNTAIN, MARYLAND. 1924. PERSPECTIVE. COLOR PENCIL AND PENCIL ON TRACING PAPER, 31 × 20". FLLW FDN# 2505.039

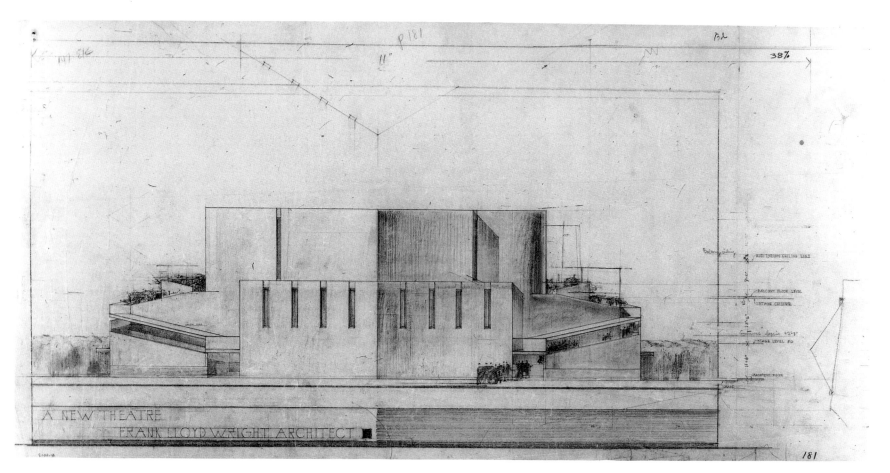

THE NEW THEATRE (PROJECT),
WOODSTOCK, NEW YORK. 1931.
CONCEPTUAL PLAN. PENCIL ON
TRACING PAPER, 23 × 20". FLLW FDN# 3106.005

THE NEW THEATRE (PROJECT),
WOODSTOCK, NEW YORK. 1931. ELEVATION.
PENCIL ON TRACING PAPER, 32 × 16".
FLLW FDN# 3106.018

PLAN OF MAIN FLOO
SCALE ⅛"=1'-0"

A NEW THEATRE
FRANK LLOYD WRIGHT ARCHITECT

AFTER THE PLANS for the Barnsdall theater complex (pages 132–135), Wright's next theater design was for Woodstock, New York. He continued to project the thrust stage further into the audience and also created a circular stage that revolved to facilitate scene changes. Backstage ramps allow access to prop rooms below. The theater was intended for a hillside site in the country, and the small sketch views demonstrate how the structure was to blend into the hills and landscape.

The initial project was abandoned, but in 1949 Wright revived the idea, still calling it "The New Theatre," for a commission he received from the town of Hartford, Connecticut. That project also was destined to remain on paper only, and it was not until 1955 that a theater of this genre was built—the Kalita Humphreys Theatre for the Dallas Theatre Center. The Dallas project was suggested by Wright's friend John Rosenfield, drama critic for one of the Dallas papers, who introduced the architect to Paul Baker, director of the theater. Baker was an innovative dramatist, and the equally innovative theater appealed to him. Architect and director worked together closely to get the theater built.

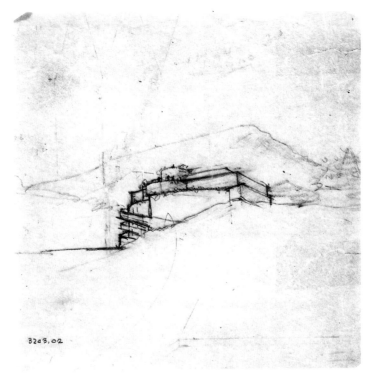

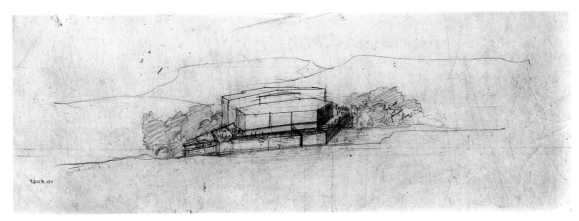

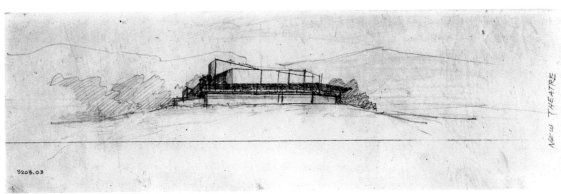

THEATER FOR FLORIDA SOUTHERN COLLEGE
(PROJECT), LAKELAND, FLORIDA. 1938. PERSPECTIVE.
COLOR PENCIL ON TRACING PAPER, 29 × 16".
FLLW FDN# 3817.001

THIS THEATER DESIGN was an adaptation of the first plans for The New Theatre (page 140), but the building is located on a flat site and provides for larger audience capacity. Several of the Florida Southern College commissions (page 224) designed by Wright, such as this theater, were not built. But Dr. Spivey, the college's president, was a miraculous fundraiser, and through his dedicated and persistent efforts some of Wright's designs were realized.

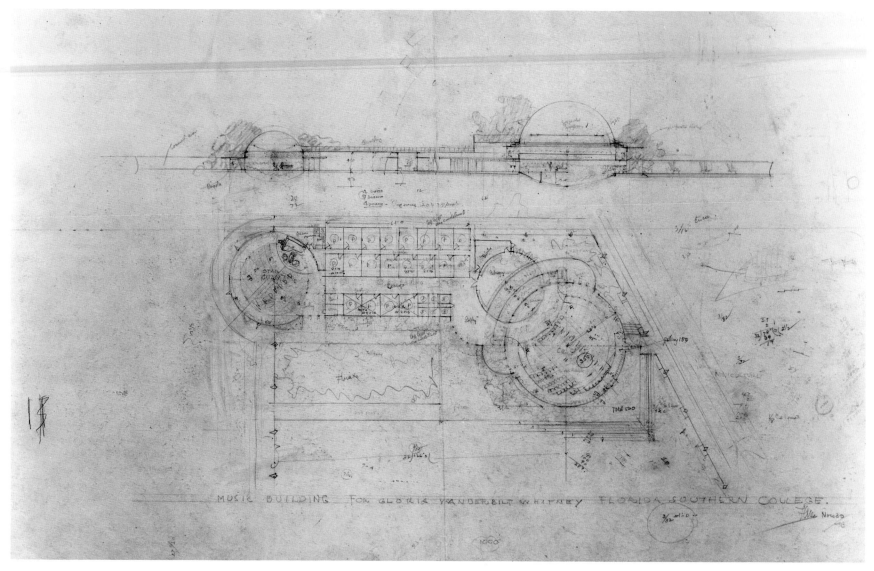

MUSIC BUILDING FOR FLORIDA SOUTHERN COLLEGE *(PROJECT)*, LAKELAND, FLORIDA. 1943.

PLAN AND ELEVATION. PENCIL ON TRACING PAPER, 36 × 25". FLLW FDN# 4211.001

THE FIRST MUSIC-SCHOOL building that Wright designed for Florida Southern College (there were eventually three plans, none of which were built) is shown in this conceptual plan and elevation and the perspective. The lines stretching out from the right side of the elevation represent a covered esplanade that was to connect all the buildings on the campus. The larger circle, designated "Symphony," was to contain 500 seats; the smaller one, the "Star Chamber," 170. In between these two structures is a series of music classrooms and practice rooms. The general grammar of the

building, as seen in the perspective, is quite different from the other structures designed by Wright for this campus.

Aside from the reading room of the library, the structures at Florida Southern are all angular in design: square, rectangular, or diamond-shaped. This music building makes ample use of circles and domes, and the perspective suggests a building of poured concrete—rather than the perforated concrete blocks that are emphasized in the other buildings by Wright.

MUSIC BUILDING FOR FLORIDA SOUTHERN COLLEGE *(PROJECT)*, LAKELAND, FLORIDA. 1943.

PERSPECTIVE. COLOR PENCIL AND PENCIL ON TRACING PAPER, 36 × 22". FLLW FDN# 4211.002

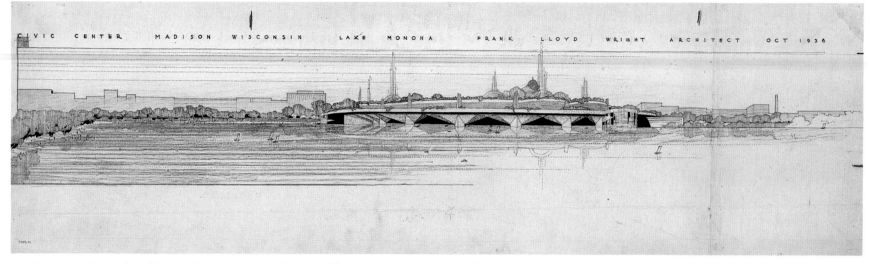

MONONA TERRACE CIVIC CENTER *(PROJECT), MADISON, WISCONSIN. 1938. PERSPECTIVE. COLOR PENCIL, PENCIL, AND INK ON TRACING PAPER, 40×12". FLLW FDN# 3909.001*

MONONA TERRACE CIVIC CENTER *(PROJECT), MADISON, WISCONSIN. 1938. PERSPECTIVE. COLOR PENCIL AND INK ON TRACING PAPER, 41×18". FLLW FDN# 3909.002*

MADISON, THE CAPITAL of Wisconsin, is built on the isthmus of two major lakes, Lake Mendota and Lake Monona. In 1939 a group of concerned citizens wished to see a civic center built for concerts, exhibitions, conventions, theater productions, and opera. Lacking such a facility, Madison found itself left off the performing arts circuit.

The center, as conceived by Wright, is sited in a terraced garden and projects over Lake Monona. It provides three levels for various functions and ample parking as well. At the water's edge, the hovering terraces protect boats and two boathouses. The placement of

the civic center over the lake seemed a natural solution: it could be approached on the level of an existing park; below, an existing highway and train tracks would be concealed by the center. In short, the project gave the citizens a fine arts and performing arts center as well as an ample, spacious park by the lake.

The project became a political football and seemed doomed from its inception to be rejected by city officials. It was revised in 1954 with slight modifications to the original scheme, only to be rejected again. On June 23, 1957, Wright addressed his apprentices with the following news: "I have just finished reading in the

newspaper that on Monday, at three o'clock, the Wisconsin State Legislature is going to kill the Monona Terrace project, 16 to 15. We will have a shining example from a state that was once quite devoted to the cause of the people. We will have an instance of where petty spite of a personal nature can deprive the people of their will and defeat their project, according to their best intentions and interest. As for me, I have been fifteen years at this thing—imagined it in the beginning, started it, stood by—and now lose very splendidly."

THE MASTERPIECE

IN 1958, while the Guggenheim Museum was under construction, Wright made a series of interior perspectives in order to show the museum's board of trustees, as well as Director James Johnson Sweeney, how exhibitions could be mounted. There was much controversy over the subject: many artists feared that the curvilinear lines of the building as well as the pitch of the ramp would make exhibition of their work impossible. Curator Hilla Rebay, the instigator of the project, feared that the building would overpower artists' works. This was never Wright's intention. "On the contrary," he wrote, "it was to make the building and the painting an uninterrupted, beautiful symphony such as never existed in the World of Art before."

For this view, Wright has created his version of a painting by Kandinsky, an artist whose work figured prominently in the Guggenheim's permanent collection. Knowing that the little girl in the foreground would have no interest in non-objective painting but would be greatly fascinated by the open court below, Wright personally included her yo-yo just before he signed the drawing.

SOLOMON R. GUGGENHEIM MUSEUM, *NEW YORK CITY. 1943. INTERIOR PERSPECTIVE, "THE MASTERPIECE." COLOR PENCIL AND PENCIL ON TRACING PAPER, 38 × 35". FLLW FDN# 4305.010*

THE MODERN GALLERY
MUSEUM FOR THE SOLOMON R GUGGENHEIM FOUNDATION
FRANK LLOYD WRIGHT ARCHITECT

SOLOMON R. GUGGENHEIM MUSEUM, *NEW YORK CITY. 1943. PERSPECTIVE. COLOR PENCIL, PENCIL, AND INK ON TRACING PAPER, 41 × 27". FLLW FDN# 4305.017*

THE DESIGN for the Solomon R. Guggenheim Museum in New York City went through many revisions, and the entire project was beset with trials and tribulations over sixteen long, arduous years. There was never, in the career of Frank Lloyd Wright, a commission that brought him more trouble and pain than this one. Wright made countless trips to New York, and the amount of correspondence for this building far exceeds that of any other in his career. During the last four years of his life he found it necessary to take an apartment at the Plaza Hotel in Manhattan so as to have a New York base of operations for the continuing demands put upon him by the project.

When it was decided, late in 1943, that the building would be in Manhattan, Wright proceeded with the concept of a multistory gallery. At one point early in the commission, other properties, not in the center of the city, were considered, which would have provoked a more horizontal and linear design. Solomon Guggenheim, in presenting the commission to Wright, gave only one stipulation: he wanted a building for his collection that would be like no other museum in the world.

There were several early versions of the spiral: rising in tiers with each tier the same size, with the tiers getting progressively smaller toward the top, or with the tiers expanding progressively in size. There was also a design of hexagonal tiers, but that was soon rejected. Wright's choice of the expanding spiral signaled his interest in finding a greater plasticity in architecture than had ever been achieved before. Settled, as Guggenheim was, on a city lot with confining restrictions of space, the spiral was a natural solution to make an art gallery in which all space within the building is related to the whole. The museum-goer is able at all times to see where he is in the building and where to go next. Space and time are linked this way.

The elevation labeled "Ziggurat" shows the building both from the outside and with a cutaway view into the arrangement of the ramps within. Three minuscule sketch elevations at the right of the main elevation show further studies for the structure as seen from the outside at different points around the plan.

Concrete, either poured in forms or sprayed, was the most appropriate material for the building's curved surfaces. At one point the architect wished for an application of thin marble veneer to seal the concrete and prevent the need for painting it, but this solution proved too costly for the budget.

In 1952, to provide the museum with further gallery space, a historical gallery, and a bookstore, Wright proposed a tall structure be built behind the "Monitor," or small office wing. He also suggested that the floors rising above, besides being a backdrop to the museum in front, would provide rentable studios to help bring in additional revenue to the museum. This "backdrop" building was conceived as a companion to the main building, set well behind it. A quiet and unpretentious pattern of small squares set within larger ones would contrast with the curvilinear forms in the foreground. In short, the tall annex behind the Guggenheim, as designed by Wright, was to have a quieting effect and not to be a strong architectural statement of its own. Its role was to conceal the ugly buildings behind the museum and to do for the museum what a park of flourishing green trees might have done had the building been on a more conducive site.

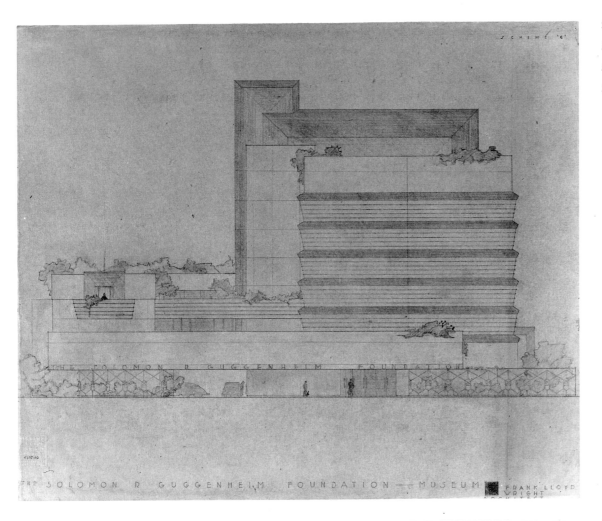

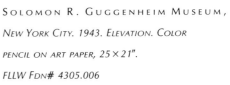

SOLOMON R. GUGGENHEIM MUSEUM,
*NEW YORK CITY. 1943. ELEVATION. COLOR
PENCIL ON ART PAPER, 25 × 21".*
FLLW FDN# 4305.006

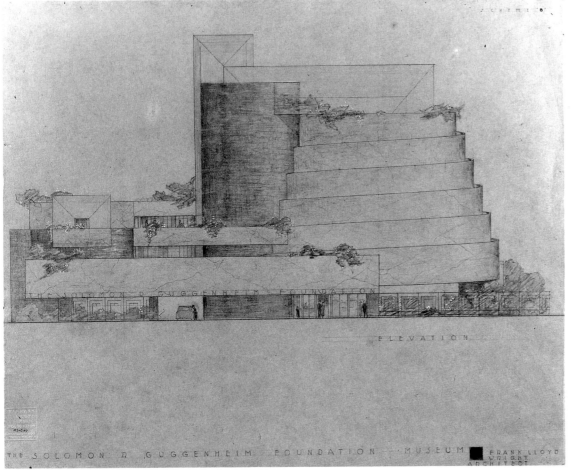

SOLOMON R. GUGGENHEIM MUSEUM,
*NEW YORK CITY. 1943. ELEVATION. COLOR
PENCIL ON ART PAPER, 25 × 20".*
FLLW FDN# 4305.007

*(OVERLEAF: SOLOMON R. GUGGENHEIM
MUSEUM. SECTION; DETAIL)*

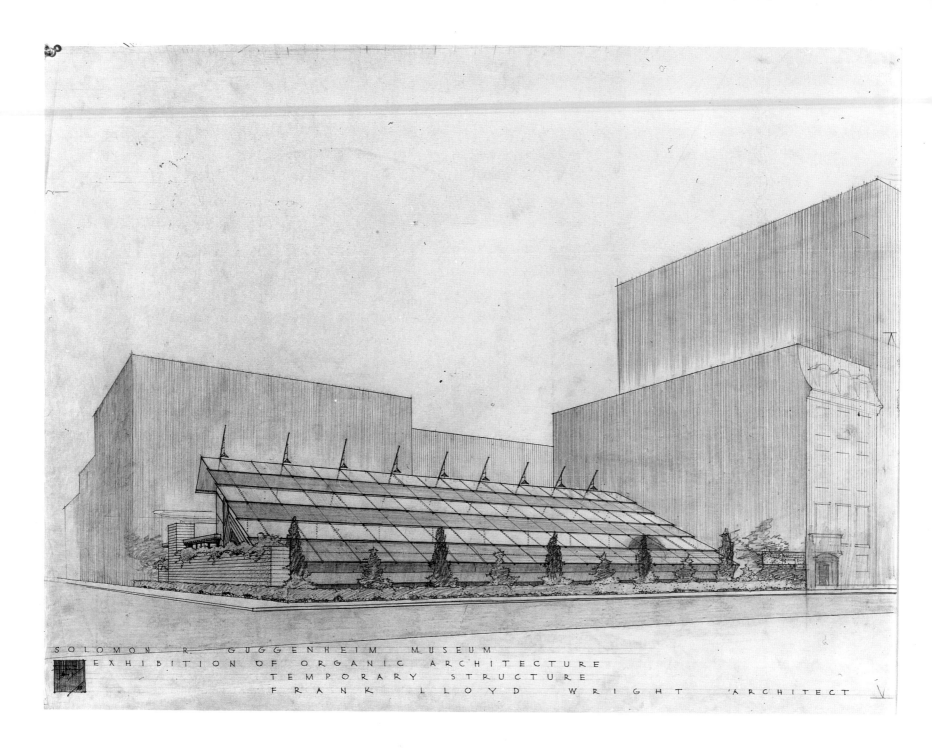

SOLOMON R. GUGGENHEIM MUSEUM
EXHIBITION OF ORGANIC ARCHITECTURE
TEMPORARY STRUCTURE
FRANK LLOYD WRIGHT ARCHITECT

"SIXTY YEARS OF LIVING ARCHITEC-
TURE" was a large exhibition of Wright's work that
toured North America and Europe from 1951 to 1954.
Sponsored originally by Arthur Kaufmann, the owner of
Gimbels, the premiere showing took place in Gimbels
department store in Philadelphia; then the exhibition
was moved to Florence, Italy. Following its European
opening in the Palazzo Strozzi in May 1951, the exhibition traveled to Switzerland, France, Germany, and
Holland. When the show came back to the United
States, it was housed in a temporary structure on the
planned site of the Guggenheim Museum in New York
City (page 148). The small, five-story building, seen to
the right of the main exhibition pavilion, was the temporary gallery for the Guggenheim collections. Entrance to the Wright exhibition was through this
building, then through a doorway cut into the wall
leading directly to the pavilion. The building was
erected on a series of pipe columns, with a roof of glass
and Masonite panels. At the far left of the pavilion, a
Usonian house was built, complete with living/dining
room, kitchen, and bedrooms, affording the public a
chance to visit one of Wright's homes.

After the exhibition was taken down, it went to Mexico City and then to Los Angeles, where a pavilion
similar to this was temporarily attached to the Hollyhock House.

EXHIBITION PAVILION FOR "SIXTY YEARS
OF LIVING ARCHITECTURE," *NEW YORK,
NEW YORK (DEMOLISHED). 1953. PERSPECTIVE.
PENCIL ON TRACING PAPER, 47 × 36".*
FLLW FDN# 5314.001

PROMPTED BY SUPPORT from his client Edgar Kaufmann, Sr., Wright made this design for a gigantic megastructure that would serve as a civic center for the city of Pittsburgh. It was to be placed where the Allegheny and Monongahela rivers meet, with bridges stretching out to it from their banks. The main spiral was to contain cinemas, convention rooms, opera and symphony halls, an arena, restaurants, shops, and other facilities. Parking places existed on each level, and the exterior ramp could be used for access and parking. A nine-acre park on top, with fountains, pools, and plantings, could also be a landing space for helicopters and hot-air balloons. Adjacent to the main ramp were an outdoor amphitheater on one side and a zoo on the other. The round structure protruding from the rivers' edge was intended to house a large aquarium, casino, and indoor swimming pool. The entire opus was meant to be a beautiful architectural feature at the juncture of the two rivers—replacing factories that were destroying the natural setting and polluting the entire city.

PITTSBURGH POINT CIVIC CENTER (PROJECT), PITTSBURGH, PENNSYLVANIA. 1947. PERSPECTIVE. SEPIA INK AND PENCIL ON TRACING PAPER, 38 × 32". FLLW FDN# 4821.004

"OASIS," ARIZONA STATE CAPITOL (*PROJECT*), PHOENIX, ARIZONA. 1957. AERIAL PERSPECTIVE. COLOR PENCIL ON TRACING PAPER, 46 × 36". FLLW FDN# 5732.001

WRIGHT'S DESIGN for the Arizona state capitol, made in April 1957, was not the result of a direct commission. Rather, it was Wright's statement about what he felt Arizona should build to house its government. Plans by other architects had been submitted to enlarge the capitol in downtown Phoenix, but to Wright's way of thinking the proposed buildings would do nothing but add to the city's congestion problems. In his design, Wright suggested that the government be moved a few miles out of urban Phoenix and into a beautiful park at the city's edge, which was backed by red rock mountains on one side and an expansive desert plain on the other.

The central portion of Wright's capitol contains the two houses of legislature, the state supreme court and governor's office extend beyond, out from the legislature, and on either side wings contain further office space. Over the entire structure was a great lattice dome of cast concrete and copper, acting as a "shade tree" for the court below. This court was to be dedicated to the citizens of Arizona and to have exhibition spaces, a restaurant, and gardens with fountains. From this last feature the project took its name, "Oasis," and on the perspective was also added the title "Pro Bono Publico Arizona."

On the aerial view, markings can be detected over the two houses of the legislature, where originally there were two tall spires for television antennae. Wright blotted these out and substituted one tower, as seen, in their stead. Fountains can be seen spraying up through the lattice dome and in the gardens of the office wings.

The view along the colonnade gives a sense of the great public space—columns were to be capped in various types of onyx and other stones indigenous to the state, along with a generous use of copper, another Arizona product, on the dome.

The night-rendering, as this genre of drawing is called, reveals the magic and charm of the project: a glowing, glistening jewel of the desert.

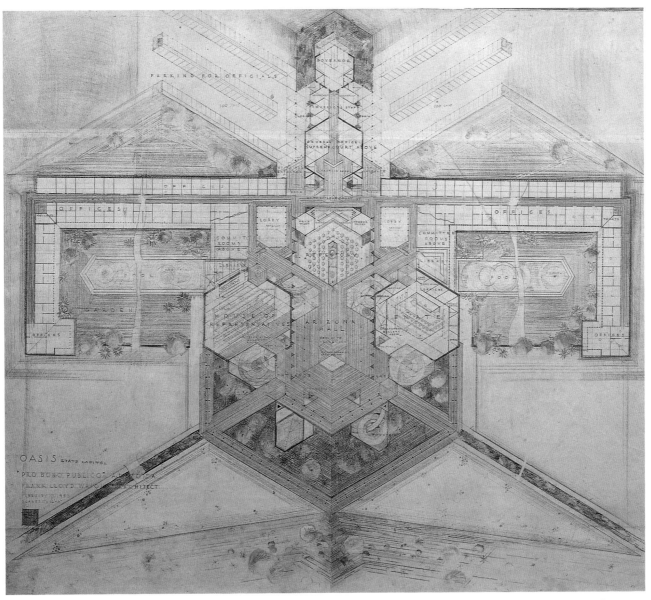

"OASIS," ARIZONA STATE CAPITOL (PROJECT), PHOENIX, ARIZONA. 1957. PLAN. COLOR PENCIL, PENCIL, AND INK ON TRACING PAPER, 60×51". FLLW FDN# 5732.008

"OASIS," ARIZONA STATE CAPITOL (PROJECT), PHOENIX, ARIZONA. 1957.
PERSPECTIVE. COLOR PENCIL ON TRACING PAPER, 46×36". FLLW FDN# 5732.002

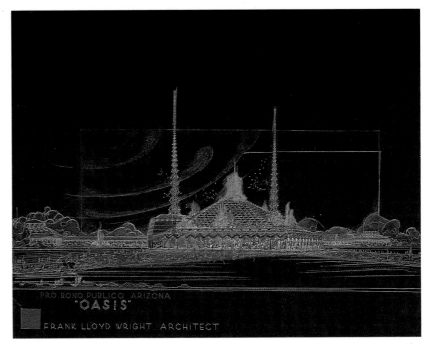

"OASIS," ARIZONA STATE CAPITOL (PROJECT), PHOENIX, ARIZONA. 1957.
NIGHT PERSPECTIVE. TEMPERA, WATERCOLOR, AND PASTEL ON BLACK ILLUSTRATION BOARD,
40×32". FLLW FDN# 5732.004

BARNSDALL PARK DEVELOPMENT
LOS ANGELES, CALIFORNIA
FRANK LLOYD WRIGHT ARCHITECT

BARNSDALL PARK GALLERY (PROJECT), LOS ANGELES, CALIFORNIA. 1957. AERIAL PERSPECTIVE.

COLOR PENCIL ON TRACING PAPER, 40×36". FLLW FDN# 5428.006

FOLLOWING the erection of the exhibition pavilion at the Hollyhock House in 1954 for *Sixty Years of Living Architecture*, Kenneth Ross, director of the Los Angeles Municipal Art Department, suggested a large gallery be built on the city's Barnsdall Park, a property Aline Barnsdall gave to the city of Los Angeles in the mid-1920s that included the Hollyhock House at the top of a hill (page 28). By the time Ross's project was conceived, much of the property at the foot of the hill had already been sold off or developed: a hospital, a service station, and a shopping center were built there. The design for the new gallery, however, was to be at a tangent to the Hollyhock House and to extend along the steep side of the hill on many levels.

The aerial view shows the approach road passing through a companion building to the main gallery, which contains museum offices. Just beyond the top of the museum, the exhibition pavilion of 1954 can be found; only a glimpse of the Hollyhock House is shown among the treetops at the hill's crown.

The perspective of the entire development belies the actual size of the museum: each full level has about 76,800 square feet of space.

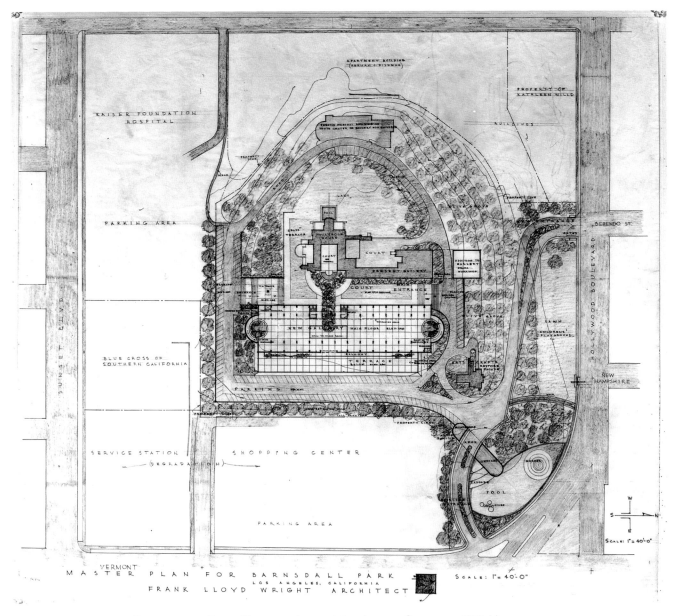

BARNSDALL PARK GALLERY *(PROJECT)*, LOS ANGELES, CALIFORNIA. 1957. MASTER PLAN.

COLOR PENCIL ON TRACING PAPER, 40 × 36". FLLW FDN# 5428.005

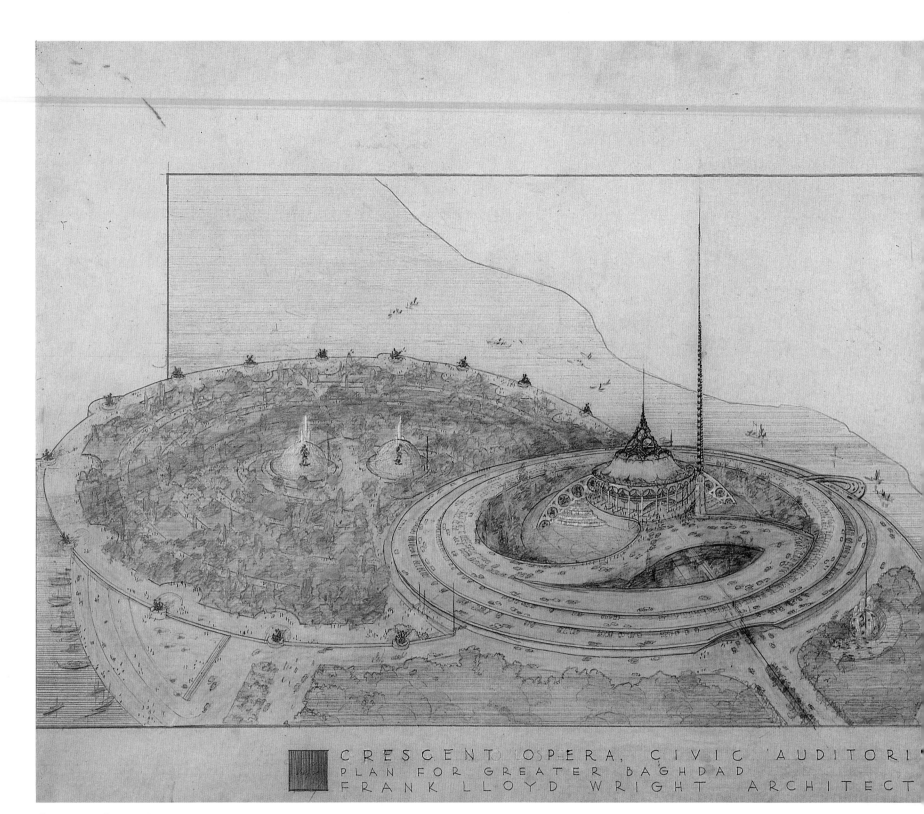

CRESCENT OPERA CIVIC AUDITORIUM,

GARDEN OF EDEN (PROJECT), BAGHDAD, IRAQ. 1957. AERIAL

PERSPECTIVE. INK, COLOR PENCIL, AND PENCIL ON TRACING PAPER, 55 × 33".

FLLW FDN# 5733.007

GARDEN OF EDEN

THE PROSPECT OF DESIGNING a group of buildings for Baghdad, Iraq, came as a splendid opportunity for Wright, who, since childhood, enjoyed the tales from *The Arabian Nights*. In the playroom that he built for his children in Oak Park in 1897, he designed a mural over the fireplace depicting the "Fisherman and the Genii," inspired by one of the Arabian legends. In 1957, he was called to Baghdad specifically to design an opera house for a new cultural center.

On his return from Baghdad, he spoke to the Fellowship about his trip. "When this commission came from Baghdad I was astonished, delighted and puzzled. I didn't know how they got a renegade like myself. A rebel, but they did! . . . And we've got a great opportunity there in the drafting room now to demonstrate that we are not destructive, but constructive, where the original forces that built the civilization of the world are concerned."

Wright realized that for an opera house his previous approaches to theater design, as presented in the Barnsdall Theatre and The New Theatre, would not be applicable. "The opera," he pointed out, "is pretty well standardized." Referring to the scenery and all the trappings required, he noted, "Those scenes are stored away in stock, and an opera house would have to be so devised that you use the stock stuff. So the opera house is not in the same plane, or in the same case, as the theater. They would be totally different."

He therefore chose to feature the proscenium arch, both within and without. A series of arches rises directly over the stage to the highest point in the house, and the final arch sweeps overhead and pierces the building's roof, extending outside and over a group of cascading pools. The arch is composed of circular openings, each containing a bronze sculpture representing a character from the tales of *The Arabian Nights*. In the words of the architect, on the top of the auditorium a "crenelated dome shelters a golden figure of Aladdin and his wonderful lamp, the symbol of human imagination."

The great ziggurat that encircles the opera house was Wright's solution to the ever-vexing parking problem. In fact, as the problems of traffic congestion grew worse and worse in the middle half of the twentieth century, Wright felt that the first concern of the architect was to consider the problem of parking the great masses of

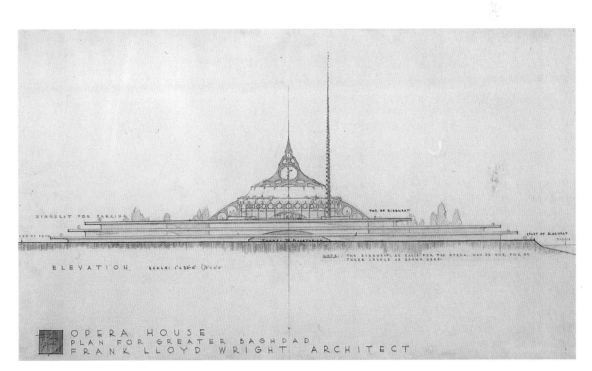

OPERA HOUSE (PROJECT), BAGHDAD, IRAQ. 1957.

ELEVATION. COLOR PENCIL ON TRACING PAPER, 43 × 24".

FLLW FDN# 5733.032

cars. On February 16, 1958, he said to his apprentices, "Have you read anything or seen anything in the architectural magazines solving the parking problem, except to clear off adjoining lots and let them pile the cars up and blot out the buildings? You can't build a building now, a beautiful building, and put it in a whole acreage of cars. And what have you got? Nothing. It will spoil it." The ziggurat ramp at the Baghdad Opera serves as an access route to the building and also provides three tiers of parking, part of the space under cover, for more than nineteen hundred automobiles. Between this architectural feature, for access and parking, lies a green park and pool as a setting for the opera away from the road. The tall spire rising beside the building itself is a television antenna. Beneath the main opera house is a planetarium.

As shown in the aerial view, the ziggurat containing the green park and opera is engaged on one side by another, much larger circular structure. This was to be a public park, named Edena, with two statues under fountain sprays in the center portraying Adam and Eve. Along the periphery of the park were other statues commemorating various peoples and nationalities. Wright maintained that it was not an apple that Eve presented to Adam, but an orange! The park was therefore to be a citrus garden.

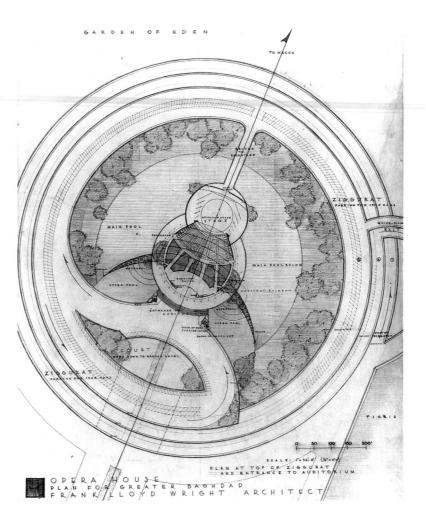

(UPPER RIGHT)

OPERA HOUSE *(PROJECT)*, BAGHDAD, IRAQ.
1957. PLAN. INK, COLOR PENCIL, AND PENCIL ON TRACING PAPER, 36 × 43". FLLW FDN# 5733.028

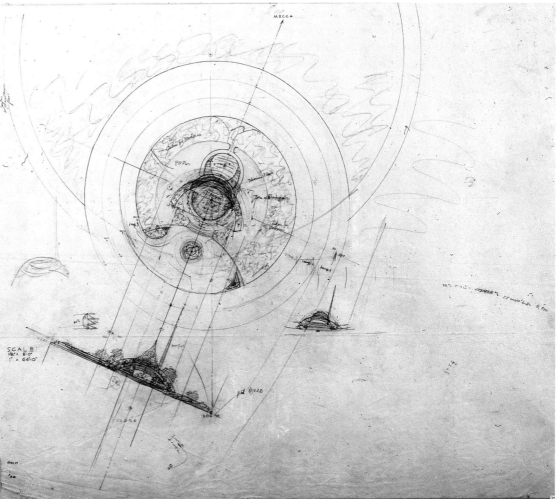

OPERA HOUSE *(PROJECT)*, BAGHDAD, IRAQ.
1957. CONCEPTUAL SKETCH. PENCIL ON TRACING PAPER, 46 × 35".
FLLW FDN# 5733.009

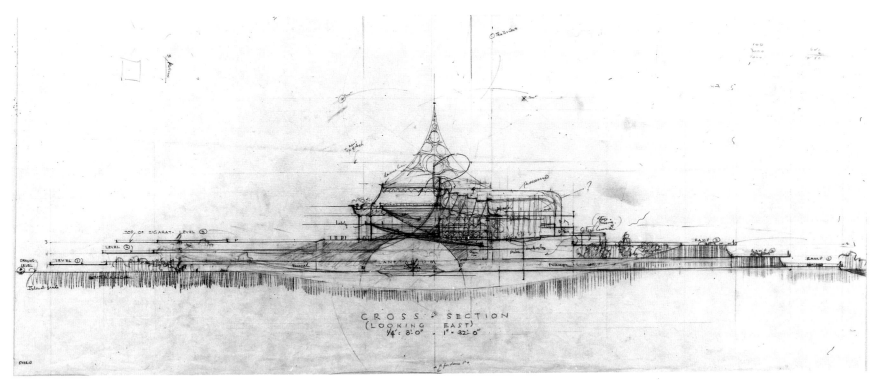

OPERA HOUSE *(PROJECT)*, BAGHDAD, IRAQ. 1957. SECTION. COLOR PENCIL AND PENCIL ON TRACING PAPER, 40 × 18". FLLW FDN# 5733.013

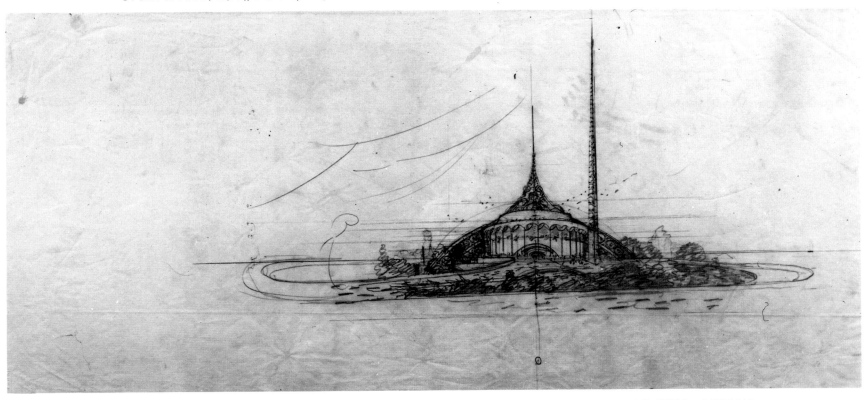

OPERA HOUSE *(PROJECT)*, BAGHDAD, IRAQ. 1957. ELEVATION. COLOR PENCIL AND PENCIL ON TRACING PAPER, 44 × 17". FLLW FDN# 5733.014

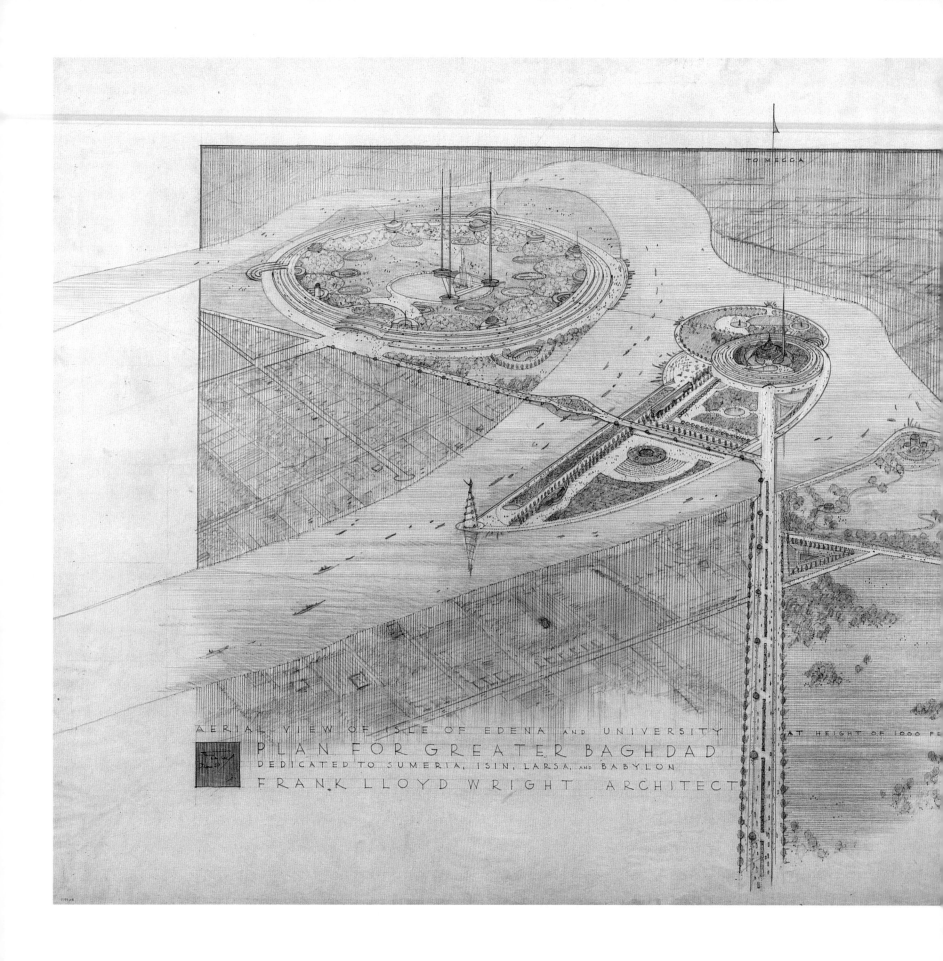

AERIAL VIEW OF ISLE OF EDENA AND UNIVERSITY AT HEIGHT OF 1000 FE

PLAN FOR GREATER BAGHDAD

DEDICATED TO SUMERIA, ISIN, LARSA, AND BABYLON

FRANK LLOYD WRIGHT ARCHITECT

TO MECCA

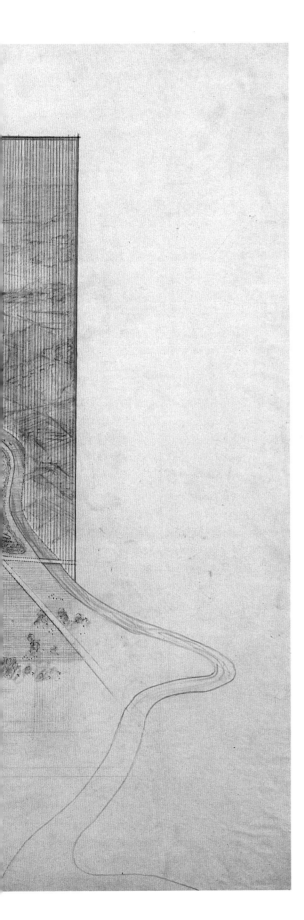

PLAN FOR GREATER BAGHDAD (PROJECT),
BAGHDAD, IRAQ. 1957. AERIAL PERSPECTIVE.
INK, COLOR PENCIL, AND PENCIL ON TRACING PAPER,
53 × 36". FLLW FDN# 5733.008

MONUMENT TO HAROUN-AL-RASHID (PROJECT),
BAGHDAD, IRAQ. 1957. ELEVATION. COLOR PENCIL AND INK
ON TRACING PAPER, 28 × 60".
FLLW FDN# 5751.004

THIS DRAWING, LABELED "Aerial View of Isle of Edena and University," is a perspective showing all of the Baghdad projects in one view, from a height of 1,000 feet.

The large circle at the upper left is the university, and on the Isle of Edena can be seen the garden, the opera house, the two art museums, the little shopping kiosks in the grand bazaar, and finally, at the prow of the island, the monument to Haroun-al-Rashid himself. An arrow, pointing through the top edge of the perspective, marks "To Mecca."

THIS IMPOSING MONUMENT to the caliph of Baghdad was to stand on the far extremity of Edena island, touching the river's edge and casting the shadow of the caliph and the spiral of camel drivers across the city. When asked by one of his apprentices why he altered the natural shape of the island—really a low sandbar—to put this feature at the end, Wright answered: "I think this is one of the privileges of architecture—if the man-made shape is architecturally fitted to the job. And also, it [the island] has to be armored and defended, or it will be washed away. So that armor is, by nature, an engineering project—and engineering is a feature of architecture. So why not make the whole thing seem like a gracious, beautiful building? In the water it would be like a tremendous ship. With the buildings that connected with it, it would all look like an architectural circumstance and the island becomes a building."

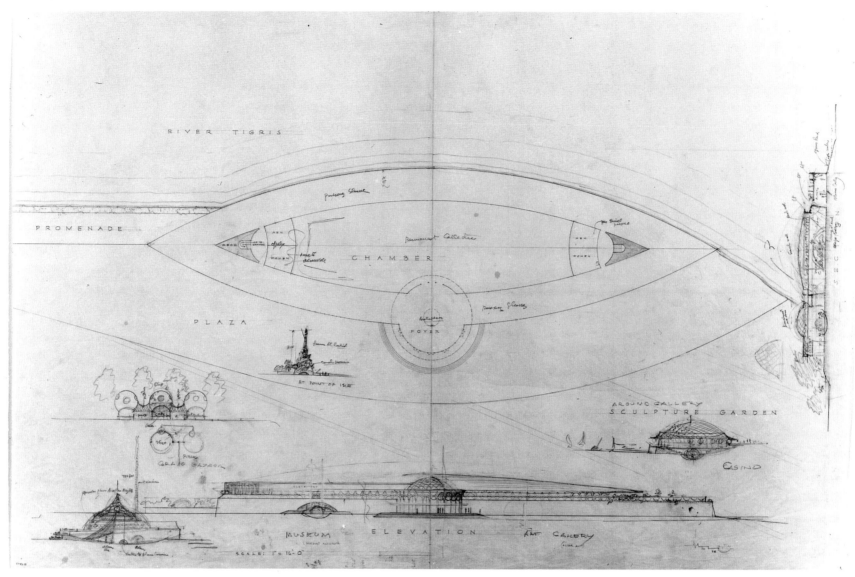

ART GALLERY (PROJECT), BAGHDAD, IRAQ. 1957. CONCEPTUAL SKETCH. PENCIL ON TRACING PAPER, 55 × 36". FLLW FDN# 5749.003

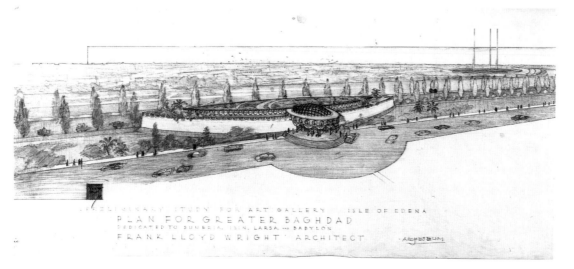

ART GALLERY (PROJECT), BAGHDAD, IRAQ. 1957. PERSPECTIVE. INK, COLOR PENCIL,
AND PENCIL ON TRACING PAPER, 48 × 20". FLLW FDN# 5749.005

THIS SHEET OF DRAWINGS has conceptual sketches for several projects, including the opera house, that Wright presented to the king of Iraq and the commission developing the cultural center. The long, lozenge-shaped plan was for an art gallery, its elevation directly below. Running up the right-hand edge of the paper is a cross section of the same gallery. In between the plan and the elevation is a monument to Haroun-al-Rashid, caliph of Baghdad, who first built the ancient city on the plan of a ziggurat. Diagonally to the left of the monument sketch is the elevation and plan for the kiosks of the grand bazaar. On the lower left is a thumbnail cross section of the opera itself.

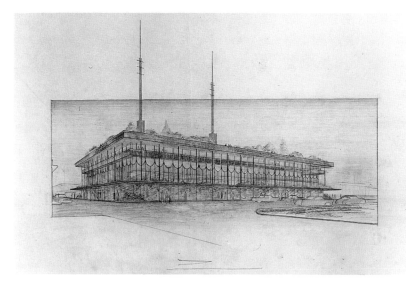

POSTAL-TELEGRAPH BUILDING *(PROJECT)*, BAGHDAD, IRAQ. 1957.

PERSPECTIVE. INK, COLOR PENCIL, AND PENCIL ON TRACING PAPER, 40×33". FLLW FDN# 5734.007

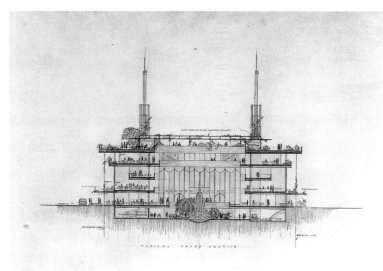

POSTAL-TELEGRAPH BUILDING *(PROJECT)*, BAGHDAD, IRAQ. 1957.

SECTION. INK, COLOR PENCIL, AND PENCIL ON TRACING PAPER, 48×30". FLLW FDN# 5734.015

WHILE THE CIVIC CENTER for the plan of Greater Baghdad—including the opera house, two museums, grand bazaar, casino, park, and monuments—was to be built on an island, the building for the Postal-Telegraph office was intended for downtown Baghdad. "The basic aim of this design," Wright explained, "has been to produce a building by extremely economical methods and greatly simplified construction. The basis of the construction is the hollow steel tube filled with concrete during construction (similar to the so-called 'Lally' column). The floors are concrete slabs cast hollow to receive wiring and air-conditioning ducts. The building is designed around a central court with a green garden at the basement level. Public rooms, offices, and equipment rooms are arranged around the court on the various floors, which cantilever beyond the columns to form balconies and sunshades. The roof slab is insulated with sixteen inches of earth planted to greenery." Cantilevered steel tubes would carry further planting as

vines, offering shade along the sidewalk level. "The whole structure," Wright continued, "provides a translucent, well-lighted interior space under adequate shelter in the hot climate of Baghdad. Trees planted in the interior court may be seen from the street through the diaphanous structure."

The overthrow of the king and his government the following year precluded the construction of any of Wright's Baghdad projects, but what we have on record manifests his sensitive and sympathetic response to the cultural needs of the Middle East.

(Below)

THE LOZENGE-SHAPED MUSEUM in Baghdad (page 164) was intended for more contemporary art collections, while this museum was specifically designed to display ancient Mesopotamian sculptures. On either side of the central portal were to be two large

winged lions, such as those found in the temples or palaces of ancient Assyria. The space within the museum would be lit by light coming through narrow openings in the concrete louvers and reflecting off a dropped ceiling onto the objects below. The small cross section diagrams this light source. The plan is divided in half, the left-hand portion showing the ground level, or main level, of the museum, the right-hand portion showing the roof.

While Wright was in Baghdad in the spring of 1957, he was taken to see the Sumerian collections and derived much inspiration from the work of the ancient sculptors. He called Sumeria the cradle of civilization, and all the designs he made for Baghdad were aimed at honoring a great tradition, in the way he had tried to honor his Japanese architectural predecessors when he built the Imperial Hotel in Tokyo. On most of the drawings for the Baghdad projects there appears a dedication "to Sumeria, Isin, Larsa, and Babylon."

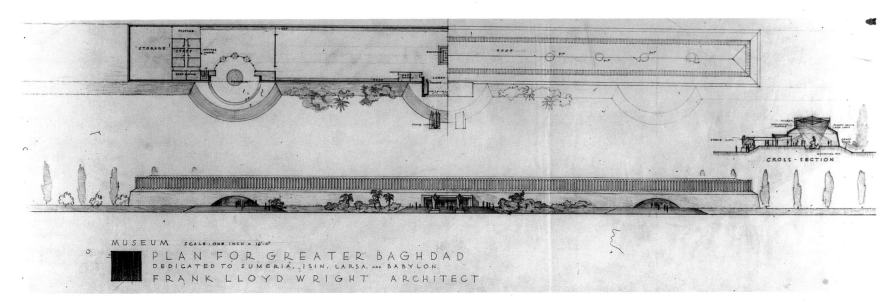

MUSEUM *(PROJECT)*, BAGHDAD, IRAQ. 1957. PLAN, ELEVATION, AND SECTION. COLOR PENCIL AND INK ON TRACING PAPER, 55×18". FLLW FDN# 5748.003

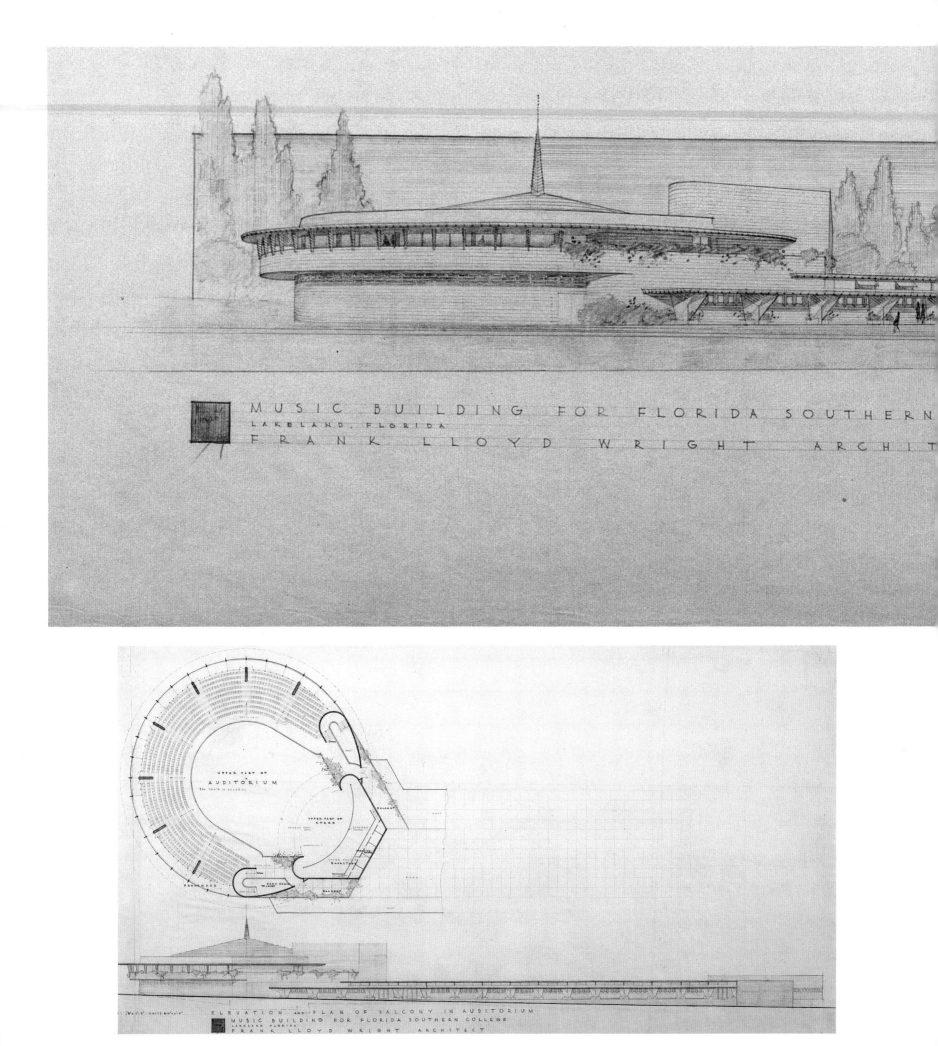

MUSIC BUILDING FOR FLORIDA SOUTHERN
LAKELAND, FLORIDA
FRANK LLOYD WRIGHT ARCHIT

UPPER PART OF
AUDITORIUM

UPPER PART OF
STAGE

ELEVATION and PLAN OF BALCONY IN AUDITORIUM
MUSIC BUILDING FOR FLORIDA SOUTHERN COLLEGE
LAKELAND, FLORIDA
FRANK LLOYD WRIGHT ARCHITECT

L L E G E

T

MUSIC BUILDING FOR FLORIDA SOUTHERN
COLLEGE (PROJECT), LAKELAND, FLORIDA. 1957. ELEVATION
AND MEZZANINE PLAN. INK, COLOR PENCIL, AND PENCIL
ON TRACING PAPER, 57 × 31". FLLW FDN# 5320.005

MUSIC BUILDING FOR FLORIDA SOUTHERN
COLLEGE (PROJECT), LAKELAND, FLORIDA. 1957.
PERSPECTIVE. INK, COLOR PENCIL, AND PENCIL
ON TRACING PAPER, 57 × 31". FLLW FDN# 5320.003

THIS WAS THE THIRD proposal for a music building for Florida Southern College; like the other two
schemes it was not built. The second design, not included in this selection, was a combination of the small
star chamber from scheme one (page 144) and a theater
design similar to The New Theatre (page 141).

Here the plan more closely resembles the general
idea of the 1942 scheme, with a large auditorium at one
end of the building and a small chamber-music hall,
again called "Star Chamber," at the other. Classrooms
and exhibition spaces are in the long connecting building between the two, with interior top-lit galleries and
exhibition spaces set among the classrooms.

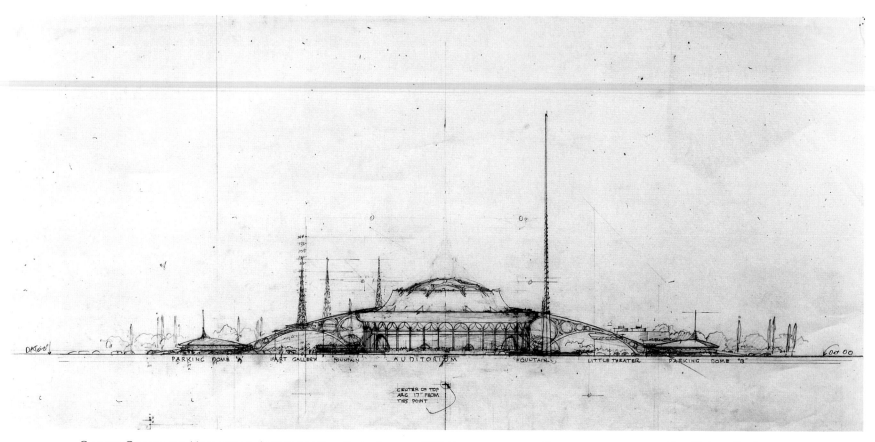

GRADY GAMMAGE MEMORIAL AUDITORIUM, TEMPE, ARIZONA. 1959. CONCEPTUAL SKETCH. PENCIL ON TRACING PAPER, 36 × 18". FLLW FDN# 5904.004

WRIGHT'S DESIGN for this auditorium is based on his design for the Baghdad Opera two years earlier. The elevation records the same theme of crescent arches, but in this design they connect to two parking domes. The motif of the columns and capitals running along the façade of the auditorium is derived from palm trees and palm fronds, which figure noticeably in the landscaping of the campus. Neither architect nor client lived to see the building completed. Upon Gammage's death, the building was named Grady Gammage Memorial Auditorium. It was dedicated in 1964, and Eugene Ormandy led the Philadelphia Symphony Orchestra in the premiere concert. Following the concert, Ormandy spoke of the greatness of the hall, not only praising its aesthetics but also its acoustics. Later, when speaking to Wright's widow, he told her that he selected the pieces for the concert he had just conducted with the architect in mind: works by Mozart and Beethoven and Richard Strauss's *Ein Heldenleben*. During the Strauss tone poem, especially, he let the orchestra perform with such volume and power that the overpowering sense of heroism was swept into the hearts of everyone in the audience. When the sound ended, there was a long and almost reverent silence before the wave of applause. "I'm sure that Frank Lloyd Wright would have been tremendously pleased," said Ormandy.

IN THIS CIVIC CENTER Wright created a building that actually is a bridge between three hills. When he was first taken out to the site in 1957 and shown the terrain upon which the county planned to build its center, he was assured that there would be plenty of flat space, that the hills could easily be leveled. "Leave them as they are," he cautioned. "We will give you a building that spans from hill to hill."

The aerial view makes this solution to the hills and valley apparent. The driveway through the building passes on the left under the Administration Building and on the right under the Hall of Justice. The wings are really double rows of offices. The perspective also shows the individual roof lines running the full length of both wings, with space between the two sides of each wing. This space is covered by a skylight, making it possible for every office in the building to look out over the landscape and for the corridors to receive natural light as well.

On the far right of the view, bordering a lagoon, is a fair pavilion, a tentlike structure intended for hosting state and county fairs as well as civic and local ones. It was not built, nor was the amphitheater that can also be seen, barely, at the lower right of the lagoon.

The civic center has proven to be a most successful and practical building. Partitions, doors, and electrical/telephone installations are all planned and built on a unit system so that they can be moved and removed as the needs and requirements of the various departments change. Like the Johnson Wax Company Building in Racine, Wisconsin (page 248), which opened in 1939, the Marin County Civic Center has become an inspiration to the people working within it.

MARIN COUNTY CIVIC CENTER, SAN RAPHAEL, CALIFORNIA. 1957. PERSPECTIVE. INK AND COLOR PENCIL ON TRACING PAPER, 75 × 36". FLLW FDN# 5746.001

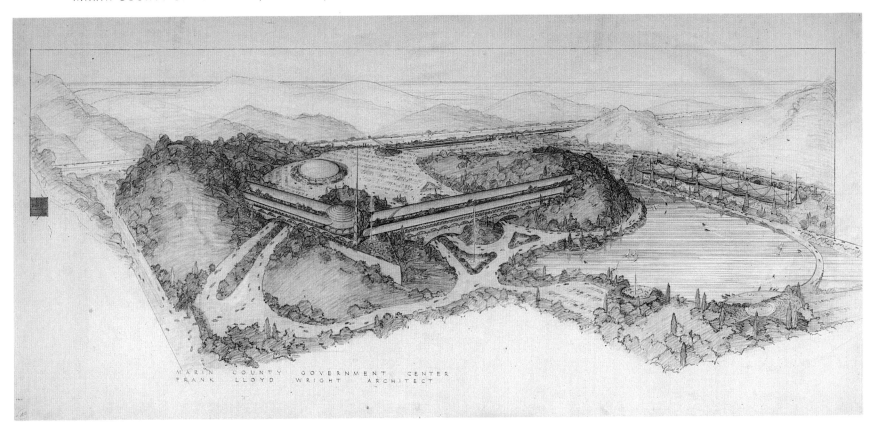

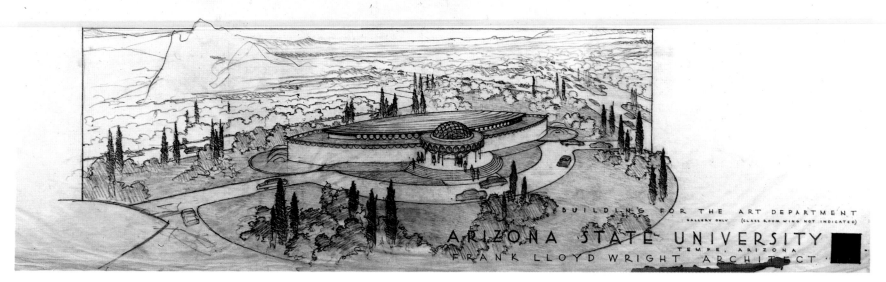

ART DEPARTMENT GALLERY FOR ARIZONA STATE UNIVERSITY *(PROJECT), TEMPE, ARIZONA. 1959. PERSPECTIVE. PENCIL ON TRACING PAPER, 60 × 36". FLLW FDN# 5912.001*

ARIZONA STATE UNIVERSITY President Grady Gammage came to Frank Lloyd Wright a couple of years before the architect's death with what seemed to be an impossible dream: he wanted to have a fine arts center of Wright's design built on the campus of what was then Arizona State College. In their first meeting to discuss the project, Wright recognized that funds were badly needed for the center to be realized, but he was willing to make some preliminary drawings so that Gammage could try to raise money and generate interest in the scheme.

The overall plan was to include an auditorium in the center of the property, an art gallery and art department along one border on the eastern side, a music department at the northwest corner, and a recital hall set alone to the east of the music department. The great sweeping curve is actually a road that passes by the site. This plan, based on the architect's sketches, was prepared posthumously to show the regents of Arizona State University in 1959.

The auditorium was the only building of this complex that was built (1964).

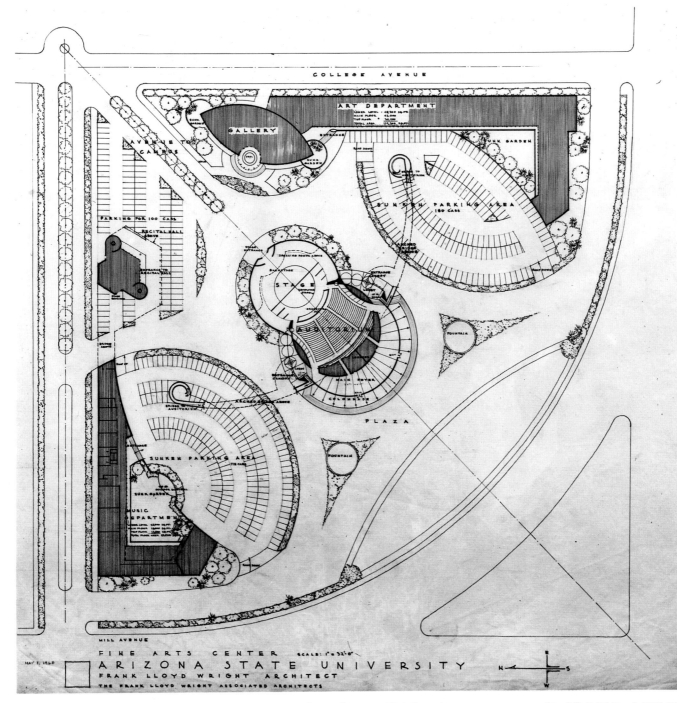

FINE ARTS CENTER (PROJECT), ARIZONA STATE UNIVERSITY, TEMPE, ARIZONA. 1959. PLAN. INK ON TRACING PAPER, 36 × 36". FLLW FDN# 5911.006

PART FIVE

HOTELS, INNS, AND RESORTS

INCLUDED IN THIS GENERAL CATEGORY of hotels, inns, and resorts are a spa Wright designed for Elizabeth Arden, a YWCA building for the city of Racine, Wisconsin, and a race track for Harry Guggenheim at Belmont Park, New York. The overall category might be understood as buildings for relaxation, entertainment, and club activities. The selection stretches from a simple board-and-batten vacation cottage at Como Orchards in Montana (1908) to a grand sports club and play resort composed of soaring disk-shaped bowls of reinforced concrete for Huntington Hartford in Hollywood, California (1947). The drawings for many of these hotel and inn projects are especially valuable in that they constitute the only record of Wright's thoughts on the works, and in some cases, such as Como Orchards and Midway Gardens, where the buildings were built, they have subsequently been demolished or fallen into disrepair. The Como Orchards scheme (page 174), for example, was only partially constructed; what little remains there today is mostly in ruins. The Hartford Play Resort (page 194) was never built, but to look at the drawings is perhaps to have a penetrating view of the twenty-second century. The most famous buildings in this section are the Midway Gardens for Chicago, built in 1913 and demolished nearly two decades later, and the great resort hotel San Marcos-in-the-Desert, planned to be built near Chandler, Arizona, in 1929, but abandoned before any ground was broken—a victim of the stock-market crash in October of the same year.

These buildings show how Wright reacted to the needs as well as to the problems of the touring public, whether on vacation or on business. San Marcos (page 184) was definitely a resort, with all aspects of the design meant to serve a vacationer, while the Rogers Lacy Hotel (page 114) was a cosmopolitan downtown Dallas establishment hosting transient guests, conventions, and social events.

There are several aspects about the draftsmanship worthy of study. One of the most obvious in the strictly perspective drawings—those intended to capture the image of the idea and best show it—is the placement of the image on the piece of paper. Naturally the building is usually presented front and center, but the variety of ways in which it can be seen—a bird's-eye view, a ground-level view, from above, from an angle, directly en face, or stretching into the horizon and almost vanishing with it—shows Wright's versatility.

Sometimes paper was added to the top or to the bottom of a sheet once the drawing was finished, so as to emphasize the placement of a building. In some of the early drawings, there was an attempt to make a frame-border for the work, as in the drawing for the Como Orchards cottage (page 174). But this type of ink or pencil margin totally encasing the drawing is relatively rare. In general the edge of the paper, as in the Japanese prints of Hiroshige, is the "frame," nothing more, nothing less. Wright admitted that the Japanese print taught him much, mostly the "elimination of the insignificant." But it also taught him an entire language of image placing, perhaps most strikingly evident in the small vertical perspective of the Thomas Hardy House (page 18).

Wright's limitless ways of rendering the foliage, the skyline, and foreground details are perpetually intriguing. Since an architect has to depict his buildings in true perspective, showing them actually as they will look when built, when Wright fantasized in his perspectives it was in the surrounding description, the arrangement of the trees and foliage—all the subordinate drawing, in other words. Only there could he indulge himself fully in artistic image making.

The placement of the titles, or title block, identifying the work, the client, the location, and Wright himself as "Architect," varied a great deal in the earlier drawings. But after 1932 the title was placed along the bottom edge of the paper. Sometimes he made the title block part of the perspective itself, as with the aerial view of the Lake Geneva Hotel (page 176). The perspective of the hotel for Odawara (page 179), on the other hand, has no title; perhaps it was merely a sketch view and the fully prepared perspective no longer exists. The image of the hotel is perched on a hillside amid a stand of trees. A framing line extends along the left, top, and right borders, but this line is interrupted by the tree branches at the top and is terminated by the foliage on either side. This particular drawing, clearly by Wright himself, manifests his special treatment of placing the building at the top of the sheet and giving the viewer a look at it from far down the hillside without any interfering foreground whatsoever. The Tahoe perspectives (pages 180–183), by contrast, occupy and practically fill the entire sheets on which they are drawn. The Tahoe drawings were also completely drawn by Wright at a time when the architect was drastically changing his method of rendering perspective drawings by using colored pencils on tracing paper rather than ink and watercolor on art paper. Taken with the other perspectives in this section, they merely prove that there was no rule of thumb in laying out the drawings: each one was considered on an individual basis, depending upon how Wright chose to reveal the building to his client.

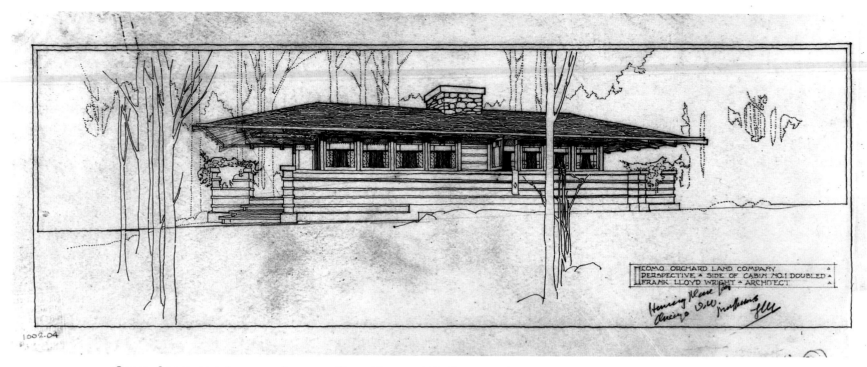

COMO ORCHARDS SUMMER COLONY, *Darby, Montana. 1908. Perspective. Ink on tracing paper, 20 × 8". FLLW Fdn# 1002.004*

THIS SMALL CABIN DESIGN was part of a much larger commission for a group of cabins of varying sizes positioned on a sloping mesa in Montana. The cabins were extremely simple; the complex was to be a summer colony for University of Chicago professors on vacation. A lodge in the center of the grouping provided cooking and dining for the cabins' occupants. Cabins such as the one shown here, "Cabin No. 1 Doubled," were occupied by two families. There were three bedrooms, two baths, and a centrally located living room. No kitchens were provided; heating was by means of the fireplace only.

This drawing is "framed" in an interesting manner: double lines run along the top edge, but on the sides the outer line continues to make the black border, while the inner line cuts across the view to become the ground line for the cottage.

THIS PAVILION for Banff National Park in Canada was built as illustrated here but was then destroyed in a forest fire. The use of black ink for a black sky drawing occurs rarely in Wright's presentation drawings, and the vertical lines for the background trees, likewise rendered in black ink, appears here for the first time. In later drawings, especially after 1932, this method of showing the trees' foliage by means of lines became a rather standard practice.

In 1951 Wright wrote on the drawing, "Banff Pavilion—Park in Canada [for the] Canadian Pacific Ry—FLLW 1911–12." At the same time he toned in the background trees with graphite pencil, leaving the foreground foliage a soft light tan, the color of the art paper itself. This work, along with other Canadian commissions, was done in association with the architect Francis Sullivan of Ottawa.

The pavilion is a simple work: fieldstone foundations and chimney mass and rough-saw lumber construction. Along the roof ridge ran a clerestory window band to bring top light into the center of the pavilion.

BANFF PARK PAVILION, *ALBERTA, CANADA (DEMOLISHED). 1911. PERSPECTIVE. INK AND PENCIL ON ART PAPER, 21 × 7". FLLW FDN# 1302.001*

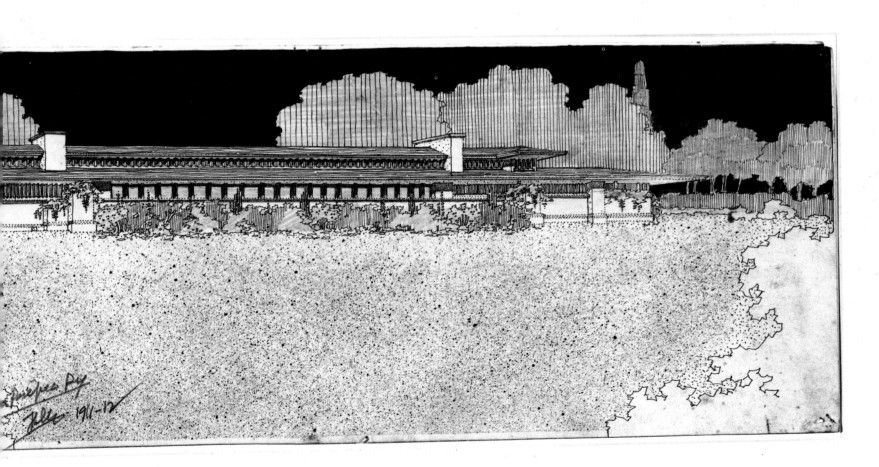

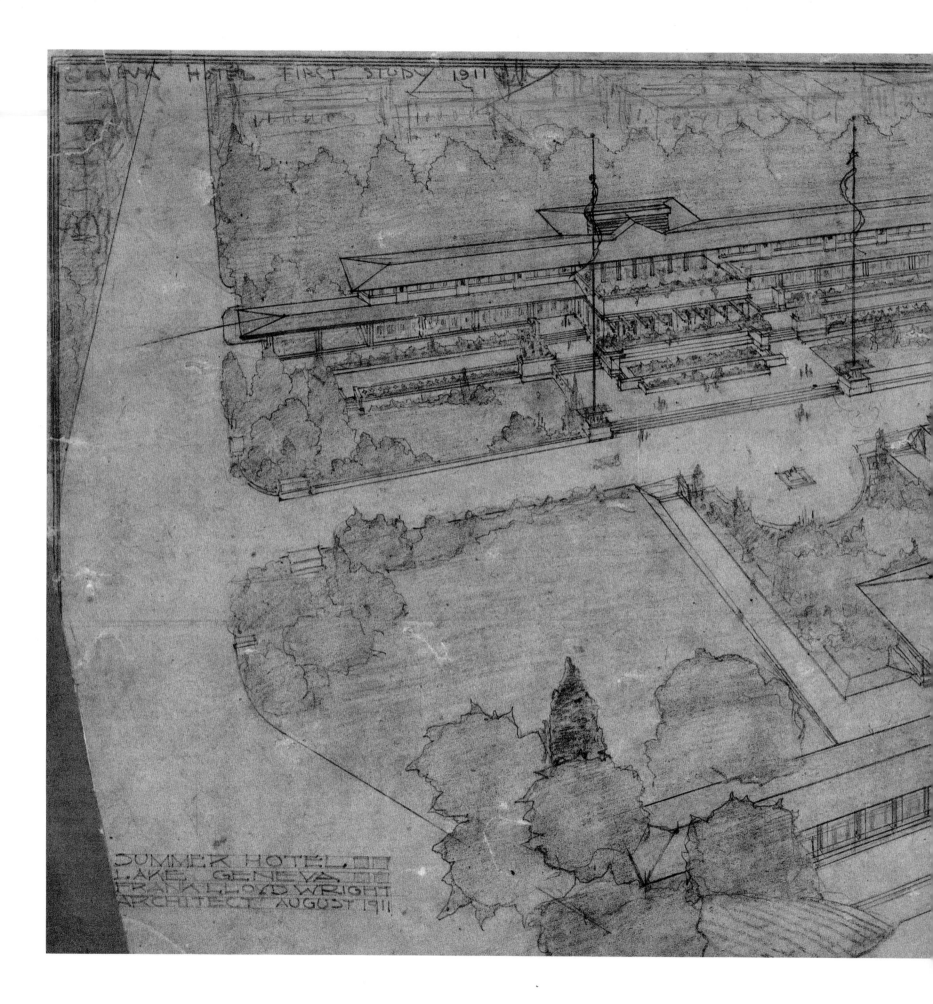

GENEVA HOTEL FIRST STUDY 1911

SUMMER HOTEL
LAKE GENEVA
FRANK LLOYD WRIGHT
ARCHITECT AUGUST 1911

THE DEPICTION OF THIS Wisconsin hotel, with its boathouse in the foreground and the town of Lake Geneva in the background, occupies the entire sheet of paper; the title block is in the roadway leading to the hotel. The drawing was laid out by one of Wright's draftsmen, but there are, nonetheless, many decided touches solely from the hand of the architect himself. There is his own title across the top, "Geneva Hotel First Study 1911 FLLW," and there are the roughly sketched buildings that give but a hint of the town of Lake Geneva behind the stand of trees at the top edge of the drawing. The triple-line border closely follows the paper's edge, from the roadway on the left, over the top of the drawing, and terminating at the water's edge on the right. A portion of the hotel, at the right, has been sketchily erased, revealing that there was originally a large mass perpendicular to the general plan that was later deleted, most probably due to cost restrictions. The building, as built, was similar in concept to this first study, but minus the boathouse. In the 1960s the hotel was demolished to make room for an apartment house.

LAKE GENEVA HOTEL, LAKE GENEVA, WISCONSIN (DEMOLISHED). 1911. PERSPECTIVE. PENCIL AND COLOR PENCIL ON TRACING PAPER, 23 × 14".

FLLW FDN# 1202.001

THE TITLE RUNNING ALONG the top edge of the Midway Gardens' perspective reads, "CONCERT GARDENS CHICAGO EDWARD C. WALLER JR. OSCAR J. FRIEDMAN OWNERS FRANK LLOYD WRIGHT ARCHITECT CHICAGO." And on the bottom left edge is the caption, "First sketch of Midway Gardens 1913," with a penciled-in square, initialed ",CL12.5FLLW." But this exquisitely and skillfully drawn rendering is hardly a "first sketch." Indeed, it conforms fairly well to the way in which the gardens were finally built. The drafting technique is an unusual one: graphite pencil on gray tracing linen, with only a few touches of color for the balloons rising from the finials, some indication of water in pools in the summer gardens behind the main structure, and minuscule touches of red—probably red tile inserts—across the street façade walls. The mechanical perspective of the drawing was done by one of Wright's draftsmen, as was the case with most of the perspectives, but the touches of Wright's own hand abound in this view, namely in his shading of the trees and foliage. By use of the overall technique of gray upon gray, with only dashes of color, the image has a certain wistful nature unlike any other drawing in the collection.

Midway Gardens was an extraordinary building. Like the great Gothic cathedrals of France, it was the work of one master builder; Wright designed and supervised all the elements in the structure, from sculpture and stained glass to murals, furniture, lamps, tableware, and table linen. Midway Gardens was Wright's first opportunity to design all the component parts of a building; it was a precedent he referred to for the Imperial Hotel.

But the building had tragic consequences, both for itself and for the architect. While it was nearing completion, Wright's home, Taliesin, was set on fire and seven people were axed to death by an insane servant. The victims included Wright's beloved companion Mamah Borthwick Cheney and her two children, who were visiting her at the time. Midway Gardens itself then suffered financial problems, was never completed fully in line with the architect's plans, was sold and resold, became a cheap beer garden, was covered with paint—in Wright's words, a beautiful woman was dragged to the level of a prostitute—and then was turned into a laundry and a car wash, until eventually, mercifully, it was demolished in the early 1930s.

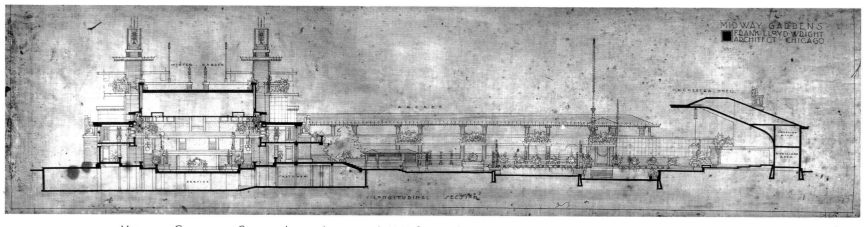

MIDWAY GARDENS, CHICAGO, ILLINOIS (DEMOLISHED). 1913. SECTION. INK AND PENCIL ON TRACING LINEN, 46 × 11". FLLW FDN# 1401.026

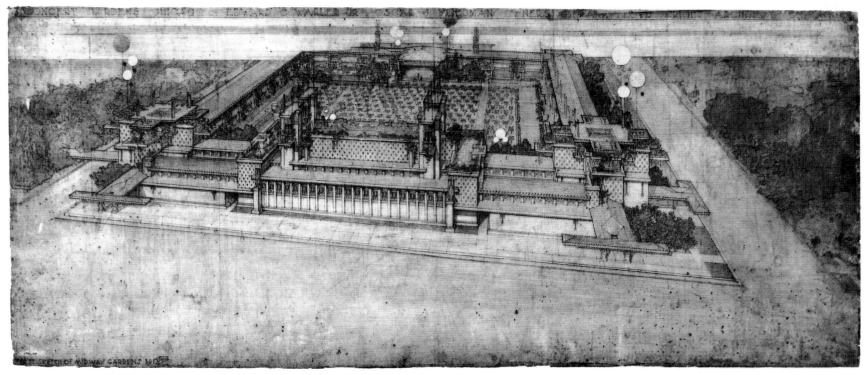

MIDWAY GARDENS, CHICAGO, ILLINOIS (DEMOLISHED). 1913. PERSPECTIVE. INK AND PENCIL ON TRACING LINEN, 39 × 16". FLLW FDN# 1401.007

ODAWARA HOTEL *(PROJECT). NAGOYA, JAPAN. 1917. PERSPECTIVE. PENCIL AND COLOR PENCIL ON TRACING PAPER, 36 × 24". FLLW FDN# 1706.003*

IN THE 1931 CATALOG of his work, Wright described this drawing as "a study for a tourist hotel in the tall pines of the Imperial estate." The perspective itself has no title block, but in later years he wrote on the lower right, "Hotel—for Hayashi—Japan. Near Kamakura." Hayashi was the general manager of the Imperial Hotel and a close personal friend of the architect's since 1913. The drawing is all in the hand of Wright: building, landscape, and forest. Very little exists in the Frank Lloyd Wright Archives on this project other than this lovely view, a sketch plan on the topographical site survey, and one more preliminary study of the general layout of the buildings. Most of the drawings for this and other Japanese projects, except for the Imperial Hotel, were left in the office of Wright's associate in Tokyo, Arato Endo, and were destroyed during air raids in the Second World War.

ONE OF THE FIRST COMMISSIONS to come to
Wright's newly established Los Angeles office in 1922
was for an inn with accompanying cabins, cottages, and
barges at Emerald Bay on Lake Tahoe, California. By this
time, Wright's technique of rendering had moved entirely away from the use of watercolor on art paper to
color pencils on tracing paper. He had discovered a
collection of color pencils made by Kohinoor, in
Czechoslovakia. The range of color was extensive, the
leads themselves soft and easy to apply. As he began to
make this change from watercolor to color pencil, he
confessed, "There is nothing more seductive than a
blank sheet of white paper lying before me and a handful of these color pencils at my disposal." Indeed, the
delicate poetry of the Tahoe drawings is unsurpassed
anywhere in the collection.

Various cabin types are identified as "Wigwam,"
where the pine-tree–inspired roof rises over the block
walls like a great wigwam; "Shore Cabin," where the
cottage is placed at the lake's edge; "Cabin Lodge,"
where the cabin is a larger, more significant dwelling
with several rooms; or "Cabin Float," where the cabin is
actually a moored barge situated on the lake itself.

Wright had just returned from Tokyo when he began
work on this project. There were few draftsmen at this
point working for him, and he was engaged in building
the Hollyhock House for Aline Barnsdall as well as two
other residences on her Olive Hill property (page 28).
To his great dismay, however, he soon discovered that
the real-estate corporation that hired him for the Lake
Tahoe projects simply wanted the use of his name to sell
property. The scheme was dropped almost as soon as it
was begun. But we are fortunate to have these few
drawings as at least part of the record of the work he
was undertaking for this ill-fated summer vacation
development.

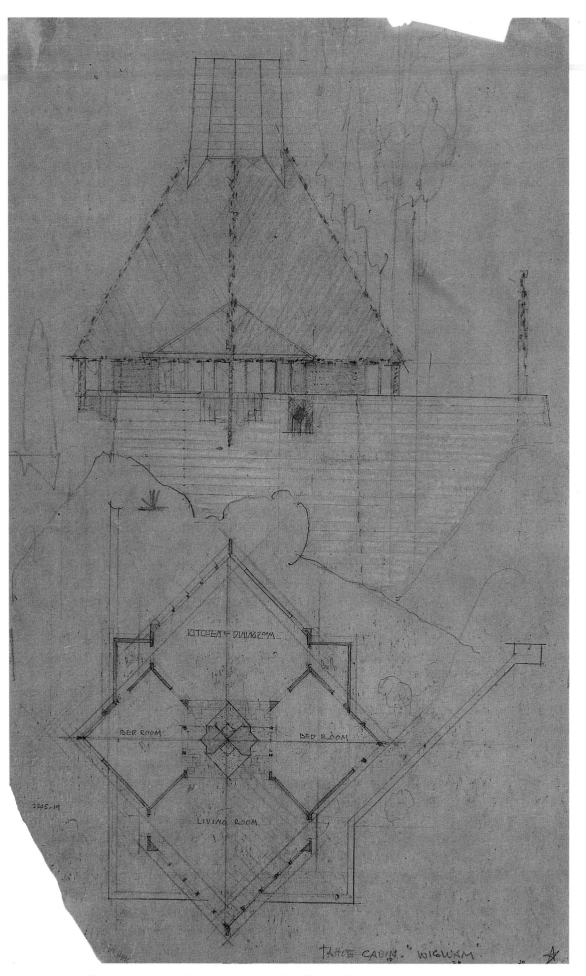

LAKE TAHOE SUMMER COLONY (PROJECT), LAKE TAHOE, CALIFORNIA. 1922. PLAN AND ELEVATION.

PENCIL AND COLOR PENCIL ON TRACING PAPER, 11 × 18". FLLW FDN# 2205.019

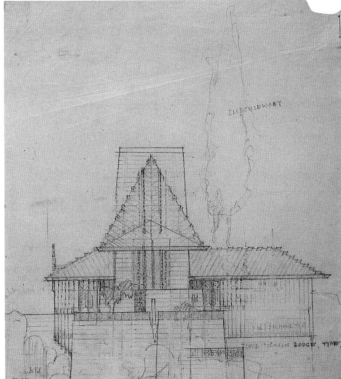

CABIN

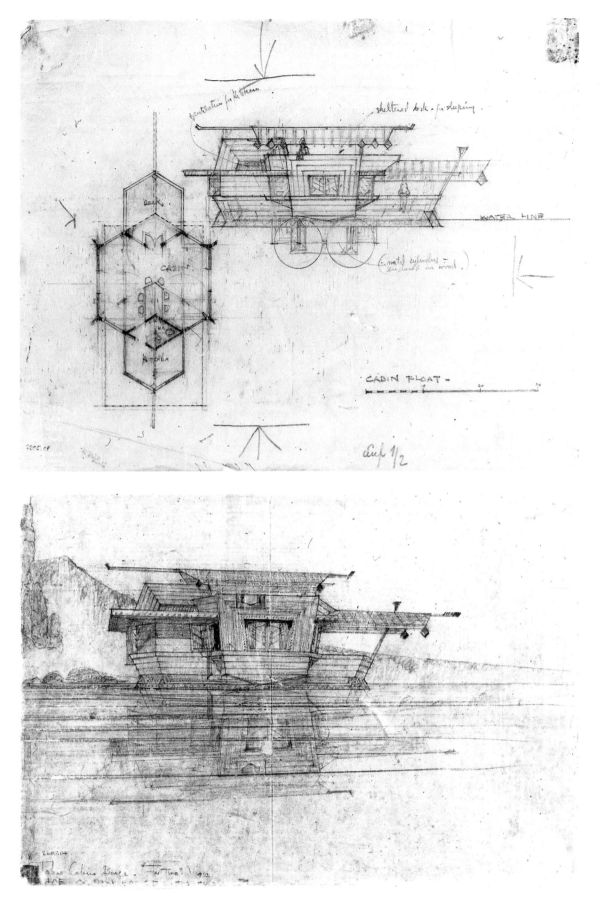

LAKE TAHOE SUMMER COLONY *(PROJECT),*
LAKE TAHOE, CALIFORNIA. 1922. PLAN AND ELEVATION.
PENCIL ON TRACING PAPER, 13 × 10". FLLW FDN# 2205.008

LAKE TAHOE SUMMER COLONY *(PROJECT),*
LAKE TAHOE, CALIFORNIA. 1922. PERSPECTIVE. PENCIL AND
COLOR PENCIL ON TRACING PAPER, 13 × 10".
FLLW FDN# 2205.004

(OPPOSITE)

LAKE TAHOE SUMMER COLONY *(PROJECT),*
LAKE TAHOE, CALIFORNIA. 1922. PERSPECTIVE. PENCIL AND
COLOR PENCIL ON TRACING PAPER, 15 × 22".
FLLW FDN# 2205.001

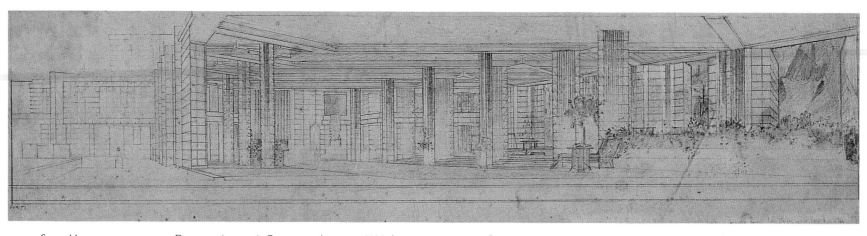

FROM THE INSTANT HE SAW the Arizona desert around Phoenix, Wright was drawn to the marvelous lessons to be learned from this environment. He not only looked about him, at the cactus, at the stark mountain ranges, at the vast, clear, open stretches, but he saw also a whole gamut of principles at work in nature. The sagauro cactus, for example, with its tall flutes, its hollow interior, its walls reinforced with long, vertical wood members, was an inspiration to him. He later said that his use of the reinforced-concrete block came directly from the rib-reinforced construction of the sagauro.

Wright was invited to the desert first in 1927–1928 to help build the Arizona Biltmore Hotel. He acted as a consultant to Albert Chase McArthur, the hotel's architect and the son of Wright's Chicago friend and client Warren McArthur. While working and living in Phoenix, Wright, his wife, and their two small children motored about the region, observing the landscape. He loved the clean, pristine, sun-drenched air.

As work came to a close on the Biltmore, he met Alexander Chandler, of the nearby town that took his name. Chandler had already built a resort hotel in the center of the town but now wished to build a larger resort in the mountains overlooking the desert. Wright drove to La Jolla, California, to meet with Chandler about this new commission; the original sketches for the resort were made while he was in La Jolla in May 1928. The next winter, with his family and seven draftsmen, Wright migrated out of a blustery Wisconsin snowstorm and set up camp on a small desert knoll not far from the site where the new resort was to be constructed. The camp that he and his draftsmen built was indeed just that: boxed board walls with canvas tops stretched over wooden frames. The triangular sections of canvas at the ends were painted scarlet red. From the view of those scarlet triangles scattered throughout the camp came the name "Ocotilla," after the cactus that has long, swaying branches reaching up from the ground and a flame-red blossom at each tip.

San Marcos-in-the-Desert, as the resort was to be named, was to be a great sun-filled series of terraces along the south slopes of the mountain range, where tourists could bask in the warm winter sunshine. Each room had its own terrace, and every corridor, bath, closet, and hallway was lit by skylights so that more sunlight could pour in. The cross section of his original sketch shows the layout of the terraces set upon the desert slopes. Entrance to the structure, from a gate lodge and parking facility, was via a deep ravine, or wash—really a dry river—that took the cars and passengers under the main terrace of the hotel. No roads, no traffic, not even parked cars would mar the beauty of either building or desert.

San Marcos was to be the very synthesis of concrete-block construction, perfectly thought out in every detail. Paul Mueller, the builder of the Imperial Hotel as well as other Wright buildings, moved into quarters at Ocotilla while the working drawings were being made. As summer approached, and as the desert heat made camp living impossible, Wright and his family and draftsmen migrated back to Wisconsin. The working drawings were finished, the specifications written, the block schedules—those special drawings that detailed all of the various types and sizes of concrete block to be used—completed.

In October the stock-market crash wiped out the finances of many of the individuals who, along with Dr. Chandler, were sponsoring the new project. And with the loss of their money also came the loss of the San Marcos.

SAN MARCOS-IN-THE-DESERT *(PROJECT), CHANDLER, ARIZONA. 1928. PERSPECTIVE. PENCIL ON TRACING PAPER, 35×20". FLLW FDN# 2704.049*

SAN MARCOS-IN-THE-DESERT *(PROJECT), CHANDLER, ARIZONA. 1928. AERIAL PERSPECTIVE. WATERCOLOR AND WATERCOLOR WASH ON ART PAPER, 65×23". FLLW FDN# 2704.048*

(OVERLEAF: SAN MARCOS-IN-THE-DESERT. *PERSPECTIVE; DETAIL)*

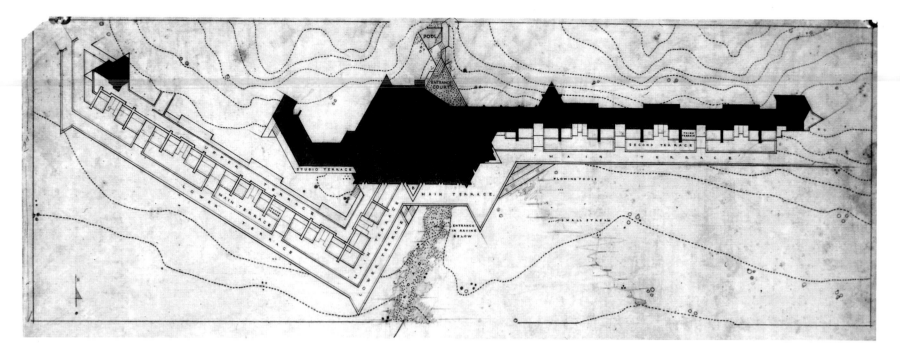

San Marcos-in-the-Desert (project),
Chandler, Arizona. 1928. Plan. Ink on art paper,
32 × 18". FLLW Fdn# 2704.052

SAN MARCOS IN THE DESERT   FOR   ALEXANDER CHANDLER · FRANK LLOYD WRIGHT

SAN MARCOS-IN-THE-DESERT (PROJECT),
CHANDLER, ARIZONA. 1928. PLAN AND ELEVATION.
PENCIL AND COLOR PENCIL ON TRACING PAPER,
41 × 21". FLLW FDN# 2704.007

SAN MARCOS-IN-THE-DESERT (PROJECT),
CHANDLER, ARIZONA. 1928. SECTION. PENCIL AND
COLOR PENCIL ON TRACING PAPER, 41 × 11".
FLLW FDN# 2704.008

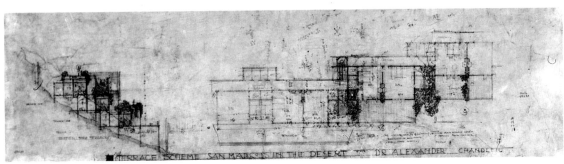

SAN MARCOS-IN-THE-DESERT (PROJECT),
CHANDLER, ARIZONA. 1928. PERSPECTIVE.
PENCIL ON TRACING PAPER, 55 × 16".
FLLW FDN# 2704.047

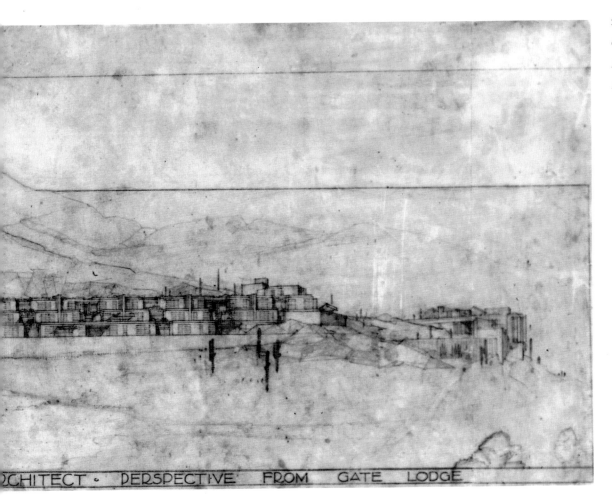

ALEXANDER CHANDLER took great pride in the small desert camp his architect had built, and would drive his friends out from town to show them Ocotilla. For winter living in a climate that had little rain, it seemed ideal as a low-cost means of construction, and he asked Wright to design a tourist facility based on the same idea. San Marcos Water Gardens was the result, but the use of concrete block and better carpentry were to make it more permanent than the hastily built camp in which Wright was living. Although he was not aware of it at the time, what Chandler got in this project was the first motor inn, designed for the transient traveler in his automobile. The aerial view shows the overall layout of the motor inn: individual cottages are grouped around a larger pavilion for dining, social events, and office work. The second view shows three typical cabins with white canvas roofs. A water course ran throughout the development, through beds of flowers and plants, to create an oasis in the desert.

From his stay in Ocotilla, during the winter of 1928–1929, Wright found the soft light coming through the canvas tents so pleasant and tranquil that he proposed a similar effect be incorporated into this project. Ten years later, he used the idea again for his own home at Taliesin West.

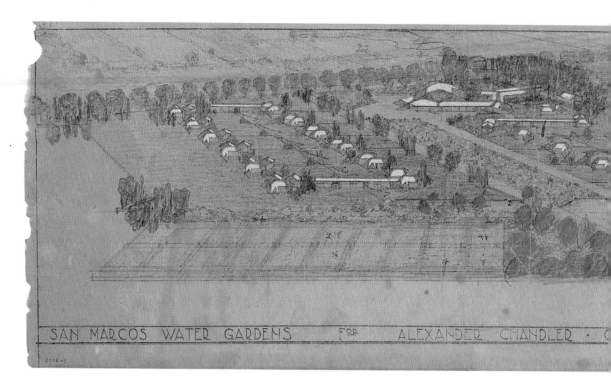

SAN MARCOS WATER GARDENS   FOR   ALEXANDER CHANDLER · (

SAN MARCOS WATER GARDENS (PROJECT),
CHANDLER, ARIZONA. 1929. AERIAL PERSPECTIVE. PENCIL AND
COLOR PENCIL ON TRACING PAPER, 41×12".
FLLW FDN# 2705.003

SAN MARCOS WATER GARDENS (PROJECT),
CHANDLER, ARIZONA. 1929. PERSPECTIVE. PENCIL AND COLOR
PENCIL ON TRACING PAPER, 26×7". FLLW FDN# 2705.002

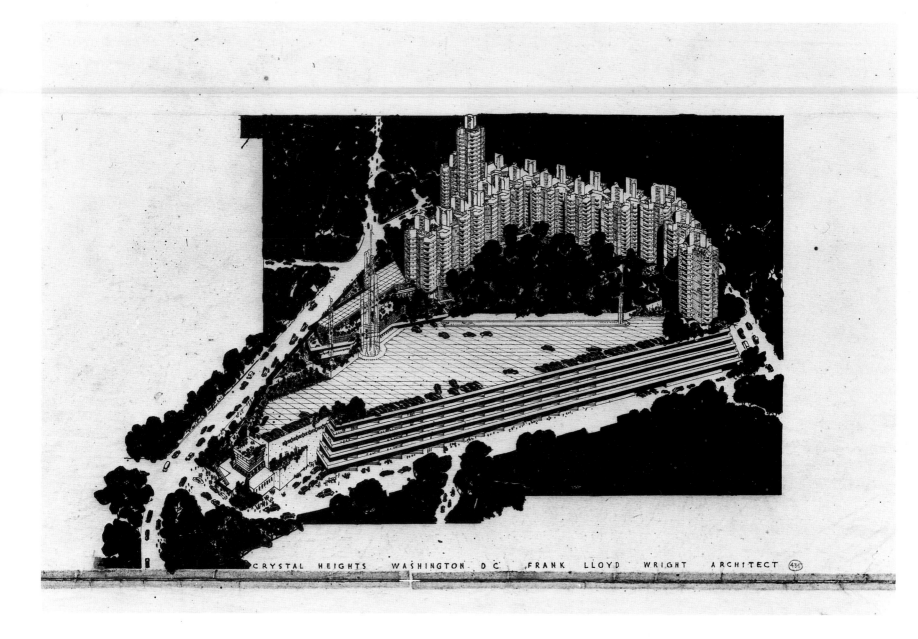

CRYSTAL HEIGHTS WASHINGTON D C FRANK LLOYD WRIGHT ARCHITECT

"*CRYSTAL HEIGHTS*" *WAS THE NAME* Wright selected for a cluster of hotel and apartment towers he designed to be set in a park of oak trees on Connecticut Avenue in Washington, D.C. The drawing, done by apprentices at Taliesin, is all in brown ink, except for the architect's personal red square, which he has dated, "Dec/39," and initialed in his usual manner. The terraces on the front of the drawing represent tiers of shops with parking spaces behind them. At the bottom left is a theater. The connections for the towers in this hotel project are similar to those Wright originally proposed in the Chicago Grouped Towers, nine years earlier (page 113).

CRYSTAL HEIGHTS *(PROJECT), WASHINGTON, D.C. 1939.*

AERIAL PERSPECTIVE. SEPIA INK ON TRACING PAPER, 34 × 24".

FLLW FDN# 4016.001

IN 1945 ELIZABETH ARDEN commissioned Wright to design a new spa adjacent to her existing establishment, "Main Chance," located on the slopes approaching Camelback Mountain in Phoenix, Arizona. Wright's proposed design would provide the services and facilities associated with what he called her "female reconstitution." Floor-to-ceiling walls of glass are set under wide, protective overheads (planted with green gardens above). The title of the project was "Sunlight," as lettered in brown ink on the drawing. But above it, in gray pencil, Wright has put the word "Moonlight," and a circle, depicting the moon, has been made by cutting out the paper to reveal a second sheet beneath it. "It would seem," he explained, "that the fundamental error in this essay lay in the emphasis placed on sunlight when twilight or moonlight was preferable."

Attached to the perspective is a note to Miss Arden:

My dear Elizabeth Arden:
So many fine things are born into "the here" and vanish . . . pass on into an unrealized future—probably the best things of all do so? This being "just one of those things" at which you glanced in passing—I thought you might like to see it again—just because.

Frank Lloyd Wright
Taliesin West
April 27th, 1945.

The drawing is very delicately rendered; the ivory-toned lines of the concrete structure shimmer against the mountain background. In his own editing of the drawing, Wright has cast a sort of "twilight" atmosphere across the landscape by graphite shading on the mountains and in parts of the sky.

DESERT SPA FOR ELIZABETH ARDEN (PROJECT), PHOENIX, ARIZONA. 1945. PERSPECTIVE. PENCIL AND COLOR PENCIL ON TRACING PAPER, 37 × 19". FLLW FDN# 4506.002

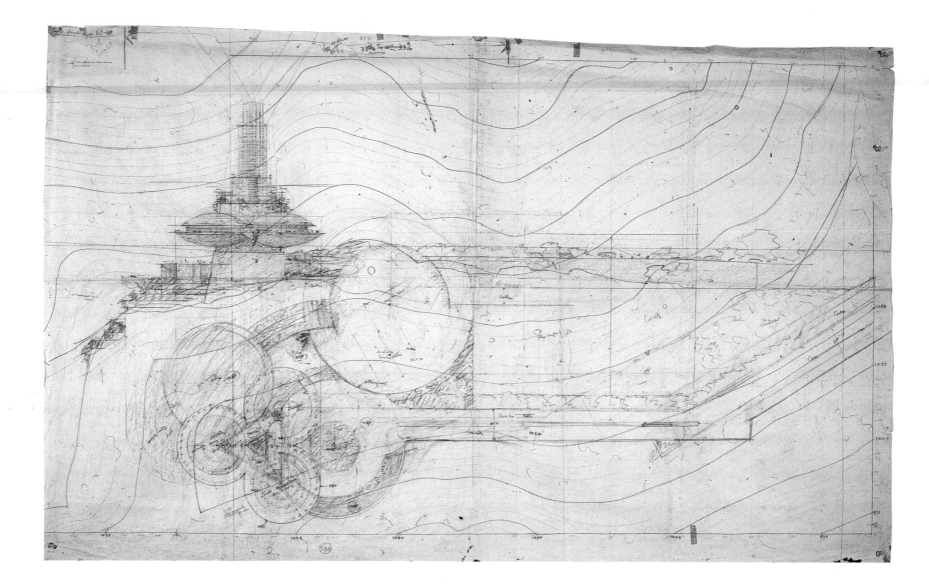

PLAY RESORT AND SPORTS CLUB FOR
HUNTINGTON HARTFORD (PROJECT), HOLLYWOOD,
CALIFORNIA. 1947. CONCEPTUAL PLAN AND ELEVATION.
PENCIL AND COLOR PENCIL ON TRACING PAPER,
76 × 44". FLLW FDN# 4731.001

WRIGHT'S PERSPECTIVES SERVE their purpose of conveying the sight and spirit of the buildings, but his most intriguing drawings are his conceptual sketches. And of those great drawings, this conceptual study for a sports club is without doubt among the most outstanding. On a topographical map of the site, laid out by his apprentices in red ink on white tracing paper, Wright made a plan and elevation revealing his scheme for three large disks projecting out from a central masonry core. These Wright has labeled as "Dining and dancing," "Lounge," and "Cabaret" rooms. Each circle is marked as having a diameter of "72'-0". The larger blue circle above these is a 75-foot-diameter swimming pool; an even larger circle, 120 feet in diameter, is labeled "Championship Tennis Matches." The encircled numbers throughout are designations related to the topographical lines of the property and the heights

of the rooms and terrace within the sports club itself. The massive stone and concrete wall that supports the disks was to contain further facilities: steam rooms, locker rooms, kitchen, elevators and stairwells, and—at the upper level—a duplex apartment for the client, Huntington Hartford himself. The smaller disk at the top was a sun deck. At the entry level are tennis courts and a large swimming pool.

The graphite pencil perspective (page 195) was drawn by a Taliesin apprentice in preparation for another, more final view, but Wright worked extensively on this. It is a hitherto unpublished drawing, practically an unknown drawing, because the two more famous views, taken from the canyon below, were not developed out of this study. The final presentation drawing that corresponds to this one no longer exists, except in a photographic record.

PLAY RESORT AND SPORTS CLUB FOR

HUNTINGTON HARTFORD *(PROJECT)*, HOLLYWOOD,

CALIFORNIA. 1947. PERSPECTIVE. PENCIL

ON TRACING PAPER, 50×37". FLLW FDN# 4731.011

METEOR CRATER INN *(PROJECT)*, METEOR CRATER,
ARIZONA. 1948. PLAN AND ELEVATION. PENCIL AND COLOR PENCIL
ON TRACING PAPER, 40 × 36". FLLW FDN# 4822.003

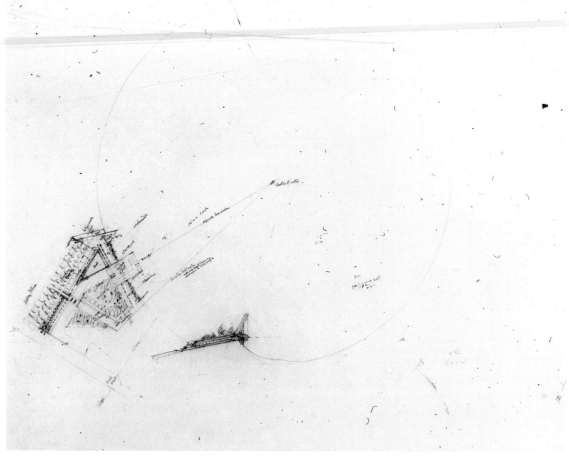

METEOR CRATER INN *(PROJECT)*, METEOR CRATER,
ARIZONA. 1948. AERIAL PERSPECTIVE. PENCIL AND COLOR
PENCIL ON TRACING PAPER, 36 × 27". FLLW FDN# 4822.002

IN NORTHERN ARIZONA there is a great crater dug out of the earth where it was struck by a meteor. In Wright's day it was an attraction for tourists, but unlike the nearby and far more famous Grand Canyon, it had no facilities for the public. This project was to provide for those needs with a resort containing a motel, dining facilities, shops, and a museum as well as access to the crater from the rim.

The conceptual plan and elevation is made on a large sheet of paper. The size of the paper and the relatively small studies on it dramatize the actual site conditions. The elevation makes it quite clear how the resort itself was to be terraced, in keeping with the sloping grade of the crater. Inside the stone mass at the crater's edge is an elevator that descends to the bottom of the crater, and above there is an outdoor lookout.

The plan is labeled with designations for all the rooms and provisions needed, from the filling station at one end to parking spaces and guest rooms. Construction was to be of stone masonry and timber with a wood shingle roof. But the project advanced no further than preliminary drawings.

In the perspective, the resort almost disappears into the desert and distant mountains; the impressionistic setting was achieved by mixing several colors of horizontal lines. The drawing is signed and dated, "FLLW May 17/48."

THE TITLE OF THIS DRAWING, "Cottage Group Center," refers to a large hotel that Wright designed for Huntington Hartford, for whom he also designed the Play Resort and Sports Club (page 194). The hotel provides general rooms and areas in the large central mass shown on the perspective and is covered by a roof garden projecting out over the tall glass enclosures. But stretching out behind and on either side of this main mass are various levels of cottagelike attached and semiattached rooms and suites. Guests would be able to enter the main structure and find their way to their rooms via elevators and corridors or to drive around in their cars and come upon the same level via a series of roadways concealed behind the buildings. Like the hotel for San Marcos-in-the-Desert, all rooms are placed adjacent to sun-filled terraces; for this southern California setting much planting and flowers are included as an integral part of the scheme.

In this second version designed for the same canyon, the resort is placed in a different location. Both this and the earlier scheme are at the entrance to the canyon, the Sports Club further up on its own promontory. But the first scheme oriented the rooms to the east. Wright rethought the placement of the guest rooms, in light of the fact that this was a resort hotel, and decided that it would be best if the rooms faced west: "They can sit on the terraces and view the sunset, which is certainly preferable to having the rising sun in the morning pouring into the rooms and awakening them. This is to be, after all, a vacation place!"

(OVERLEAF: COTTAGE GROUP CENTER.
PERSPECTIVE; DETAIL)

A G E   G R O U P   C
U N T I N G T O N   H A R
N K   L L O Y D   W R I G H T
L L O Y D   W R I G H T

N T E R

F O R D   ⑴⑴5

R C H I T E C T

S S O C I A T E

YWCA *(project), Racine, Wisconsin. 1949. Perspective. Pencil and color pencil on tracing paper, 36 × 28". FLLW Fdn# 4920.027*

THE COMMISSION FOR WRIGHT to build the YWCA in Racine, Wisconsin, came about at the instigation of one of the city's leading citizens, Herbert F. Johnson, president of the S.C. Johnson and Son Company. Learning that the Y needed new facilities, he was eager to see them have a Frank Lloyd Wright building (in 1936 he had commissioned the Johnson Wax Company Building), and he offered to engage the architect and pay his preliminary fees. The organization, however, was not so keen on the idea, and although a second proposal was made to try to fulfill their needs, the project suffered from the usual fate of a typical "committee" and was dropped.

The plan was fully developed, with provisions for a bowling alley, a restaurant, crafts shops, meeting rooms, and a library. The top floor was to contain a large swimming pool under a translucent glass enclosure, opening onto a terrace in summer but closed against the cold in winter.

With all of the various requirements the building had to meet, this is an interesting example of Wright designing a relatively small multipurpose structure. Even at this early date, he specified ramps for access to all floors, making them a feature of a large central court as well as providing for the handicapped.

MANY TIMES DURING HIS CAREER Wright took an unexecuted design, a project that had been abandoned, and modified it for another client. Obvious among these cases is the Saint Mark's Tower of 1929, which became the Price Tower in 1952 (pages 112 and 120). In some instances it was the idea of the past project that became the new building, such as the Steel Cathedral, which finally emerged as the Beth Sholom Synagogue (pages 98–99).

How literally the new design would be translated depended upon the circumstances and the conditions to be met. The tourist camp he designed for Alexander Chandler in 1927 (page 184) seemed the perfect solution for a tourist facility for officials of the U.S. Plywood Corporation in Leesburg, Florida. The site was a lake with floating islands, and the program called for a motel, a pavilion for dining and entertainment, and an aquacade with a bandstand for performances. The large aerial view is almost like a plan, outlining the entire scope of the project, while the closer view focuses on the pavilion. Although the plan is almost identical to the San Marcos Water Gardens project (page 190), the materials were to be more permanent: concrete block walls with an all-plywood roof were used—rather than the canvas of the earlier plan. Even the tall pylon, or tower, was to be of plywood, rising from a concrete base, with pendant lanterns hanging from the triangular sections all the way up the structure.

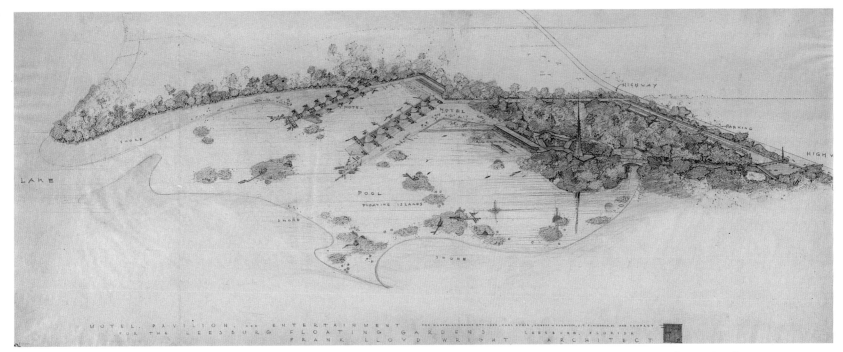

FLOATING GARDENS (PROJECT), LEESBURG, FLORIDA. 1952. AERIAL PERSPECTIVE. PENCIL AND COLOR PENCIL ON TRACING PAPER, 63×36". FLLW FDN# 5216.002

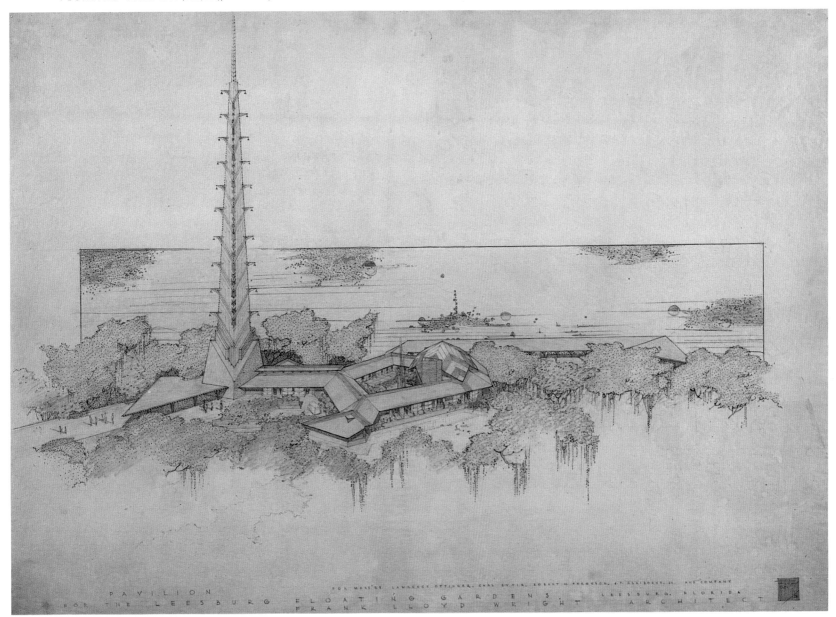

FLOATING GARDENS (PROJECT), LEESBURG, FLORIDA. 1952. AERIAL PERSPECTIVE. PENCIL AND COLOR PENCIL ON TRACING PAPER, 58×36". FLLW FDN# 5216.001

Your Excellency!

That you might be interested in
the type of Motel we are building in the US. instead of HOTELS
F.LL.W.   (kindly preserve and return—
These are originals)

MOTOR HOTEL FOR MR DANIEL WIELAND, HAGERSTOWN, MD.
FRANK LLOYD WRIGHT, ARCHITECT

WIELAND MOTEL (PROJECT), HAGERSTOWN, MARYLAND.
1956. AERIAL PERSPECTIVE. PENCIL AND COLOR PENCIL ON
TRACING PAPER, 36 × 19". FLLW FDN# 5521.001

DESIGNED FOR A CLIENT in Hagerstown, Maryland, this motel was to be set in a gardenlike field, with the office and restaurant in one large circular building and the motel units, two stories high, in a gentle arc on the right. The cars would park in or under a portion of the second level, keeping them safe from bad weather as well as partially concealed within the building rather than surrounding it. On the upper-left corner Wright has written, "Your Excellency! That you might be interested in the type of motel we are building in the U.S. instead of hotels. FLLW. (Kindly preserve and return— these are originals)." The note is a record of his intention to send the drawing to the king of Iraq and his cultural commission, but the fact that the drawing has remained in the collection leads us to believe that the revolution in Iraq intervened, and the drawing was never sent.

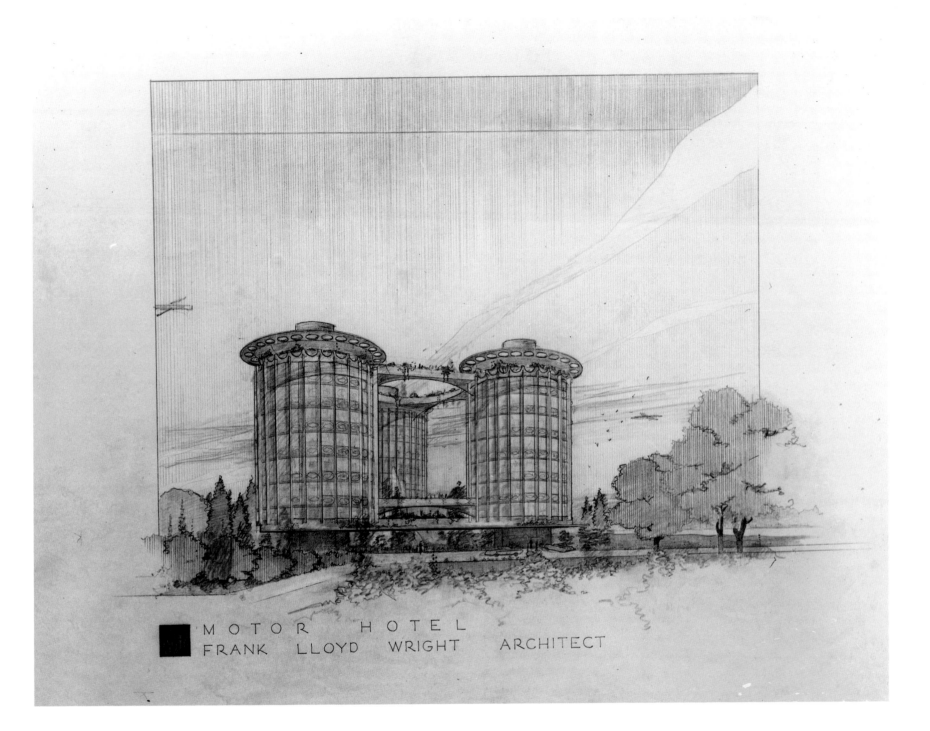

MOTOR HOTEL
FRANK LLOYD WRIGHT ARCHITECT

WHILE THE MOTEL FOR WIELAND was to be placed in a large field at the edge of town (page 202), this design for Memphis, Tennessee, was in a more urban setting. The group of three towers rises from a small park in the city. At the top level the towers are connected by a restaurant with outdoor dining, when desired. The image is placed rather formally on the sheet, and at one point the skyline has been dropped down so as to change the building's relationship to it. The perspective drawing is rather clumsy and somewhat inaccurate. But Wright went to work on it, adding foliage, details, clouds, and shadows, to try to save the situation without discarding the drawing and starting all over again.

BRAMLETT MOTOR HOTEL (*PROJECT*), MEMPHIS, TENNESSEE. 1956. PERSPECTIVE. PENCIL AND COLOR PENCIL ON TRACING PAPER, 36 × 29". FLLW FDN# 5620.004

HARRY GUGGENHEIM (Solomon Guggenheim's nephew) wanted Wright to design a new race track at Belmont Park, New York, in 1956. In describing the project, Wright commented, "A massive slab, with four levels reached by twelve or sixteen escalators (depending on size of stand), covered by a translucent plastic roof, suspended on a lacework of slender tensile steel cables." This was his typical approach to the use of steel, which he always called "the spider spinning." Most twentieth-century architecture continued to employ steel in the context of traditional wood-building techniques: post-and-beam construction. Here, by contrast, the steel is flexible and therefore stronger. As was demonstrated by Roebling's Brooklyn Bridge, steel could be used in ways more appropriate to its inherent characteristics.

Notes by the architect on the rendering refer to the seating capacity and the heating system: "Concrete slab floor and seats slab floor heated. Canopy defrosted."

Of the seventeen works illustrated in this section on hotels, inns, and motels, only four were built, and those all in the earlier part of Wright's career. And of those four, three were demolished—the only one remaining, Como Orchards, is practically demolished. Yet these buildings represent some of his most innovative designs from the point of view of architectural and engineering innovation. To Wright, the two disciplines were synonymous: he was designing twentieth-century buildings in total accord with twentieth-century building techniques. It is erroneous, therefore, to refer to his work as fifty years ahead of its time; it was really right in keeping with the technology of the time, but the clients and contractors, indeed the American public, were fifty years behind.

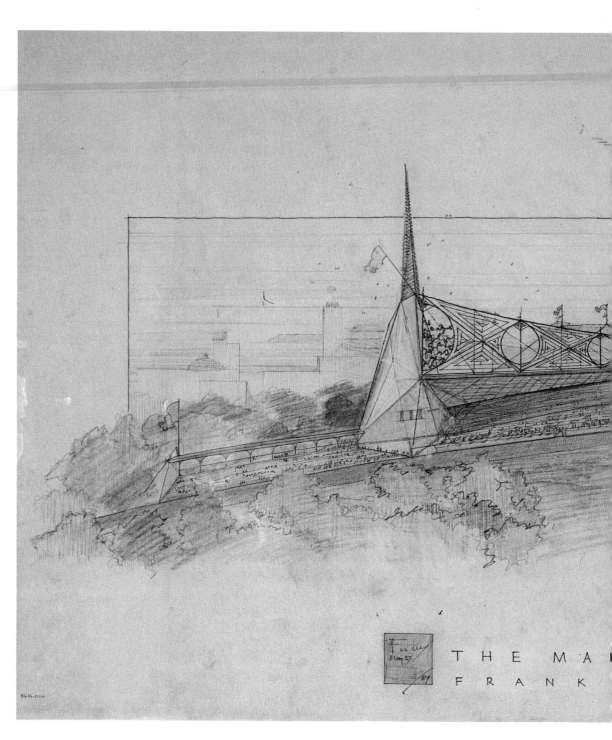

NEW SPORTS PAVILION (PROJECT), BELMONT PARK, NEW YORK. 1956. PERSPECTIVE. PENCIL AND COLOR PENCIL ON TRACING PAPER, 58 × 26". FLLW FDN# 5616.020

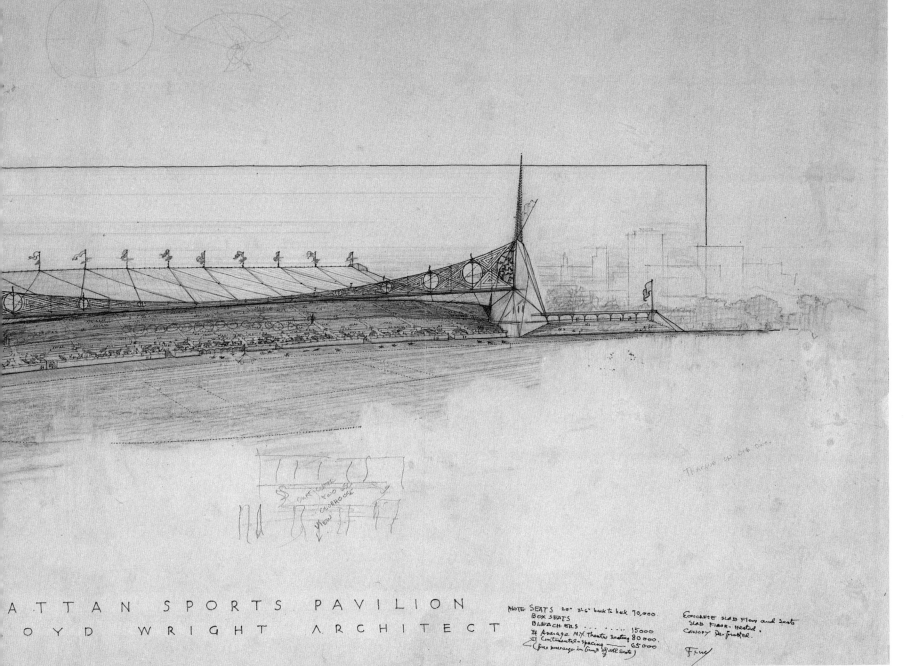

ATTAN SPORTS PAVILION

OYD WRIGHT ARCHITECT

NOTE SEATS 20" 3'6" back to back 70,000.
BOX SEATS
BLEACHERS 15000
Ⅱ Average N.Y. Theatre seating 80 000.
Ⅲ Continental-spacing 65 000
(free passage in front of all seats)

CONCRETE SLAB FLOOR and Seats
SLAB FLOOR - Heated
CANOPY De-frosted.

PART SIX

COMMERCIAL AND
EDUCATIONAL BUILDINGS

THE DRAWINGS IN THIS SECTION range from a small dress shop Wright sketched for Oak Park, Illinois, in 1937 to a department store in India he designed in 1946. Included are banks and educational buildings, a fraternity for Indiana University, and a student pensione in Venice. The buildings for educational purposes encompass a kindergarten for his mercurial client Aline Barnsdall, a group of playhouses for the Oak Park Playground Association, his own Taliesin Fellowship complex (in a much larger scheme than was finally realized), a two-room country schoolhouse for Wisconsin, a college in Lakeland, Florida, and a large university for Baghdad, Iraq.

Education was in Wright's blood; his two aunts and mother were educators who founded the Hillside Home School, the first coeducational home school in the nation, which took in children from the ages of five to eighteen. They offered a revolutionary curriculum by rejecting any kind of segregation: boys and girls were taught the same classes, from home economics to chemistry and algebra. Each child was also responsible for duties on a farm connected with the school, learning to care for animals, tend a garden plot, and raise vegetables. The young Wright visited the school often, and from his association with its teachers and the families of the students, several commissions as well as lifelong friendships evolved.

Indeed, Wright's earliest commission, in 1887, was to design one of the Hillside Home School buildings, called the "Home Building." It revealed the influence of Lyman Silsbee's "shingle style." Ten years later Wright took another commission from his aunts, this time for a windmill tower on a hill above the school buildings. He called the construction "Romeo and Juliet." In 1902 he again designed and built a school building for his aunts, which still stands as the Hillside Home School and is now part of the Frank Lloyd Wright School of Architecture. In 1928, after both aunts died, he purchased the buildings, which had been deserted for several years and were in dreadful condition. He had made a promise to his aunts that he would somehow continue the tradition of what he called "congenital education" that was deeply rooted in the family. In 1928 he proposed creating an extension of the Hillside Home School buildings with new structures added to the existing ones. This proposal, called the Hillside Home School for the Allied Arts, was to be a new school for one hundred students of architecture, painting, sculpture, music, crafts, and drama. But the scheme proved too ambitious and was dropped. The Taliesin Fellowship, originated in 1932, grew out of that concept and still flourishes.

Wright's delight and joy in pleasing and developing a young child's mind is evident in his kindergarten designs. His own playroom, in the Oak Park house that he built for his wife and their six children, bespeaks this same concern: the room is scaled in every detail to children, and it clearly aims to delight them. The kindergarten for Aline Barnsdall, called the "Little Dipper," is an illusory fantasy of the starry constellation (page 214); the Oak Park playhouses are four fantasies, each with completely different elevations but all based on the same plan (page 216).

In his architecture for institutions of higher education, such as the campus Wright designed for Florida Southern College in 1938 and the University of Baghdad in 1958, his desire to have students relate to their time and their natural surroundings is clearly apparent. These are not the ivy-clad structures of higher learning so long considered appropriate to the academic world in the United States; instead, they address problems and seek solutions that are of today, not yesterday (pages 224 and 234).

With Wright's commercial structures as well, it was always the purpose of each building that determined its space and its form. Banks, Wright maintained, should give the customer a sense of protecting his property and investments. A bank building should have, foremost, this quality of a "strongbox," as he called it. In his earliest bank building, a concrete and brick monolith begun in 1894 and revised in 1901 (page 209), this "strongbox" quality is imposing, almost monumental. Light comes into the interior from windows above a high wall-frieze. The City National Bank Building of 1909 likewise emits interior light from above a blank, protective brick wall (page 210). Almost forty years later, the two buildings Wright designed for the Valley National Bank in Arizona (page 226) have more light and space on the ground level but still maintain the sense of protection and well-being that he believed a bank must have. One bank, called the "Daylight Bank," is top lit; the other's light comes from tall clerestory glass on the second-floor level.

MONOLITHIC BANK (PROJECT). 1894.

PERSPECTIVE. INK ON ART PAPER,

18 × 11". FLLW FDN# 9408.001

WRITING ABOUT THIS PROJECT when it was published in *The Brickbuilder* in August 1901, Wright said, "While there is probably little romance about a bank—less poetry in the bray of Sancho Panza's substantial, positive gray donkey than in the sound of Rosinante's spirited neighing—yet the community likes to feel that this same bank is there to stay. It is, in fact, the town strongbox, and it is a temple to the God of Money, as modern temples go."

This is one of Wright's projects that has a wide variety of dates assigned to it. The perspective drawing is labeled "EARLY STUDY CONCRETE MONOLITH BANK 1894." The 1931 European exhibition catalog lists it, in Wright's own handwriting, as 1897. The version as published in 1901, despite the phrase "CONCRETE MONOLITH BANK," was intended as a building built of brick: "The building is constructed entirely of brick. The ornamental members throughout are of terra cotta, except the windowsills and the caps, which are cast in bronze, finished in antique vertigris. The floors in the public space are laid with a mosaic of unglazed ceramic." In the cast ornament set between the piers and

at their capitals there is a strong hint of Sullivanesque design, although a more geometric feeling is employed here than in most works by Louis Sullivan. If we assume the date of Wright's design to be 1894, it was done one year after Wright had been in private practice.

On the plan Wright has attributed the drawing to "Birch Burdette Long, Del.," a notation put on the drawing in the 1950s. But the ink instructions on the plan and cutaway view, "Return to Frank Lloyd Wright Steinway Hall," must have been written in 1897, when his office was located in that building in Chicago.

MONOLITHIC BANK *(PROJECT). 1894.*

CUTAWAY PERSPECTIVE. INK ON ART PAPER,

22 × 13". FLLW FDN# 9408.002

MONOLITHIC BANK *(PROJECT). 1894.*

PLAN. INK ON ART PAPER, 22 × 12".

FLLW FDN# 9408.003

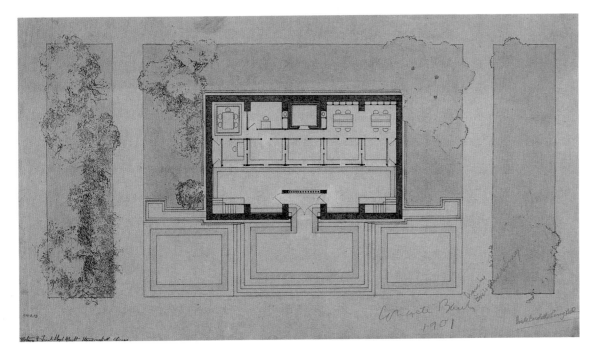

THIS BUILDING, CONSTRUCTED in 1909 in Mason City, Iowa, is a remarkable example of a multipurpose structure. The long wing with the blank brick wall and high windows above is a bank. To the right, in a more residential style, is a small hotel. Between the two buildings are further office spaces for a law firm, and there is room for a restaurant, café, and two stores on the street level. But the two main elements, the commercial bank and hotel, are held together in a quiet harmony that pervades the entire design.

The drawing containing two elevations, one from the side and one head on, seems most likely to have been laid out originally by one of Wright's draftsmen. But the manner in which the architect has gone to work on it, with shading and the addition of ornamental details, is strongly characteristic of Wright's ability to instill a sense of vibrant life and romance into an otherwise simple architectural development drawing.

The perspective is likewise rich in detail, the draftsmanship of the highest caliber. The building has suffered dreadful additions and modifications over the years as subsequent owners have wrought undesirable changes, but from this carefully made and delicately rendered perspective the pristine quality of the original structure can be sensed.

CITY NATIONAL BANK, MASON CITY, IOWA. 1909.
ELEVATIONS. PENCIL ON TRACING PAPER, 36 × 12".
FLLW FDN# 0902.012

CITY NATIONAL BANK, MASON CITY, IOWA. 1909.
PERSPECTIVE. INK ON TRACING PAPER, 36 × 11".
FLLW FDN# 0902.001

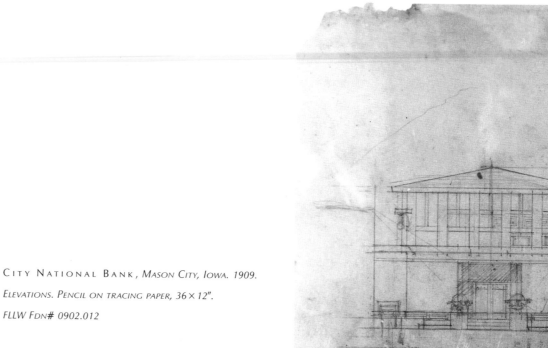

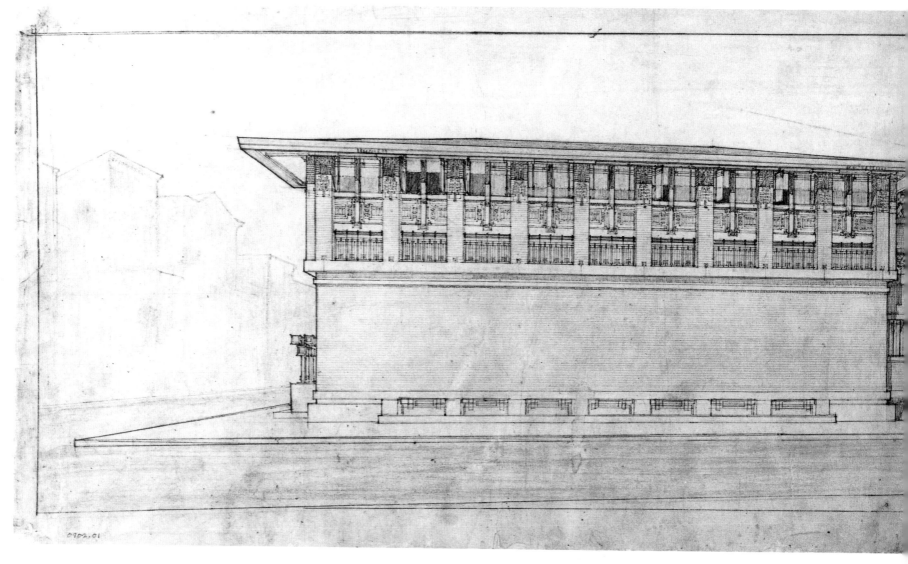

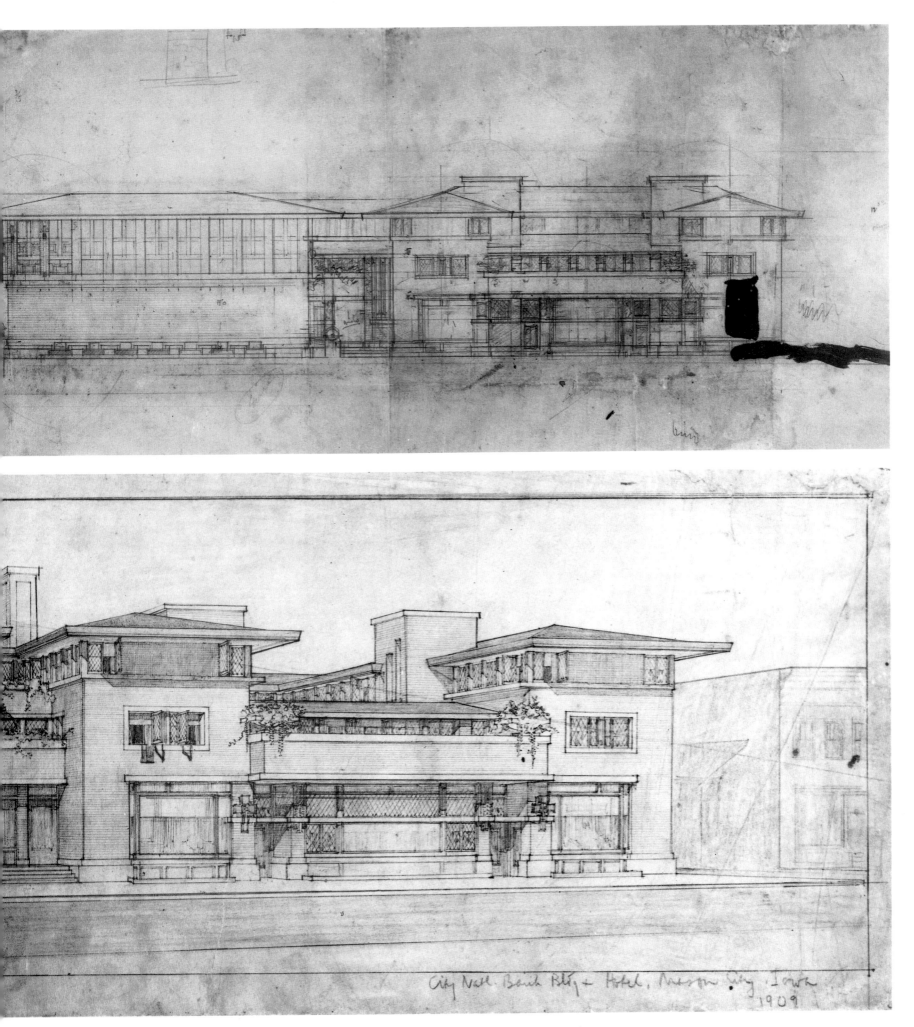

City Natl. Bank Bldg + Hotel, Mason City, Iowa
1909

211

WRIGHT DESIGNED THIS BANK for Spring Green, Wisconsin, a small farming community near his own home in Taliesin. The building that he proposed has, like the early concrete Monolithic Bank (page 208), the character of a "strongbox." Here, however, the elevation has more architectural variation, noticeably in the treatment of the window walls and the extended planting features at the entrance. The conceptual plan, totally drawn by Wright, is almost all freehand, while the elevation, also his, is more carefully drafted with the addition of his usual freehand touches.

The large presentation perspective is a magnificent drawing done in graphite pencil on tracing linen, with shades of green representing foliage and plants. Most presentation drawings were done either on heavy art paper or on tracing paper. It is rare to see one on tracing linen, which was usually reserved for the making of working drawings.

STATE BANK OF SPRING GREEN (PROJECT),
SPRING GREEN, WISCONSIN. 1914. PERSPECTIVE.
PENCIL AND COLOR PENCIL ON TRACING PAPER,
30 × 20". FLLW FDN# 1405.001

STATE BANK OF SPRING GREEN *(PROJECT)*,
SPRING GREEN, WISCONSIN. 1914. ELEVATION.
PENCIL ON TRACING PAPER, 20 × 11".
FLLW FDN# 1405.002

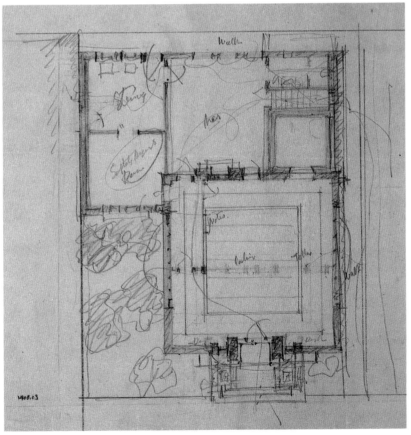

STATE BANK OF SPRING GREEN *(PROJECT)*,
SPRING GREEN, WISCONSIN. 1914. PLAN.
PENCIL AND COLOR PENCIL ON TRACING PAPER,
12 × 11". FLLW FDN# 1405.003

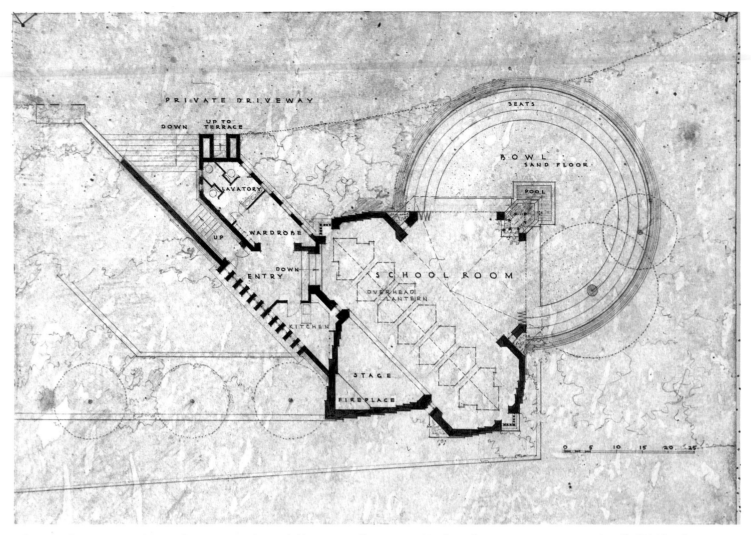

LITTLE DIPPER FOR ALINE BARNSDALL *(PROJECT)*, HOLLYWOOD, CALIFORNIA. 1921. PLAN. PENCIL ON TRACING PAPER, 18 × 13". FLLW FDN# 2301.007

ON THE OLIVE HILL PROPERTY of Aline Barnsdall, where Wright constructed her Hollyhock House (page 28) and Residence A and Residence B, he also planned this kindergarten school and playhouse. Various theater projects (pages 132–135) were planned for Miss Barnsdall as well, but like the school they never were carried out. Part of her interest in the dramatic arts extended to the education of children, and this kindergarten was laid out so that the main schoolroom could be used as a stage, with an outside bowl for the audience. The overhead lantern roof, as marked on the plan, would bring top light into the classroom and performing area. The configuration of the plan, with schoolroom and entry wing, suggested the shape of the Little Dipper to Wright.

This school was to be built of cast concrete and concrete block, the patterns of the blocks clearly evident in the perspective drawing. The building is nestled into the side of a steep hill; the entrance stepped down from the private driveway, with an external stairway leading up to a roof terrace.

The view might suggest a rather imposing and fortresslike building due to the great retaining walls that carry the kindergarten up the steep hill. But the delicate block patterns soften the wall, and the actual building itself looks onto a garden and sand court on one side and a swimming pool bordered by flowers on the other. A centrally placed "lantern," or raised clerestory, filters daylight into the building from above.

Little Dipper for Aline Barnsdall *(project)*, Hollywood, California. *1921. Perspective. Pencil and color pencil on tracing paper, 26×17". FLLW Fdn# 2301.008*

NO PROJECT MORE evidently portrays Wright's love of delighting small children than this one for a group of four playhouses in Oak Park, Illinois. Even the title suggests the romance of the scheme, "Kinder-symphonies." The names he selected for the playhouses further suggest the gaiety of the project: "The Goblin," or "Scherzo," "Two-for-a-Penny," "The Iovanna," after his daughter's name, and "The Anne Baxter," after his granddaughter.

On the original plan, he has explained the nature of the playhouses: "GROUND PLAN: Same for all four buildings. Modifications made above main roof only, and in front windows outside prowside of gutter line." Other notes on the plan designate placement of flowers and lights at the corners of the buildings. The plan that has an elevation placed beneath shows roof-line modifications, and the note accompanying the cluster of circular globes reads, "Cast in colored concrete, same in all buildings. Perforated light globes." Inside each was to be a centrally placed fireplace in the main play-room, with two toilets and a kitchen along the back walls. The project went no further than these sketches.

The perspective, a drawing done completely by Wright himself, shows a playhouse with colored globes and a reflecting pool. Along with his own drawings for the Lake Tahoe project, these renderings intimately reveal his personal touch.

"KINDERSYMPHONIES" KINDERGARTEN (PROJECT), OAK PARK, ILLINOIS. 1926. ELEVATION AND PLAN. PENCIL AND COLOR PENCIL ON TRACING PAPER, 13 × 10". FLLW FDN# 2601.003

"KINDERSYMPHONIES" KINDERGARTEN (PROJECT), OAK PARK, ILLINOIS. 1926. PLAN. PENCIL AND COLOR PENCIL ON TRACING PAPER, 13 × 10". FLLW FDN# 2601.005

"KINDERSYMPHONIES" KINDERGARTEN (PROJECT), OAK PARK, ILLINOIS. 1926. PERSPECTIVE. PENCIL AND COLOR PENCIL ON TRACING PAPER, 13 × 10". FLLW FDN# 2601.007

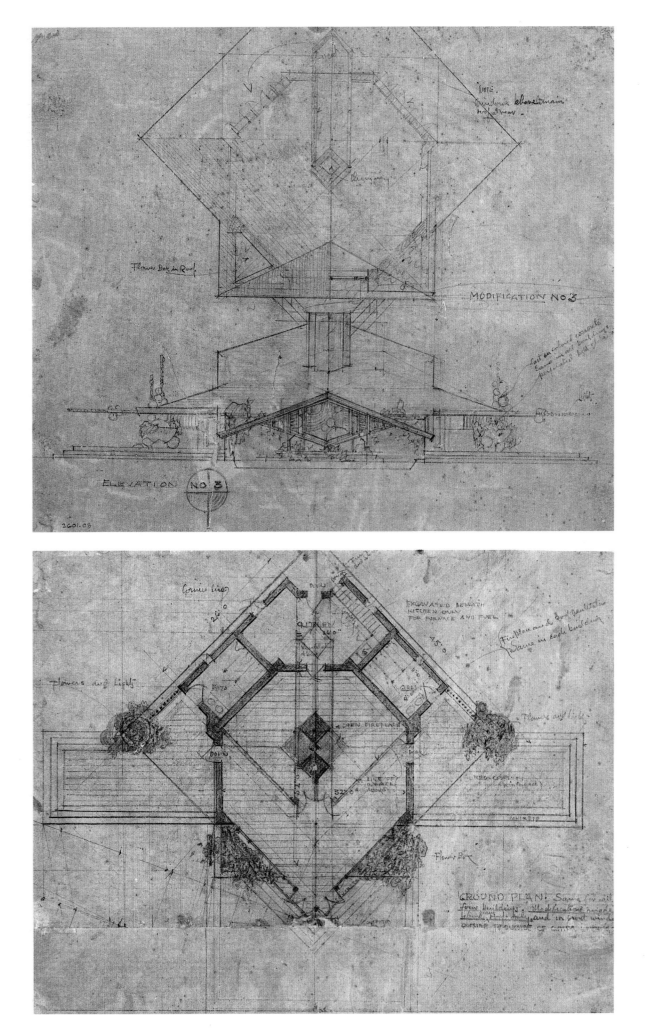

WHEN FRANK LLOYD WRIGHT and his wife established the Taliesin Fellowship as an apprenticeship-training school for architects, they had already taken over the Hillside Home School buildings that he had designed for the Lloyd Jones sisters in 1902. Hillside, as it is now called, is located over the hill from Taliesin. At the top of the view is the "Romeo and Juliet" windmill tower that he built in 1897. Down the meadow, on the other side of the hill and out of sight, lies Taliesin. The hill on the far right of the drawing conceals Midway, a farm complex that is also part of the Taliesin Fellowship buildings. The main Hillside buildings from 1902 are drawn here; other outlying buildings were planned for further shops, studios, and dormitory facilities but were never realized.

The drawing style throughout is definitely Wright's, and the image, more like a great landscape, fills the entire sheet from edge to edge. It conveys the lush pastoral setting of southern Wisconsin, yet the architectural lines are crisp and graphic.

TALIESIN FELLOWSHIP COMPLEX,
SPRING GREEN, WISCONSIN. 1932. AERIAL PERSPECTIVE.
PENCIL AND COLOR PENCIL ON TRACING PAPER, 21×18".
FLLW FDN# 3301.001

THIS DRAWING IS UNIQUE to the collection. Its placement of the shop within a circle (interrupted by the sidewalk) and its mounting on two different shades of backing paper sets it apart.

The shop was intended for a busy street in downtown Oak Park; the two floors above the shop were for an apartment for Leo Bramson, the client. The glass front is louvered—that is, protected with a movable series of horizontal shades that control the amount of sunlight entering the shop's interior. There is a subtle but masterful massing of the poured-concrete forms, one in the cantilevered balcony stretching across the front on the second level, another in the smaller balcony projecting out from a glass window over the street front on the third level. A chimney rises in the rear.

BRAMSON DRESS SHOP (PROJECT),
OAK PARK, ILLINOIS. 1937. PERSPECTIVE.
PENCIL AND COLOR PENCIL ON TRACING PAPER,
16 × 15". FLLW FDN# 3706.001

(OVERLEAF: TALIESIN FELLOWSHIP COMPLEX.
AERIAL PERSPECTIVE; DETAIL)

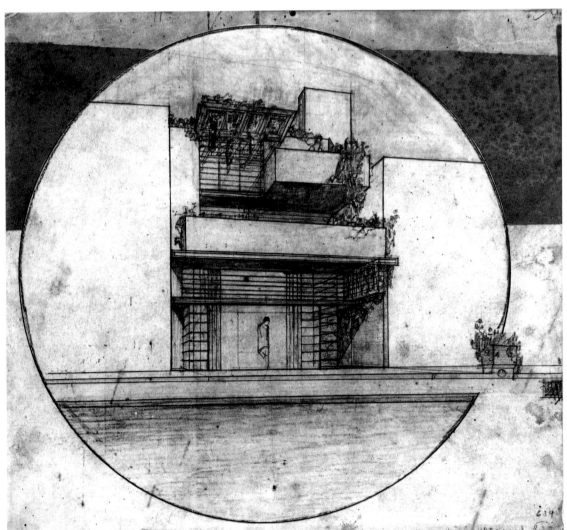

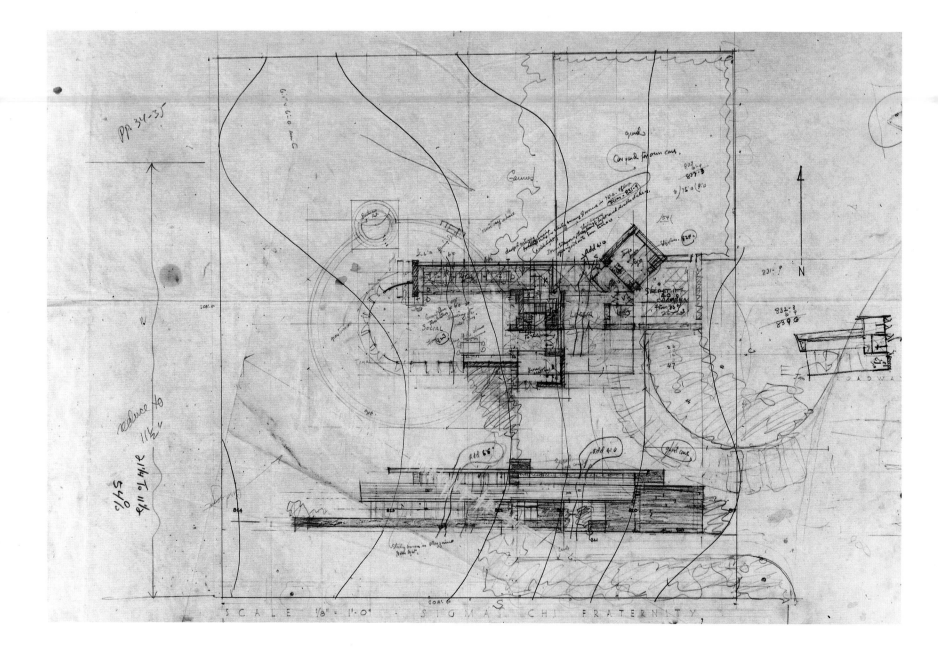

THE CLOSE RELATIONSHIP of plan to elevation, each one an integral part of the other, is made graphically manifest in this conceptual drawing done entirely by Wright. In architecture, he explained to his apprentices at Taliesin, "a good plan should reflect itself in the elevation, just as the elevation should reflect the plan. If there is a harmonious interconnection between the two, the design is a good one. But so often I see someone's elevation that has little or no bearing with the same person's plan, they are disconnected and the resulting building will be so, as well."

This drawing bears out Wright's innate gift of making that connection between plan and elevation. Also typical of his conceptual sketches, especially on a site that is not absolutely flat, is his attention to the slope of the ground and the building's orientation. The students' bedrooms and studies are kept purposely small, the emphasis being on the large social hall, on ground level, which rises two stories. As with most fraternities at that time, the design had to have national support from the parent chapter. In 1941 their tastes were decidedly too conservative to permit a design of this nature.

SIGMA CHI FRATERNITY HOUSE *(PROJECT)*,
HANOVER, INDIANA. 1941. PLAN AND ELEVATION.
PENCIL AND COLOR PENCIL ON TRACING PAPER, 44 × 36".
FLLW FDN# 4108.001

THE SARABHAI FAMILY, owners of a vast cotton-mill industry in India, commissioned Wright to design a department store for exhibiting and selling calico cloth in Ahmedabad, India. The perspective, at first glance, would seem to represent a large structure, if each of the window openings on the exterior wall of the tower were considered as a separate floor level. Such is not the case. The figures in front of the shop window indicate the accurate scale. The cantilevered concrete parapet above the plate-glass windows at street level acts as a sun shield for the pedestrians. So that the textiles within the window will not be cast in shadow and require extensive, artificial lighting, as they ordinarily would on bright days, the windows reach above the parapet line to admit natural daylight into the display space below.

The various floors are kept free from the exterior screen wall. There are two open courts throughout the entire structure, and air circulation from the slab edge around the open courts provides a novel and innovative type of natural air-conditioning in the humid, hot cli-mate. A café is on the uppermost floor, with a pent-house apartment for the owners rising above a roof-garden terrace.

In 1946 the problems of engineering a structure of this complexity in India proved insurmountable, and the project was finally abandoned.

SARABHAI CALICO MILLS STORE (PROJECT), AHMEDABAD, INDIA. 1946. PERSPECTIVE. PENCIL AND COLOR PENCIL ON TRACING PAPER, 24 × 36".
FLLW FDN# 4508.001

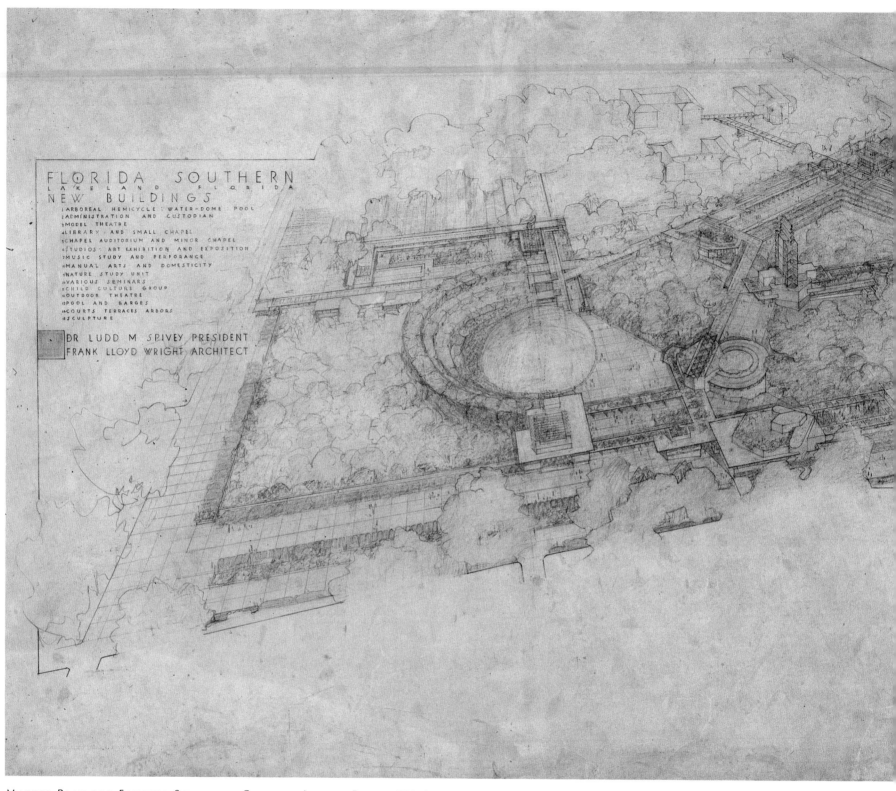

FLORIDA SOUTHERN
LAKELAND FLORIDA
NEW BUILDINGS
1 ARBOREAL HEMICYCLE WATER-DOME POOL
2 ADMINISTRATION AND CUSTODIAN
3 MODEL THEATRE
4 LIBRARY AND SMALL CHAPEL
5 CHAPEL AUDITORIUM AND MINOR CHAPEL
6 STUDIOS ART EXHIBITION AND EXPOSITION
7 MUSIC STUDY AND PERFORANCE
8 MANUAL ARTS AND DOMESTICITY
9 NATURE STUDY UNIT
10 VARIOUS SEMINARS
11 CHILD CULTURE GROUP
12 OUTDOOR THEATRE
13 POOL AND BARGES
14 COURTS TERRACES ARBORS
15 SCULPTURE

DR LUDD M SPIVEY PRESIDENT
FRANK LLOYD WRIGHT ARCHITECT

MASTER PLAN FOR FLORIDA SOUTHERN COLLEGE, LAKELAND, FLORIDA. 1938. AERIAL PERSPECTIVE. PENCIL AND COLOR PENCIL ON TRACING PAPER, 47 × 23". FLLW FDN# 3805.002

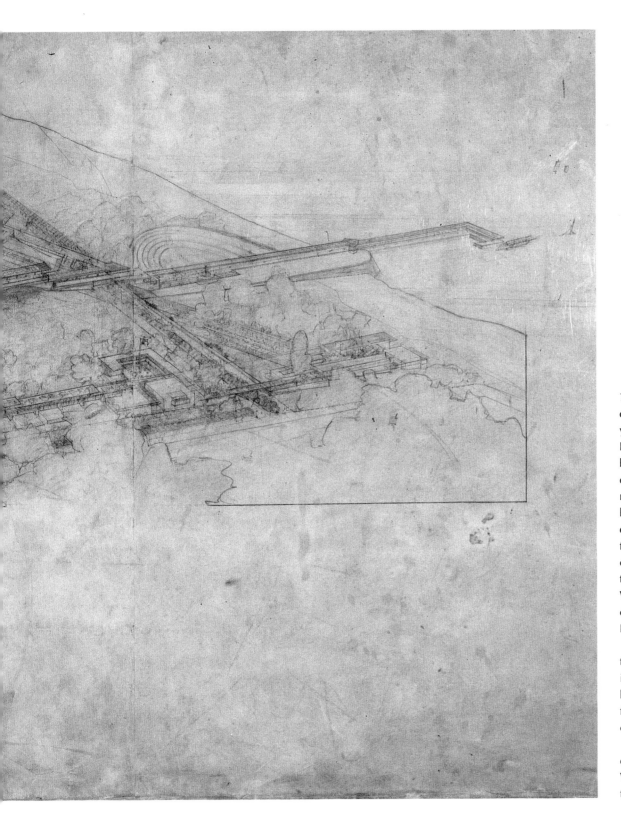

THIS AERIAL VIEW of the Florida Southern College campus projects an overall scheme that took many years to realize, with some buildings remaining unbuilt. In 1938 Wright's design for this campus was a radical break from the staid and steady academic tradition of college campuses in English Gothic, Georgian Colonial, or Classic Revival idioms. Here Wright has set the buildings in a Florida landscape of citrus groves on the edge of a lake and let them take their general character from the environs. All the buildings are connected by a covered esplanade as shelter against tropical rains in the winter and hot sun in late spring and summer. Wright often referred to this scheme as the truly American college, for the America of today rather than the Europe of yesterday.

The Pfeiffer Chapel, Minor Chapel, library, administration building, "various seminars," manual arts building (called "Industrial Arts"), and the water dome were built. Not listed on the master-plan perspective but in fact constructed was a building for the science and cosmography department.

The value of this drawing is greatly enhanced by the extensive amount of personal work done on it by Wright and also by the fact that the campus, as it stands today, has been neglected almost to the point of ruin.

THIS DESIGN, TO INCLUDE SHOPS as well as a bank, was proposed for the Valley National Bank in Sunnyslope, Arizona, a suburb of Phoenix. The sketch plan and elevation places the bank itself at the center, on a little park of its own, with shops flanking it on both sides. Vehicle circulation permits access to drive-in windows, and the angle of the shop wings permits parking space behind them. Like the "Daylight Bank" for Tucson (pages 228–229), this building is windowless on the ground level but lighted from a large clerestory window seen in the perspective as it faces a roof terrace. The materials were to be desert masonry—stones placed in wooden forms with concrete poured around them (the architect used this for his own home and studio at nearby Taliesin West).

The bank's president, Walter Bimson, was a close friend of Wright's, and throughout their association there were many projects on which they collaborated. Bimson, however, seemed beset with a certain conservatism that always, in the final analysis, prompted him to seek more traditional architects to design his buildings. Despite the disappointment of not having built a building for him—although he designed many—Wright held his banker friend in high esteem, and they remained friends throughout their lifetimes. Although not willing to subscribe to his architect's architecture, Bimson was steadily helpful in providing whatever financial assistance Wright needed to run his home and studio.

VALLEY NATIONAL BANK *(PROJECT),*

SUNNYSLOPE, ARIZONA. 1947. PERSPECTIVE.

PENCIL ON TRACING PAPER, 44 × 18". FLLW FDN# 4734.010

VALLEY NATIONAL BANK (PROJECT),
SUNNYSLOPE, ARIZONA. 1947. PLAN AND ELEVATION.
PENCIL AND COLOR PENCIL ON TRACING PAPER,
38 × 33". FLLW FDN# 4734.001

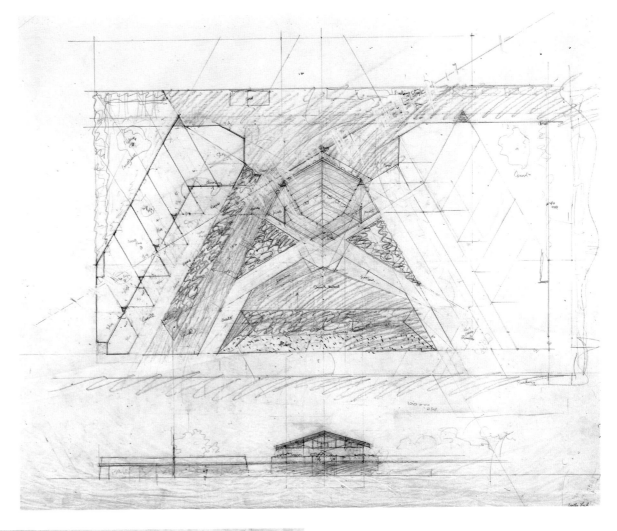

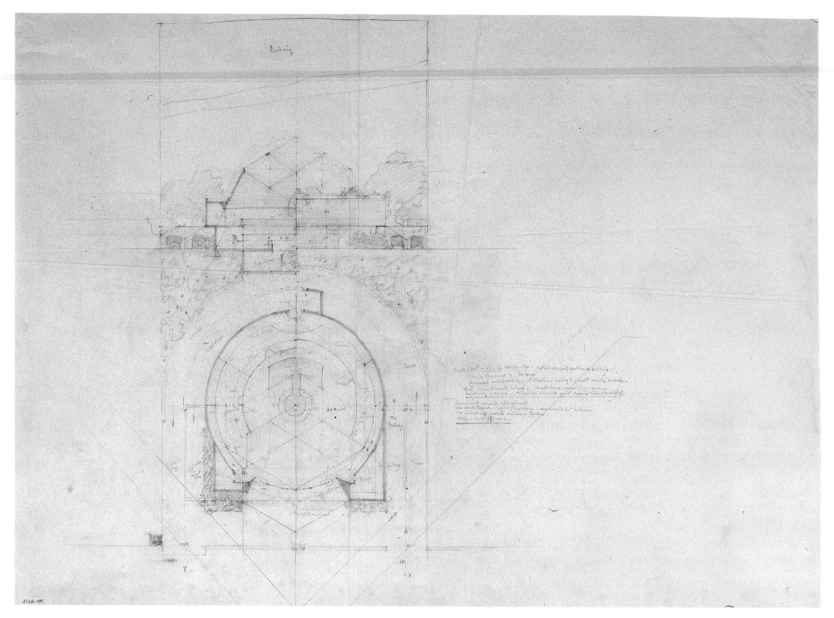

"DAYLIGHT BANK" FOR VALLEY NATIONAL BANK (*PROJECT*), TUCSON, ARIZONA. 1947. PLAN AND ELEVATION.
PENCIL AND COLOR PENCIL ON TRACING PAPER, 39 × 27". FLLW FDN# 4722.001

THIS DRAWING IS A FINE EXAMPLE of one of Wright's conceptual studies, showing a plan and elevation with explanatory notes on the side. The notes for this "Daylight Bank," as Wright called it, describe in detail aspects of the project that the drawing omits:

Bank—Unit 1—for 100' frontage. Outside deposit system on 2 levels. May be decreased to 75'-0 or increased indefinitely. Alterations owing to growth easily made. Safe-deposit vault below—Vault door seen from main banking room. Structure simple and easily standardized. Reinforced concrete throughout. Air-conditioned—double glass dome—air circulated between. No windows except entrance feature. Airy—light—secure.

An open well on the main floor looks onto the lower level, where the bank vault is located. A mezzanine level is arranged with further offices. Both the ground-floor level and the mezzanine level have provisions for drive-in windows; an access ramp allows vehicles to reach the upper level. This idea of Wright's for a drive-in window was highly controversial at the time; officials of the bank thought it an unnecessary added expense. The architect maintained that it would be a most necessary provision. Working drawings were made for the pro-

ject, but the modern aspects of the design seemed to frighten the "authorities," and the project was eventually dropped.

The perspective shows the ramp that wraps around the rear of the building and rises to the second level. The architect's concluding note, "Airy—light—secure," can be explained by this perspective: light comes in from the top, mainly, through an insulated double-glass, or plastic, dome with panels of copper as well. The rest of the building is windowless, except for the glass doors at the front. It forms another one of those "strongboxes," as Wright regarded his bank designs, but it is much more liberated than the earlier ones.

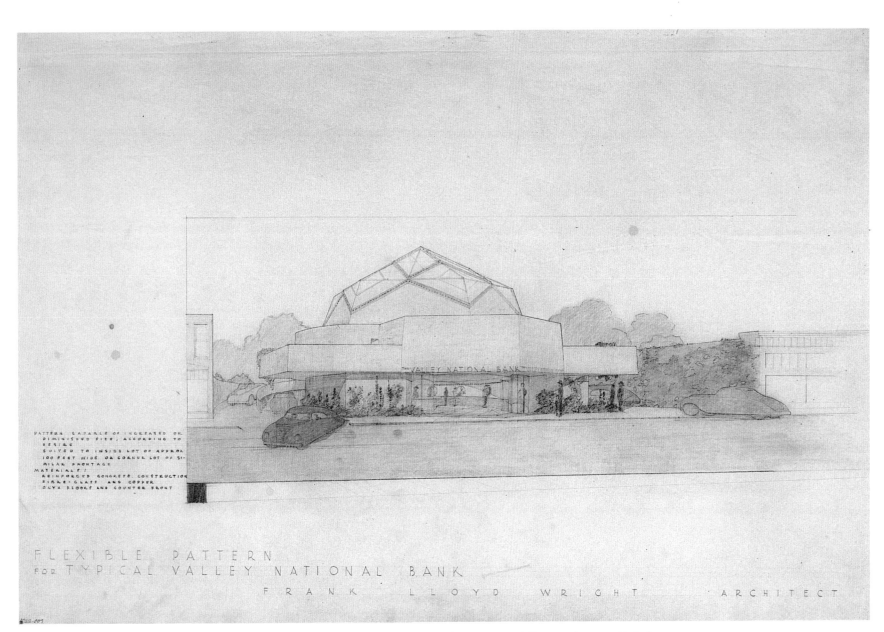

PATTERN CAPABLE OF INCREASED OR
DIMINISHED SIZE, ACCORDING TO
DESIRE
SUITED TO INSIDE LOT OF APPROX.
100 FEET WIDE OR CORNER LOT OF SI-
MILAR FRONTAGE
MATERIALS:
REINFORCED CONCRETE CONSTRUCTION
PIREX-GLASS AND COPPER
ONYX BLOCKS AND COUNTER FRONT

THE VALLEY NATIONAL BANK

FLEXIBLE PATTERN
FOR TYPICAL VALLEY NATIONAL BANK
FRANK LLOYD WRIGHT ARCHITECT

''DAYLIGHT BANK'' FOR VALLEY NATIONAL BANK *(PROJECT), TUCSON, ARIZONA. 1947. PERSPECTIVE.*

PENCIL AND COLOR PENCIL ON TRACING PAPER, 39 × 26''. FLLW FDN# 4722.007

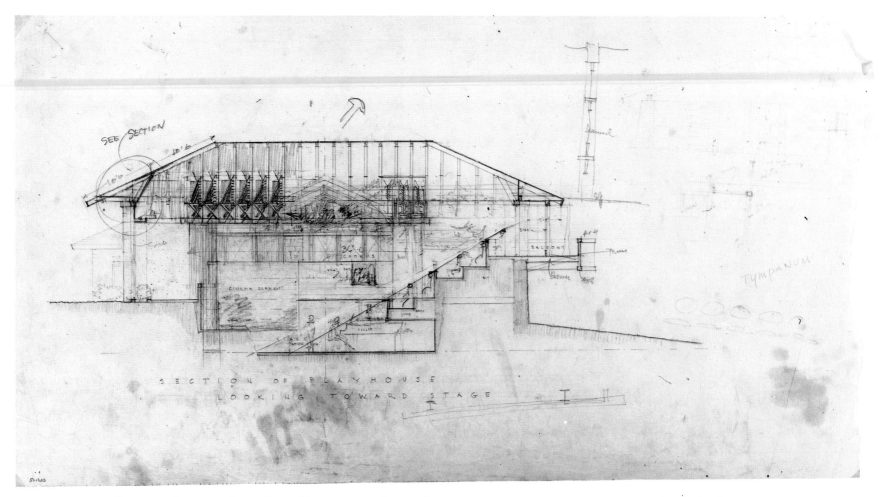

IN THE SPRING OF 1952 Wright was clearing away leaves and brush at the Hillside Home School and setting fire to the assembled piles of branches and foliage. A wind swept the flames up against the main building and under the roof overhang. Within moments, the wing containing classrooms, dining room, and theater was in flames. Most of the apprentices were still in Arizona; there was only a small group with the Wrights who had made the advance trip north to open the buildings for the summer season. As the fire raged through the theater and dining room, consuming a weaving gallery and seven classrooms as well, Wright and the apprentices went into the nearby drafting room

and dragged approximately nineteen thousand of his original drawings onto the lawn outside, the record of his entire life's work up to that time. Fortunately the fire was stopped at the large living room and did not spread to the other galleries or drafting room.

The fire demolished the theater roof and interior but left the massive sandstone walls intact. In rebuilding the school, Wright decided to change the angle of the seating and lower the stage area and the roof line. On this conceptual section he has drawn a decorative pattern to be made out of plywood and inserted in between the roof beams. Although this particular pattern was not effected, a similar design was used instead as a folding

screen between the dining room and the theater. The various sketches within the drawing are views in various directions: the drawing is like a memo by the architect to himself, a jotting down of thoughts that later on he would develop on other drawings. Many of the actual construction details he solved in the process of building the building itself. He came in each day and supervised the work carried on by his apprentices. (The theater curtain, which he designed especially to replace the one that was burned, is also illustrated in this volume; page 293).

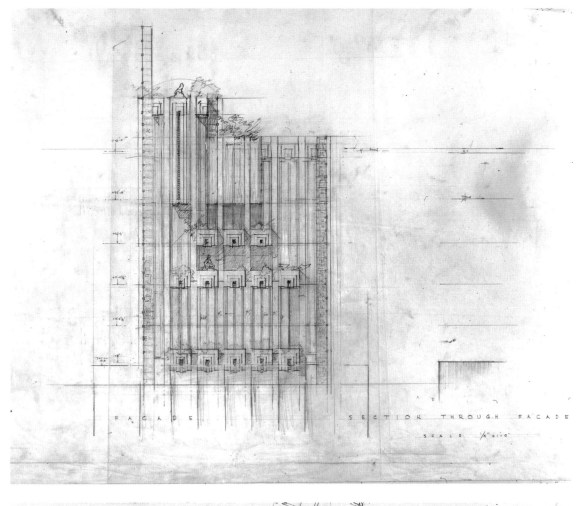

F A C A D E   S E C T I O N   T H R O U G H   F A C A D E

SCALE ⅛"=1'-0"

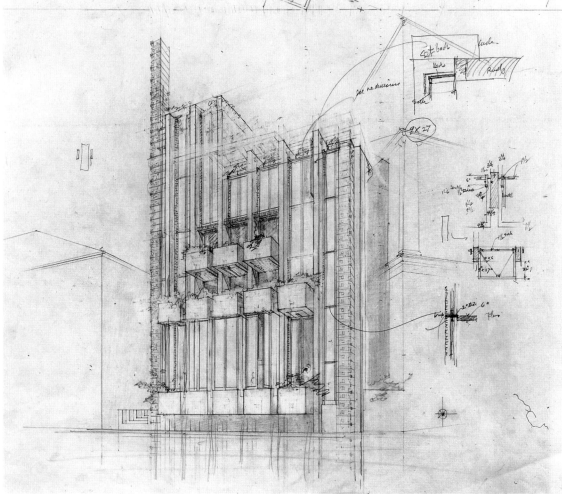

IN 1952 ANGELO MASIERI, a young Italian architect, visited the United States with the express desire to meet Frank Lloyd Wright. After the meeting, Masieri was killed in an automobile accident returning from Wisconsin to the East Coast. His wife and family wished to memorialize him in some manner and wrote to Wright asking if he would design a pensione domicile for architectural students at the university in Venice. The final perspective prepared by Wright for the project has been widely published, but these two drawings, published here for the first time, record Wright's early thinking on the work. The site was a triangular-shaped lot on the Grand Canal, near the Palazzo Rezzonico. Concrete piles, driven into the mud beneath the waters, were to rise and hold the marble-faced concrete piers that carry all floor slabs, likewise of reinforced concrete. On either side of the elevation are running bands of bronze and glass light features. Bedrooms, a library, and a living room open onto projecting balconies overlooking the canal. The library, which was to serve also as the main social gathering room, is open to all three levels; a little belvedere at the top opens onto a roof garden. Essentially Venetian in character, with its delicate scale, its use of marble facing on balconies overlooking the canal, and its slender bronze lighting poles, the memorial was also to be a well-built twentieth-century building respecting its city's character. However, British and American tourist bureaus did not see it that way; they resented the thought of a modern building on the Grand Canal and prevented the scheme from getting built. Ernest Hemingway also sent word that it would be better if Venice burned to the ground than have a Frank Lloyd Wright building on its famous main waterway. To which Wright replied, "Just a voice from the jungle!"

MASIERI MEMORIAL BUILDING (PROJECT),

VENICE, ITALY. 1953. ELEVATION.

PENCIL ON TRACING PAPER, 36 × 26".

FLLW FDN# 5306.009

MASIERI MEMORIAL BUILDING (PROJECT),

VENICE, ITALY. 1953. PERSPECTIVE.

PENCIL ON TRACING PAPER, 36 × 27".

FLLW FDN# 5306.020

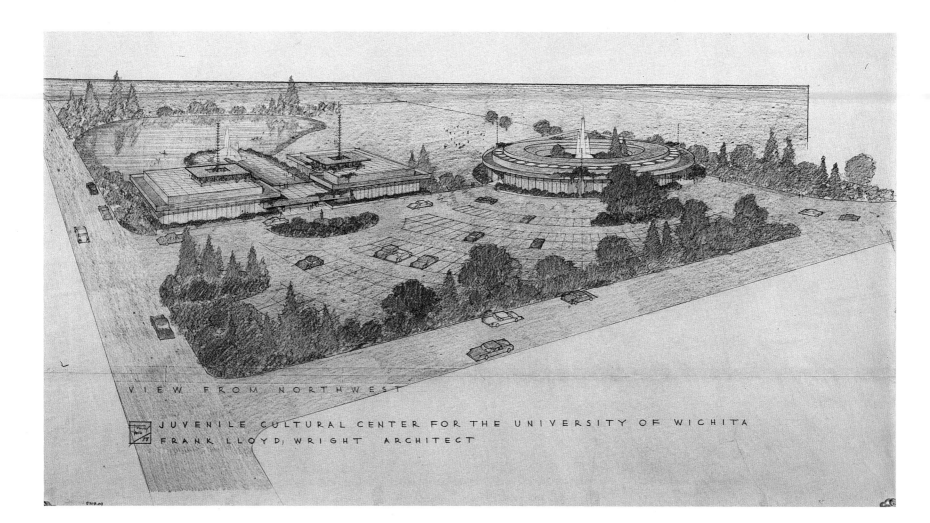

VIEW FROM NORTHWEST

JUVENILE CULTURAL CENTER FOR THE UNIVERSITY OF WICHITA
FRANK LLOYD WRIGHT ARCHITECT

OF THE TWO BUILDINGS designed for this educational center, the square building on the left of the aerial view was built; the circular one remains unexecuted. The commission came in 1958, a year before Wright died, and the working drawings for both buildings, as well as the supervision of the one that was constructed, were carried out by his apprentices following his death. The building, as built, is constructed out of brick and reinforced concrete, the workmanship excellent, the general breadth of the scheme elegant.

Consistent with the character of most of Wright's later work, a general simplicity prevails. This simplicity is something he prophesied exactly half a century before this building was designed, when he wrote, "As for the future—the work shall grow more truly simple; more expressive with fewer lines, fewer forms; more articulate with less labor; more plastic; more fluent, although more coherent; more organic."

JUVENILE CULTURAL CENTER FOR THE
UNIVERSITY OF WICHITA, *WICHITA, KANSAS. 1958.*
PERSPECTIVE. PENCIL AND COLOR PENCIL ON TRACING PAPER,
42 × 28". FLLW FDN# 5708.004

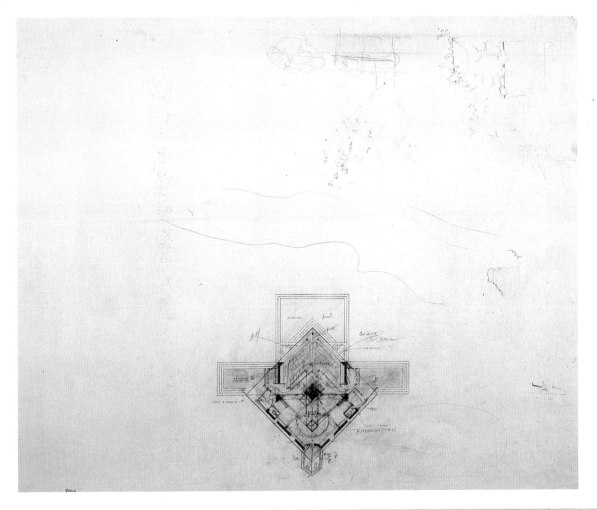

WYOMING VALLEY IS ADJACENT to Taliesin in Wisconsin. For the design for a two-room schoolhouse there, Wright took his earlier scheme for the Kindersymphonies (page 216) and revised the plan. The new school's requirements demanded a larger plan than the Kindersymphonies, and Wright expanded the scheme accordingly. This is, therefore, another instance where an unrealized earlier project was able to be redesigned and applied to a later situation. The perspective shows the building constructed out of native Wisconsin limestone, but the material used was standard concrete block. Two large classrooms, an assembly room, bathrooms, and kitchens complete the scheme.

WYOMING VALLEY SCHOOL,
WYOMING VALLEY, WISCONSIN. 1956. PLAN.
PENCIL AND COLOR PENCIL ON TRACING PAPER, 35 × 28".
FLLW FDN# 5741.001

WYOMING VALLEY SCHOOL,
WYOMING VALLEY, WISCONSIN. 1956. PERSPECTIVE.
PENCIL AND COLOR PENCIL ON TRACING PAPER, 35 × 27".
FLLW FDN# 5741.003

VIEW FROM SOUTHEAST

WYOMING VALLEY SCHOOLHOUSE
FRANK LLOYD WRIGHT ARCHITECT

BAGHDAD UNIVERSITY *(PROJECT)*,

BAGHDAD, IRAQ. 1957. AERIAL PERSPECTIVE.

PENCIL AND COLOR PENCIL ON TRACING PAPER, 71 × 34".

FLLW FDN# 5759.006

AERIAL VIEW OF THE UNIVERSITY   AT HEIGHT OF 300 FEET
PLAN FOR GREATER BAGHDAD
DEDICATED TO SUMERIA, ISIN, LARSA AND BABYLON
FRANK LLOYD WRIGHT   ARCHITECT

ON THE SAME ISLAND IN BAGHDAD that was to hold the opera (page 160), two museums, and a monument to Haroun-al-Rashid (page 163), Wright proposed this solution for the grand bazaar—the Middle East's version of the shopping mall. The drawing that shows the art museum (page 165) contains also a minuscule sketch elevation and plan from which this presentation rendering was made. The skill and expertise that Wright diligently invested in his apprentices paid off in their ability to take his small sketches and develop them according to his original idea. This plan, elevation, and section is a fine example of that process. The little kiosks are domes of reinforced concrete balanced along a continuous support wall. Each dome provides shelter for the quasi-outdoor market space, with a storage loft inside the dome itself. When the bazaar is open, temporary tables are set up under the dome and outside, in keeping with the regional tradition of putting goods and merchandise on view for sale. At night, when the shops are closed, the tables and merchandise are hauled into the storage loft located within the dome.

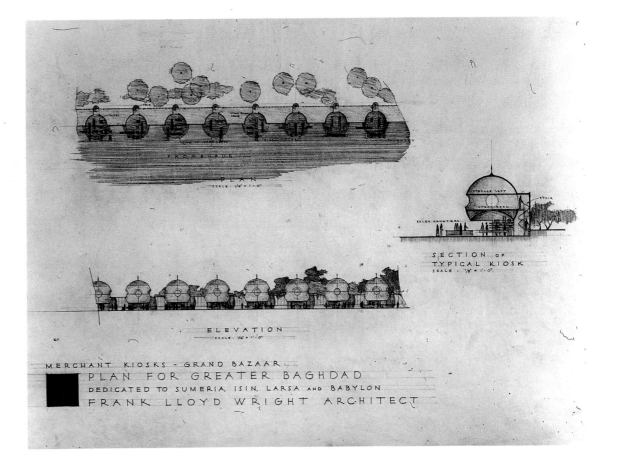

KIOSKS (PROJECT), BAGHDAD, IRAQ. 1957.
PLAN, SECTION, AND ELEVATION. PENCIL AND
COLOR PENCIL ON TRACING PAPER, 36 × 23".
FLLW FDN# 5750.003

SPEAKING ABOUT HIS DESIGN for Baghdad University Wright noted:

Here, the ziggurat is the generic form for parking the entire traffic of the various buildings of the university. The campus itself is thus free of cars with entrances easily available from each level by way of multilevel courts in the various department buildings which are placed at the inner circumference (curriculum) of the ziggurat. As a matter of course, as many buildings as are necessary could join the curriculum.

On the far right edge of the drawing, the opera and the Park of Edena can be detected (page 162). The tall spires are for television transmission. The large circumference of the outer ziggurat provides the necessary flexibility and space for future expansion. The open space within the circle is reserved for green parks, fountains, and gardens.

The buildings as shown on the perspective are widely spaced, allowing for at least two or three more structures in between each one—planning for, in other words, a 300-percent expansion, if needed.

PART SEVEN

ARCHITECTURE AND ENGINEERING

WORKS FROM SEVERAL DIFFERENT CATEGORIES of architecture and design—none in itself large enough to constitute an entire section of Wright's output—are grouped together here. Included are a laundry, a mortuary, a parking garage, a service station, an airplane hangar, an embassy for the United States Department of State, a prefabricated farmhouse, two large office buildings, and an electronics factory. There are also studios for a sculptor, a painter, and two offices for Wright himself, one in Fiesole, near Florence, Italy, the other in Chicago. Four bridge designs show how Wright's ideas for bridge engineering progressed from a simple, rural bridge for Glencoe, Illinois, executed in 1915, to a great reinforced structure for San Francisco in 1949 that utilized the longest and highest single span yet conceived. The section culminates with Wright's design of 1958 for "The Living City" (a revision of his early plan for Broadacre City), made for the 1958 book of the same title. Along with his vision of an American city integrated into the landscape are designs for helicopters, cars (which he called "road machines"), and a railroad train for the future. The variety emphasizes the flexibility of Wright's imagination and his constant ability to respond to challenges.

THE LARKIN BUILDING was a "first" in many ways: it was the first air-conditioned office building; the first to use plate-glass doors swinging on pintle hinges set into the floor rather than on the jamb at the side; the first office to have all steel sheet-metal furniture (specially designed by Wright and made by the Van Dorn Company in Cleveland); and the first building to use the wall-hung water closet and wall-hung toilet partition, facilitating the cleaning of the toilets. The main offices were on the ground floor in a great atrium; all other offices were on the six balconies on the building's sides,

overlooking the court. The top level contained a restaurant and conservatory. The roof deck above was a squash court. All managers and employees of this mail-order company worked in one great space, with private consultation rooms for use when needed. The dominant impression created by the architecture was of one large family working harmoniously together in a thoroughly modern, functional, and beautiful environment.

No sooner was the building built in 1906 than it received great acclaim, first in Europe, as heralding the advent of modern office planning. Wright called his

approach "The affirmative negation," meaning new, clean lines in architecture had replaced dated and senseless applied ornament. On another drawing of the building he later wrote, "The Grammar of the Protestant," once more pointing out the simplicity of forms, the utilitarian aspects of the building and the ability of architecture to inspire those working within. In 1950 the building was torn down to make way for a parking lot.

Wright's variety of perspective drawing plays a strong and evident role in this chapter, from the rather formalized "framing" of the Larkin perspective here to

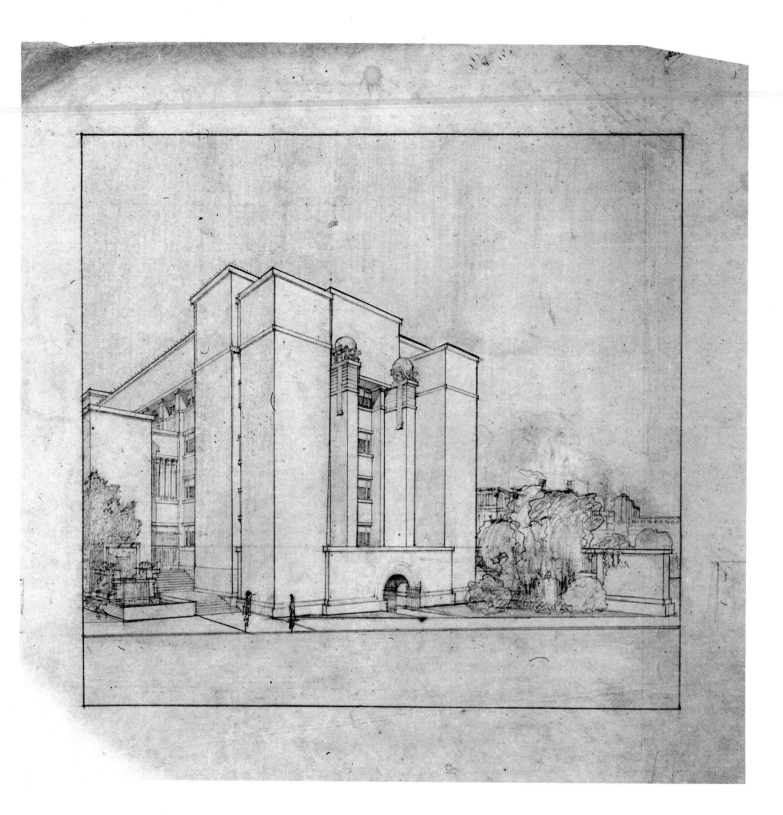

the whimsical sweep of clouds and air trails in the airplane hangar of 1958 (page 264). Even with the double ink line that contains another Larkin view (page 237), an unexpected effect takes place. The view shows only the lower part of the office structure; before its lines reach the edge of the border, a notanlike cloud engulfs the building. This "notan" was a typical device used in most of the scenic prints of Hiroshige, usually in the form of a band along the top edge of the print designating the time of day (blue for midday, rose or yellow for sunset or sundown, black for stormy condi-

tions or night). In the Larkin drawing the cloud obscures the termination of the building's lines against the constriction of the frame. It is an odd drawing; one wonders what Wright was trying to demonstrate by it. Perhaps he was emphasizing the separation of the entryway and annex, on the right, from the main structure itself on the left.

LARKIN COMPANY ADMINISTRATION BUILDING, *BUFFALO, NEW YORK (DEMOLISHED). 1903. PERSPECTIVE. PENCIL ON TRACING PAPER, 23 × 17".* FLLW FDN# 0403.022

RICHARD BOCK, a Chicago sculptor, was a friend of Wright's. The architect employed him several times to make sculpted ornaments for his buildings. In 1906 Wright designed this studio residence for him. The front part of the studio contained a living and dining space as well as a bedroom and bath; behind was a large two-story workroom. The drawing shown here was rendered by Marion Mahony, one of Wright's most skilled draftsmen in the Oak Park studio; there she met and fell in love with another draftsman, Walter Burley Griffin. They both eventually left the studio, were married in June 1911, and established their own architectural practice.

The studio for Bock was never built, but many years later—sometime in the 1950s—Wright took out the working drawings and converted the large studio at the rear into three bedrooms. Why this latter-day change was done is not recorded in the archives.

As the drawing reveals, Mahony delighted in featuring blossoms and leaves. The influence of the Japanese print can be seen in her style, which prompted Wright to note on one of her drawings, "Drawn by Mahony—after FLLW and Hiroshige."

RICHARD BOCK STUDIO (PROJECT), MAYWOOD, ILLINOIS. 1906. PERSPECTIVE. INK ON TRACING PAPER, 23 × 12". FLLW FDN# 0612.001

WHILE LIVING IN FIESOLE, near Florence, in 1910 to prepare the plates for the Wasmuth portfolio of his work, Wright made this study for a residence for himself and his companion Mamah Borthwick Cheney. On the upper left his lettering reads, "Studio for the Architect. Florentine study—Florence 1910." And below, in barely perceptible script, he has written, "Florence—Italy, Via Verdi—Madame Illingworth—1910. Feb."

In keeping with the traditional planning of the Italian region, the studio-residence is built along a high garden wall facing the street. There is a small entrance at the left. At one point in the plan the building juts out and engages the garden wall. There Wright has included a sculptural frieze in the upper level. The rest of the building is set back from the wall, letting gardens and lawn surround it, and secluded from street noises and pedestrians.

Wright returned to the United States in 1911. The little studio-residence was never built, but in 1956, for a client in Cuernavaca, Mexico, he revised the project, which seemed appropriate to the Mexican setting. That revision, also, was not built.

FRANK LLOYD WRIGHT RESIDENCE AND STUDIO (PROJECT), FIESOLE, ITALY. 1910. PERSPECTIVE. PENCIL AND COLOR PENCIL ON TRACING PAPER, 28 × 11". FLLW FDN# 1005.001

ON HIS RETURN from Italy in 1911, Wright elected to live in Chicago, having closed his Oak Park studio and separated from his wife, Catherine. (One of the first things he did on his return was to remodel the Oak Park studio and home into three apartments, so Catherine could derive an income by renting them.) The studio-residence he designed for himself on Goethe Street was a large and expansive structure, both a home and an office. There is another, more widely published view of this same building, but the one chosen for publication here is a drawing entirely by Wright. As the view suggests, the building is a tall, narrow townhouse set between other buildings, with a small garden at the entry to the reception area. Inside, three levels are grouped around an open hall, or well, with many variations in the split-levels. Above the open hall is a roof garden.

The plan proved far too expensive, and the project was abandoned. At the same time, Wright was building a hilltop house for his mother in Wisconsin; she saw his plight of having no place to work and live and encouraged him to take over her house for himself and Mrs. Cheney. He accepted the offer and named the house "Taliesin," the Welsh word meaning "shining brow."

FOR THE 1931 CATALOG of his European exhibition, Wright captioned this drawing with the simple statement, "Study for combining all functions of government in a foreign country." This type of embassy building, of 1914, hardly meets the requirements for an embassy today, which needs to be a veritable fortress unto itself. But in these different times, while Wright was living and working in Tokyo on the Imperial Hotel, an embassy's needs were far simpler. Although used for official purposes, the structure is treated more like a residence, which indeed it was for the ambassador and his family. Spread out among trees and gardens, the embassy is designed in the idiom of Wright's later prairie houses.

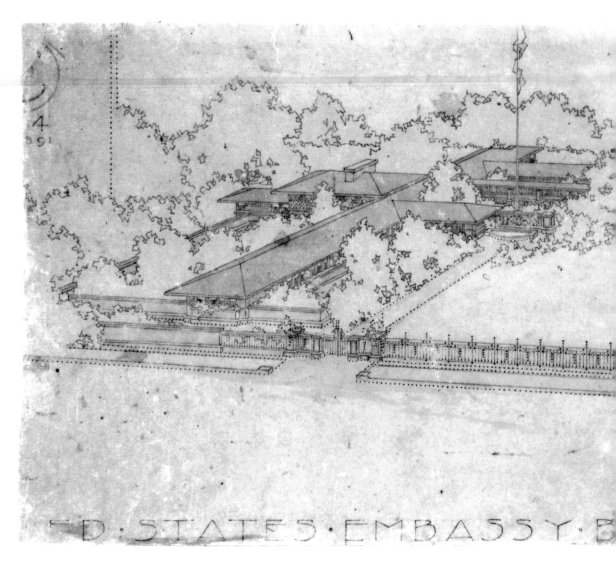

UNITED STATES EMBASSY BUILDING (PROJECT),

TOKYO, JAPAN. 1914. AERIAL PERSPECTIVE.

WATERCOLOR AND WATERCOLOR WASH ON ART PAPER,

31 × 10". FLLW FDN# 1406.007

RAVINE BLUFFS was the name of a housing project designed by Wright and built by Sherman Booth, a lawyer and friend of Wright's involved in land speculation and development. For the same woodland glen Wright had designed a house for Booth, but it was never built.

This drawing, watercolor and gouache on heavy art paper, is not by Wright, but of all the "painting-drawings" in the collection it is among the loveliest: the details of the white concrete bridge glisten in the semi-darkness of the forest, and the flowers and foliage are quietly subdued — as if stunned by the pristine architectural intrusion in their midst.

RAVINE BLUFFS BRIDGE, GLENCOE, ILLINOIS. 1915.

PERSPECTIVE. WATERCOLOR AND WATERCOLOR WASH

ON ART PAPER, 24 × 18". FLLW FDN# 1505.001

LD'NG · FRANK · LLOYD · WRIGHT : ARHIT

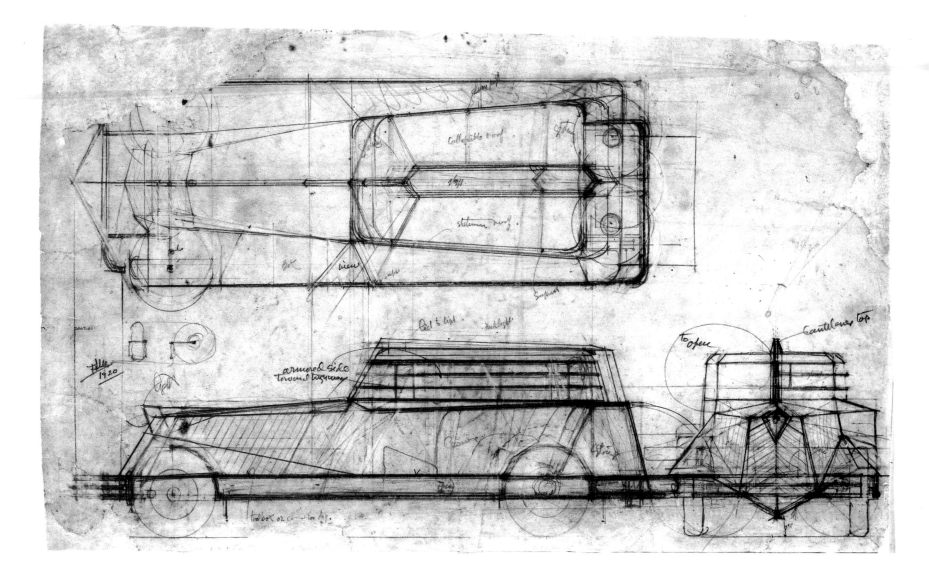

WRIGHT LOVED AUTOMOBILES. In fact, they were one of his passions. Regardless of the condition of his personal finances, he always drove marvelous cars. At various times he owned a Cord, a Cadillac, a Lincoln Zephyr, an Acedes, a Riley, a Jaguar (he had three of them in his life), a Mercedes, and a Bentley. He was always striving to find that sense of design that seemed most appropriate to a moving vehicle. He regarded the great mass of American car designs as infinitely inferior to the European designs, as witnessed by his preference for German and English cars. In Paris, in 1956, he saw the new model of the Citröen Pallas DS 19, which was not available for export at the time. He admired the design and the engineering, and if he could have, he would have taken one home with him.

Here we see his design for a car he called an "Automobile with a cantilevered top." Part of the roof, divided down the center from front to back, was to open (Wright enjoyed convertibles), but the driver's portion was fixed. Notes on the drawing, somewhat enigmatic and quite startling, reveal his thinking on the project: "Armored side toward highway"; "Lid to lift"; "backlight"; and the most startling, "Cantilever top." The driver's side is shielded by metal louvers to afford full view but to shield him from the sun's rays.

AUTOMOBILE WITH CANTILEVERED TOP *(PROJECT)*.
PENCIL AND COLOR PENCIL ON TRACING PAPER, 27 × 16".
FLLW FDN# 2001.001

FRANK LLOYD WRIGHT had an intrinsic respect for farming that dated from his early childhood, when his mother, considering him a dreamer, trimmed his long, blond curly hair and sent him to work during the summers on her brothers' farms in southern Wisconsin. It was a hard decision for her to make; she cherished the thought that her young boy was going to be a great architect (a plan she had made before he was born). But as he grew, and as she watched him sitting by the shores of the Wisconsin River drawing designs in the sand with a twig in his hand, she knew, instinctively, that he needed the force and mettle that hard farm work would give him. She was, herself, brought up on a farm in her father's ancestral valley, near Spring Green, Wisconsin.

The lessons Wright learned on the farm never left him. He established a farm of his own at Taliesin, and it played an integral part in the life of the Taliesin Fellowship. He regretted to see the American nation turn from an agrarian nation to an industrial one; he had faith, however, that the country would eventually reconsider the importance of its agrarian roots. "Agronomy," he wrote in 1945, "the equal of industrialism or superior, is the gifted source of our national culture—even now—if you take a fair view at our country. As the natural agronomy we are describing proceeds, there will be a new farmer and his family in Broadacres. He will, by intensive methods, gradually take the place of the 'dirt' farmer and his family of pioneer days."

In 1932 Wright made designs for what he called the "Prefabricated Farm Unit," or the "Unified Farm," to be built entirely of sheet metal and assembled on the site. Wright's intention was to replace a typical farm's arbitrarily scattered buildings and sheds with facilities organized under one roof (particularly helpful in inclement weather). As he wrote:

This composite farm-building would be made up of assembled prefabricated units. Shelter for cars, a comfortable dwelling, greenhouse, a packing and distributing place, a silo (narrow and tall or short and wide), stables for cows and horses, and diversified animal shed for sheep, pigs, etc. The whole establishment would be good architecture. Good to look at. Emancipation for the life of the farmer. As such the whole farm-unit could well be delivered to the farmers at low cost by machine production intelligently expanded and standardized.

PREFAB FARM UNIT (PROJECT). 1932.
AERIAL PERSPECTIVE. PENCIL AND
COLOR PENCIL ON TRACING PAPER, 26 × 13".
FLLW FDN# 3202.008

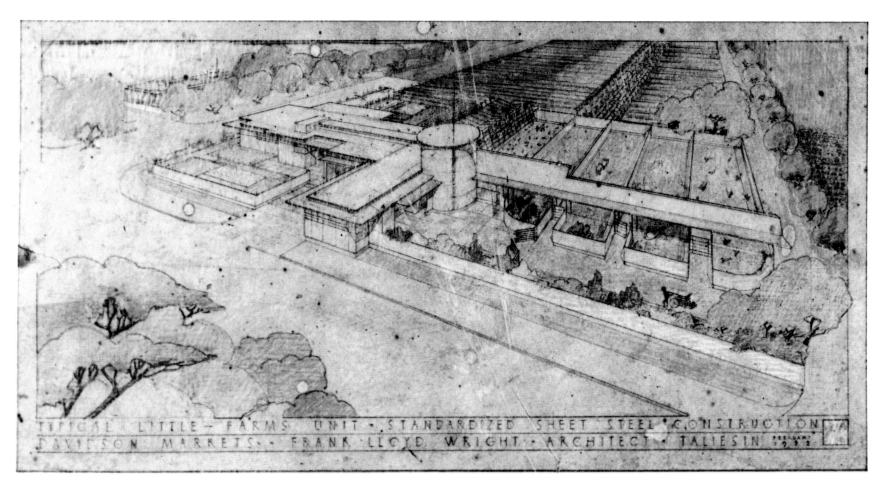

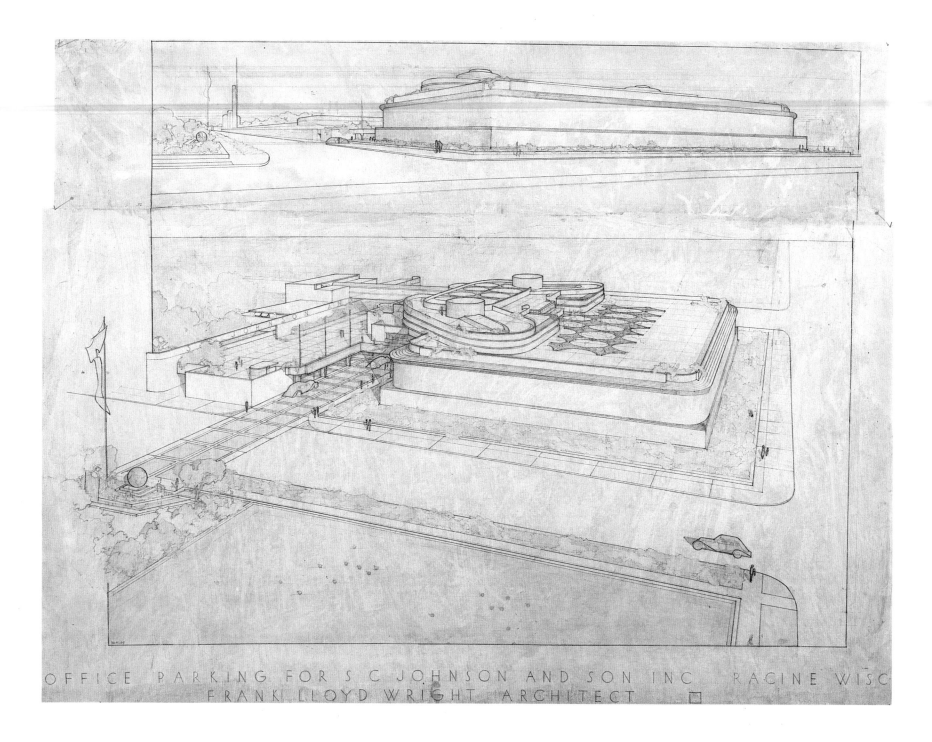

OFFICE PARKING FOR S C JOHNSON AND SON INC RACINE WISC
FRANK LLOYD WRIGHT ARCHITECT

S. C. JOHNSON & SON, INC.

ADMINISTRATION BUILDING,

RACINE, WISCONSIN. 1936. PERSPECTIVES.

PENCIL AND INK ON TRACING PAPER,

40 × 29". FLLW FDN# 3601.002–003

FOR THE JOHNSON WAX COMPANY'S office building, two perspectives were made. One is a ground view, as though the viewer were standing across the street from the building. The other is an aerial view, showing the overall building and its relation to the city block and entrance drive. But the views were later attached together to make a single drawing. We know the two drawings must have been made separately because the title on the lower drawing bears no relationship to the upper drawing. The way in which the two have been joined is most intriguing: the border lines of the upper drawing are interrupted, as was often the case in Wright's perspectives, by the city street in front, but only to continue below to become the upper border for the lower drawing, whose left-hand edge terminates in the flag pendant. This treatment is not

Hiroshige-inspired, as many of Wright's devices were, but rather is an invention of Wright himself that occurs frequently in drawings after 1936.

In the midst of an industrial zone, Wright achieved in this building what he had previously achieved in the Larkin building (page 237): he created a sealed environment with light coming in from above, instead of a building where windows looked out onto an unpleasant factoryscape. He often compared the two buildings, saying the Johnson opus was the feminine counterpart to the more masculine Larkin one. The beneficent effect of working in a large spacious toplit room was immediate on the employees: they grew to love their building. Johnson himself noted that "people I tried to get to come and work for me before the building was opened now came of their own accord and asked for jobs." The

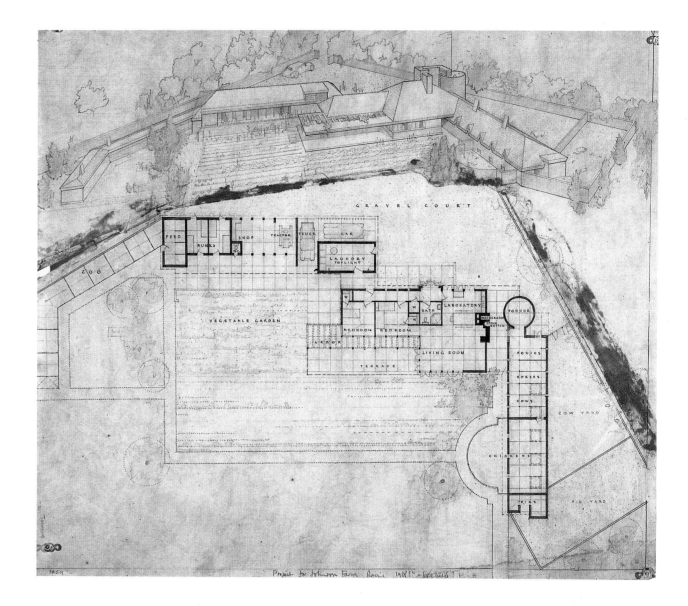

FARM UNIT FOR H. F. JOHNSON *(PROJECT),*
WIND POINT, WISCONSIN. 1938. PERSPECTIVE AND PLAN.
PENCIL ON TRACING PAPER, 28 × 24".
FLLW FDN# 3815.001

streamlined atmosphere of the work area made the spaces within clean and light, without being cold or impersonal. In contrast to the usual dingy gray or bilious green, the interiors were a soft rust red and the columns shimmering white with the glistening skylights above.

The building itself became famous the moment it opened in 1939. Wright commented on its celebrity:

When the building was opened the world seemed to have been waiting for the event because it was there outside trying to get in to see it. When finally it did get in, reams of newspaper copy began to pour from the press, and such talk! Everyone who saw the building tried to describe it, "It is like a woman swimming naked in a stream. Cool, gliding, musical in movement and in manner.". . . Meanwhile the stream of

visitors from all over the world went on and continues to go on to this hour. Why? Because of something in the universal air, that's why. It was high time to give to our hungry American public something truly "streamlined," so swift, sure of itself and clean for its purpose, clean as a hound's tooth—that anybody could see the virtue of this thing called Modern. Many liked it because it was not "modernistic," but seemed to them like the original from which all the "streamlining" they had ever seen might have come in the first place.

The architect's intention was that it be "as inspiring a place to work in as any cathedral was in which to worship."

THIS FARM BUILDING for Herbert F. Johnson, president of the Johnson Wax Company, was designed as an adjunct to his private estate near Racine, Wisconsin. The main house, called "Wingspread" (page 46), was built by Wright the year that this farm design was made, and many of the construction materials and details that applied to the main house were to be incorporated here: the fine brickwork, the walls capped with white sandstone, the hipped roofs and trellises. The farmer's living quarters are placed in the central part of the plan, with the farm animals' pens in one wing near the silo, and the laundry, workshops, and garages in the other. The L-shaped building looks onto a vegetable garden; the rear side contains runs and yards for the animals, bordered by a brick wall—in keeping with the type of brick construction at the main house beyond.

THIS WAS A SMALL STUDIO dwelling designed
for an artist who wished to live and work in solitude on
the New Jersey coast. The entire structure, except for
the poured-concrete supports and chimney mass, is of
wood siding, with lapped boards extending on a sloped
line and mitering at the corners. The studio is indeed the
absolute symbiosis of carpentry-built design, explicitly
expressing its materials, construction, and details.

The lower level contains a carport under the projecting balcony and a "private" area with kitchen, dining,
and sleeping rooms. The upper level is entitled, simply,
"Franklin Watkins Studio." At one end of the room, tall
windows face north and open onto a balcony; a seat
nestles around the fireplace hearth at the other end.

"WINDSWEPT," FRANKLIN WATKINS
STUDIO (PROJECT), BARNEGAT CITY, NEW JERSEY. 1940.
PERSPECTIVE. PENCIL AND COLOR PENCIL ON
TRACING PAPER, 36 × 18". FLLW FDN# 4021.006

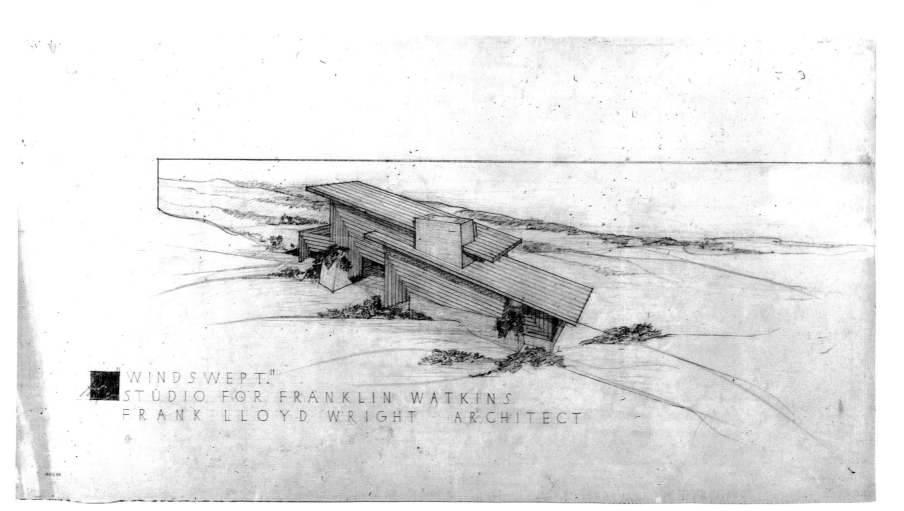

GARAGE AND RESTAURANT
FOR GLENN AND RUTH RICHARDSON

FRANK LLOYD WRIGHT ARCHITECT

GARAGE AND RESTAURANT FOR
GLENN AND RUTH RICHARDSON (PROJECT),
SPRING GREEN, WISCONSIN. 1943. PERSPECTIVE.
PENCIL AND COLOR PENCIL ON TRACING PAPER, 36 × 19".
FLLW FDN# 4306.003

GLENN AND RUTH RICHARDSON were
friends of Wright's who lived in nearby Spring Green,
Wisconsin. They owned and operated a Pontiac service
station in the town and performed most of the servicing
on the Taliesin Fellowship vehicles, even those owned
by the students. At one point they considered buying
the property bordering Taliesin. This design was what
Wright proposed they build. It contained a small restaurant overlooking the Wisconsin River and a service
station as well. The second level was to be their residence. The project was never realized, but the drawing
of the building and its relationship to the hills above is
an especially fine example of architecture integrated
into the landscape.

(OVERLEAF: GARAGE AND RESTAURANT FOR
GLENN AND RUTH RICHARDSON.
PERSPECTIVE; DETAIL)

251

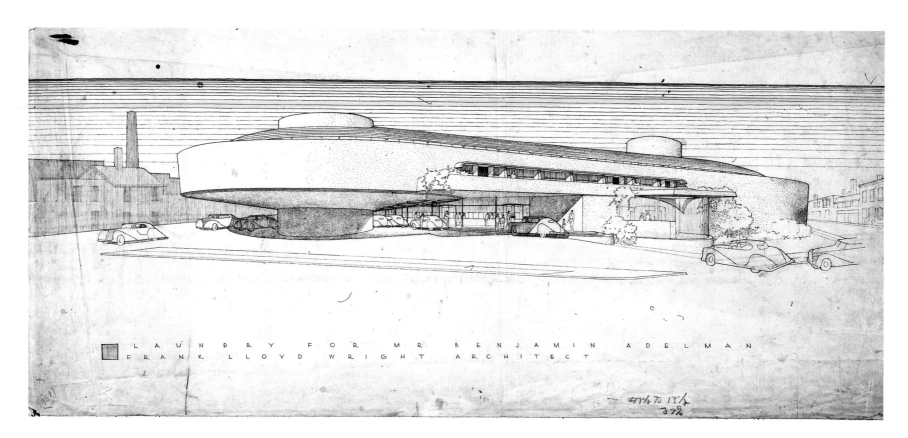

ADELMAN LAUNDRY (PROJECT),
MILWAUKEE, WISCONSIN. 1945. PERSPECTIVE.
SEPIA INK ON TRACING PAPER, 55 × 25".
FLLW FDN# 4507.001

BOTH PERSPECTIVES for the Adelman Laundry, its exterior and its interior, are done in sepia with occasional touches of black ink. No coloring whatsoever has been added, and only a few strokes of graphite pencil were used to create shadows in the foreground of the interior view. In general, the shading required to make the perspectives read more accurately has been achieved by the spacing of the ink dots: closer together for shade, further apart for more light.

The building was intended to be a thoroughly modern dry-cleaning and laundry establishment for Milwaukee, Wisconsin, with provisions for drive-in as well as walk-in service. Designed as two levels, the main laundry and customer lobby is on the ground floor with private offices and a cafeteria above. (The cafeteria itself is on a balcony overlooking the laundry room below.) The laundry room, a large air-conditioned space, occupies both levels. A special lobby and secure storage area are set aside for furs. The rear of the building has machinery rooms and loading space for the delivery trucks.

A totally fireproof building, the laundry was to be constructed of reinforced poured concrete with clerestory lighting for the main workrooms and glass doors opening onto an outdoor balcony next to the cafeteria.

ADELMAN LAUNDRY (PROJECT),
MILWAUKEE, WISCONSIN. 1945. INTERIOR
PERSPECTIVE. SEPIA INK ON TRACING PAPER,
35 × 17". FLLW FDN# 4507.013

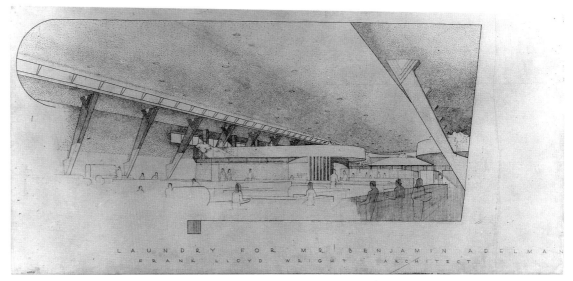

FOR WRIGHT, a man much in love with life, with nature, with all things living and growing, this commission to design a mortuary chapel was often depressing. Naturally he had to do a certain amount of research. He said he would come home to his residence at night sometimes "wondering if I felt as well as I should. But Nick [the client] had a way of referring to the deceased, always, as the 'merchandise,' and that would cheer me up. I pulled through and you behold the result."

Five chapels are grouped around garden courts, each one with a separate access. All preparation is carried on in the space below the chapels; the wrought-iron gate to this area can be seen in the foreground of the perspective. A detached building on the left contains space for flower and casket selection, as well as offices for Nicholas Daphne and his staff. "The plan of the whole,"

Wright wrote, "was an attempt to take some of the curse off the customary undertaker's official proceeding. I didn't expect to make even the funeral of one's enemies exactly cheerful, but I did think I could give the obsequities some beauty without destroying their integrity. . . . Every possible convenience designed to make the place helpful to the bereaved is here incorporated. The emphasis is here laid not on Death but on Life."

The drawing is very subdued, mostly showing the concrete building's white surfaces with a little shading of the foliage in brown and sepia and the rooftops in light blue. The buildings in the background have been shaded in gray to let them remain rather unnoticed in the general prospect. A large piece of tracing paper has been added to the original rendering to place the chapels further away from the viewer.

DAPHNE FUNERAL CHAPELS (PROJECT), SAN FRANCISCO, CALIFORNIA. 1945. PERSPECTIVE. PENCIL AND COLOR PENCIL ON TRACING PAPER, 36 × 24". FLLW FDN# 4823.001

SAN FRANCISCO FUNERAL CHAPELS FOR NICHOLAS P DAPHNE

FRANK LLOYD WRIGHT ARCHITECT

IN THREE SUCCESSIVE YEARS—1947, 1948, and 1949—Frank Lloyd Wright made designs for three bridges, each more innovative than the preceding one. The bridge that he designed in 1915 for Ravine Bluffs (page 243) was a simple engineering solution; the three solutions he proposed here had never before seen in the field of engineering, much less architecture.

The first bears the title "REGIONAL DEVELOPMENT WITH HIGHWAYS AND PARK SYSTEMS PROPOSED BY THE FRANK LLOYD WRIGHT FOUNDATION." The site was in a part of Wisconsin near Taliesin for which he had designed a series of approaches, parks, and a bridge over the Wisconsin River. The standard bridge at that time was an ugly overhead steel girder span. At best it was a hazard because of the threat of rust: it had to be constantly painted to coat and protect it. (In fact, a bridge that crossed the Wisconsin at Spring Green had collapsed because its steel supports weakened after years of exposure to rain and frosts.)

Wright referred to the design shown here as the "Butterfly wing bridge" and described it as follows: "We prepared a standardized unit system cantilever bridge, staunch and easy to repeat any number of times anywhere—either independent of shop fabrication or employing it. The type is called Butterfly because the wingspread of the spans concentrates the load upon a deep central girder economical up to spans of 200 ft. The low sweeping arches become an asset to any landscape."

Steel reinforcing, deep within the poured concrete, is kept safe from erosion. But the project was rejected.

Wright explained, "Without success our Foundation made an attempt to change the routing and the design and placing of the Wisconsin Highway Commission's projected bridge over the Wisconsin River near Spring Green and Taliesin." The local citizens of Spring Green strongly supported the project, but neighboring towns felt that the scheme was too favorable to Spring Green.

BUTTERFLY BRIDGE (PROJECT), SPRING GREEN, WISCONSIN. 1947. PERSPECTIVE. PENCIL AND COLOR PENCIL ON TRACING PAPER, 37 × 23". FLLW FDN# 4723.001

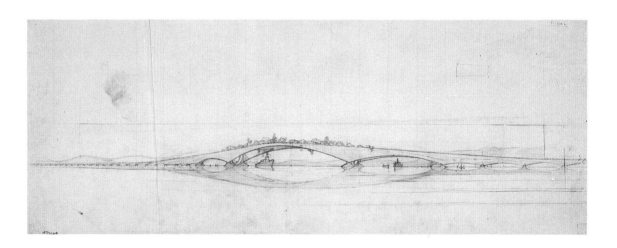

SAN FRANCISCO BAY BRIDGE (PROJECT), CALIFORNIA. 1949. PERSPECTIVE. PENCIL ON TRACING PAPER, 36 × 14". FLLW FDN# 4921.006

WHEN THE FIRST civic center that Wright designed for Pittsburgh proved to be too large for the community's needs, he made this design for a smaller scheme. Part of the project this time, as well as the first, was the need for two bridges to cross the Monongahela and Allegheny rivers. At first glance this perspective might lead one to believe that he designed a suspension bridge because of the cables engaging the roadbed. But that is not the case. Instead, there are two cantilevered bridges supported by the great concrete mass, like a huge sail. This drawing shows only one of the bridges; the other—its twin—proceeds over the river. The cables are called "stayed cables," and they act as a steadying element, providing equal tension along the bridge. The decorative weaving of the cables, seen partway down their length, is in reality the tension-reinforcing that keeps them taut at all times. The roadbed itself is divided into three levels: the lowest one for trucks, the next for automobiles, and the top is a garden for pedestrians. To further stabilize the bridge the cross section of these three roadbeds is triangular, like the keel of a ship.

Grouped around the base of the concrete sail are the component features of the civic center: auditorium, opera, cinema, and restaurants, with spiral ramped buildings for parking.

TWIN BRIDGES FOR POINT PARK (PROJECT),
PITTSBURGH, PENNSYLVANIA. 1948. PERSPECTIVE.
PENCIL AND COLOR PENCIL ON TRACING PAPER, 44 × 29".
FLLW FDN# 4836.004

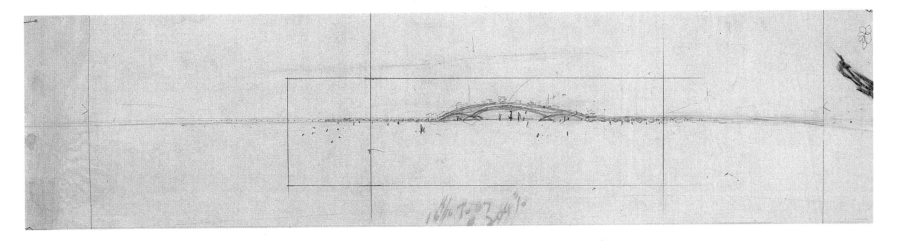

FOR THE SECOND crossing of Southern Bay near San Francisco, Wright proposed a reinforced-concrete bridge based on the project he had done two years previously for the Wisconsin River. The long stretch of bridge goes over the bay in a series of butterfly wing arches, but where the ships need to sail, the bridge rises in a great concrete span. If built, this would have been the longest concrete span in the world, a thousand feet long and up to one hundred and seventy-five feet above the water. Approaching the top of the span the roadbed divides to make a green park so that motorists can turn off, stop, and take in the view. The project was defeated by the steel companies' lobbying group, who preferred an all-steel traditional bridge to this more economical suggestion in which steel is used only to reinforce the poured concrete.

SAN FRANCISCO BAY BRIDGE (PROJECT),
CALIFORNIA. 1949. PERSPECTIVE. PENCIL ON TRACING PAPER,
30 × 8". FLLW FDN# 4921.001

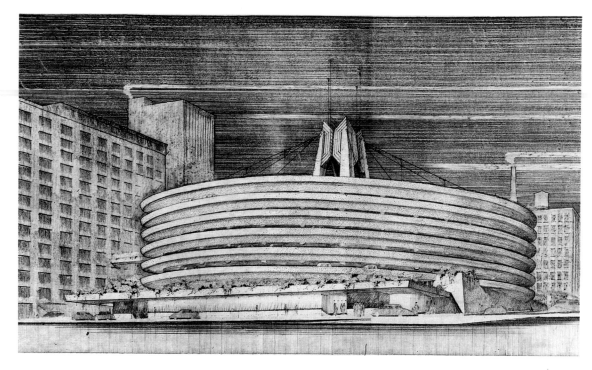

"SELF-SERVICE" GARAGE (PROJECT),
PITTSBURGH, PENNSYLVANIA. 1949.
PERSPECTIVE. PENCIL AND COLOR
PENCIL ON TRACING PAPER, 47 × 36".
FLLW FDN# 4923.054

EDGAR J. KAUFMANN, SR., for whom Wright built Fallingwater (page 41), was responsible for Wright's commissions for both of the Pittsburgh civic centers (pages 152 and 257). Kaufmann was a civic-minded individual and wanted to see his city have the very best architecture possible. However, he seems to have been defeated each time he proposed a building. This proposal for a self-service garage, to be built adjacent to his department store, was among his defeats.

The garage would naturally have served his store, but it also would have helped the general downtown community's desperate need for parking spaces. The building is a great structure of access ramps. The central pylon, seen rising out of the garage, anchors cables that engage the ramps through a detailed and well-engineered system for supporting the building. Wright made two versions of the project, both basically the same in treatment of parking and circulation. One has

four support masses at the corners of the ramps. The other—shown here—dispenses with the support corners and is planned in much the same way as the Guggenheim Museum (page 147).

For such an imposing structure the drawing, by contrast, is in delicate rose sepia color pencils with only a small amount of graphite pencil used to point up some of the decorative elements at the top of the pylon and to sharpen the curved edge of the individual ramp levels.

LENKURT ELECTRIC COMPANY (PROJECT),
SAN CARLOS, CALIFORNIA. 1955.
INTERIOR PERSPECTIVE FOR OFFICE.
PENCIL ON TRACING PAPER, 23 × 14".
FLLW FDN# 5520.012

ONCE AGAIN ADDRESSING parking space as a necessary evil that must be solved in a satisfactory manner if a building is to be beautiful, Wright has here, in this electronics factory for California, placed a garage beneath the second-floor workrooms. In this way each worker could park his car beneath the area in which he worked; stairways and elevators taking him directly from nearby parking to his place of work. The aerial view (page 206) shows the repetitive nature of the design; standardized spaces allow the factory to be easily expanded. The large square area at the lower-left corner contains administration offices on the periphery, and the great dome covers the patio, restaurant, café, and auditorium—the social center for all members of the firm. The elevations and sections explain in more detail the way in which the parking is integrated into and beneath the factory, which itself is all on one level. Wright used the dendriform, or mushroom-shaped, columns that were so successful in the Johnson Wax Company's administration building (page 248), but the difference here is in the handling of the spaces between the columns. In the Johnson building, those spaces are flat skylights; in the Lenkurt building, small pagodalike domes of copper and glass rise up to protective louvers that can open and close depending upon the need for shielding from the hot Californian sunshine but always allowing natural daylight to fill the interior work space. The furnishings of the offices, including those of the executives, were designed in keeping with the whole opus, and a group of six perspectives was made to illustrate this aspect of the design. On the office draw-

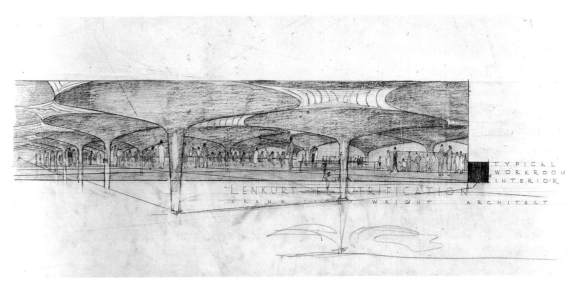

LENKURT ELECTRIC COMPANY (PROJECT), SAN CARLOS, CALIFORNIA. 1955. INTERIOR PERSPECTIVE FOR WORKROOMS. PENCIL AND COLOR PENCIL ON TRACING PAPER, 36 × 26". FLLW FDN # 5520.009

ing, Wright has penciled in the suggestion, "Note—In the open center frames of the chair backs—a metal emblem of LENKURT could be set. FLLW"

Complete working drawings were prepared for the project, but a sudden change in ownership and the equally sudden need for a quick, expedient factory building rather than an architectural masterpiece put a halt to the execution of the Frank Lloyd Wright design.

LENKURT ELECTRIC COMPANY (PROJECT), SAN CARLOS, CALIFORNIA. 1955. ELEVATION AND SECTION. PENCIL AND COLOR PENCIL ON TRACING PAPER, 63 × 36". FLLW FDN # 5520.001

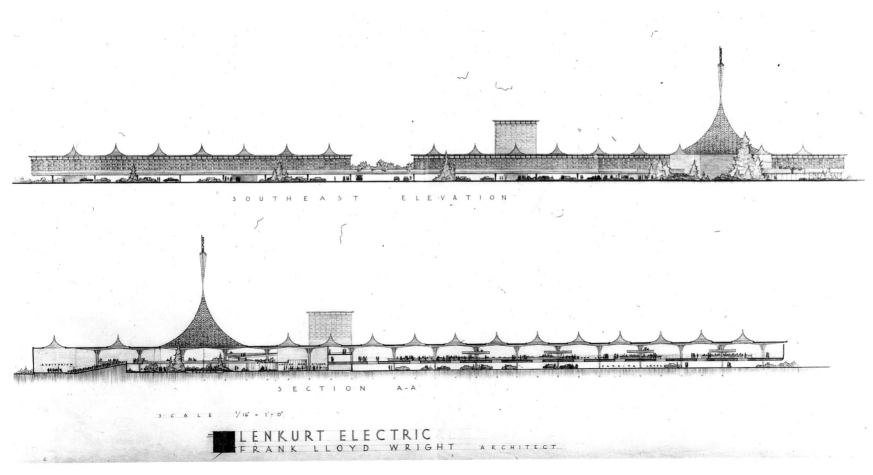

SOUTHEAST ELEVATION

SECTION A-A

SCALE 1/16" = 1'-0"

LENKURT ELECTRIC
FRANK LLOYD WRIGHT ARCHITECT

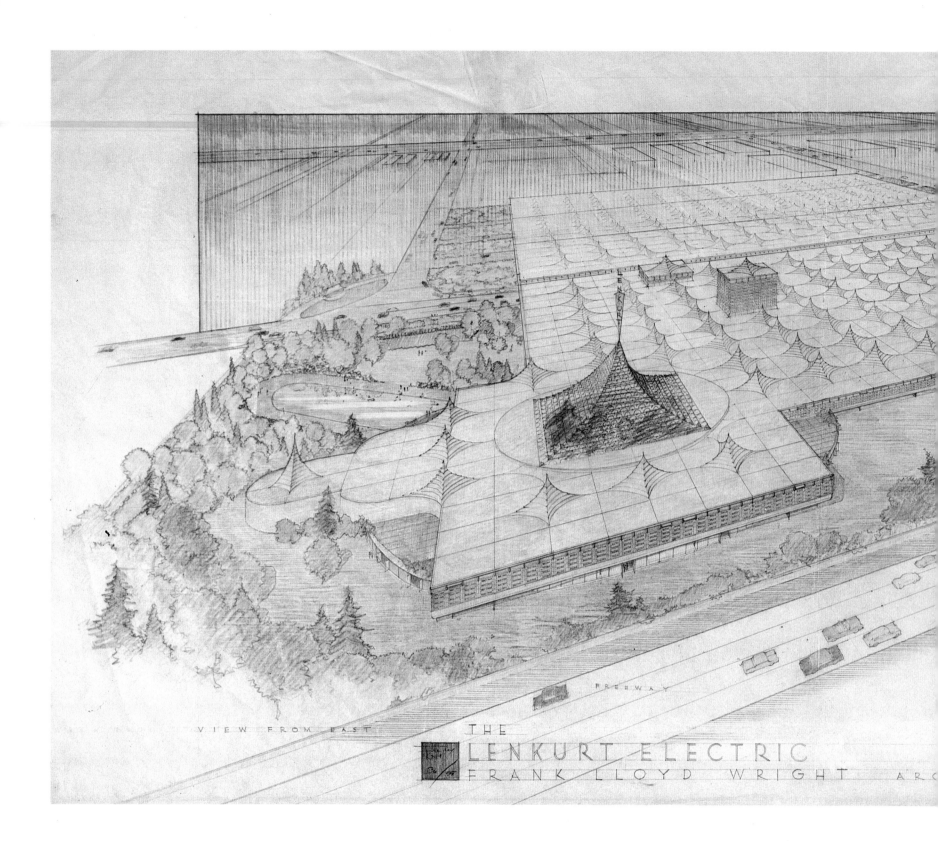

VIEW FROM EAST   THE
LENKURT ELECTRIC
FRANK LLOYD WRIGHT ARC

FREEWAY

ECT

LENKURT ELECTRIC COMPANY *(PROJECT)*,
SAN CARLOS, CALIFORNIA. 1955. AERIAL PERSPECTIVE.
PENCIL AND COLOR PENCIL ON TRACING PAPER, 64 × 37".
FLLW FDN# 5520.003

IN KEEPING WITH Wright's interest in automotive design is this design for what he called a "Road Machine." One of the tractors used on his farm in Wisconsin was an International Harvester Tractor "M," and the car design here is patterned after some of that vehicle's features. The driving force goes directly from the motor to the two large wheels; the front wheel is placed in the center. The driver sits behind and above the passengers—the machine was intended to be a taxi—in his own separate compartment with clear vision all around. The general aim of the design, Wright said, was to produce a motor vehicle that had more flexibility in traffic: "Most American cars are designed like shoeboxes going down the highway. But a car should be designed with sleek lines, like fish in a school of fish."

At the bottom edge of this sheet of paper Wright has made some sketches for a helicopter design.

ROAD MACHINE (PROJECT). 1955.
PLAN AND ELEVATION. PENCIL AND COLOR
PENCIL ON PAPER, 42 × 29".
FLLW FDN# 5826.005

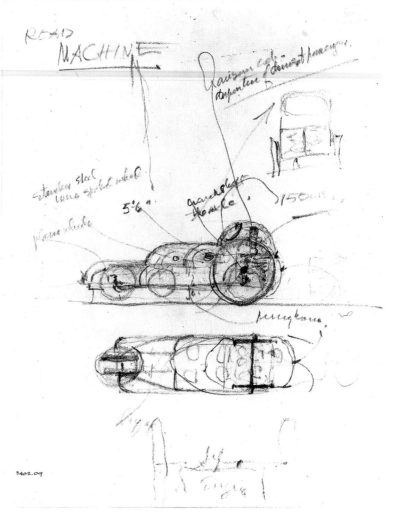

ROAD MACHINE (PROJECT). 1958. PLAN AND ELEVATION. COLOR PENCIL ON
TRACING PAPER, 9 × 11". FLLW FDN# 5826.008

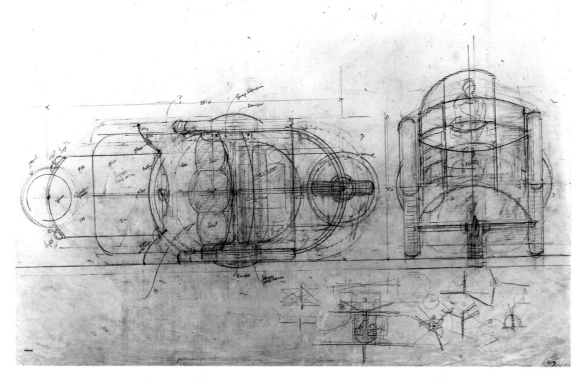

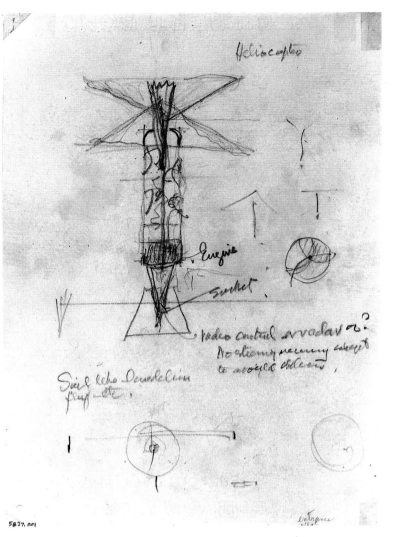

THESE THREE DRAWINGS in blue color pencil on sheets of typing paper are grouped together to demonstrate Wright's ideas about three types of transport: a helicopter, a train, and a taxicab (called "Road Machine").

The study for the helicopter was later modified into a more saucerlike design (as seen on the rendering of Broadacre City; page 265). The basic idea of the vehicle was that it was to run on radio beams, or radar, as Wright's note indicates, and to be self-steering. Some of his notes are difficult, if not impossible, to interpret, but the final version of this helicopter shows a machine with four doors, giving access to eight seats (or more, if a larger model were needed). The machine rests in a socket device with its entrance doors level with the station platform. When all four doors are closed, the helicopter rises and goes on its course to the next socket landing, either on the ground level of a building or on a roof terrace.

The train was to be a cylinder, air-driven by a propeller above the engine car, riding on a monorail or on ball bearings. On the elevation of the train Wright has written "track or monorail." And his suggestion to use ball bearings was his solution for avoiding noisy train wheels. In the section the corridor is on one side, sitting room and upper berth on the other.

The sketch below the train designs is called the Broadacre City "Right of Way" and is a highway design, yet most of the notations are illegible. But in other writings Wright specified what a highway should have:

a fast zone, a zone for trucks and semis, and a regular passenger car zone, each segregated from the other. A central lane would carry the trains, sometimes on raised tracks above concrete structures that would contain warehouses—transportation and storage would thus be combined in one centrally located convenience. The lights for the highway would be placed in the curb edge, like the aisle lights in a theater, doing away with tall poles and glaring lamps and turning the highways into what he called "ribbons of light."

The Road Machine is here labeled "Hansom cab—separation of driver and passenger," referring to its use as a taxi. The elevation, albeit very much of a sketch, more fully explains the earlier drawing shown for the same vehicle.

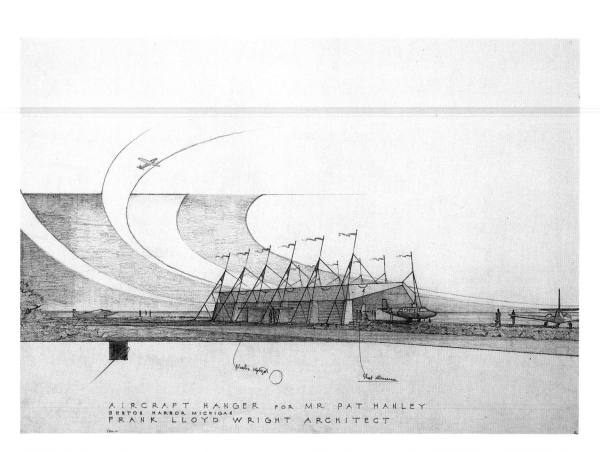

HANLEY AIRPLANE HANGAR (PROJECT),
BENTON HARBOR, MICHIGAN. 1959. PERSPECTIVE.
PENCIL AND COLOR PENCIL ON
TRACING PAPER, 36 × 25".
FLLW FDN# 5816.002

THIS "AIRCRAFT HANGAR for Mr. Pat Hanley" was to be a small structure in Benton Harbor, Michigan. The hangar was to be built of standard concrete-block walls on the long sides, with a suspended aluminum roof overhead. The perspective has a certain "aviation" quality expressed by the soaring steel pylons and cables that carry the roof. Throughout the section the notes on the drawing fully explain the scheme: "Concrete block pier, 4" steel struts, 6" steel tension 'T,' 8" steel compression 'T,' sheet aluminum roof, continuous 12" steel beams hung from cables at pylons, light open-web steel purlins, rolling doors."

Wright has left the perspective pretty much as his apprentice drew it, except to insert some circular skylights on the roof with a line connecting to his note on the bottom, "plastic skylight," and a circle to designate its form. The other line and corresponding note at the bottom points to the roof and reads, "sheet aluminum."

The building seems so lightweight in appearance it almost resembles a glider poised for an instant on the ground before taking off into flight once more.

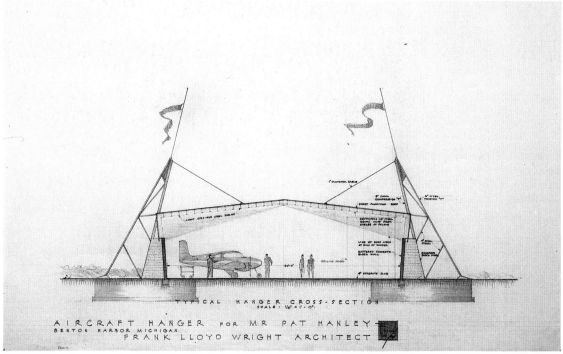

HANLEY AIRPLANE HANGAR (PROJECT),
BENTON HARBOR, MICHIGAN. 1959. SECTION.
PENCIL AND COLOR PENCIL ON PAPER,
36 × 25". FLLW FDN# 5816.003

FRANK LLOYD WRIGHT wrote three books about urban design and the problems with cities, offering his own solutions. In 1932 he wrote *The Disappearing City.* Two years later he and the Taliesin Fellowship built Broadacre City, a twelve-foot-square model showing a city integrated into a natural landscape. Other models of bridges, overpasses, service stations, and houses were made to accompany Broadacre's tour in 1935 to several major American cities. In 1945 Wright revised *The Disappearing City* text and published a new book called *When Democracy Builds,* illustrated with photographs of the Broadacre City models. The year before he died, 1958, he extensively rewrote the text and published it under the title *The Living City.* This last book was also illustrated with photographs of drawings and models. To amplify the photographs of the Broadacre

City model, Wright made a series of perspective views of the city, some of which were published in the book.

The drawing illustrated here was not published at that time. It shows the city as an integral part of the landscape, which is the main thesis of Broadacre. A river is in the foreground, hillslopes rising beyond. Into this drawing Wright has placed several of his own buildings, some of which were built, though others were not. In the center of the work rises the Rogers Lacy Hotel, and dotted through the hilly landscape can be found such projects as the Self-Service Garage (page 258), the Golden Beacon apartment tower (page 116), the Gordon Strong Automobile Objective and Planetarium (page 136), the Pittsburgh Civic Center #1 (page 152), the Huntington Hartford Play Resort (page 194), and subsequently completed buildings such as the Marin

County Civic Center (page 169) and the Beth Sholom Synagogue (page 99). The architect has drawn a line connecting one of the barges on the river to his note below, "Atomic Barge," and again at the top, he has written "Taxi-copter"—an accurate prediction of things to come, in view of today's new forms of transport power.

THE LIVING CITY *(PROJECT). 1958.*
PERSPECTIVE. PENCIL ON TRACING PAPER,
42 × 34". FLLW FDN# 5825.006

PART EIGHT

THE IMPERIAL HOTEL

EIGHTEEN NINETY-THREE WAS THE YEAR in which Frank Lloyd Wright began his independent architectural practice in Chicago. Coincidentally, it was the same year in which Clarence Buckingham, a prominent Chicago businessman, began to collect Japanese prints. From 1893 until his death in 1913, Buckingham amassed a collection of more than thirty-six hundred prints, which started with the work of Moronobu (1625–1694) and continued through the era of *Ukiyo-e* prints, or "Images of the Floating World," represented by such great artists as Utamaro, Hokusai, Shunko, Eishi, and Hiroshige. Advising him with the collection was Frederick Gookin, a leading expert in Japanese art. Japanese prints first came to Gookin's attention, as well as to Wright's, at the Columbian Exposition of 1893, and from this time on there was a select "club" of Chicagoans devoted to collecting them. (Buckingham's collection is now in the Art Institute of Chicago.) Through his association with these early Chicago collectors Wright himself began collecting Japanese prints, as well as studying the existing collections of people such as Buckingham. Soon he developed a keen fascination with the prints. In the years to come he avidly purchased the masterworks of the Japanese woodblock print not only for himself but also for other now-famous collections at the Museum of Fine Arts, Boston, the Metropolitan Museum of Art in New York, and the Spencer Museum in Lawrence, Kansas, as well as the Art Institute in his native Chicago.

"During my later years at the Oak Park workshop," Wright observed, "Japanese prints had intrigued me and taught me much. The elimination of the insignificant, a process of simplification in art in which I was myself already engaged, beginning with my twenty-third year, found much collateral evidence in the print." In February 1905, "after building the Larkin building and the Martin residence, all but tired out," Wright made his first journey to Japan with his wife, Catherine, and his clients Mr. and Mrs. Ward Willits. Armed with funds from the Larkin commission, he avidly purchased prints, folding screens, kakemonos (scrolls), surimonos, and bronzes.

In 1913 Wright returned to Tokyo, and at this point secured the commission for the new Imperial Hotel. Although the formal commission came the next year, in 1914, the archives have a letter from the hotel's manager, Aisaku Hayashi, to Wright dated August 19, 1913: "Glad to hear from you

and to know that you are once more settled in your own surroundings. Things must keep you quite busy but hope something will come of the hotel plan. Please see that the concrete facing exposed to all sorts of weather such as we have in this part of the world will stand the test of time and is practical. I think this is quite important. I have been getting several inquiries from manufacturers in America to whom I have referred you. The ground question [site] is not settled, but there is every hope of deciding before long."

For the most part, Japan's architecture before the Second World War was a carpentry architecture. Tokyo was a wood and paper city, primarily, but with roofs of heavy tiles. During earthquakes the tiles were dislodged and fell onto people running in panic through the streets, and following each earthquake came an inevitable conflagration that swept through this highly combustible type of construction. Considering these factors, Wright realized that his design for the new hotel must solve two problems: the movement of the trembler and the fires that came in its wake. Reinforced concrete would allow the building to have the necessary flexibility to move with the shocks, not oppose them, and then return to normal. The cantilever would place supports in the center, rather than at the edges of the walls. When discussing this idea with officials from the hotel at lunch one day in Chicago, Wright pointed to a waiter carrying a tray over his head, balanced on the outstretched palm of his hand: "There is your answer: balanced loads, concrete reinforced with steel, the walls of brick, also reinforced with concrete and steel, and a lightweight roof of copper." He further explained that to try to resist the quake with stolidly rigid construction would place any building in jeopardy of breaking under extreme pressure. What he proposed in the design of the Imperial Hotel was, for the first time in the history of architecture, a building that forces could push and pull. When speaking of this he would invariably interlock his fingers, move his wrists in many directions, and say, "You've heard me talk about tenuity 'til I'm black in the face. What is tenuity? That's the new thing in building. No ancient architect and no ancient builder ever had it. He could only make superimpositions of materials upon materials. When you could make several materials become as one, and weld them together from within, you got what we call the principle of tenuity, which built the Imperial Hotel. It brought it through the earthquake."

For eight years Wright traveled back and forth from the United States to Japan; the last four years saw him spending most of his time at the construction site of the hotel. He prepared preliminary drawings in 1914 while at Taliesin in Wisconsin, but when he went over to Tokyo that same year, he drastically revised his scheme. The basic plan, a large "H" with public rooms in the central area and the two wings reserved for guest rooms, was kept in the revised proposal, but treatment of the elevation was tempered from a rather modern, flat-plane, slab-roof construction to a more conventional one, "I have been sometimes asked why I did not make the opus more 'modern.'" Wright noted. "The answer is that there was a tradition there worthy of respect and I felt it my duty as well as my privilege to make the building belong to them so far as I might. The principle of flexibility instead of rigidity here vindicated itself with inspiring results. But the A.I.A. commission sent to study conditions in Japan subsequent to the great trembler of 1923 made no mention of the structure."

The foundations for the building were made up of a network of slender concrete piles, nine feet long, tapered and sunk into the soil two feet beneath the entire structure. An early survey of the site showed that the earth nine feet below the topsoil was mud, the result of filling in what had once been a bay of water. Wright presented the idea of connecting the building above with the spongy cushion of mud below. Across this network of concrete piles were laid the foundations themselves, made of reinforced concrete. Brick courses at the lower level were spread heavy and wide, with hollow bricks used for the building's higher levels. The "grammar of the structure," as the architect wrote on one of the drawings, "was a low center of gravity." Further explaining the structure, in a talk to his apprentices, he said: "It was built with brick shells, filled with concrete and all the bricks had dovetailed backs so that the concrete flowed into the bricks. And you could not get a brick away without splintering it and taking it away, splinter by splinter, from the wall. It was integral, you see. It was a very fine type of construction for what we wanted to do because there was steel in tension in the wall, giving it tensile strength. We could use the wall as a cantilever whenever we wanted to."

From early in his career, Wright insisted on carrying out the design of not only his buildings, but their furnishings as well. In the Imperial Hotel, however, we have an almost unparalleled example of the architect as master of all the arts: furniture, sculpture, murals, tableware, linen, silver, glass, carpets, upholstery fabrics, even wastepaper baskets and cuspidors. From the copper roof overhead down to the carpets underfoot, everything was designed by Wright. In this context the Imperial Hotel is a highly important work, and although the building was demolished in order to build a tall high-rise hotel in its place, the documentation—both in photographs and drawings—is complete and extensive: over 278 photographs, including construction photographs, and 715 drawings for the building and all its features exist in the archives.

Many times Wright promised his third wife, Olgivanna, that he would someday take her to Japan and show her the great culture he so deeply admired, the monuments, the treasures, the life itself of the Japanese people. That was never to happen, but she did go to Tokyo in 1967, eight years after her husband had died, on the urgent call of several Japanese architects to see if she could save the Imperial Hotel from pending demolition. When she arrived at the hotel, it was late in the afternoon on an October day. The low sweeping rays of the sun glowed on the oya carving and yellow-gold color of the bricks of the building. The moment Mrs. Wright emerged from her car, the press was waiting, with microphones and cameras. One reporter stepped forward and asked, "Mrs. Wright, how does it feel to be here in the courtyard of the Imperial Hotel?" She slowly turned, looked around her, turned back to the reporter, and said, with a quiet smile, "It is as if I were once again embraced by the arms of my husband."

The drawings in this section of the book document the many facets of design and drafting that made up the remarkable building and all its component parts. There are working drawings, beautifully delineated in ink on tracing linen by Japanese draftsmen; there are Wright's own conceptual drawings for the building and its decorative features; there are development drawings for sculpture carefully laid out by the draftsmen and then copiously edited by the architect; and there are drawings for furniture, murals, carpets, glass designs, and a silver tea service. This section, therefore, reveals the vast complexity of one of the most significant buildings of the twentieth century.

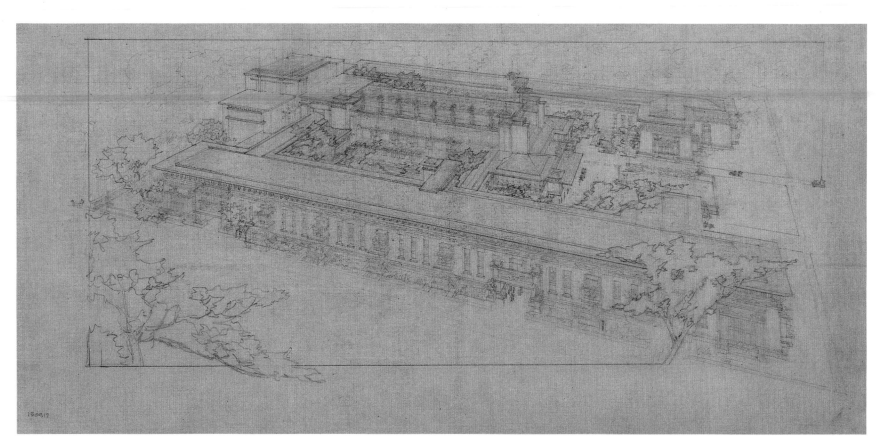

IMPERIAL HOTEL, TOKYO, JAPAN (DEMOLISHED). 1915.
PERSPECTIVE. PENCIL ON TRACING PAPER, 23 × 12".
FLLW FDN# 1509.017

THIS RELATIVELY small aerial view gives an idea of the plan of the building: the two long wings contain three floors each of private guest rooms and suites. The central portion, which is bordered on both sides by inner gardens, contains a dining room, lobby, and foyer at the entrance side on the right, and the tall portion at the rear of the building contains a cabaret, theater, promenade, and banquet hall. Throughout the public-room areas are smaller private dining rooms, parlors, and tea balconies. The basic plan, as shown here in its earlier stages, remained the same when the building was constructed. This drawing is predominantly by the hand of Wright himself.

THE BANQUET HALL, sometimes known as the Peacock Room, was on the top level of the hotel. This sketch perspective gives some idea of the size of the room, with its elaborate balconies, ceiling decoration, and hanging crystal lights. The mechanical lines of the drawing were laid out by one of the Japanese draftsmen working with Wright in Tokyo. From the printing it would appear that the drawing was done by Arato Endo, an architect himself, but the indications of ceiling decoration and the hanging lights are distinctly Wright's.

Throughout his sojourn in Japan, from 1916 to 1922, Wright had much valuable assistance from a staff of Japanese draftsmen, foremost among them being Endo, who, in fact, was Wright's right-hand man not only for the design and supervision of the Imperial Hotel but also for many other projects and buildings designed and built in Japan during these years.

IMPERIAL HOTEL, TOKYO, JAPAN (DEMOLISHED). 1915.
INTERIOR PERSPECTIVE. PENCIL ON TRACING PAPER, 18 × 20".
FLLW FDN# 1509.020

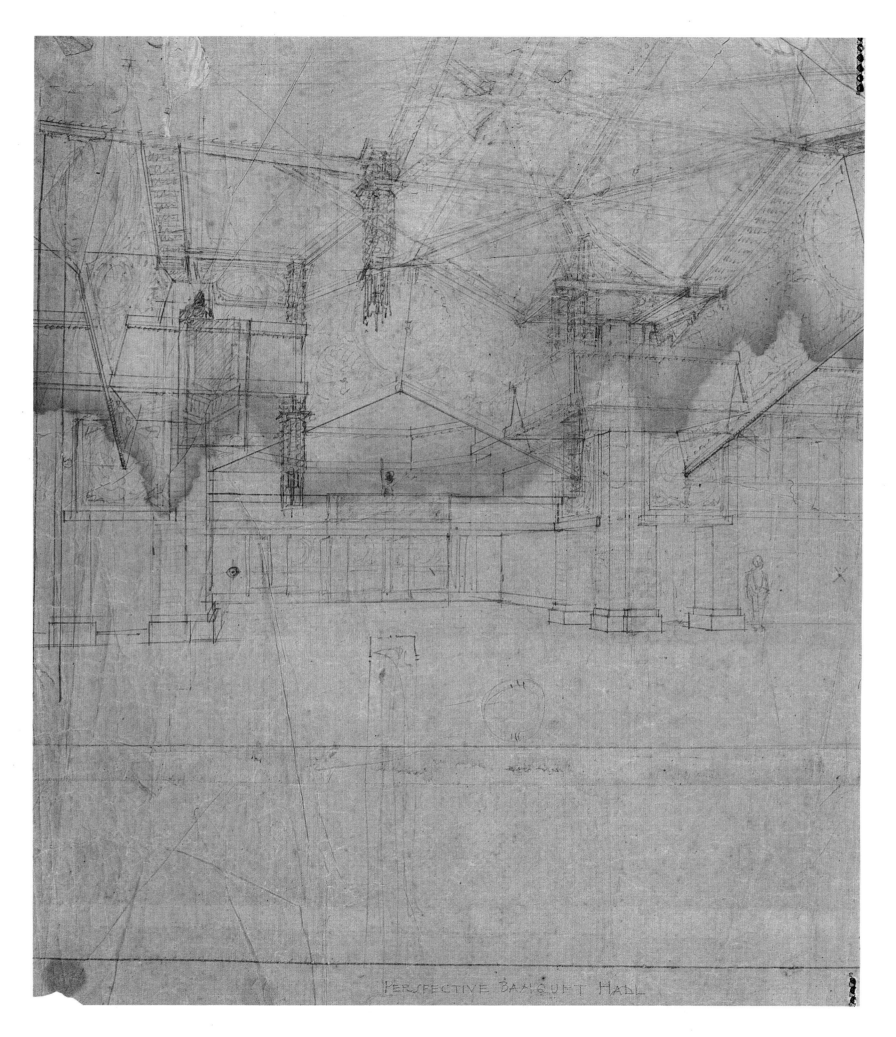

PERSPECTIVE BANQUET HALL

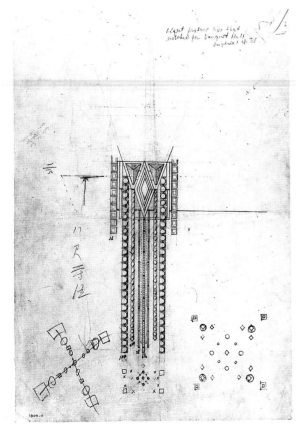

IMPERIAL HOTEL, TOKYO, JAPAN (DEMOLISHED). 1915.
CONCEPTUAL SKETCH. PENCIL ON TRACING PAPER, 11 × 16".
FLLW FDN# 1509.011

A DRAWING for a crystal light fixture, this sketch
gives the elevation of the design; the dots below show
the plan of the strings of crystals. A Japanese draftsman
has written on the top of the sheet, "Light fixture like
that sketched for Banquet Hall Imperial Hotel," simply
as a way of identifying the sheet for later use when it
would be drawn up in more detail for actual production
of the item.

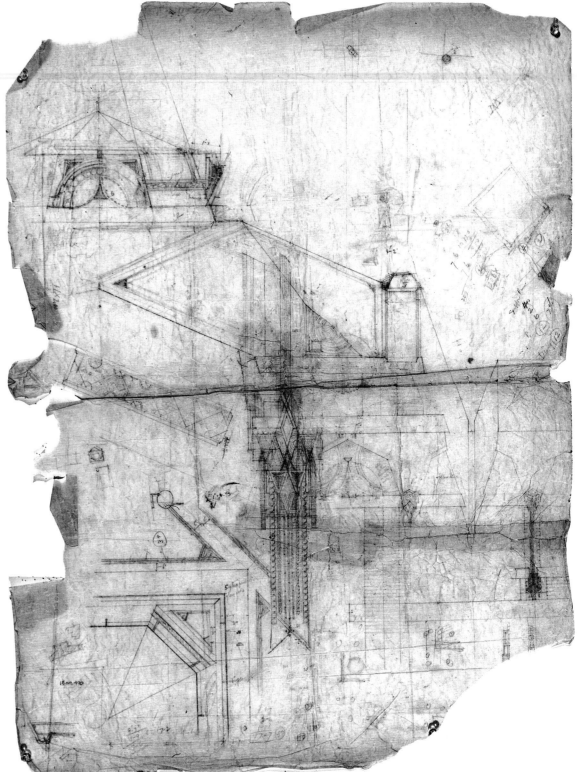

WRIGHT'S OWN WORK on this drawing is evident
throughout this sheet of details for a crystal light in the
hotel's banquet hall. There are additional sketches for
ceiling decoration and oya stone carvings as well. At the
uppermost part of the drawing can be seen a mural
design for the ceiling done as an abstraction of the
peacock. This, like all Wright's abstractions, has been
rendered by using a T-square and triangle rather than
freehand forms. Indeed, the decorative elements
throughout the Imperial Hotel were rendered in this
manner.

IMPERIAL HOTEL, TOKYO, JAPAN (DEMOLISHED).
1915. CONCEPTUAL SKETCH. PENCIL AND COLOR PENCIL
ON TRACING PAPER, 27 × 36". FLLW FDN# 1509.490

ALL THE FINAL architectural working drawings for the hotel were drawn in india ink on gray tracing linen. A drawing of this genre was done by the draftsmen in the office at that time—and most likely done in Tokyo, although the sheet bears the address "FRANK LLOYD WRIGHT ARCHITECT CHICAGO." Wright was in and out of Japan between 1916 and 1922, but he still considered Chicago to be his main office address. This section shows the relationship of cabaret, theater, and banquet hall, stacked one above the other with careful detailing included for all the decorative carvings and murals. The special fascination of this drawing is the extensive work Wright has done in graphite pencil and color pencil both for decorative and structural elements. Although only a sample of the full section of the building, it gives some of the scope of the hotel's size and complexity.

IMPERIAL HOTEL, *TOKYO, JAPAN (DEMOLISHED).*
1915. WORKING DRAWING. INK AND PENCIL ON
TRACING LINEN, 41 × 58". FLLW FDN# 1509.674

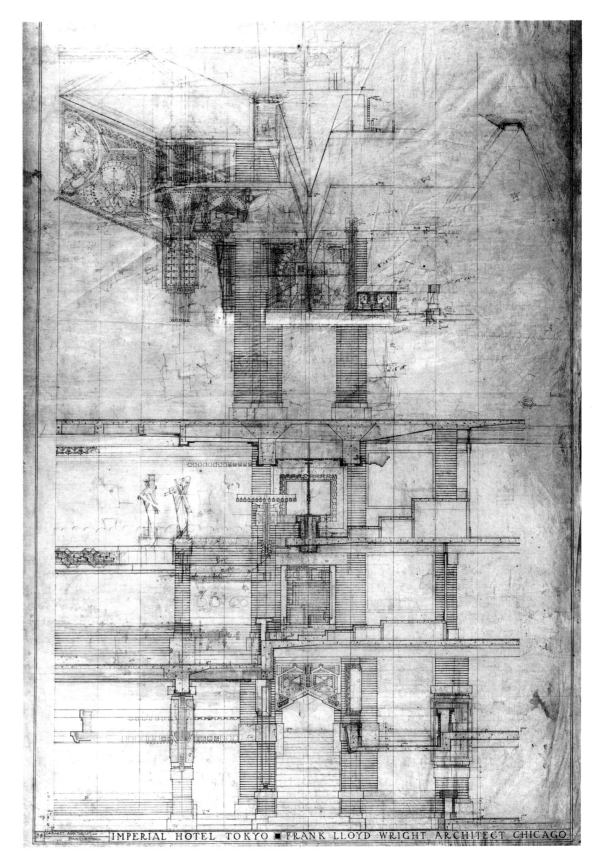

IMPERIAL HOTEL TOKYO ■ FRANK LLOYD WRIGHT ARCHITECT CHICAGO

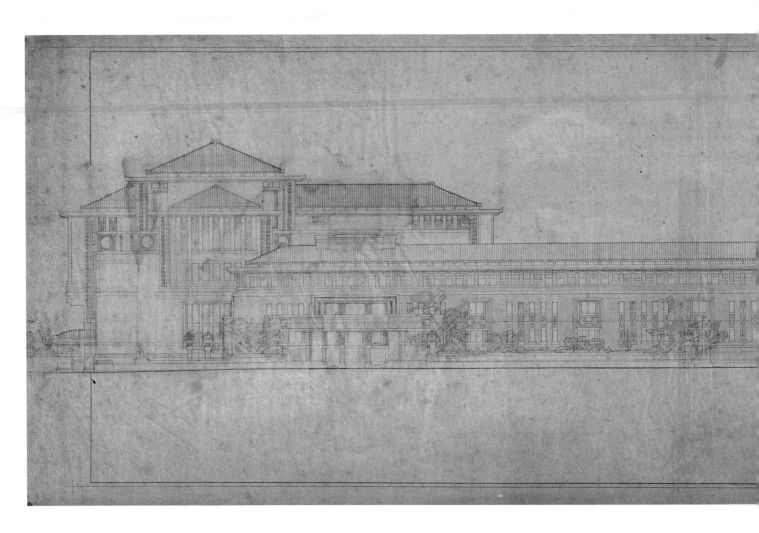

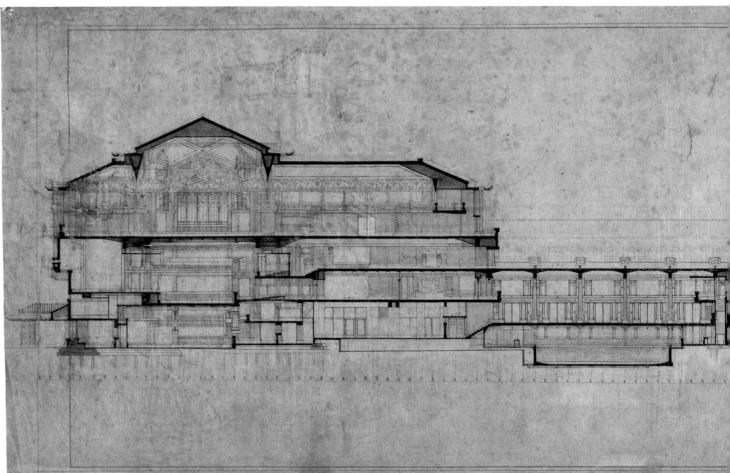

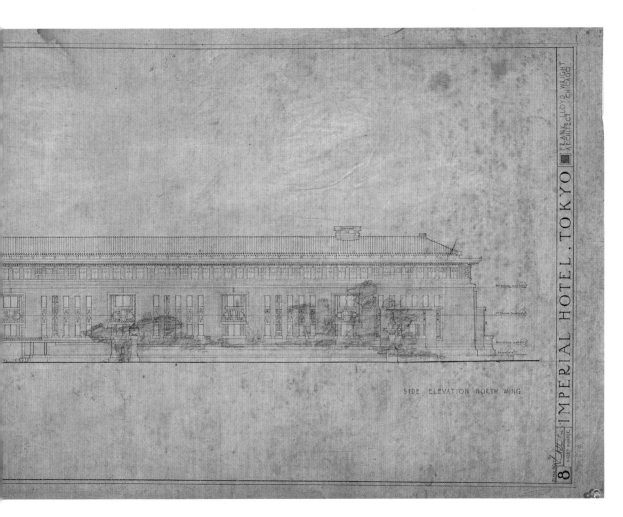

SIDE ELEVATION NORTH WING

IMPERIAL HOTEL, TOKYO

FRANK LLOYD WRIGHT
ARCHITECT CHICAGO

8

SHEET NUMBER 8 in this working-drawing series is an elevation of the hotel's south wing, with the tall mass containing the cabaret, theater, and banquet hall on the left-hand side. Like all the drawings in this set, the medium is india ink on gray tracing linen, and, like all the work by Wright's draftsmen of this period, it is beautifully executed. The graphite pencil trees and shrubs, sort of hastily drawn around the base of the building, were added by Wright at a much later date.

IMPERIAL HOTEL, TOKYO, JAPAN (DEMOLISHED). *1915. WORKING DRAWING. INK AND PENCIL ON LINEN, 58 × 41". FLLW FDN# 1509.647*

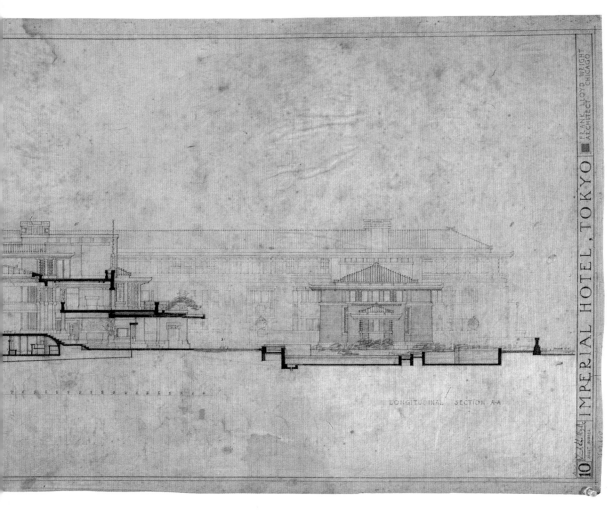

LONGITUDINAL SECTION A-A

IMPERIAL HOTEL, TOKYO

FRANK LLOYD WRIGHT
ARCHITECT CHICAGO

10

THIS SHEET, Number 10, is lettered below the building, "Longitudinal Section A-A." It reveals the building all the way from the banquet hall, theater, and cabaret at the left, through to the two parlors that overlook the two-story dining room, into the lobby with its balconies, and out across the entrance court. The swimming pool beneath the dining room was never executed. Construction of the building began in 1920–1921, at which time more drawings were made. Other drawings, as required for decorative details, furnishings, carpets, and so forth, were also prepared in 1921 while Wright was supervising the work in Tokyo. Once again, at a later date, he went over the drawing and penciled in some planting in the entrance court.

IMPERIAL HOTEL, TOKYO, JAPAN (DEMOLISHED). *1915. WORKING DRAWING. INK AND PENCIL ON LINEN, 58 × 41". FLLW FDN# 1509.650*

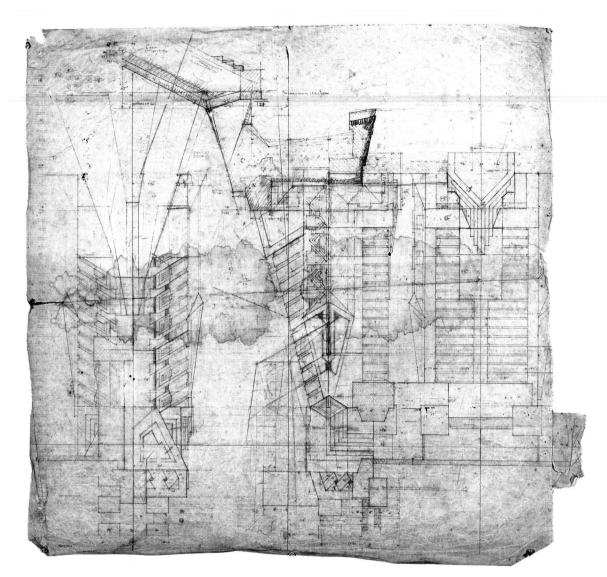

FOR INTEGRAL ORNAMENT throughout the hotel Wright chose a stone called oya that had to be quarried out of a lake near Nikko. This stone was formed by lava dust falling into the lake eons ago and compacting into a buff gray green pockmarked stone. It was the pockmarked character of it that appealed to the architect. Even though the Japanese regarded this stone as too lowly to use in buildings of any prestige, Wright selected it and insisted upon it because, when freshly quarried, it had the consistency of hard cheese, could be easily carved, and, when dried, was relatively lightweight. In its use in the Imperial Hotel it was secured, inside and outside, to the fabric of the building by means of steel rods and poured concrete. This was typical of the manner in which Wright regarded all ornament: as natural and as integral to the structure as the blossoms of any flower are to its stock.

IMPERIAL HOTEL, TOKYO, JAPAN (DEMOLISHED).
1915. WORKING DRAWING. PENCIL ON TRACING PAPER,
40×40". FLLW FDN# 1509.528

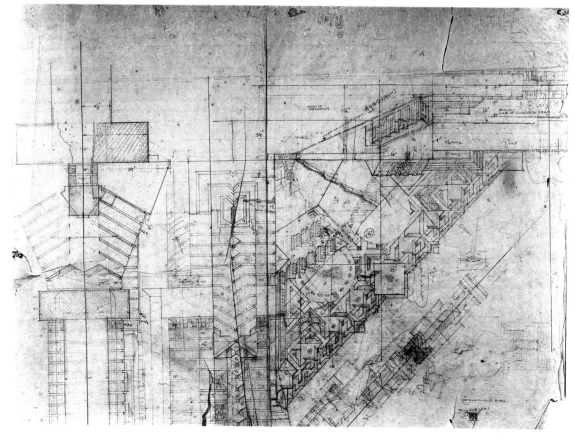

THIS RICHLY DETAILED drawing for the oya stone carving was made for the hotel's dining-room piers. It is signed and dated "OK FLLW July 20, 1921." Wright made numerous alterations and changes in the details, but he must have felt that the stone cutters did not need a revised drawing. Their skill had become legion, as was his admiration for their fine craft and diligent workmanship.

IMPERIAL HOTEL, TOKYO, JAPAN (DEMOLISHED).
1915. WORKING DRAWING. PENCIL ON TRACING PAPER,
38×32". FLLW FDN# 1509.298

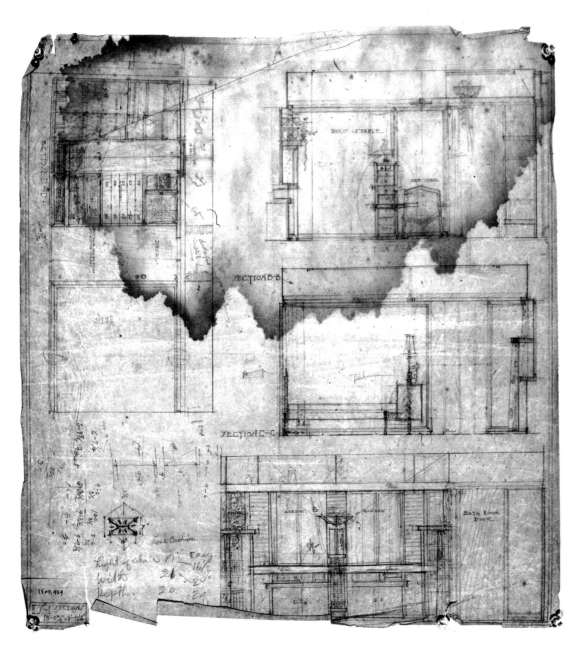

THE TYPICAL BEDROOMS of the hotel had little brick, except on the exterior window walls, and no oya stone carving, simply a plain stone lintel beneath the window frames. The rooms were partitioned by plaster walls with wood paneling. The drawing for a typical room, done by Wright himself, shows the four interior elevations with built-in cabinets, shelves, and free-standing furniture. Above the stack of built-in wardrobe drawers is a square door with a special lock from inside: laundry deposited here could be picked up via a corresponding door opening into the hallway and then returned and retrieved by the guest.

IMPERIAL HOTEL, TOKYO, JAPAN (DEMOLISHED). 1915. INTERIOR ELEVATION. PENCIL ON TRACING PAPER, 21 × 22". FLLW FDN# 1509.434

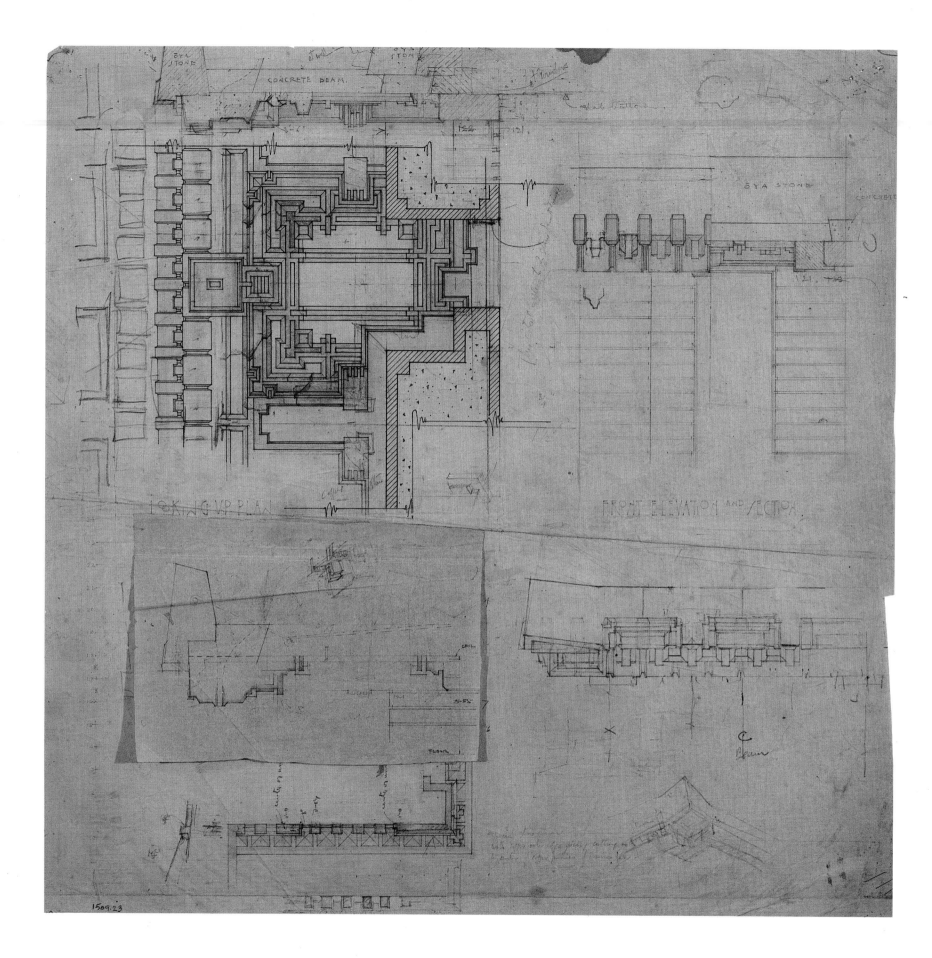

CONCRETE BEAM.

BYA STONE

LOOKING UP PLAN

FRONT ELEVATION AND SECTION

C
Plan

1509.23

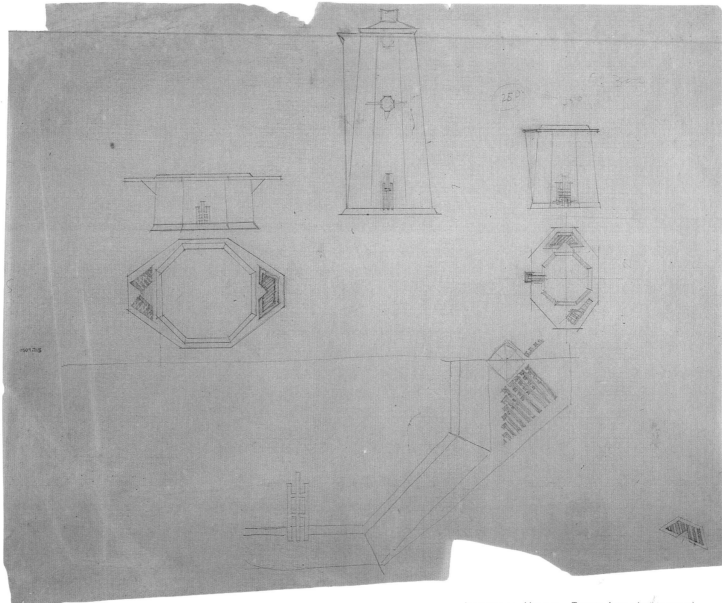

THIS IS A PARTICULARLY complicated drawing showing the details and construction of the cornice of the roof, which combined a reinforced-concrete slab, oya stone carving, and copper. The upper-left drawing is a plan looking up at the projecting cornice, a front view set to the right of it. The sketches below are more in the nature of initial studies done by Wright, while those above are a translation of those studies done by his draftsmen. A typical thumbnail sketch by Wright of the cornice at the corner is barely visible on the lower right of the sheet. The plan looking up has been rendered in color pencils to make it more readable.

AMONG THE IMPERIAL HOTEL'S 715 drawings is this design for a tea service. This sheet presents a teapot, sugar bowl, and creamer. Sketches for a tray to hold them all are incomplete, and the design for the perforated pattern is shown differently on each lid, but a prototype exists in the Frank Lloyd Wright Archives of at least the creamer. For years it stood on Wright's desk at Taliesin, a holder for his pencils and pens.

The monogram for the hotel, a combined I and H, appears on these designs in different variations, but it does not appear on the little creamer. There exists no finite record whether any, or how many, of these tea services were actually made and used in the hotel. Now that the hotel has been demolished, any hope for such a record seems dim, indeed.

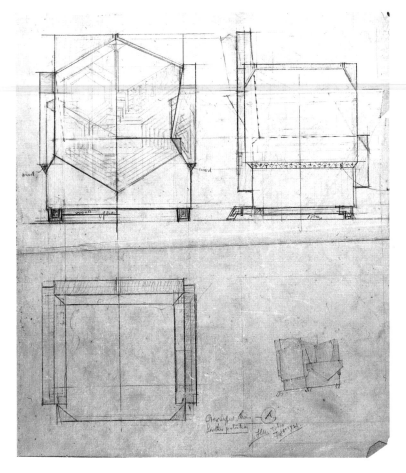

THESE TWO SMALL DRAWINGS made by Wright in green pencil indicate his designs for two chairs: an overstuffed chair and a small dining chair, called the "Peacock chair," for use in the banquet hall. Each drawing contains a delightful little perspective sketch of the intended chair. His note for the overstuffed chair reads, "Overstuffed Chair-A. Leather protection. FLLW Tokio Feb 4, 1921." The writing accompanying the other reads "FLLW Feb 3, 1921—Tokio." Oddly, this spelling of Tokyo occurs consistently in all his writings and notations during these years in Japan.

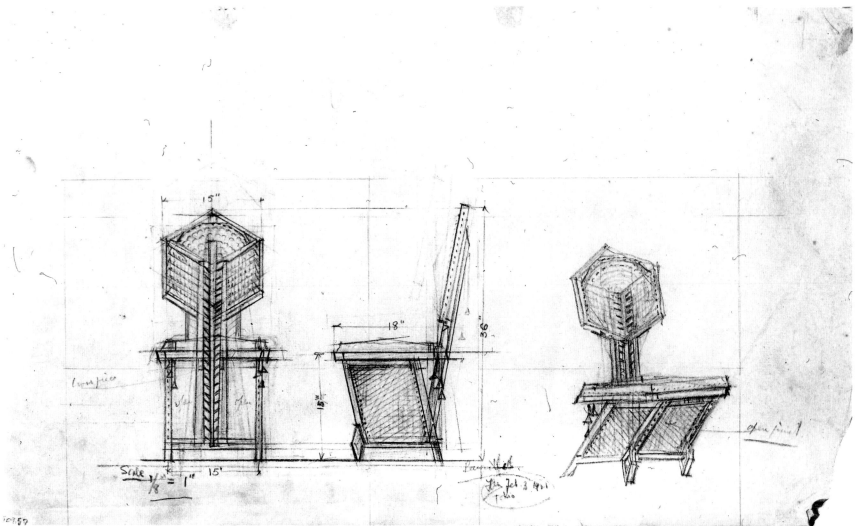

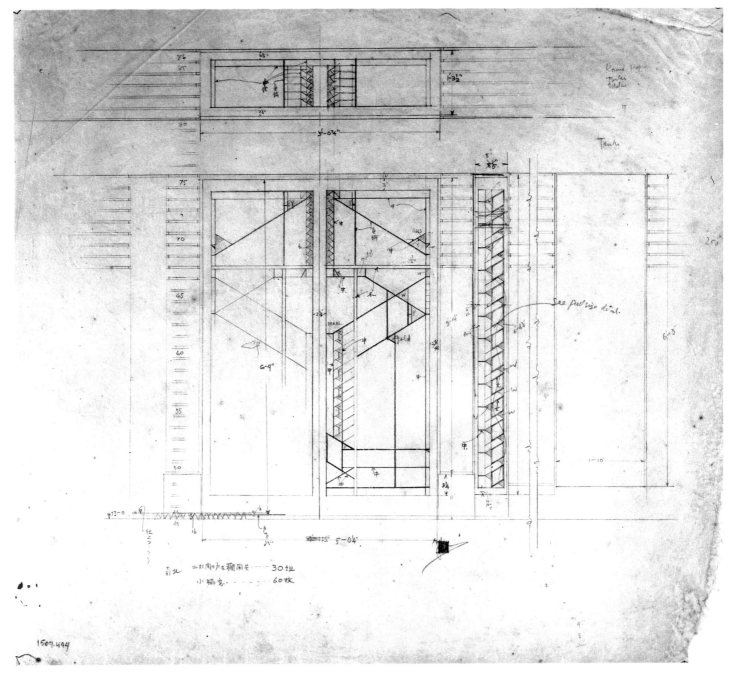

IMPERIAL HOTEL, TOKYO, JAPAN (DEMOLISHED).
1915. WORKING DRAWING. PENCIL ON TRACING PAPER,
22 × 20". FLLW FDN# 1509.494

IN CONSIDERATION of the earthquakes in Japan, Wright designed the larger areas of glass, such as these French doors, to be made of composite smaller panes arranged in an interesting and artistic pattern. Clear sheets of this size could prove hazardous in the movement of a quake. Unlike the stained-glass windows of his prairie houses, which employed stained, iridescent, and flashed glass, these windows for the Imperial employed clear glass throughout.

IMPERIAL HOTEL, TOKYO, JAPAN (DEMOLISHED).
1915. RENDERING. PENCIL AND COLOR PENCIL ON
TRACING PAPER, 29×17". FLLW FDN# 1509.068

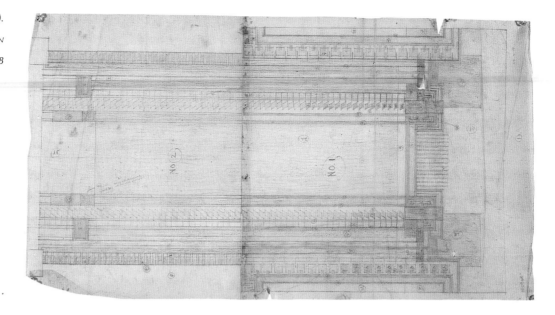

IMPERIAL HOTEL, TOKYO, JAPAN (DEMOLISHED).
1915. RENDERING. PENCIL AND COLOR PENCIL ON
TRACING PAPER, 29×17". FLLW FDN# 1509.036

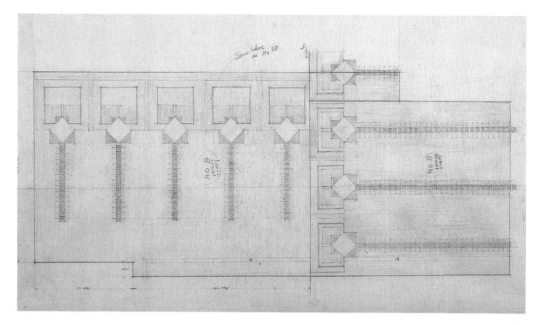

IMPERIAL HOTEL, TOKYO, JAPAN (DEMOLISHED).
1915. RENDERING. PENCIL, COLOR PENCIL, AND GOLD INK ON
TRACING PAPER, 36×23". FLLW FDN# 1509.004

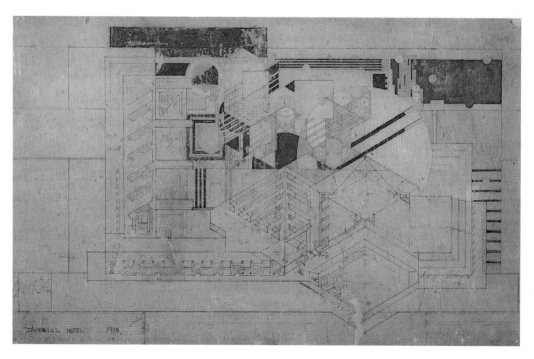

(*Opposite top*)

ALL THE CARPETS in the hotel were designed by Wright and custom woven in China. The basic color for the overall field was a soft buff, the designs in varying shades of blue and amber. Over twelve hundred carpets were required, many of them small pieces sewn together to go around columns and piers and to connect with larger carpets. This carpet design, designated as Number 1 and Number 2, was woven for the foyer and lobby, to run from the entrance to the dining room, into the main lobby, and down the steps to the front doors.

Wright was not always able to design carpets for his homes and buildings. He did so on certain rare occasions, such as for the Heurtley, Coonley, Robie, Meyer May, and Bogk houses in his early work, and the Price, Gillin, David Wright, and Hoffman houses in the later part of his career. But of all these works, the most extensive was unquestionably the carpet designs for the Imperial Hotel.

(*Opposite middle*)

CARPET DESIGNS Number 8 and Number 9, employing a simpler pattern to Numbers 1 and 2, were used in the promenade adjacent to the banquet hall and private dining rooms and in the parlor, a large social room connected to the promenade. The drawing indicates how the various sections are to be pieced together so as to flow as one carpet throughout the public rooms, around columns and piers and up or down steps as required.

IMPERIAL HOTEL, TOKYO, JAPAN (DEMOLISHED). 1915. RENDERING. PENCIL AND COLOR PENCIL ON TRACING PAPER, 45×45". FLLW FDN# 1509.044

(*Opposite bottom*)

ADJACENT TO the hotel's promenade was a large spacious room called "The Parlor," and used for private social functions in a more homelike atmosphere than the usual rather cold, convention-center type of arrangement. There were two fireplaces in the parlor facing each other from opposite walls, and over each was a mural designed by Wright and executed in cut oya stone and polychrome (paint applied to the prepared plaster surface).

The drawing shown here is one of those murals, and it is labeled "IMPERIAL HOTEL 1913 Stone Carving and Polychrome Decoration—Ladies' Parlor." The fireplace opening is at the bottom of the sheet, three brick courses on each side supporting the lintel stone of oya, with a triangular section pro-

truding down. The parts of the drawing that denote the stone carving are done in graphite pencil, the parts in polychrome on the plaster in gold ink and color pencils.

Again Wright in later years dated the work here, as he had done on several Imperial Hotel drawings, as 1913. This corresponds to the date of his second trip to Japan, his meeting with the hotel's general manager, Hayashi, and Hayashi's letter concerning the new building. To Wright, the hotel was "in the making" in 1913, if only in his own fertile imagination.

AT THE TOP LEFT edge of this carpet design, Wright has lettered, "Full Size Detail—Imperial Hotel—One unit in Banquet Hall Rug—Woven in Peking—1917—FLLW." As the note would indicate, this unit, which measures forty-five square inches, was but one in a connected series that formed the entire rug. The pattern is based on the peacock, with outstretched wings and eyes of the feathers made into a beautiful and colorful abstraction.

(*OVERLEAF: IMPERIAL HOTEL. RENDERING; DETAIL*)

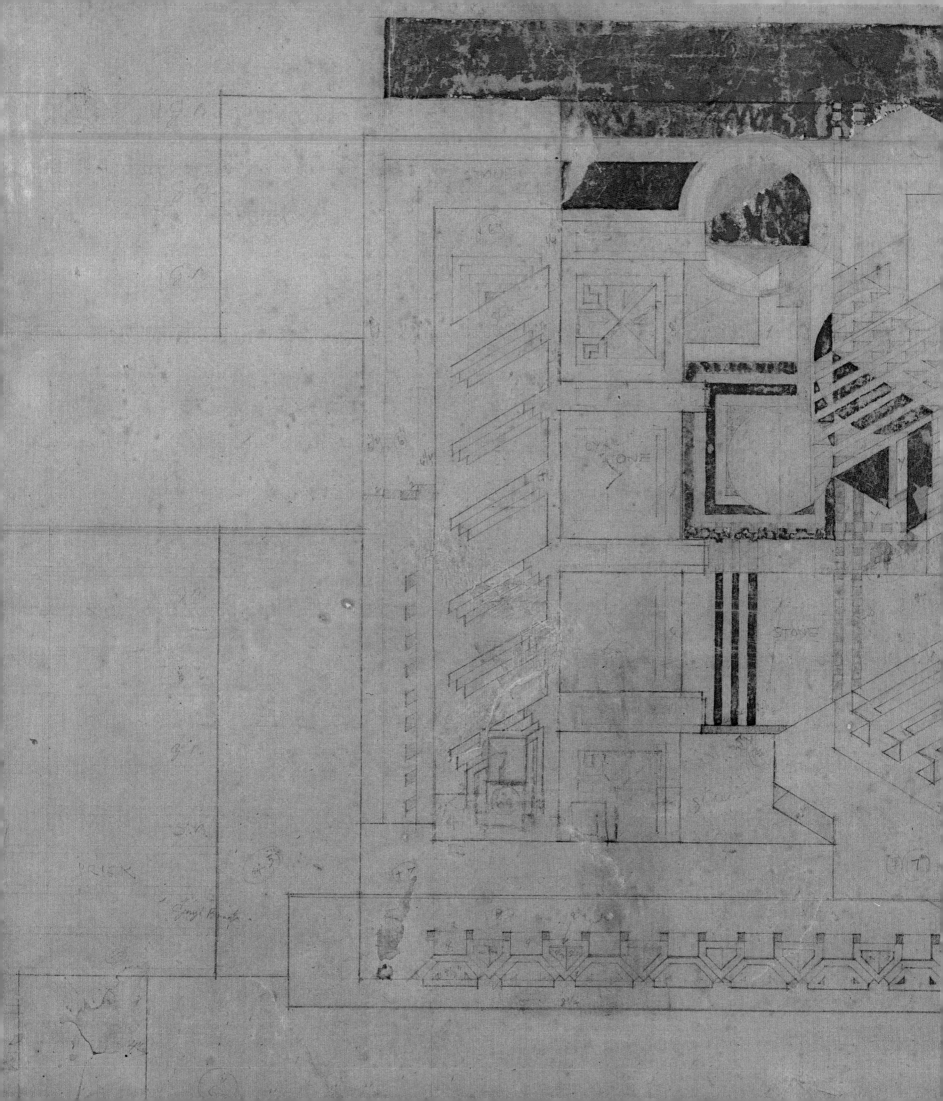

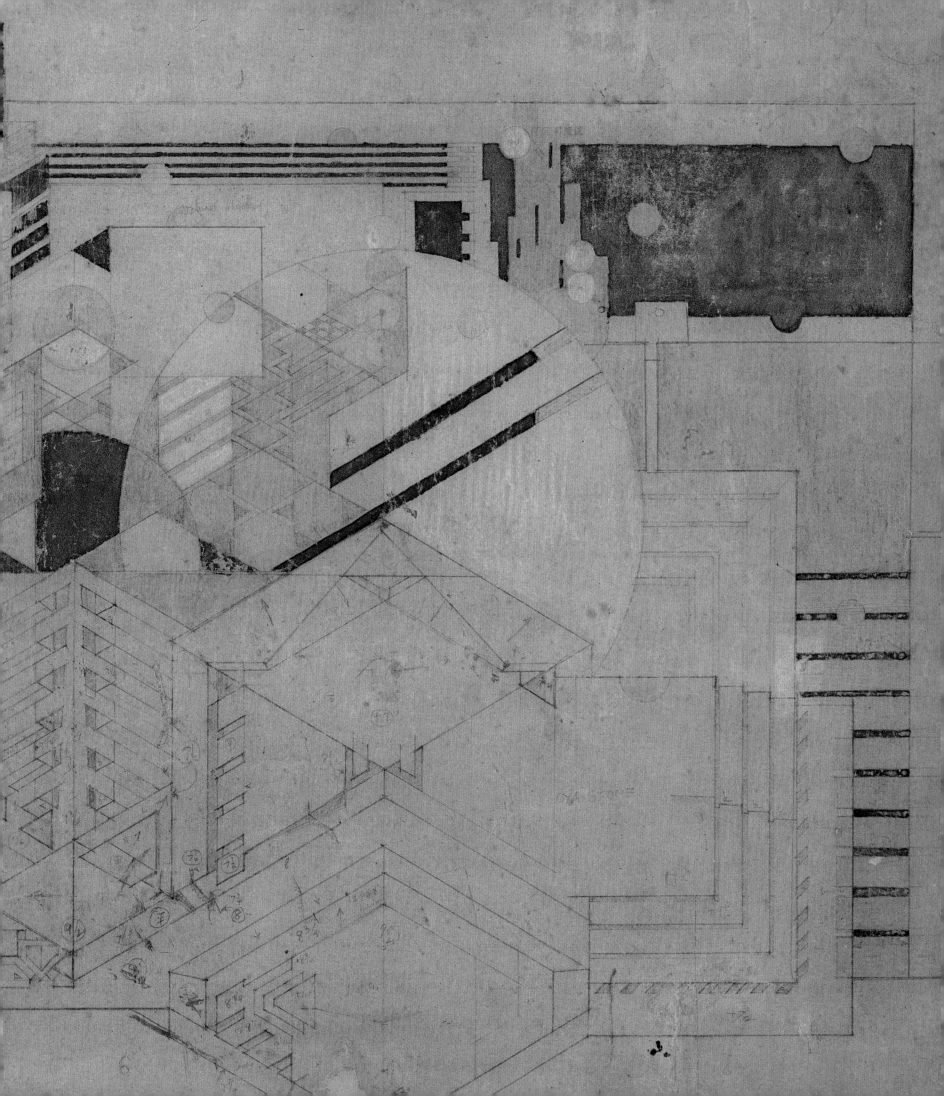

PART NINE:

GRAPHIC AND DECORATIVE DESIGNS

EARLY IN HIS CAREER Wright frequently experienced the disappointment of finishing a fine new house for a client and then witnessing the client decorating it with a motley collection of Victorian furniture. To avoid this, little by little he began designing built-in items—sideboards for the dining room, cases and cabinets for the living room, seat and end tables built as part of the fireplace inglenook. The casement draperies of the time were as hideous to him as the standard store-bought furniture, and so he designed glass patterns, usually in stained glass, that would permit people inside the house to look out but also give them some privacy from the passersby outside. Gradually he expanded his designs to include freestanding chairs, tables, dining-table sets, bed frames, hassocks, coffee tables, and, eventually, carpets and rugs.

Organic architecture, to his way of thinking, innately expresses this sense of the parts related to the whole. This approach would automatically encompass all the interior furnishings and decorative features as well as the walls and floors and ceilings of a building. Wright's architecture is the most successful where he was given the opportunity to create designs for all aspects of a dwelling or building. In those works there is a congruity and integrity that arises as a result of that interrelation of all parts harmonious with the whole. Where he was denied the chance to integrate those final, but so important, interior details, or where they have been subsequently removed from their original context, the building suffers from a lack of aesthetic fulfillment.

In his designs for book covers, bookplates, magazine covers, murals, and wall hangings he was careful always to keep in mind the nature of the material out of which the object would be made. Graphics are flat, by nature, printed on the page or paper, as are murals, and in studying his work in these fields we never see one surface lying across another. With great skill and dexterity he kept all the lines and planes absolutely flat. This was one of the features that most appealed to him about Japanese prints and folding screens: there was no attempt at shading or perspective. All his designs belonged to and expressed the relevant medium.

Wright loved to make abstractions in color pencils—taking the germ of an idea and elaborating on it in his own way without imitating the original idea itself. As with his architectural drawings, the designs for graphics and decorative features again attest to his enjoyment of drawing in itself.

WILLIAM C. GANNETT, a Unitarian preacher, was a friend of Wright's uncle Jenkin Lloyd Jones, also a preacher. In an essay of six chapters, entitled *The House Beautiful,* Gannett describes the experience of building, furnishing, and living within a home in transcendental, Unitarian-like terms inspired by Ralph Waldo Emerson. During the winter of 1896–1897 Wright and his first client, William H. Winslow, designed and handprinted the essay in a leather-bound volume, which they made on Winslow's own private press. The edition was limited to ninety copies, each signed by the designer, Wright, and the printer, Winslow, and then distributed as gifts to their friends.

The plate for the chapter "Our Guests" in Gannett's book demonstrates a truly phenomenal facility in drawing: it is done freehand with a quill pen and china ink. There are aspects of the design that would appear "Sullivanesque"—Wright had only left Sullivan's office some three years before this was made—but woven throughout are other, newer aspects in the straight-line patterns that would eventually become his personal vocabulary.

An interesting footnote to this graphic design of 1896 lies in the Frank Lloyd Wright Archives: in 1956 Wright took a copy of the volume and, still keeping the bulk of his prior design intact, he made an entirely new layout for each page. On the final page, where his signature of 1896 lay beside that of Winslow's, he once again signed the book, reverting from his now usual upright handwriting to the original slanted style he had used sixty years earlier, and dated it "1956."

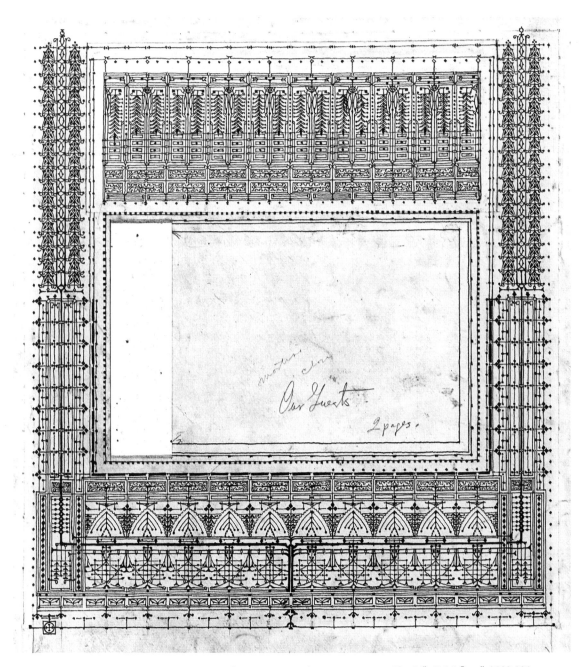

THE HOUSE BEAUTIFUL. *1896. GRAPHIC DESIGN. INK ON ART PAPER, 15×21".* FLLW FDN# 9609.006

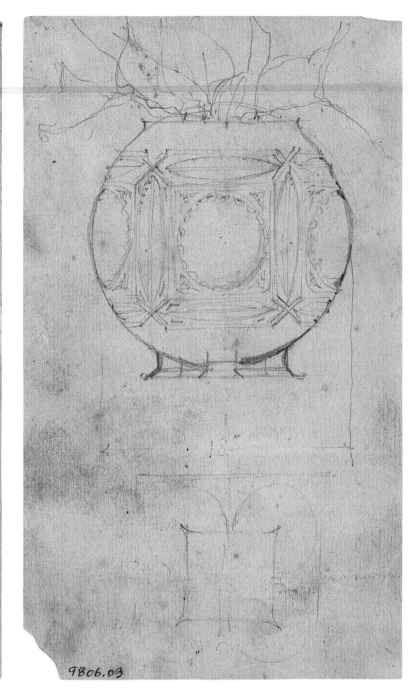

DESIGNS FOR VASES AND FLOWERHOLDERS.

1898. CONCEPTUAL SKETCH. PENCIL ON TRACING PAPER, 5 × 7".

FLLW FDN# 9806.002

DESIGNS FOR VASES AND FLOWERHOLDERS.

1898. CONCEPTUAL SKETCH. PENCIL ON TRACING PAPER, 5 × 7".

FLLW FDN# 9806.003

A SMALL SERIES of sketches, most of them measuring no more than four by seven inches each, is grouped together in the archives under the heading "Vases and Flowerholders." These are designs for objects intended to be produced in copper or bronze. The one here marked "Lilac" is more freehand in style than we expect of Wright, but the second one is his original pencil sketch of the famous bronze urns that recently garnered high prices on the auction block. Below the elevation of the urn can faintly be seen a sketch of its plan.

THE GLASS throughout the Susan Lawrence Dana House was regarded by Wright as among his best efforts in the medium. The two panels of glass designs in the working drawing are for hanging screens, like draperies, placed between the entrance hall and gallery so that a view from one to the other is not blocked by, but rather is enhanced by, the rich autumnal colors of the stained-glass patterns. In the 1950s Wright noted on the drawing, "Dana—Brass Screen—brass grille—glass filled."

Hanging above the dining-room table are suspended lamps of stained-glass shades; the complicated study for a lamp shows the architect's detail in coloring, style, and pattern and has his notes, "Butterfly hanging lamp Dana D.R."

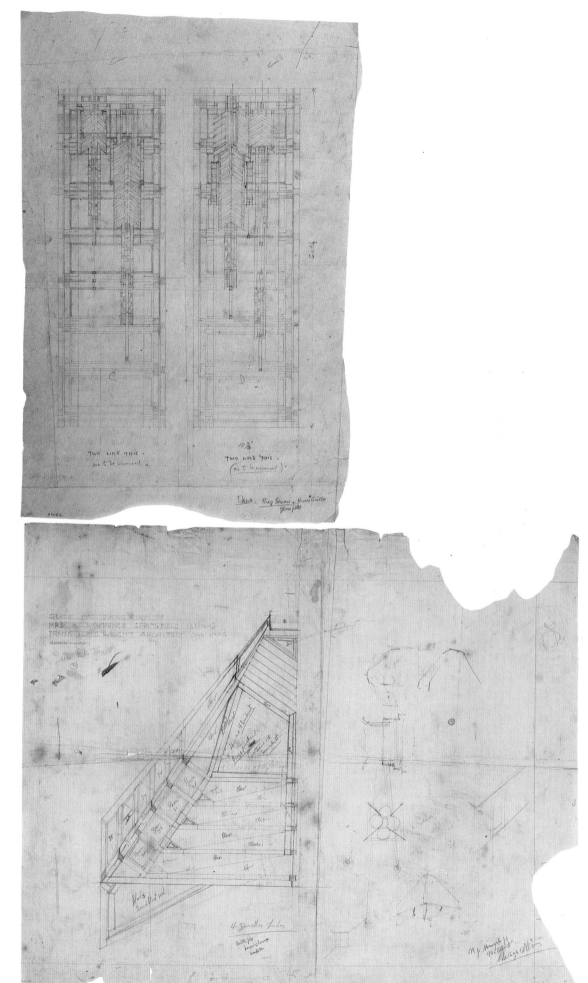

SUSAN LAWRENCE DANA RESIDENCE,
SPRINGFIELD, ILLINOIS. 1900. WORKING DRAWING
FOR STAINED GLASS. PENCIL ON TRACING PAPER,
15 × 23". FLLW FDN# 9905.012

SUSAN LAWRENCE DANA RESIDENCE,
SPRINGFIELD, ILLINOIS. 1900. STUDY FOR LAMP.
PENCIL ON TRACING PAPER, 31 × 26".
FLLW FDN# 9905.008

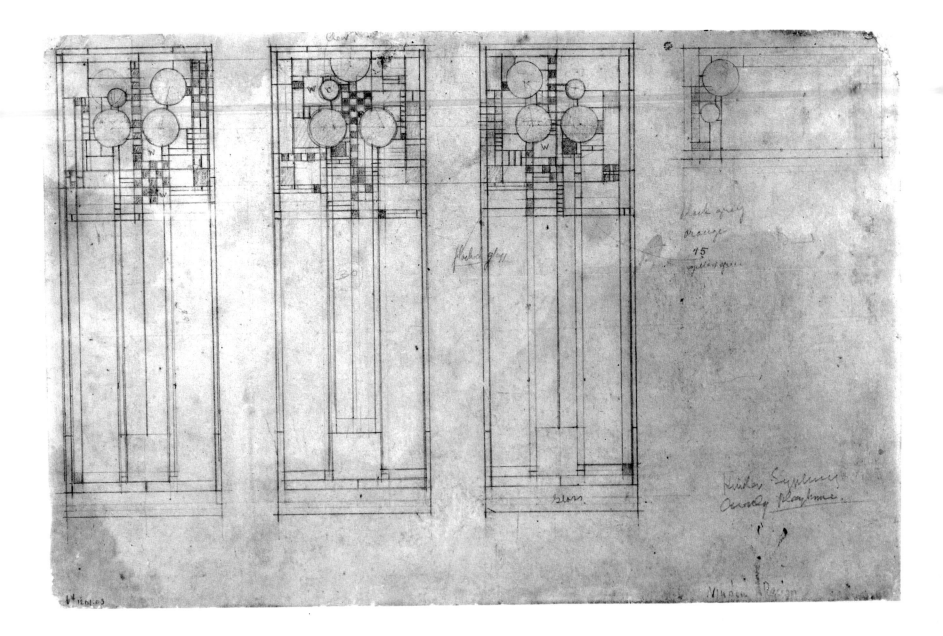

FOR THE WINDOWS in a children's playhouse, Wright chose a theme he thought would please youngsters: balloons and confetti, associated with parties and good times. On his drawing for the three tall windows in the front of the building, he later wrote, "Kinder Symphony—Coonley Playhouse."

In a letter of October 2, 1912, Avery Coonley wrote to Wright:

Last night I took home the drawing of the balloon scheme for the play-house windows. We all think the balloon part of it charming, and although certainly daring, an extremely happy conception most skillfully worked out. It has greatly improved since you left me.

All seem to be equally unanimous, however, that the confetti part of the idea is not successful, and both Mrs. Coonley and I favor abandoning the confetti for some more easily understood arrangement, particularly as I have never seen the two associated.

How would a band going across like the frieze on the wall of the room in which the balloons are supposed to be floating do? Or, some pure decoration around the edge of the glass? We very much like the simplicity of the lower part of the windows, and hope you will work out something which will please you, at the same time keeping the effect simple, and the number of pieces as small as possible. I feel sure this can be worked out into a most charming result.

Wright, however, prevailed upon the Coonleys to accept the confetti, and in the end they were immensely pleased.

AVERY COONLEY PLAYHOUSE, RIVERSIDE, ILLINOIS. 1912. PRESENTATION DRAWING FOR STAINED GLASS. PENCIL AND COLOR PENCIL ON TRACING PAPER, 18×12". FLLW FDN# 1201.003

ON THIS SMALL but meticulously rendered drawing are a wealth of designs for furniture and objects:
metal chairs and table, metal lamp with attached flower
holder, tablecloth and napkins, dinnerware, a silver
fruit bowl, and some indication of a floor covering,
either of tiles or a rug. Midway Gardens (page 178) was
never fully completed to the architect's wishes, and
most of these objects and furniture were not realized.
Lamps were made, however, based on this design but
greatly modified, and the silver fruit bowl was recently
produced.

MIDWAY GARDENS, CHICAGO, ILLINOIS (DEMOLISHED).
1913. PRESENTATION DRAWING FOR FURNITURE. PENCIL ON
TRACING PAPER, 13 × 15". FLLW FDN# 1401.006

THIS DESIGN FOR A MURAL at Midway Gardens
is done in gouache, watercolor, gold ink, and color
crayons, with some touches in graphite pencil. Above
the colorful drawing is attached a small sketch, signed
"FLLW" in two places, indicating the architect's own
hand in the work. A note on the side, also by Wright,
says "Bar," for the mural was indeed executed on the
wall above a black marble slab in the gardens' bar. A
circle is shown in the design protruding out of the
roofline, where it turns and goes onto the ceiling with
an indication of the wood strip passing through it.

MIDWAY GARDENS, CHICAGO, ILLINOIS (DEMOLISHED).
1913. PRESENTATION DRAWING FOR MURAL.
PENCIL, COLOR PENCIL, GOLD INK,
WATERCOLOR, AND COLOR CRAYON ON
TRACING PAPER, 31 × 33". FLLW FDN# 1401.120

(OVERLEAF: MIDWAY GARDENS.
PRESENTATION DRAWING FOR MURAL; DETAIL)

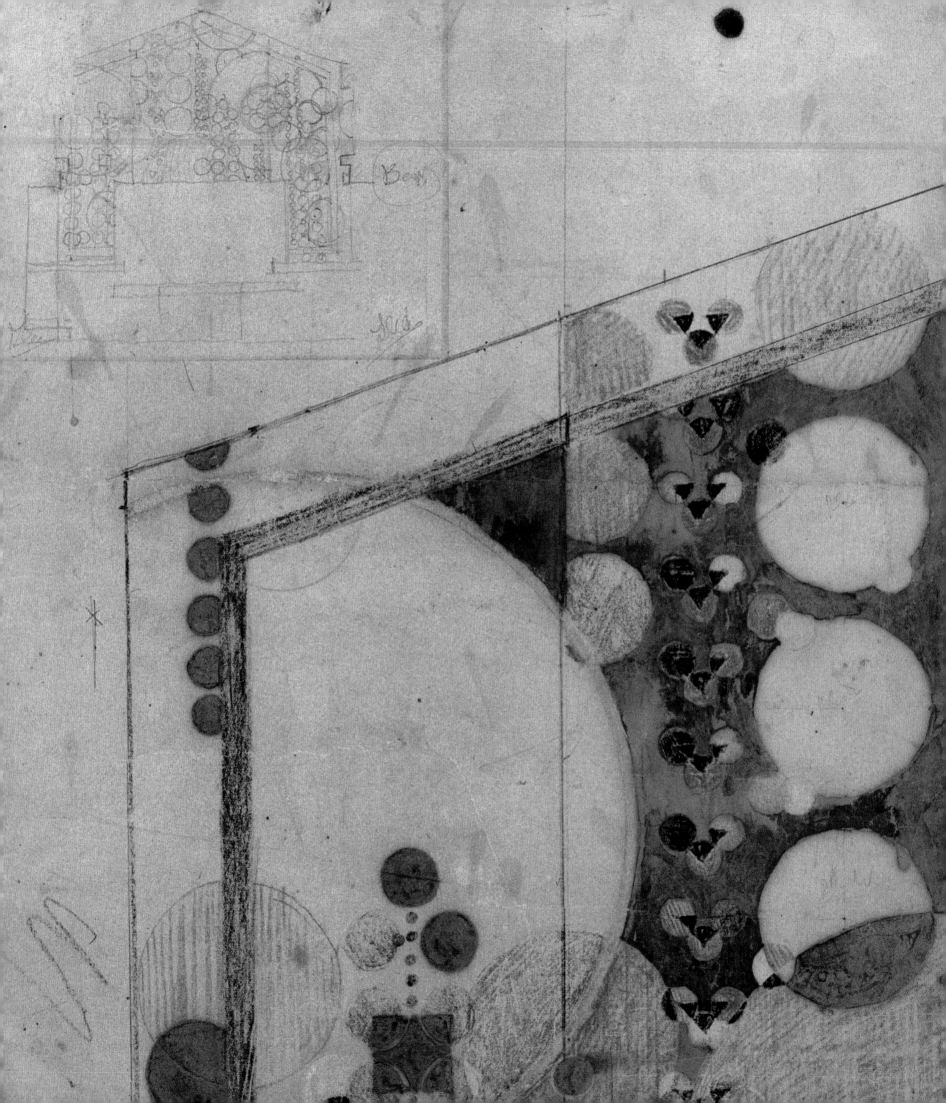

IN 1929 THE DUTCH COMPANY Glasfabriek Leerdam commissioned Wright to design a series of vases, flower holders, dinnerware, glassware, and goblets to be executed in glass and china. The design for the coffee cup shows the general style for the tableware—a hexagonal pattern with the corners embossed or stamped with triangular designs.

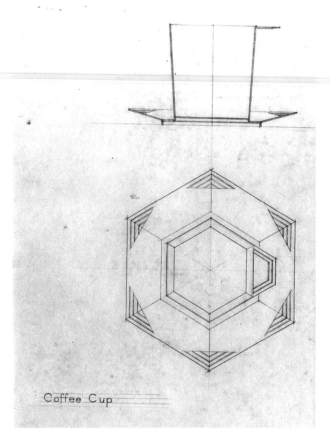

Coffee Cup

FOR MAX HOFFMAN, who built Wright's design for a Mercedes showroom on Park Avenue in New York, Wright also designed a home. It was the third attempt at the house design that finally pleased Hoffman after two more lavish and expansive proposals were abandoned. As the house neared completion, Wright suggested a carpet design for the living room with a runner for the long hall. The drawing here is actually a plan and drawing in one, with the placement of tables, chairs, hassocks, and fireplace represented in relation to the carpet. Hoffman's timid reaction to the residential designs that Wright prepared for him extended to the carpet as well. He refused it. Following the architect's death in April 1959, Wright's widow had the carpet made by V'Soske in Puerto Rico for her living room at Taliesin in Spring Green.

WHEN WRIGHT published *An Autobiography* in 1932, with Longmans Green of New York, he made graphic designs for each of the main sections of the book. This one was for "Book One—Family" and was used on the cloth binding as well as the dustcover.

On the upper-right corner he wrote to his editor, Frank E. Hill at Longmans Green: "My dear F.H. You won't like this design at first—I have disobeyed instructions and altered anymore suggestions somewhat. But you will like it much when you see it on the bookstands in contrast to the other books. Where every cover is barking loud (like the samples you sent) no one hears (or sees) anything in particular. It is contrast that catches the eye or the ear—I am sure of this and I ought to know? FLLW."

A note on the lower margin reads: "Red Square— Scarlet Embossed. Note—All black lines stamped in gold on either paper or cloth as case may be. [For Jacket] suggest glossy white paper with black and red printed just as here shown (glossy white will keep clean enough). The lettering is separate drawing so it may be different color. Suggest deep sepia—almost black for lettering and embossed—Note—I like the paper cover of the 'Gentle Art of Making Enemies' as before suggested. Color too."

Each of the graphic designs illustrates the prelude to a section of the book. In this case the contradiction of the two main lines, one firm and straight and unyielding, the other darting about it to the right and left, illustrates the story of a boyhood walk through the snow in early spring Wright took with his Uncle John. John proceeded straight across the meadow to the next hill, veering neither right nor left, while the young Frank— fascinated by the wildflowers growing through the snow, ran from side to side gathering an armload of them. At the end of their walk, Uncle John pointed back to the tracks in the snow and admonished the young boy clutching his armload of flowers for his jagged, ragged, hither and thither path as opposed to his uncle's straight, direct one.

"Uncle John's meaning was plain," as Wright described it. "NEITHER TO THE RIGHT NOR TO THE LEFT, BUT STRAIGHT, IS THE WAY. The boy looked at his treasure and then at Uncle John's pride, comprehending more than Uncle John meant he should. The boy was troubled. Something was left out."

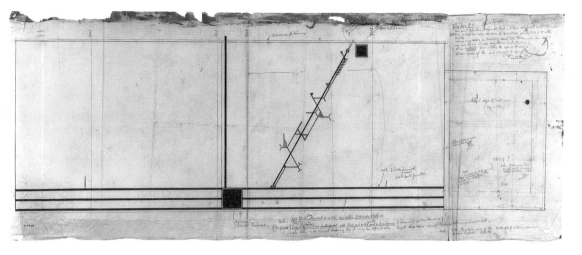

"FROM GENERATION TO GENERATION." 1931.
GRAPHIC DESIGN. INK ON ART PAPER, 40×15". FLLW FDN# 3104.005

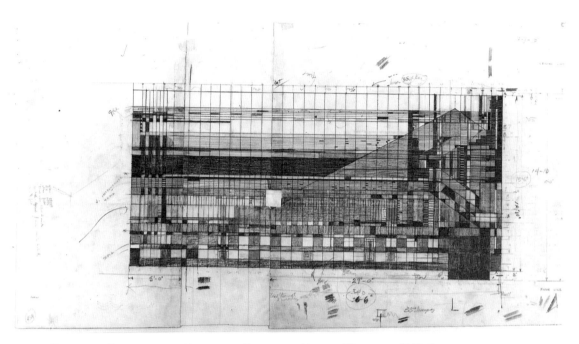

CURTAIN DESIGN FOR HILLSIDE THEATRE, HILLSIDE, WISCONSIN. 1952. CONCEPTUAL SKETCH.
PENCIL AND COLOR PENCIL ON TRACING PAPER, 38×21". FLLW FDN# 5223.001

WHEN THE HILLSIDE Theatre of the Taliesin Fellowship complex, burned in 1952, lost with it were the special curtains and draperies that Wright had designed, including the main stage curtain. His replacement design is an abstraction of the Wisconsin landscape: fields and hills, red barns, crops, furrows of freshly plowed ground on a great hanging tapestry. The curtain was executed by the Taliesin Fellowship, under the direction of Olgivanna Lloyd Wright, as a surprise for the architect. The background was an off-white Belgian linen, the designs cut-out appliqué in red, black, and green felts, the lines in wool yarn and gold cording. The felt square and patches were tacked at the top corners only, so that when the curtain moved or was drawn back, they responded either by folding in or out.

After it was finished and hung, Wright was immensely pleased to see the result. The yarn lines, however, were often altered, in situ, by Wright when he came to review the pattern. He would cut certain ones so that they hung vertically rather than horizontally. Just as he worked on the drawing, he worked on the "finished" product.

The design shows a space of six inches between the actual curtain and the curtain bar; strips of yarn attached to the top of the curtain then were attached to the track. On the floor, likewise, the curtain is placed six inches above the stage level, with his emblem, the red square, at the far right corner.

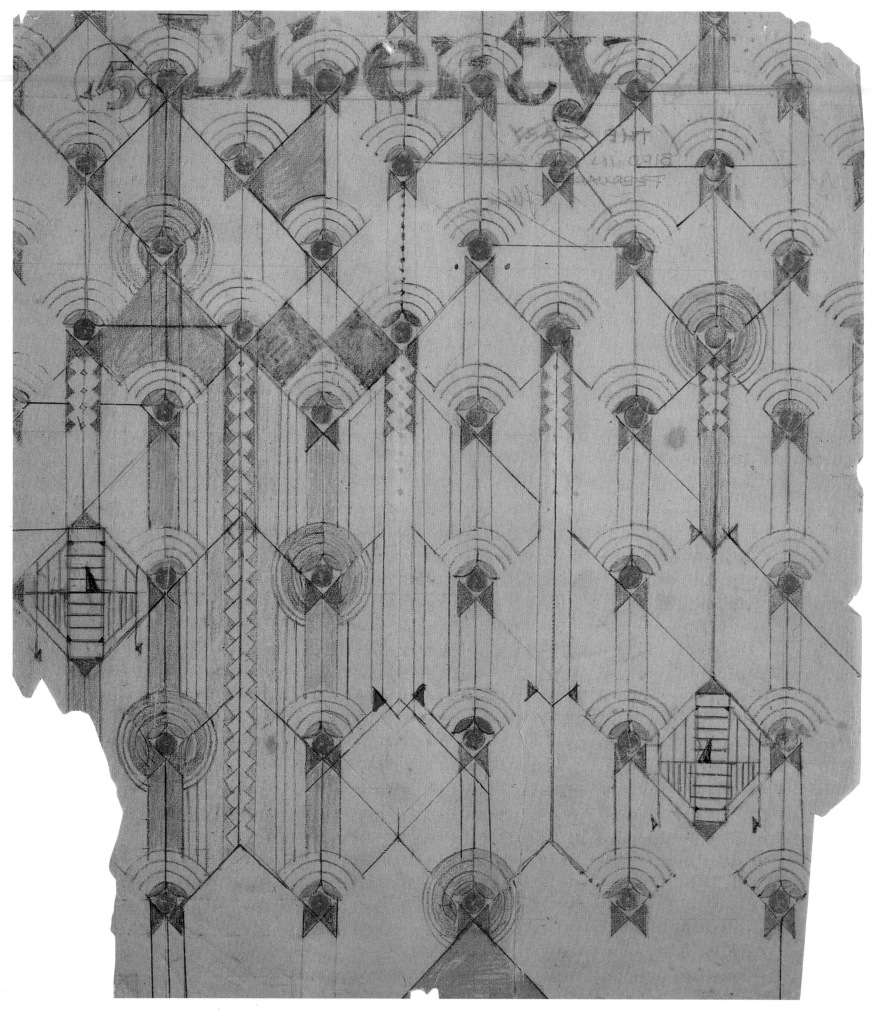

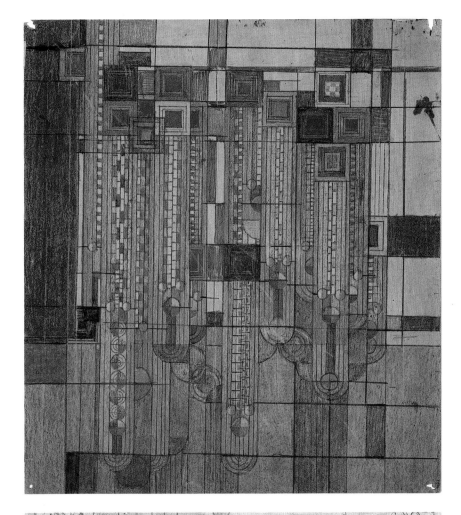

FRANK LLOYD WRIGHT was commissioned in the winter of 1926–1927 to make a series of designs for covers of *Liberty* magazine. Twelve designs were produced, each devoted to a specific month. The drawings that the architect made proved too "radical" for the publisher, and they were all rejected. Over the years Wright changed the titles for them, even changing some of the months that had originally been designated.

April Showers was later called *The Canary—Bird in the Cage—February,* and later still, *Scherzo.* On this drawing can be detected the lettering for *Liberty* magazine and its price, five cents. *Saguaro Forms and Cactus Flowers* first appeared in muted, quiet colors on the cover of an anthology of lectures Wright gave at Princeton in 1930 entitled "Modern Architecture." From time to time Wright continued to work on this particular abstraction and relabeled it *November—Autumn—Phoenix.* The curved arms of the saguaro, a great desert cactus tree, can be seen in green colors, the cactus ribs outlined in red color pencil. *The Jewelry Shop Window,* sometimes called *The Jeweler's Window,* he later retitled *December.*

When this group was exhibited in Europe in 1931, he composed the caption to read, "For the Children, obvious arrangements of familiar objects or easy abstractions—intended to be 'not too difficult'."

(ABOVE)

COVER DESIGNS FOR *LIBERTY* MAGAZINE
"SAGUARO" (PROJECT). 1926. CONCEPTUAL SKETCH. PENCIL AND COLOR PENCIL ON TRACING PAPER, 12 × 13".
FLLW FDN# 2604.010

(OPPOSITE)

COVER DESIGN FOR *LIBERTY* MAGAZINE
"SCHERZO" (PROJECT). 1926. CONCEPT SKETCH. PENCIL AND COLOR PENCIL ON TRACING PAPER, 12 × 13".
FLLW FDN# 2604.009

(LEFT)

COVER DESIGN FOR *LIBERTY* MAGAZINE
"THE JEWELRY SHOP WINDOW" (PROJECT). 1926. PRESENTATION DRAWING. PENCIL AND COLOR PENCIL ON TRACING PAPER, 12 × 12". FLLW FDN# 2709.001

CHRONOLOGY

1867
Frank Lloyd Wright born in Richland Center, Wisconsin, on June 8. He is the first child of William Russell Cary Wright and Anna Lloyd Jones Wright.

1874
The Wright family moves to Weymouth, Massachusetts.

1876
Anna Lloyd Wright introduces the Froebel "Kindergarten" training to her son.

1877
The Wright family moves to Madison, Wisconsin. Frank spends the summer months at the James Lloyd Jones farm near Spring Green, Wisconsin.

1885
Wright's father leaves Madison and abandons his family. Wright enters the University of Wisconsin at Madison and works for Allan D. Conover, a professor of engineering.

1887
Wright witnesses the collapse of the Wisconsin State Capitol Building in Madison.
   Leaves Madison for Chicago, finding employment first at the office of Joseph Lyman Silsbee and eventually with the architectural firm of Adler and Sullivan.

1889
Wright marries Catherine Lee Tobin.

1890
Wright is assigned all residential design handled by Adler and Sullivan.

1891
Son Frank Lloyd Wright, Jr. (Lloyd), born.

1892
Wright leaves offices of Adler and Sullivan.
   Son John Lloyd Wright born.

1893
Wright opens his own practice in Chicago, Illinois.

1894
First exhibition of Wright's work is held at the Chicago Architectural Club.
   Daughter Catherine Lloyd Wright born.

1895
Exhibition of Wright's work is held at the Chicago Architectural Club.
   Son David Samuel Wright born.

1896
Wright writes the lecture "Architecture, Architect, and Client" and a credo entitled "Work Song."

1897
Wright moves his office to Steinway Hall, Chicago.

1898
Exhibition of Wright's work is held at the Chicago Architectural Club.
   Daughter Frances Lloyd Wright born.

1899
Exhibition of Wright's work is held at the Chicago Architectural Club.

1900
Wright delivers a lecture, "The Architect," at the Second Annual Convention of the Architectural League of America. He writes the lectures "A Philosophy of Fine Art" and "What is Architecture?" as well as articles on Japanese prints and the culture of Japan.
   Exhibition of Wright's work is held at the Chicago Architectural Club.

1901
Wright reads his lecture "The Art and Craft of the Machine" at Hull House in Chicago.
   Exhibition of Wright's work is held at the Chicago Architectural Club.

1902
Wright meets William E. Martin and Darwin D. Martin, future clients and patrons.
   Exhibition of Wright's (and others') work is held at the Chicago Architectural Club.

1903
Son Robert Llewellyn Wright born.

1904
Wright attends the Louisiana Purchase Exposition in Saint Louis.

1905
Wright and his wife, Catherine, make their first trip to Japan, accompanied by Wright's clients Mr. and Mrs. Ward Willits.
   Wright begins collecting and dealing in Japanese prints.

1906
Wright exhibits his collection of Hiroshige prints at the Art Institute of Chicago.

1907
Exhibition of Wright's work is held at the Chicago Architectural Club.

1908
German philosopher Kuno Franke meets with Wright in Oak Park; the Wasmuth portfolio would be the result of this meeting.
   Japanese prints from Wright's collection are exhibited with other collections in a major exhibition at the Art Institute of Chicago.

1909
Wright leaves his practice and family for Europe, accompanied by Mamah Borthwick Cheney.

1910
Wright travels to Berlin and then to Fiesole. In Fiesole, Wright, son Lloyd, and others prepare the illustrations for *Ausgeführte Bauten und Entwürfe von Frank Lloyd Wright,* published that year in Berlin by Ernst Wasmuth.
   Edwin and Mamah Cheney divorced.

1911
Wright returns from Europe and begins building a new home and studio near Spring Green, Wisconsin. The complex is called Taliesin.

1912
Wright opens an office in Orchestra Hall, Chicago.
   Publishes "The Japanese Print: An Interpretation" (Seymour, Chicago).

1913
Wright visits Japan to secure the commission for the Imperial Hotel and to acquire Japanese prints for American clients.

1914
Julian Carlston kills Mamah Cheney and six others, then sets fire to Taliesin.
   Wright meets Miriam Noel. Anna Lloyd Wright moves to Taliesin.
   The exhibition *Frank Lloyd Wright* is held at the

Art Institute of Chicago. Work on the project began in 1911.

1915
Wright sails to Japan with Miriam Noel and opens an office in Tokyo.

1916
While working on the Imperial Hotel, Wright makes several trips back to the United States to supervise work going on in his Los Angeles office.

1917
Prints from Wright's collection offered in a sale exhibition.

1918
Wright goes to Peiping, China. He visits the monuments and art treasures of China as a guest of Ku Hung Ming, a noted Chinese writer and secretary to the empress dowager.

1919
Wright receives his first citation, "Kenchiko Ho, Royal Household Japan," conferred by the Imperial Household.

1920
Wright's mother, Anna, visits him in Tokyo.

1921
Construction begins of Wright's Imperial Hotel in Tokyo.

1922
Wright opens an office in Los Angeles.
Wright and Catherine are divorced.

1923
Wright's mother, Anna, dies.
Kanto earthquake demolishes much of Tokyo. The Imperial Hotel survives.
Wright publishes "Experimenting with Human Lives" (Los Angeles Fine Art Society), concerning the earthquake and the Imperial Hotel.
Marries Miriam Noel.
Construction begins on Wright's Textile Block houses in Los Angeles.

1924
Wright separates from Miriam Noel Wright.
Louis H. Sullivan dies.
Wright meets Olgivanna Lazovich Hinzenburg.

1925
Second major fire occurs at Taliesin.
Publication of "The Life-Work of the American Architect Frank Lloyd Wright," edited by H. Th. Wijdeveld (Wendingen, Holland).

Daughter Iovanna born to Frank Lloyd Wright and Olgivanna Hinzenburg.

1926
The Bank of Wisconsin takes title to Taliesin, due to Wright's indebtedness.
Wright and Hinzenburg are arrested near Minneapolis for allegedly violating the Mann Act.
Wright starts work on his autobiography.

1927
Wright is made an honorary member of the Académie Royale des Beaux Arts, Belgium.
Wright begins a series of articles under the heading "In the Cause of Architecture," subsequently published monthly in *The Architectural Record*.
Wright divorces Miriam Noel Wright. Travels with Hinzenburg to Puerto Rico. Spends the winter in Phoenix, Arizona, with Hinzenburg while working on the Arizona Biltmore Hotel.

1928
Wright marries Olgivanna Hinzenburg at Rancho Santa Fe, California.

1929
Wright is made an "Extraordinary Honorary Member" of the Akademie der Kunst, Berlin. The honor is conferred by the state.
Construction of the "Ocotilla" camp begins in January in Chandler, Arizona.
Wright leaves Arizona in May for Wisconsin and then New York City to discuss plans for Saint Mark's Tower with William Norman Guthrie.
Work continues on projects for Chandler, but following the stock-market crash on October 29, these projects come to a halt.

1930
Wright delivers the Kahn Lectures at Princeton University, Princeton, New Jersey, and publishes them under the title *Modern Architecture* (Princeton University Press, 1931).
Wright continues work on his autobiography with Olgivanna and works on *The Disappearing City*.

1931
The Wrights visit Rio de Janeiro, as guests of the Pan American Union, to judge a series of designs for the Columbus Memorial.
Exhibition of Wright's life work travels to New York City, Amsterdam, Berlin, Frankfurt, Brussels, Milwaukee, Wisconsin, Eugene, Oregon, and Chicago.
Wright publishes *The Hillside Home School of the Allied Arts: Why We Want This School* (The Taliesin Press).

1932
The Wrights found the Taliesin Fellowship and

convert the Hillside Home School buildings at Hillside, Wisconsin, into the Taliesin Fellowship Complex.
Wright publishes *An Autobiography* (Longmans Green, New York) and *The Disappearing City* (William Farquhar Payson, New York).
Wright is made an honorary member of the National Academy of Brazil.
Exhibition of Wright's work included in the *International Style* at The Museum of Modern Art, New York City.

1933
Wright publishes "The Taliesin Fellowship" (The Taliesin Press, January 1933 and December 1933).

1934
Wright and apprentices begin construction of a scale model of a section of Broadacre City.
Wright meets Edgar Kaufmann, a future client.
The first issue of *Taliesin,* a magazine founded by Wright is published by The Taliesin Press.

1935
Construction of the Broadacre City model continues at "La Hacienda" in Chandler, Arizona. The completed model is exhibited at the Industrial Arts Exposition at Rockefeller Center.

1936
Wright meets H. F. Johnson at Taliesin.
Visits Phoenix, Arizona.

1937
The Wrights are invited by the Soviet Union to attend the World Conference of Architects.
Wright and author Baker Brownell write and publish *Architecture and Modern Life* (Harper, New York).

1938
"Taliesin Eyes I," the first in a series of brochures by The Taliesin Fellowship is published by The Taliesin Press.
Wright designs the January issue of *Architectural Forum*, which is dedicated to his work.
Wright appears on the cover of *Time* magazine.
Wright begins work on his winter residence and studio, "Taliesen West," in Arizona.

1939
Wright is invited to London to deliver a series of lectures at The Sulgrave Manor Board. They are published as *An Organic Architecture* (Lund Humphries, London).
Wright is awarded an honorary master of arts by Wesleyan University, Middletown, Connecticut.
Taliesin is published by The Taliesin Press.

1940

The Work of Frank Lloyd Wright, a major retrospective exhibition is held at The Museum of Modern Art, New York City.

Wright founds the Frank Lloyd Wright Foundation.

1941

Wright is made an honorary member of The Royal Institute of British Architects and receives The Royal Gold Medal for Architecture; the honors are conferred by King George VI. Wright is awarded the Sir George Watson Chair by the Royal Institute of British Architects and honored by The Sulgrave Manor Board.

Wright and Frederick Gutheim publish *On Architecture* (Duell, Sloan and Pearce, New York).

The second issue of *Taliesin* is published by The Taliesin Press. Five issues of "A Taliesin Square-Paper: A Nonpolitical Voice from Our Democratic Minority" are published by The Taliesin Press (January, May, June, July, August).

1942

Wright is made an honorary member of the National Academy of Architects, Uruguay.

1943

Wright publishes a revised edition of *An Autobiography* (Duell, Sloan and Pearce, New York).

Wright publishes "Book Six: Broadacre City" (The Taliesin Press).

Wright is made an honorary member of the National Academy of Architects of Mexico. The honor is conferred by the state.

1944

An issue of "A Taliesin Square-Paper" is published.

1945

Wright publishes *When Democracy Builds* (University of Chicago Press).

Two issues of "A Taliesin Square-Paper" are published (May and August).

1946

Wright is made an honorary member of The National Academy of Finland. The honor is conferred by the state.

Stepdaughter Svetlana dies on September 30.

An issue of "A Taliesin Square-Paper" is published.

1947

Wright is awarded an honorary doctorate of fine arts by Princeton University, Princeton, New Jersey.

An issue of "A Taliesin Square-Paper" is published.

1948

The January issue of *Architectural Forum* is dedicated to Wright's work.

An issue of "A Taliesin Square-Paper" is published.

"Taliesin to Friends," a brochure, is published by The Taliesin Press.

1949

Wright publishes *Genius and the Mobocracy* (Duell, Sloan, and Pearce, New York).

Wright is made an honorary member of The American National Institute of Arts and Letters.

Wright is awarded the Gold Medal of the American Institute of Architects.

Wright is awarded The Gold Medal of the Philadelphia Chapter of the American Institute.

Wright is awarded an honorary degree by The Peter Cooper Foundation for the Advancement of Art.

Two issues of "A Taliesin Square-Paper" are published (March and November).

1950

Wright is awarded an honorary doctorate of laws by Florida Southern College, Lakeland, and the Centennial Award by *Popular Mechanics* magazine.

1951

Wright and his apprentices design and construct an exhibition of Wright's work entitled *Sixty Years of Living Architecture*. It includes models, photomurals, and original drawings. The show opens at the Palazzo Strozzi in Florence.

Wright is awarded the Medici Medal, conferred by the city of Florence and awarded at the Palazzo Vecchio.

The Star of Solidarity is awarded to Wright in the Doge's Palace in Venice.

An issue of "A Taliesin Square-Paper" is published (January).

Wright opens West Coast office in San Francisco with Aaron Green, Associate.

1952

The exhibition *Sixty Years of Living Architecture* travels from Florence to Zurich, Paris, Munich, and Rotterdam.

A fire partly destroys Wright's Hillside Home School buildings in Spring Green, Wisconsin.

1953

The exhibition *Sixty Years of Living Architecture* is on view in Mexico City and New York.

Wright is made an honorary member of The Akademie Royale des Beaux Arts, Stockholm. The honor is conferred by the state.

Wright is made honorary member of The National Academy of Finland. The honor is conferred by the state.

Wright publishes *The Future of Architecture,* (Horizon Press, New York).

Hugh Downs interviews Wright for television.

Wright publishes *In the Cause of Architecture* (The Taliesin Press); "Organic Architecture: Language of

an Organic Architecture" (The Taliesin Press); "A Taliesin Square-Paper"; and "Taliesin Tract, Number One" (The Taliesin Press).

1954

The exhibition *Sixty Years of Living Architecture* concludes its run at Wright's Hollyhock House in Los Angeles.

Wright is awarded a citation and Brown Medal by The Franklin Institute of Philadelphia. Wright is awarded an honorary doctorate of fine arts by Yale University, New Haven, Connecticut.

Wright publishes *The Natural House* (Horizon Press, New York).

Wright opens office and residence in New York City, "Taliesin East."

1955

Wright is awarded an honorary doctorate of fine arts by the University of Wisconsin, Madison.

Wright is awarded an honorary degree by The Technische Hochschule of Darmstadt, Germany.

Wright is awarded an honorary degree by The Technische Hochschule of Zurich, Switzerland.

Wright and Edgar Kaufmann, Jr., publish *An American Architecture* (Horizon Press, New York).

1956

Wright publishes *The Story of the Tower* (Horizon Press, New York).

The Wrights travel to Wales.

Wright is awarded an honorary doctorate of philosophy by the University of Wales, Bangor.

Mayor Richard Daley of Chicago declares October 17 "Frank Lloyd Wright Day." Wright presents the "Mile High Illinois" at an exhibition at the Hotel Sherman.

Construction of the Solomon R. Guggenheim Museum begins in New York City.

1957

Wright is invited to Baghdad, Iraq, to design an opera house, cultural center, museum, university, and postal-telegraph building.

The Wrights visit London, Paris, and Cairo.

Wright publishes *A Testament* (Horizon Press, New York).

Wright is interviewed twice on television by Mike Wallace in New York City.

1958

Wright publishes *The Living City* (Horizon Press, New York).

Wright is awarded the Gold Medal by the National Concrete Masonry Association.

1959

Wright begins work on a history of architecture for teenagers. It is to be called *The Wonderful World of Architecture*.

Wright dies April 9.

INDEX

Note: Page numbers in *italics* refer to illustrations.

302

ACKNOWLEDGMENTS

FEW ARTISTS LITERALLY change the way generations of people see and think. Frank Lloyd Wright was such an artist: he remains the most important architect of the twentieth century. His concepts regarding domestic architecture at the turn of the century are ingrained in our thinking, as are many of his ideas on urban planning and modern living. His fertile mind wandered across the built landscape with such dexterity that it is almost unimaginable in today's world of specialization. He saw architecture not only as an organization of spaces and of decoration but also as an opportunity to challenge contemporary engineering, science, and technology. Thus, he developed an organic architecture, paying specific attention to the site, to the nature of materials, and to how innovative industrial methods could be utilized.

To have the ability to explore Wright's concepts through this publication is indeed a rare treat. Even more so is the opportunity to view the drawings assembled for this undertaking in the galleries of the Phoenix Art Museum. The exhibition and publication, coordinated with the Frank Lloyd Wright Archives housed at Taliesin West in Arizona, will draw attention to Taliesin's massive holdings. They *are* truly a national treasure. Over twenty thousand drawings are at Taliesin West. To be able to share with the public the very best is a rare opportunity for which our museum feels quite privileged.

The staff at Taliesin West, under the leadership of Richard Carney and Bruce Brooks Pfeiffer, has been exceedingly cooperative in generating an exhibition that addresses the casual viewer as well as the practicing architect and architectural historian. We at the Phoenix Art Museum are pleased to have participated in this project, which, for the first time in almost thirty years, offers a major retrospective look at this towering architectural figure. We are also gratified that the museum has participated in this treasure's future by enabling so many of the drawings to be conserved as a result of a grant from the Flinn Foundation of Arizona. Such activity is a strong focus at Taliesin West as the future of the Frank Lloyd Wright Archives unfolds.

James K. Ballinger
Director, Phoenix Art Museum

FOR ANY PROJECT AS LARGE as this presentation, a great many people from different organizations participate in various aspects of work and preparation. Three organizations in particular must be cited: the Frank Lloyd Wright Archives, the Phoenix Art Museum, and the Northeast Document Conservation Center. Without their personal, as well as professional, advice, the exhibition and this book would not have been possible.

For their assistance in typescript and text proofing I am grateful to Indira Berndtson and Dixie Legler. For their assistance in selecting the drawings, cataloging, and data-base maintenance I am grateful to Oscar R. Muñoz and Sharon Paty Monar. For assistance in photography of the drawings, especially those images retaken for this publication, I am grateful to Greg Weiland. For his careful study and selection of those drawings that needed special conservation at the Northeast Document Conservation Center in Andover, Massachusetts, I am grateful to conservator T. K. McClintock. The results of their painstaking work at the center is nothing short of a miracle. For his valuable assistance and curatorial work in the initial and then final selection of drawings to be exhibited, I am grateful to Phoenix Art Museum Director James K. Ballinger. And, finally, I wish to thank Margaret Kaplan, Charles Miers, and Bob McKee at Harry N. Abrams, Inc., for their enthusiastic support and patient work.

Bruce Brooks Pfeiffer
Director, The Frank Lloyd Wright Archives

303